CHRISTIAN RENEWAL

IN A CHANGING WORLD

CHRISTIAN RENEWAL IN A CHANGING WORLD

A New Approach to Moral Theology

BERNARD HÄRING, C.SS.R.

Translated by Sister M. Lucidia Häring
Missionary Sister of the Most Sacred Heart of Jesus

DESCLEE COMPANY · NEW YORK
TOURNAI · PARIS · ROME

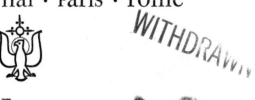

First published in German under the title: *Christ in einer neuen Welt,* by Erich Wewel Verlag (Freiburg im Breisgau, 1961). The present English translation is a revised and updated edition of the German original.

First Printing, December 1964
Second Printing, April 1965
Third Printing, August 1965
Fourth Printing, October 1966

IMPRIMI POTEST
Most Rev. William Gaudreau, C.SS.R.
Superior General
Rome, September 14, 1964

NIHIL OBSTAT
Daniel V. Flynn, J.C.D.
Censor Librorum

IMPRIMATUR
✠ Francis Cardinal Spellman
Archbishop of New York
November 5, 1964

The nihil obstat and imprimatur are official declarations that a book or pamphlet is free of doctrinal or moral error. No implication is contained therein that those who have granted the nihil obstat and imprimatur agree with the contents, opinions or statements expressed.

© *1964 by Desclee Co., Inc.*
Library of Congress Catalog Card Number: 65–12896
Printed in the U.S.A. by H. Wolff, New York

AUTHOR'S PREFACE

The present book which had been published in German before the beginning of the Second Vatican Council is now appearing in English at a time when the Third Session of the same Council is discussing the schema, "The Presence of the Church in Today's World." May this volume help God's chosen priests, as well as all the faithful, to understand more perfectly the message of the Council which bids them to become "the salt of the earth" through their specific witness and sincere collaboration with all men of good will.

It is a special satisfaction for the author to present the English text in the careful translation of his own sister and to express to her his deep gratitude. He also conveys his sincere appreciation for all those aiding in the preparation and reading of the manuscript, especially Father Albin V. Veszelovszky, St. Norbert Abbey, DePere, Wisconsin; and Sister Angelita Myerscough, Ad.PP.S., St. Louis University, for their careful and painstaking review of the manuscript.

During the past three years the author had the enjoyable experience of listening and speaking to generous priests and religious, as well as innumerable open-minded lay people, in the U.S.A., Canada, England, and Ireland. This privilege makes him confident that the book may reach many of his friends. To all his readers and acquaintances he expresses his best wishes and personal regards.

Bernard Häring, C.SS.R.
Washington, D.C.
June 1964

contents

3 GOD AND THE HEART OF MAN 91

4 THE SOUL'S INTIMATE ENCOUNTER WITH GOD 174

INTRODUCTION

We are living in a changing world. This statement together with the title of this book is filled with far-reaching implications.

Contemporary man is reminded of the stupendous transformations apparent in all phases of his material existence. Impressive signs of a new age have appeared in the second industrial revolution with the introduction of automation, the smashing of atoms, the utilization and control of atomic energies, and man's daring venture into space. All these epoch-making achievements are unmistakable indications of "a new era—a new world."

The Christian living in this age of material progress and innovations may not abandon the world to its relentless fate but should act in full accord with God's exhortation at the dawn of creation: "Fill the earth and subdue it" (Gen. 1:28). The world is God's indisputable dominion.

The cross, the sign of the world's redemption, is a forceful challenge to the Christian to bear witness to Christ in both private and public life. Toward this noble end of Christianizing the entire world, God has bestowed on man the gift of His Holy Spirit.

The Christian, like his Lord and Master, is not only a stranger in this world (cf. John 17:14), but must prove himself in the struggle against evil as "the salt of the earth and the light of the world" (Matt. 5:13-14). He is to proclaim the glorious works of God, who has called him out of darkness into His marvelous light (cf. Pet. 2:9).

In such an eventful hour of history it would indeed be deplorable if the Christian, prompted by narrow concerns for personal salvation, would abandon to the corrupt and subversive this new world so full of adventurous possibilities and threatening tensions. Furthermore, a stubborn adherence to empty forms and conventions would prove no less detrimental in such a momentous epoch in history because only those things which are truly vital and deeply rooted shall survive the upheavals of transition periods. The Christian should free himself from all undue attachments to failing social systems and from all inordinate desires for innovations for the sake of mere change.

Only faith can fully reveal the deep significance of the phrase: *The Christian in a new era—in a new world.* Supernatural faith directs our attention to *a truly new world* which had its glorious dawn in the Incarnation and which is beginning to shape itself in the Church and in the hearts of Christians as a prelude to a "new heaven and a new earth" at the end of time (Apoc. 21:1). The Christian derives his unfaltering trust and joy from his authentic adaptation to this new world which has revealed its fundamental laws in the cross of Christ and manifested its marvelous victory in Christ's glorious resurrection. Truly, these are good tidings announced to us. The same profound joy, experienced by the neophytes in mission territories at the time of their first encounter with the glad tidings of the gospel truths, should also animate the Christian in our modern society.

This book aims to ascertain both the requisite means and sources of strength for a genuine Christian renewal in our changing, modern world. The author makes no attempt to discuss or to solve all the various problems confronting man in general or man living in this particular age, but rather to present a synopsis of the marvelous riches of our faith, of the blessed fulness of divine grace, and of the beauty and genuine value of a truly Christian life. Such a general survey of the Christian way of life shall necessarily unfold the fundamental laws and principles which should govern our moral behavior and at the same time present some concrete guides for the solution of individual problems.

A *treatise on moral theology*, written for today's Christian who courageously labors under the great task of *aggiornamento* (the late Pope John's term for modernization), should not be confined to explanations regarding the signs and needs of our present time, nor limited to simple enumerations of duties and obligations. The unquestioning faith in "the height and depth of the love of Christ, which surpasses all understanding" (Eph. 3:18 ff.), is an indispensable prerequisite for a fruitful Christian life in compliance with Christ's command "to be the light of the world." The Christian's obligations and duties reveal their genuine beauty and deep significance only in the context of the glad tidings of the gospel.

God has given us His Law, but has not placed us under the Law as slaves by imposing a multiplicity of regulations. He has called each of us in a most intimate and personal way, addressing us by name as He created us according to His own image and likeness (cf. Gen. 1:26 ff.). In baptism we have received the name of children of God so that now, full of confidence, we may call Him "Abba" (Father) (Rom. 8:15). "See what kind of love the Father has bestowed on us that we should be His children not merely in name but in reality. The world does not recognize us, because it has not recognized Him" (I John 3:1).

The Christian's way of life stands the test of time only to the extent that it is lived in agreement with the word of God. In its essence, it is an answer of love. "Speak Lord, Your servant hears" (I Kings 3:9). Such will be the response of the Christian who begins to comprehend that the Law of Christ is essentially a message of joy, inspired by God's love for men (cf. Gal. 6:2). (Chapter I)

With the cheerful and willing acceptance of God's word, the Christian is beginning to see his own existence in the light of the gratuitous, beneficent will of God; and, therefore, is ready to surrender himself unreservedly to the guidance of divine grace, thereby realizing and tasting *the blessed freedom of the children of God.* (Chapter II)

God is speaking to the heart of man. Therefore, purity of heart, manifest in *the undefiled conscience* and pure intention, is the most essential prerequisite for intimate union with God. (Chapter III)

God desires our heart: "My son, give Me your heart" (Prov. 23:26). If in a childlike spirit we try to enter into the thoughts of His Heart, and if we begin to recognize the revelations of His truths, promises and admonitions as expressions of His boundless love for us, then our response to His invitations will always be the answer of love. The expositions of the three divine virtues—*faith, hope, and charity*—present the Christian life as a heart-to-heart dialogue with God, a colloquy of love. (Chapter IV)

The virtue of religion imbues the individual and the entire community of Christians with reverence before the transcendence of God who reveals His glory and sanctifies His children. In the celebration of the Holy Sacrifice, in the reception of the sacraments, and in every prayer offered, we become aware of God's personal approach to our soul as He calls us by our name, and we respond with faith, hope, love and adoration. (Chapter V)

The actions of our daily life must be seen as the fruits of an undivided love of God and neighbor and as elevated into the sphere of the supernatural, into the adoring colloquy of faith, hope, and charity. *The moral virtues:* truthfulness, fidelity, sincerity, patience, respect and care for the good name of self and others, as well as the cardinal virtues: prudence, justice, fortitude, and temperance are shown as the fruits of an undivided charity to God and neighbor, raised to the adoring colloquy of faith, hope, and charity. They are means of transforming our life according to faith. (Chapter VI)

How does the sinner arrive at this generous response to the bountiful, beneficent will of God? How may we gradually attain the full measure of joy in the Law of God, the blessed freedom of the children of God, purity of heart, and an intimate union with God? The answers are found in the glad tidings about conversion and growth in charity. (Chapter VII)

Throughout these meditations our hearts should remain open to God's word as given to us in Holy Scripture. "Lord, to whom shall we go? You have the message of eternal life!" (John 6:69).

CHRISTIAN RENEWAL
IN A CHANGING WORLD

1 THE LAW OF CHRIST as TIDINGS OF GREAT JOY

Man's very nature calls for a moral code. This holds true in our day as much as in pre-Christian times. However, before the coming of Christ, the burden of the Law was totally unbearable because man lacked the moral strength to fulfill its relentless requirements. Is this then the essence of the renewal through Christ that the Christian has received the strength to live up to the demands of the Law?

It would indeed be far from the truth, and even detrimental, to appraise Christian life and perfection in the light of the *ought* and to look upon Christ merely as the source of strength in the fulfillment of the Law. This, in the final analysis, would keep man self-centered and a slave "under" the Law. Such an attitude would prevent the Christian from entering into a desirable and meaningful relationship with Christ. *Through His love and the renewal by grace, Christ Himself has become for us the*

*Way, the Truth, and the Life. He Himself is the Law
for the Christian.* In the joyful recognition of the Law as
God's covenant of love, the inspired poet of the Old Testament triumphantly exclaimed: "Your Law, O Lord, is my
joy" (Ps. 118:77). How much more should the Christian
recognize the moral law as an expression of the bountiful
love of God and the overflowing charity of Christ; *for the
charity of Christ is our Law.*

SYNOPSIS OF CHAPTER ONE

The keynote to an understanding of the new world and
the New Law is found in: (1) the Sermon on the Mount,
(2) the mystery of Christ's resurrection, and (3) the happenings of Pentecost. (4) We understand the primacy of
the virtue of religion over the moral obligations, the sublimity of the virtue of charity in comparison with the commandment of charity, and again, the primacy of the commandment of charity over all other commandments. (5)
The New Law is a precept engraved in the mind and heart
of man, designed to lead the Christian to authentic conformity with Christ through the graces of the sacraments.
(6) There are many aspects of law for the Christian: the
law of nature, the law of grace, the positive laws, and the
duties arising from the need of each moment. These obligations are all embraced in the life of union with Christ.

Section I. The Eight Beatitudes as the New Law

The Sermon on the Mount, the epitome of Christ's message, opens with the nine times repeated "Blessed" (Matt.

5:3-11).* This *blessed* from the lips of our Savior is a direct invitation to participate in the mutual love celebrated by the Father and the Son in the Holy Spirit. Through the mediation of Christ, the Triune God wishes to introduce the creature into His own blissful love. The ninefold promise contained in the "blessed" is the preface to Our Lord's teaching on "the new justice" and the New Law of His love.

"Do not think that I have come to destroy the Law or the prophets. I have not come to destroy but to fulfill them" (Matt. 5:17). The Sermon on the Mount is Christ's plea for absolute purity of intention and an undivided, wholehearted devotion to His cause. This utter dedication to God's kingdom is the prerequisite for "becoming the salt of the earth and the light of the world" (Matt. 5:13 ff.). Christ insisted that the mere *hearing* of the good tidings is far from authentic discipleship. He closed the Sermon on the Mount with these solemn and serious words: "And everyone who hears My words and does not act upon them, shall be likened to a foolish man who built his house on sand. And the rain fell, and the floods came, and the winds blew and beat against the house, and it fell, and was utterly ruined" (Matt. 7:26-27).

In this present time of grace and salvation we have received the glad tidings of the *new heart*. This is definitely indicated in God's demands for absolute purity of intention and unconditional love for neighbor. Even the threat of catastrophe for those failing to implement Christ's teaching must be seen in the light of God's unfailing love and as a proof of His serious and earnest endeavors in His

---

* Although we generally speak of eight beatitudes, the gospel of St. Matthew contains a nine times repeated "blessed" because the eighth beatitude is paraphrased.

dealings with man. God's message is a personal one addressed to each soul in a most intimate way and, therefore, penetrates the very depth of man's being.

Christ's invitation to a life animated by love, and built on the eight principles of happiness, is an expression of God's respect for human dignity. He could have placed us under minimum requirements of the Law in the manner of slaves. The sublimity of the challenge no longer presents a burden when seen in the light of the gospel or "good news." The Law is contained in the nine times repeated "*blessed*," the beatitudes of the new life.

Christ's Law, in all the seriousness of its demands, does not detract from the joy inherent in the glad tidings of God's love. In reality, this Law is the keynote of the nine times repeated "blessed" of the beatitudes—because God's goodness manifests itself in His commandments as well as in His gifts. *God shows Himself bountiful in His Law and bestows blessings in His demands. His Law is always a personal expression of His love for us.*

The following questions may arise: Is the good news, promulgated in the Sermon on the Mount, meant only for those far advanced on the road of perfection? Is Our Lord's "blessed" addressed only to those whose life has been sinless and filled with the fruits of good works? It is true that God expects a rich harvest "in true justice and holiness." We are unable to participate in God's blissful glory and to behold Him face to face until we are completely purified and perfect. And yet, the words of the Sermon on the Mount are an incontestable proof that the jubilant "blessed" was meant for the weak and miserable, the heavily burdened, the poor and little ones of the land who come to God like needy beggars.

"Blessed are the poor in spirit; for theirs is the kingdom of heaven" (Matt. 5:3). We can offer Our Lord only what

He Himself has given us—His own gratuitous gifts. This explains why Our Lord made the bestowal of His bountiful blessings dependent on this one prerequisite, namely, that we become *like little children* and gratefully acknowledge our utter dependence on His inexhaustible goodness and mercy (cf. Matt. 18:3). "I thank You, Father, Lord of heaven and earth, for hiding these things from the learned and wise, and revealing them to the simple. Yes Father, such was Your choice" (Matt. 11:25-26). After this exultant address to the heavenly Father, Our Lord immediately invites the poor in spirit: "Come to Me, all you who labor and are burdened, and I will give you rest" (Matt. 11:28). If we accept the nine times repeated "blessed" of Our Lord in the genuine spirit of God's children, we shall fully experience the significance of the words: "My yoke is easy, and My burden light" (Matt. 11:30).

"Blessed are they who mourn, for they shall be comforted" (Matt. 5:5). Although this beatitude is addressed to all "who labor and are burdened" (Matt. 11:28), it is, nevertheless, spoken in a special way to those suffering under the burden of sin and guilt. The "blessed" of this third beatitude is applicable to our own soul provided we are sincerely sorry for our sins because they are offenses against God. The contrite of heart, who turns away from his evil ways and returns to the Lord, will find his true comforter even if, like the prodigal son, he may appear empty-handed before his heavenly Father who through the prophet assures us: "I Myself will comfort you . . . soon the prisoner shall be free of his chains. He shall not die and see utter destruction" (Is. 51:12-14). God's joy and consolation, reserved for the elect in heaven, will be ours even in this mortal life in direct proportion to our detachment from sin by means of true contrition.

The remaining beatitudes clearly indicate the sublime perfection which Christ expects of all those who wish to abide in His special grace and friendship. We are to love Him with a *"pure heart"* if we desire to recognize His presence in this earthly life and to see Him face to face in the life to come (cf. Matt. 5:8). Our utter dependence on God's goodness and mercy should dispose our hearts to genuine *meekness and compassion* toward others so that we may contribute to the extension of God's kingdom in a renewed world (cf. Matt. 5:7). If we wish to bear the exalted title of children of God, we must prove ourselves as "peacemakers" in all our dealings with men (cf. Matt. 5:9). The thought of God's gratuitous grace should enkindle in us a consuming zeal ("hunger and thirst") for God's justice so that we shall become "filled" at the fountains of grace and salvation (cf. Matt. 5:6).

"Blessed are they who suffer persecution for justice' sake, for theirs is the kingdom of heaven" (Matt. 5:10). If united with God and for the sake of His love we willingly accept reproach, persecution, and suffering, we shall be blessed with overwhelming joy and abundant reward in heaven (cf. Matt. 5:11). Only the disciple who follows his Master on the painful journey of suffering and dereliction can rejoice with Him in the celebration of the resurrection.

Section II. The Law of Christ Transfigured by the Paschal Mystery

In the infinite wisdom and condescension of His heart, Our Lord allowed His chosen apostles, Peter, John, and James, to witness His signs and wonders before He announced His impending Passion and before He allowed them to behold His utter dereliction in the Garden of Olives. Similarly, His first intimation of His intention to go to Jerusalem for His bitter Passion was given only after Peter, profoundly stirred by Christ's overpowering personality and miraculous power, had made his solemn profession of faith in the divinity of his Master (cf. Matt. 16:21). The second prediction of Christ's Passion was preceded by His glorious transfiguration on Mount Tabor (cf. Matt. 17:22). Only the firm conviction and belief in Christ's glorious resurrection can enable the Christian to follow in his Master's footsteps on the road of suffering. Christian life receives its true meaning and significance, its genuine joy, and utter detachment from the things of this world, from no other source than the paschal mystery, namely, the final exaltation of the crucified Savior.

The night before His sacrificial death on the cross, Christ, the eternal High Priest, prayed to His heavenly Father: "Father, the hour has come! Glorify Your Son, that the Son may glorify You. . . . I have glorified You on earth; I have accomplished the work that You had given Me to do. And now, Father, glorify Me with Yourself with the glory which I had with You before the world existed" (John 17:1-5). Christ's pain-wracked body gave ample testimony to God's boundless love. The incarnate Word offered the most worthy sacrifice of love and obedience to His Father. The heavenly Father graciously manifested His acceptance of the worthy holocaust in the exaltation of His Son in the resurrection and ascension into heaven. *Christ's Passion and Resurrection are two inseparable mysteries.* Our Lord indicated this truth before His bitter Passion: "The hour has come for the Son of Man to be glorified. Amen amen, I say to you, unless the grain of wheat falls into the ground and dies, it remains alone. But if it dies, it brings forth much fruit" (John 12:23-25).

Jesus clearly foresaw the terrible anguish connected with His sacrificial death. " 'Now My soul is troubled. And what shall I say: Father, save Me from this hour? No, this is why I came to this hour. Father, glorify Your name!' There came therefore a voice from heaven, 'I have glorified it, and I will glorify it again' " (John 12:27-28). In His earthly sojourn Christ was not solicitous for His own glory (cf. John 8:50), but for the glory of His Father who sent Him (cf. John 7:18). Therefore, in turn, the Father glorified His Son because of His faithful obedience in accepting the ignominious death on the cross.

Our divine Savior emphatically outlined the prospect of His disciple when He stated: "He who loves his life loses it; and he who hates his life in this world, keeps it unto life everlasting. If anyone serves Me, let him follow Me; and where I am, there also shall My disciple be, if anyone serves Me, My Father will honor him" (John 12:25-27). *In the glorious light of the paschal mystery we begin to realize the lofty dignity connected with our imitation of Christ.* God does not withhold our divine adoption until the end of our life as a reward for our fidelity. The entire Christian life, from its inception to its consummation is spent in the splendor of the glory of God's love, in the light of Christ's resurrection and in the certain expectation of His return "in power and glory."

Every grace is the fruit of Christ's Redemption and, therefore, loudly proclaims: "A great price was paid to ransom you" (I Cor. 6:20; I Pet. 1:18-19). Each grace is a testimony to Christ's boundless love in His sacrificial death on the cross and therefore obliges us to an unbounded and everlasting gratitude. Every grace urges us to walk in the footsteps of our crucified Savior. At the same time, every actual grace is not only a ray of glory emanating from our risen Lord, but also a pledge of our own resurrection.

The mystery of Christ's resurrection confirms and ratifies the profound declaration on Christian living promulgated in the Sermon on the Mount.

Section III. The New Law as the Gift of the Holy Spirit

It was on the Mount of the Beatitudes that Christ, the incarnate love of God the Father, announced the glad tidings concerning Christian living. By His cross and resurrection, Our Lord proved the infinity and magnificence of His own love and the dignity inherent in His discipleship. In the bestowal of the Holy Spirit He confirmed these blessed events of our salvation as the very law of our new life.

The Holy Spirit is our risen Savior's precious gift to us. He has become the dispenser of the new principle of life and the pledge of our future glory. After Christ had suffered His Passion, He rose from the dead and ascended into heaven for our sake. The truly intimate relationship between the Passion and glorification of Christ is lucidly expressed in Holy Scripture. The occasion was at the feast of the Tabernacles, celebrated in commemoration of the event occurring during the long pilgrimage in the desert when Moses touched the rock with his rod to bring forth life-giving, sparkling waters. At the time of the celebration of this event, "Jesus stood and cried out saying: 'If any man is thirsty, let him come to Me, and drink; yes, if a man believes in Me, as the Scripture says, fountains of living water shall flow from his bosom'" (John 7:37-38).

To which St. John adds: "He was speaking of the Spirit, which was to be received by those who learned to believe in Him; the Spirit which had not yet been given to men, because Jesus had not yet been raised to glory" (John 7:39). Christ is the Rock. From His Sacred Heart flow the living waters of salvation. These are transmitted to us through the Holy Spirit who is the love of God as Person. Our divine Savior had to return to the Father in order to make us partakers in His sublime life of love. He explained to His disciples: "It is expedient for you that I depart. For if I do not go, the Advocate will not come to you; but if I go, I will send Him to you. . . . He shall glorify Me, because He shall receive of Mine and shall show it to you" (John 16:7-14).

The Holy Spirit dwells and operates in our inmost being. Yet, in addition to this interior action in the depth of our soul, the Holy Spirit works toward the renewal of "the face of the earth" (Ps. 103:30). Our personal cooperation with God's Holy Spirit in the work of our sanctification, as well as our readiness to share in the renewal of the world, will increasingly form our soul to Christ's own image and likeness. The Holy Spirit produces in our hearts "charity, joy, peace, patience, kindness, goodness, faith, modesty and chastity" (Gal. 5:22).

The Christian eager to fulfill his obligations in a new world—a world renewed through the death and resurrection of Christ—must guard against the corruption arising from "the spirit of this world." He must crucify the old self with its unruly desires and tendencies. "If a man wishes to come after Me, let him deny himself, and take up his cross, and follow Me" (Matt. 16:24; Luke 9:23). Since the Holy Spirit has been bestowed on the Christian as the risen Savior's precious gift, all depressing and self-tormenting anxieties must give way to holy joy. *The nine times repeated "blessed" of the Sermon on the Mount, the joy of the Easter message, and the peace of the Holy Spirit, must shine forth in the life of each Christian. Only thus shall we renew "the face of the earth"—the earth which God, the Creator, entrusted to man at the beginning of time.*

In the farewell discourse at the Last Supper, Our Lord made the astounding promise to His disciples: "Amen, amen, I say to you, he that believes in Me, the works that I do, he also shall do, and greater than these shall he do; because I am going to the Father" (John 14:12-13). In the Incarnation, Christ "dispossessed" Himself and took the "nature of a slave" (Phil. 2:7). "The Son of Man has not come to be served but to serve, and give His life as a ransom for many" (Matt. 20:28). He willingly took upon Himself the sufferings and the opprobrium of the cross. It was only in His glorious resurrection and ascension that He revealed Himself as the triumphant victor ascending into eternal glory. Christ sent us the Holy Spirit so that He may accomplish in us and through us the all-surpassing task of the world's renewal and final return to God in the interval between the first Pentecost and His second coming in glory and majesty.

Separated from Christ, the Christian is weak and powerless (cf. John 15:5). This sincere conviction of our utter dependence on God should animate our prayers offered "in the name of Christ." Then Our Lord will grant us all things "so that the Father may be glorified in the Son" (John 14:13). Trusting in the Father's willingness to hear our petitions made in the name of Christ, and confident in the love of the Father and the Son, we ask for "the Spirit of Truth" to remain with us always. We are no longer frightened by the loftiness of God's expectations: "If you love Me, keep My commandments" (John 14:15).

14

God's commandments are graces and blessings which call for the answer of filial love. "He who has My commandments and keeps them, he it is who loves Me. And he who loves Me shall be loved by My Father; and I will love him and will manifest Myself to him" (John 14:21).

The reward for a truly Christian life is not confined to promises of future happiness in the life to come. The *"blessed"* or "happy" of the beatitudes is meant to become effective in this present life. The glory of Christ's resurrection penetrates and illumines the entire Christian life. Such a life is the fruit of the Holy Spirit whom the glorified Savior continues to bestow on His elect. Thus the mission, which is prompted by love and demands love for its fulfillment, gains in impetus. No law imposed from without nor any intellectual comprehension of virtue can compare with the experience: "The love of Christ impels us" (II Cor. 5:14).

Section IV. The Primacy of Charity over Law

The ninefold "blessed" of the beatitudes, the Alleluia of the Easter message, and the rejoicing in the Holy Spirit, re-echo in the great commandment which tells us that we are permitted to love God Himself "with our whole heart, and with our whole soul, and with all our mind" (Matt. 22:37; Deut. 6:5). We may love Him because "He has first loved us" (I John 4:10), and because "the charity of God is poured forth in our hearts by the Holy Spirit" (Rom. 5:5). The great commandment, therefore, is a blessing or "beatitude" coming from the heart of God, a joy-giving commandment: "Rejoice in the Lord always; again, I say, rejoice" (Phil. 4:4).

God's love for us is so deep and true that He most ardently desires our wholehearted love in return for His own boundless charity. God cherishes our love more than our accomplishments. Our works are pleasing to Him only if they are motivated by love. God's commandments—without exception—are expressions of His benevolent charity. His condescending love not only permits us but even commands us to love Him in return. All our actions, be they the routine duties of daily life or organized endeavors for the expansion of God's kingdom, should become the expressions of a genuine charity; all should be drawn into the loving dialogue with God which is the resonance of that love with which the Father and the Son love each other eternally. "The Father Himself loves you because you have loved Me, and have believed that I came forth from God" (John 16:27).

The charity, whereby God loves us and we return His own love, is not only the center and aim of all other commandments and our entire spiritual life, but the knowledge of Christ's innermost secrets of love proves to us *that our Savior's primary mission is charity.* "No longer do I call you servants, because the servant does not know what his master does. But I have called you friends, because all things whatsoever I have heard from My Father I have made known to you" (John 15:15). It is important that not only our faith and prayer life be animated by the secrets of God's love as announced to us by Christ, but that all our moral obligations and duties to men and lawful authority should be seen in the light of the blessed mysteries of salvation.

This preeminence of charity finds expression in all the truths of faith which deal with the reality of grace as a mysterious sharing in the life of the Triune God. This is especially evident in the *sacraments,* the efficacious signs of the saving and sanctifying love of Christ, and in the doctrine of the *divine virtues* (faith, hope, and charity), which constitutes an intimate dialogue of confident surrender between the self-revealing and self-giving God and the heart of man. The primacy of grace over our personal endeavors confirms not only the supernatural dignity of the Christian life in general but, particularly, the sublimity of man's moral endeavors and strivings. The divine assistance of grace is not superimposed, so to speak, on our finite human powers. The preeminence of grace means much more—it means that all our actions are transfigured and elevated by the unfathomable love and condescension of God, which sanctifies and ennobles our entire existence beyond all expectations and merits. *Man's entire moral striving should manifest the basic truth that we are sanctified for God and endowed by His bountiful grace.*

St. Peter, who in his second letter warned the Christians regarding the immoral deeds of the heretics, based his exhortation on two main aspects of religion, namely, *the Christian's participation in the divine nature through grace and the expectation of Christ's second coming in glory and majesty.*

"His divine power has bestowed on us everything that makes for life and true religion, enabling us to know the One who called us by His own splendor and might. Through His might and splendor He has given us His promises, great beyond all price, and through them you may escape the corruption with which lust has infected the world, and come to share in the very being of God. With all this in view, you should try your hardest to supplement your faith with virtue, virtue with knowledge, knowledge with self-control, self-control with fortitude, fortitude with piety, piety with brotherly kindness, and brotherly kindness with love" (II Pet. 1:3-7). What clearer terms could express the basic truth that the powerful action of grace initiates and supports all our moral endeavors? If seen in this light, the admonitions of the prince of the apostles gain their full weight and significance.

If we are truly imbued with the joyous conviction of possessing the incomprehensible treasures of grace, we shall concentrate all our efforts on growing in faith and charity, hopeful for the full revelation of God's love. The Apostle continues: "These are gifts which, if you possess and foster them, will keep you from being either useless or barren in the knowledge of Our Lord Jesus Christ" (II Pet. 1:8). As "eye witnesses of the exaltation of Christ" (II Pet. 1:16) the apostles announced "the power of Our Lord Jesus Christ and His second coming" (II Pet. 2:16). This message of the glory of God, as already foretasted and expected in its final and full revelation, is "like a lamp diffusing its light into the darkness until the breaking of the dawn and the rising of the morning star in your hearts" (II Pet. 1:19).

One of the chief roots for man's moral aberrations is his attachment to transitory treasures, manifested in his desire for the false glory of this world, in the face of which moral teachings and threats of punishment fade into oblivion. No one will be able to withstand the temptations of this world, unless in authentic faith he has received a foretaste and a presentiment of the renewal which the love of God has already accomplished in men and firmly believes in yet greater things to come, as pledged by Christ's resurrection and guaranteed by the seeds of glory placed in us: "Seeing therefore that all these things are to be dissolved, what manner of men ought you to be in holy and pious behavior, you who await and hasten toward the coming of the day of God . . . But we look for new heavens and a new earth, according to His promises, wherein dwells justice" (II Pet. 3:11-13).

Recalling the marvelous events of our salvation, the Apostle addresses the solemn and serious words of warning to those unfortunate ones who "after escaping the defilements of the world through the knowledge of Our Lord and Savior Jesus Christ, are again entangled therein and overcome" (II Pet. 2:20). *These moral admonitions gain their full weight and significance from the glad tidings of a salvation already in process.*

Even Our Lord's revelation about hell and eternal damnation is a confirmation of God's love; not only in the sense of a timely warning but as a powerful proof of God's earnestness in His love-suit. *Our final "yes" to God's loving invitation will find its consummation in heaven. Our final "no" to God's love-suit will find its eternal petrification in the icy loneliness of hell.* The thought of hell is not only conducive to arousing salutary fear but is a penetrating sermon concerning the majestic greatness of God's love. Hell is one of the great signs which unquestionably prove that the issue in our moral life is that of totality: either permanent friendship or eternal enmity with God.

The life of the baptized is not based on a keynote of threat and fear but rather on the Christian's solidarity with Christ. As "children of light" with Christ's own declarations of happiness in our hearts, we possess the courage to stand firm and ready for action in the dreadful struggles of life. The more confirmed we are in an authentic Christian optimism rooted in the glad tidings of salvation, the more determinedly we shall fight against the powers and principalities of evil.

The primacy of grace over moral demands is apparent. Grace, as the gratuitous gift of the beneficent love of God, does not minimize the importance of moral laws, but, rather, reveals their full power and victory in overflowing joy. The keen realization of the treasure of graces received and the future glory promised to us, directs our gaze heavenward in the full expectation of the new heaven and the new earth and thereby liberates our hearts from all earthly attachments. We become valiant soldiers for God's cause in the Christian renewal of the world.

The primacy of love over law implies an unconditional acknowledgment of God's redemptive dominion in the world. Man's moral struggles, as well as his endeavors to improve the world, will be doomed to failure if his attention is centered on his own abilities and obligations. God's surpassing power will manifest itself in and through men to the extent that they correspond to His redemptive plan and reciprocate His incomprehensible love. "For when I am weak, then I am strong" (II Cor. 12:10).

Section V. The Law Written in Minds and Hearts

The magnificence of the New Covenant and the New Law was announced by God through the prophet Jeremias: "Behold the days shall come, says the Lord: I will give My law in their inmost being, and will write it into their heart" (Jer. 31:31-33). The letter to the Hebrews particularly aims to extol the sublimity of Christ's priesthood in comparison with the priesthood of the Old Testament: "For when the priesthood is changed, it is necessary that a change of law be made also" (Hebr. 7:12). After paying tribute to the High Priest Jesus Christ, who had received the solemn promise from the Father: "Thou art a priest forever" (Hebr. 7:21), the Apostle adds that the prophecy of Jeremias had been fulfilled both in the new priesthood and in the New Law (cf. Hebr. 8:8 ff.). Now God has really written His Law, namely the life in Christ, "into their minds and upon their hearts" (Hebr. 8:10).

1. Sacramental Assimilation and Imitation of Christ

In the sacraments Christ the new High Priest seals His covenant with men. This is especially true of the sacrament of the Eucharist, the center of all the sacraments. In their deepest essence, the sacraments are not expressions of *law* or demands.* They are incomprehensible gifts flowing from Christ's redemptive love. By means of the sacraments, Christ, in virtue of His death and resurrection, enters into a personal and close union with each of us. With indelible characters He engraves in our hearts His redemptive acts as the law of our new life, thereby making us members of the priestly race of God. Thus, endowed by Christ and assured of His singular love and predilection, we are no longer under the severe regime of external law but are living under the mild yoke of grace (cf. Rom. 6:14).

The honor implied in Christ's invitation: "Come follow Me," exceeds all human comprehension because He summons us in a personal and intimate manner, addressing us by name. What could equal the sublimity of the discipleship of Christ which permits us not only to meditate on but also to fulfill His covenant and law of love? Weighed down by our sins, and so unlike Christ, we may question our ability to follow Christ in wholehearted love and obedience. *Yet, "the following" of Christ is not meant to be an external imitation of Christ's actions, which to a great extent are beyond our finite human powers, nor does*

* Cf. Vatican Council II, Liturgy Constitution, art. 10.

*it simply imply an emulation of His sublime dispositions
and sentiments. Christ desires to confirm our discipleship
by giving us a share in His own life and by transforming
our souls into His own image and likeness.*

This truth, that the essence of the Christian life is a
much more profound reality than a mere matter of external
relationship to law or a mere outward obedience to Christ,
is strikingly evident in the writings of the Fathers of the
Church. *St. Cyril of Jerusalem,* whom we quote as a witness of tradition in the early days of the Church, thus
describes the interior and intimate relationship existing
between Christ and the baptized: "Having been baptized
into Christ, and put on Christ (cf. Gal. 3:27) you have
been made conformable to the Son of God (cf. Rom.
8:29). God who has predestined us to be His adopted
children (cf. Eph. 1:5), has molded us into the image of
Christ's glorified body (cf. Phil. 3:21). Being, therefore,
made partakers of Christ, you are truly called Christs
(anointed) to whom God referred when He said, 'Touch not
my Christs' (Ps. 104:15). The term anointed signifies special favor and predilection. You were made other Christs
by receiving the resembling image of the Holy Spirit. All
these things were done figuratively in you because you are
images of Christ. . . . When Christ permitted Himself
to be baptized in the River Jordan, the Holy Spirit de-
scended upon Him in a visible form. . . . In like manner,
after you came up from the pool of the sacred baptismal
waters, you received the Unction or anointing with the
Holy Spirit. . . . Anointed with oil you received participation with Christ to an eminent degree" (*III Myst.
Catechesis*). Christ invites us to His imitation by giving us
a share in His own life and mission. By His own words,
filled with wisdom, He teaches us most intimately and
effectively in the very depth of the soul through the in-

spirations of the Holy Spirit. To follow Christ means to correspond faithfully to the interior realities of grace.

St. Cyril takes his orientation from the liturgy of baptism since this was highly meaningful and deeply significant in his time. The sacraments effect what they indicate and express in a symbolic language what they actually produce in the soul. Consequently, they teach us the fundamental truths about the law of the imitation of Christ which is engraved in our heart: "First you were anointed on your forehead to free you from the disgrace which has disfigured man since his shameful fall in paradise, so that now you may behold Christ's glory face to face (although merely as a faint reflection in a mirror); next your ears were anointed in order that the sense of hearing for the divine mysteries might be given to you as predicted by Isaias. 'He opens my ear, that I may hear Him as a master' (Is. 50:4), and again as stated by Christ Himself in the gospel: 'Listen, you that have ears to hear with' (Matt. 11:15). The anointing of the nose was performed so that enriched with this divine unction you could say: 'We are the fragrance of Christ for God' (II Cor. 2:15). You received the anointing of your chest to strengthen you with the breastplate of justice, thereby enabling you to stand firm against the cunning of the devil (cf. Eph. 6:14, 11). Christ, after His baptism and the descent of the Holy Spirit at the River Jordan, went out to meet and to overcome His adversary. In a similar manner, you, also, after your baptism and mysterious anointing, are equipped with the complete armor of the Holy Spirit in opposition to the vile powers of the enemy whom you shall overcome with the avowal: 'I can do all things in Him who strengthens me' (Phil. 4:13). . . . Since you have become the anointed ones by means of the holy unction of the sacraments, keep yourselves free and undefiled from every stain of sin and continue in the performance of good works so that you may become pleasing to Christ, the author of your salvation, to whom be honor and glory through all eternity" (*III Myst. Catechesis*).

St. Cyril saw the whole Christian life in the light of sanctifying grace. This grace, implanted in our beings, invites us to a Christ-like life marked by perfect docility to the inspiration of the Holy Spirit. Through the mediation of the sacraments, God creates within us a new heart and a new spirit. Consequently, we received the mission of grace: "Disciples of the new covenant and in possession of the holy mysteries through grace, renew your heart and spirit" (*I Catechesis*). "Those who have received the spiritual seal are to respond to grace by their own personal effort. . . . It is God's privilege to bestow graces. It is your responsibility to respond to grace and to abide in it" (*Ibid.*).

In relation to the sacramental efficacy as visualized in the liturgy, St. Cyril considered charity, love of enemy, kindness, chastity, the spirit of concord, and the untiring struggle to overcome the dominion of the devil, as Christ's specific tasks—missions deeply impressed in our hearts by the fruitful reception of the sacraments. "Since, in the manner of priests you are partakers of the name of Christ, and having received the seal of communion with the Spirit . . . walk worthy of the grace received by word and in deed so that you may enjoy eternal life. . . . In addition: 'Rejoice in the Lord always; again I say, rejoice'" (Phil. 4:4) (*XVIII Catechesis*).

The sacramental assimilation with Christ is a law inherent in grace, a law which in itself is good tidings or happy news. In order to understand the New Law we must open our hearts to the fulness of joy. Then, only, will the impelling force of this law reveal itself in our lives:

"For all who are moved by the Spirit of God, are sons
of God. The spirit you have received is not a spirit of slavery leading you back into a life of fear, but a spirit that
makes you sons (Rom. 8:14-15). It does not profit us to
have received the title *Christian*, unless we are bringing
forth the true fruits of Christians" (*VII Catechesis*).

2. *"The Spiritual Law of the Life in Christ Jesus"*

Just as Christ allows us to participate in His own divine
life through the action of the Holy Spirit, He also grants
us His New Law through the intervention of the Paraclete.
The Law of Christ is nothing else but the promptings of
the Holy Spirit whereby, as truly docile disciples, we become receptive to His teachings. The Holy Spirit not only
makes us sharers in the life of Christ, but also grants us a
thorough understanding and appreciation of the Law of
Christ, which is but a life in perfect correspondence to the
invitations of God's grace.

St. Augustine and St. Thomas, the two great Doctors of
the Church, followed the example of St. Paul, who, in his
emphatic and daring teaching called the Holy Spirit bestowed on us *the fulness of the New Law*. "What are the
laws of God, which are written in our very hearts by
God Himself, if not the gifts of the same Holy Spirit,
whose presence in our hearts pours forth charity, which is
the fulness of the Law" (Augustine). "By enkindling in
our hearts charity, which is the fulness of the Law, the
Holy Spirit proves Himself to be the New Law (the New
Covenant)" (Thomas Aquinas).

St. Paul's words to the Romans: "For the law of the
Spirit of the life in Christ Jesus has delivered me from the
law of sin and death" (Rom. 8:2), found the following
explanation by St. Thomas: "This law can be called the

Holy Spirit in the sense that *the Holy Spirit is the Law*. The purpose of law is to guide man towards the good. . . . The Holy Spirit dwelling in our hearts teaches us not only by enlightening our intellect concerning the things to be done, but likewise disposes the soul towards the good. . . . In addition 'the law of the Spirit' can truly be considered the working of the Holy Spirit; namely, faith effective in charity, which teaches from within and impels the heart towards the good" (*Commentary to Rom.* 8:2).

The New Law, the law of "following" Christ, is basically a *law of life* of interior dynamism leading towards growth and development in the supernatural life bestowed by grace. It is a law which the Life-Giver, the Holy Spirit, sustains by His personal indwelling in the souls. It is a law of life which makes us perceptive of the supernatural meaning of our existence so that we are no longer satisfied with the minimum requirements of the law for the sake of avoiding punishment, but in a childlike spirit respond to the impulses of divine grace while living God's own life. *Indeed, the true disciple of Christ may never become so engrossed in the mere letter of the law that he becomes oblivious to the interior realities of grace and the demands of charity.*

St. Paul urges us to open our hearts to the powerful action and impulses of the Holy Spirit when he says: "For the letter kills, but the spirit gives life" (II Cor. 3:6). The fact that the words of the Apostle may not be quoted for the sake of advocating a lawless "religion of the spirit" which despises the written word of God, is evident from the words of Christ which He spoke to the Jews who took offense at His promise of giving His flesh and blood for their food and drink: "It is the spirit that gives life; the flesh profits nothing" (John 6:64). These words are far from a concession indicating that Jesus took back His promise. The reception of Christ's body in Holy Communion has not become superfluous by the outpouring of the Holy Spirit. On the contrary, both realities of grace form a marvelous unity. In like manner, there exists an intimate relationship between the interior workings of grace wrought by the Holy Spirit and the written law of God and the Church.

The interior operations of the Holy Spirit open our hearts to the true meaning of Sacred Scripture and make us docile to the Church and her directions. Our Lord solemnly affirmed that His words are expressions of His Spirit: *"The words that I have spoken to you are spirit and life"* (John 6:64). The words of Sacred Scripture have been written under the inspiration of the Holy Spirit, the Paraclete bestowed by Christ on His Church and the apostles. *The same Lord Jesus* who sent us the Holy Spirit has also given us words of wisdom and the authority of the Church. The Paraclete, who interiorly urges each faithful to an authentic life in Christ, is the same Holy Spirit whom Christ had promised to His Church as the teacher of truth. "These things I have spoken to you while yet dwelling with you. But the Advocate, the Holy Spirit, whom the Father will send in My name, He will teach you all things, and bring to your mind whatever I have said to you" (John 14:25-26).

Mere external, mechanical conformity to the letter of the law is diametrically opposed to an intelligent and docile acceptance and implementation of Christ's message. Herein, the Christian is called upon to make an inexorable decision. *A fruitful Christian life is not subject to the dead letter of the law but is subject to the life-giving spirit of a personal God.* It is guided by the "Law of the Spirit" which in the words of Holy Scripture is the "Life in Christ Jesus" (Rom. 8:2). Sacred Scripture uses various phrases, such as: "to be in Christ," "to follow Christ," "to respond to the inner call of grace"—in order to express the sublime and blessed reality which forms the basis of our transformation into authentic Christians or other Christs. Such a life presupposes a constant openness to the invitations of divine love and a sensitive responsiveness to the needs of others. Fidelity to grace will triumph in a truly inventive and sensitive response to the needs of others.

Section VI. The Law of Christ and the Many Laws

"There is one Lord, Jesus Christ, through whom all things have come to be, and we through Him" (I Cor. 8:6). There can be no real conflict between the natural moral law and the revealed "law of grace"; for it is through the one Word of the Father that all things have been created, and this Word shared our human nature in order to manifest the overflowing, boundless love of the Father. The same Lord, who implanted in our inmost being the natural moral law as a basic guide for our actions, continues to reveal His will and good pleasure to us in the ever changing demands of the hour, in the special events of our life, and in the inspirations of the Holy Spirit.

SYNOPSIS OF SECTION SIX

The Christian, who desires to gain a clear insight into the beauty of Christian morality and who aims for maturity of judgment in the face of certain trends in our time, should understand the true relationship of the various aspects of law, such as: 1. the distinct difference and, at the same time, inner harmony between the natural moral law and the law of grace; 2. the immutable basic and essential laws in contradistinction to mere precepts and regulations which are conditioned by circumstances of time and place (statutes); 3. laws which are universally applicable and obligations arising from particular circumstances of life; 4. the unity of laws in the light of the great law of grace.

1. The Natural Moral Law and the Law of Grace

It is in praise of the undeserved grace of God to make a clear distinction between the natural moral law, rooted in man's very nature as a rational creature, and the law of the supernatural life revealed by Christ.

The natural moral law is so deeply rooted in man's being that the fall in paradise, followed by a life of sin, could not abrogate it, nor could even Redemption itself supplant it.

It is true that Moses, by reason of man's "hardness of heart," tolerated certain violations of the natural law as is indicated by his restrictions regarding divorce followed by remarriage, and polygamy. Even before his time these perversions had been practiced without restraint. Moses, therefore, tolerated the lesser evil in order to prevent more serious moral disorders. But his juridical limitations in no way implied a seal of approval and approbation on the aberrations. However, the mere fact that for the sake of maintaining the juridical order, Moses, even in the Law of the Covenant, permitted some mitigations intrinsically opposed to the original designs of the Creator and contrary to the dignity of man and woman, proves the deep distortion wrought by original sin which opened the floodgates to the pernicious stream of sin inundating the world.

Even unredeemed mankind retained the ability to recognize the most essential moral laws deeply engraved in the hearts of men. What God had manifested on Mount Sinai, amid thunder and lightening, and had inscribed into the two Tables of the Law as an everlasting pledge of the covenant of love, is a fundamental summary of the most important natural laws and precepts. These have been recognized as God's laws by all the noble and pious pagans of the past.

In the words of St. Paul, the gentiles although not in possession of the law of Moses but living by the law of their nature, as summarized in the Decalogue, "show the work of the law written in their hearts. Their conscience bears witness to them" (Rom. 2:15). God obviously manifests His dominion in the works of His creation, so that those refusing to pay homage to Him "are without excuse" (Rom. 1:20-32). St. Paul points to the fact that the gentiles' increasing darkness of intellect is the consequence of sin in general and, in particular, the sin inherent in the refusal to acknowledge and adore God (cf. Rom. 1:28 ff.).

With the revelation of salvation and the promulgation of the New Law of grace, Christ also deepened our insight into the natural moral law, while, at the same time, renewing its inexorable demands in a way which was alarming even to the apostles (in the question of the indissolubility of marriage) (cf. Matt. 19:10).

But the full impact of the natural moral law presupposes the new order of grace which enables the faithful to "accept" and fulfill its inexorable demands (Matt. 19:10). Likewise, without supernatural revelation, mankind in its present wounded state would "not easily, nor with certainty and freedom from error" arrive at a full understanding of all the moral truths within reach of the human mind, as manifested in the order of creation (Vat. Council, Denzinger No. 1716, Thomas Aquinas *S.Th.* I, q 1, a 1).

After it had pleased God "to re-establish all things in Christ, both those in the heavens and those on the earth"

(Eph. 1:10) "for in Him were created all things in the heavens and on the earth" (Col. 1:16), we may not separate the natural and supernatural domain as two completely unrelated spheres of human existence. The realm of natural morality, which to a considerable extent is open even to unbelievers, may not be neglected nor made autonomous by the Christian. It is fortunate that these truths provide a common meeting-ground for a fruitful dialogue with non-Christians of good will. But in regard to our personal life and our mission for the extension of God's kingdom, the natural and supernatural truths are related in a similar manner as the natural virtues are rooted in supernatural charity. *All that is good and noble has its origin and its goal in the person of Jesus Christ.* The important aspect in all our actions is their conformity with the established order of God and their contribution to His greater honor and glory.

The natural moral law is woven both into the order of creation and into the heart of man as a *foundation law.* The law of grace, on the other hand, presupposes an explicit revelation from God. This is not to say that the natural moral law is the only interior law in harmony with the essence of things and the rational nature of man. On the contrary, the "Law of Christ" manifested by Our Lord in words full of wisdom and power and interpreted by the Church, is even more deeply engraved in our hearts than the law of nature. *It is essentially an expression of the inner reality of the life of grace.* We shall begin to realize God's fondest expectations in our regard if in the light of faith we begin to recognize the rich treasures of grace bestowed on us. Similarly, as the natural moral law is a magnificent image of creation and man's true nature, so also the New Law of Christ is a faithful expression of man's rebirth and renewal through grace. All men are subject to this law of grace since all are called to a share in the life of grace. Yet only those in the state of sanctifying grace are truly living within this Law.

Just as an undepraved, good man has a natural inclination to what is naturally good, so the Holy Spirit working within us makes us docile toward the Law of Christ and inclines us to fulfill Christ's demands willingly and with connatural ease.

The natural moral law is not a code of external rules and regulations but rather a challenge to act in full accord with our rational nature. This does not deny that its main principles can be expressed in general, universally valid statements. The law of grace, likewise, is primarily an essential law of God's kingdom transmitted to us and engraved in our hearts by sanctifying grace. The law of grace does not only respect our natural gifts and abilities but also perfects them in a manner far surpassing all our expectations. Its essential demands are faithfully expressed in the pages of Holy Scripture and in the teachings of Holy Mother Church.

It is important that the mature Christian does not cling to mere forms and external expressions of the New Law. The Law of Christ will prove itself life-giving and blessed to the extent that the Christian sees in it the revelation of the New Covenant of love. This truth finds fitting expression in the highly significant words of Holy Scripture: "This is eternal life: that they know You, the only true God, and Jesus Christ whom You have sent" (John 17:3). Just as the supernatural moral law unfolds its true essence and beauty only as far as man recognizes all created orders in the universe as expressions of God's personal love, *so to an even greater extent is an understanding of "Christ's Law" centered in the knowledge of God the Father and Our Lord Jesus Christ.*

On the other hand, it is true that a lack of responsiveness to Christ's invitation as expressed in His Law is one of the chief obstacles to an authentic knowledge of Christ. This has its counterpart in the natural moral order where failure to respond to the dictates of the natural law tends to destroy the harmony in man's nature and thereby deters man from arriving at a true knowledge of the good in keeping with the natural law and his own abilities. Whoever estranges himself from his own true self will also become a stranger to God and the good. He will become increasingly blind to the good and his own aim and direction in life.

2. *Immutable Natural Laws and Positive Precepts*

There are certain basic demands, either inherent in man's rational nature or resulting from the supernatural order of grace, which are laid down unconditionally for all times and all men. Nevertheless, it is in the nature of man, who has helped to shape history and is himself influenced by the events of time, that he be subject to timely regulations and standards of human existence. Each epoch has its own challenge by reason of its favorable or unfavorable heritage and contingent events. Ordinarily, particular circumstances allow a variety of responses in the application of general norms or principles. *If it is a question of community responsibility, it is the duty of the legitimate authority to select one of the several possible courses of action and express it in precise and definite terms.* This results in the formulation of positive laws and regulations; "positive," not as opposed to negative but in the sense of fixed statutes, "posited" or "written" rights laid down by competent authority. Such positive laws from legitimate superiors are needed in view of original sin and for the protection of mankind. If all men were of good will there would be no need for so many laws.

In the final analysis, in a rapidly changing society, necessary guidance and directions from legitimate authority are expressions of divine wisdom. This does not dispense the individual from a personal search for the good in agreement with the natural law and the call of grace.

Equitable laws, passed by competent, legitimate authority, are binding in conscience even if they have something of the "accidental" when compared with the *implanted* natural law.

Laws or commands passed by man which are in direct opposition to a divine law, either in the natural or supernatural order, impose no moral obligation on anyone. In fact it would be sinful to observe such regulations because "we ought to obey God, rather than men" (Acts 5:29).

For example, a soldier who has been commanded to drop an atom bomb over a heavily populated district or to carry out any similar order of inhuman revenge on civilians, would be obliged in conscience to disobey such pernicious commands. If unjust civil laws are disobeyed because of loyalty to the Christian faith and its principles, such transgressions may not be reported by either citizens or government officials even though an unjust human ordinance might demand such action.

Human regulations which, although not directly opposed to God's laws, are paltry or infringe on our well-founded right, have no binding power in themselves because they lack the justice of the law. It is important, however, to decide whether our disregard for such laws or commands is in keeping with the common good (peace, respect for authority, etc.) and love of neighbor and of self.

No sensible official will adhere to regulations of the law

which constitute obstacles to the prompt and efficient discharge of his duties ("red tape"). But, on the other hand, he will abide by them if their transgression would cause great inconvenience to himself or others through the contestable nature of a document or a contract.

It is not easy for those in authority and power to adapt to present conditions laws which had been passed under different circumstances, because we are living in times of rapid change. This human limitation should be a source of deep humility for those in authority. The same holds true for those in subordination. It is not fitting that every imperfect command and every untimely regulation be unkindly criticized or spitefully disregarded. We should not expect too much of human authority.

In the last analysis, even the imperfections inherent in human legislation must be seen in the light of God's loving designs. They are a check on our pride and the unrestricted despotism of imperfect rulers. Above all, the humble acceptance of such frailty and the willing subordination to faulty laws are part of the following of Christ who, for love of us, subjected Himself to imperfect human laws and superiors. Our "dying with Christ" is accomplished in the humiliating experience of obedience, which at times may be painful and agonizing in view of the imperfections of men and the faultiness of laws. This is the task we have received in baptism. Those in authority, however, should strive to command according to the mild nature of the Law of Christ.

The Law of Christ, namely, the blessed challenge inherent in sanctifying and actual grace, is in reality "a light yoke and a sweet burden" (Matt. 11:30). The *natural law*, likewise, is not a code of rigid rules but a noble challenge implanted by God in the very nature of man, in perfect conformity with the true desires of the human heart. On the other hand, *human laws,* including parental regulations and positive laws of the Church and State, may to a greater or lesser degree become unfitting and oppressive, irrespective of the faultiness of laws. Such regulations prove detrimental to the degree that they detain man from entering fully into the blessed Law of Christ. *Human laws, despite their imperfections, may become sources of blessings if we are able to perceive their true relationship to the law of grace and thereby draw them into the "Law of the Spirit in the life of Christ" in faith, hope, and charity.*

Imbued with gratitude, we should accept the *positive laws of the Church* as authentic gifts from God transmitted to us through the hands of Holy Mother Church. On the other hand, it is not the Church's intention to present her book of statutes as a final and exhaustive reference book for Christian living. The Church's chief function is the preaching of the gospel and the celebration of the mysteries of salvation. The Law of Christ, as a law of grace and joy, is implied in this mission. The Code of Canon Law does not contain the fulness of the "Christian Law" or Christian living but acts as its safeguard and protective wall. Since God wishes to effect our salvation in the community and in the framework of history and historical changes, it is one of the fundamental missions of the Church to help us through positive, adaptable directions to fulfill our essential and timely mission and to successfully meet the difficulties and needs of the respective epoch and culture. This, too, must be considered as an expression of the historical realities of salvation and our communion with Christ, who for our sake assumed a human nature and subjected Himself to the circumstances of the particular, historical hour, thus accomplishing salvation in history.

The recent legislative modifications, enacted by the Church for the sake of adaptation to the changing circumstances of our time, should renew our incentive to enter more fully into the spirit and intentions of the Church as expressed in her laws and aiding us realize the tremendous difference between the immutable essential laws and the changeable human laws. A few examples may help to identify the true spirit of loyal acceptance in regard to the numerous adaptations prepared by a special commission for the renewal of Canon Law.

(a) To many of us, *the new legislation regarding the eucharistic fast* may seem a tremendous innovation as well as a surprise because the Church is granting such liberal mitigations in a matter in which we ourselves have been scrupulously exact. What is really at stake? It still remains the Church's concern, as it always has been, that we receive the body of Our Lord with the greatest possible reverence and that we are aware of the distinction between it and all earthly food, and that by our willingness to mortify ourselves we may manifest our sincere appreciation for God's heavenly gift. The purpose of this mitigation of the Church is that no one of good will should be prevented from the reception of Holy Communion, and good will includes the readiness to make sacrifices. Good will is synonymous with sacrifice. This legislation, therefore, is meant to encourage generosity. The Christian will freely manifest his readiness for sacrifice rather than act under the threat of sin.

(b) A similar example may be cited concerning the *law of Friday abstinence*. In the past, this law has become the "standard law" in confession for a good number of Catholics. Transgressions in this regard have been made the subject for confession even if these were due to forgetfulness or any other justifiable excuse. Today's exemptions by the Church, granted to whole groups of Christians, clearly indicate that the point at issue is not the enforcement of an external regulation. According to the intentions of the Church, abstinence from certain foods is to aid the Christian to a spirit of renunciation and sacrifice in gratitude for the bitter Passion and death of Our Lord. The other factor in the observance of this law, as in any other law of the Church, is the consideration for the community. Christians, as a community, should confess themselves to the imitation of the crucified Savior by the common observance of this sign. Today's manner of living has called for a modification of this precept. Many Catholics, at present, are living in non-Catholic surroundings. In addition, the modern ways of living and working all too often may create difficulties in the observance of this law. However, it remains essential that, on principle, we comply with the intentions of the Church and try to manifest our readiness to submit to the regulations of this commandment. Rather than to adhere to the letter of the law while yet essentially avoiding mortifications, as for example in the partaking of a luxurious meal (without meat), it would be more in agreement with the mind of the Church to make use of the dispensations without hesitation and render proof of our gratitude in other ways, such as refraining from smoking or other cherished habits. The Church's chief concern is the spirit of the law which, however, as far as possible, should take concrete form in agreement with her directions.

(c) Another innovation is the permission for celebrating *evening Mass* and, under certain circumstances, allowing the faithful to fulfill their weekly Mass obligation on Saturday. The Church in the past had set aside Sunday morning for the celebration of Holy Mass, in conformity with the rhythm and activity of life in order to permit all Christians to attend the Holy Sacrifice. Today she has adapted to the changing conditions of our social life.

(d) *The liturgical renewal in Holy Week* marked the beginning of a far-reaching movement in agreement with tradition and in the spirit of today's adaptations, paying due attention to modern man's mentality as influenced by technical advances and revolutionary changes in social life. The Church, in the Second Vatican Council, is cognizant of the need for a more profound adaptation to the various cultures. The use of the vernacular, as practiced in the Churches of the Orient, is now being allowed in the Roman Rite liturgy also. After a long and careful discussion, the overwhelming majority of Council Fathers have agreed on the great blessings of a liturgy celebrated in the mother tongue. The underlying reason for a possible delay in carrying out this renewal is due to the fact that the Church, acting in the best interests of all people and all nations, must also accommodate those still unprepared for this reform.

3. *Universal Laws and the Call of the Moment*

The term *"universal law"* applies, in the first place, to the unchangeable laws in the natural and supernatural order and, in the second place, but distinct from the first, it refers to the changeable human laws. The need or call of the moment (Kairos) includes the mission inherent in the invitations of grace and the external circumstances of our existence, especially those relating to the needs of our neighbor.

In the relationship between the universal law and the special call of the moment there are two equally reprehensible and contrary extremist attitudes.

On the one side there is the fanatic for the law, guided by the letter rather than the spirit of the law. Such may have been the priest and the levite in the gospel (cf. Luke

10:30 ff.). Always concerned about the external observances of the law even to its minutest detail, they remained untouched and unresponsive when confronted with the extreme misery of a fellowman who had been ill-treated by bandits. The written regulations of their law, "to pay tithe on everything they had," meant more to them than the crying needs of their neighbor. In contrast to this legalistic attitude, there was the moral responsiveness of the good Samaritan which Christ so vividly depicted: ". . . and seeing him he was moved with compassion. And going up to him, bound up his wounds, pouring in oil and wine . . ." (Luke 10:33 ff.).

The extreme opposite of the juridical approach, as exemplified by the "fanatic of the law," is manifested in the type of person who, carried away by feelings, loses all consideration for even the most sacred of laws. Such a person is depicted by Graham Greene in his novel *The Heart of the Matter*. This book tells the story of a good-natured adventurer who becomes an adulterer out of compassion for a poor creature. As a result of the arising conflicts—his fear of hurting his wife, the unfortunate girl, and even God Himself—he ended his life by committing suicide. The underlying trouble in such "kind-heartedness" was the failure to adhere to the universal moral laws. This caused misfortune for himself, while at the same time it entangled those nearest and dearest to him into his own ruin. Such cases are by no means confined to fiction. Thus, a poor woman living in concubinage with a crippled war veteran, touchingly implored the priest during a mission to admit her to the sacraments. Her desire was sincere. But she had no intentions of breaking the sinful union, although no sensual love was present, to judge from her words: "I am unable to hurt the poor man by leaving him, neither do I want to marry him." It took much patience and effort on the part of the priest to convince this woman that this was far from true love, and that her actions were not violating merely an "arbitrary" law but the protecting and saving order established by God, and that at the same time she was making herself an accomplice in the sins of others.

The bureaucracy of today has favored the evolution of the so-called "law-conscious" man, not only in civil but also in ecclesiastical circles. Many a priest in hearing confessions has overemphasized the responsibilities arising from the positive law with insufficient understanding for the special needs and graces of his penitents. A real scandal is created by those "pious" people who keep the Friday abstinence so meticulously that they examine their soup for the minutest particles of meat, while at the same time they remain indifferent to the basic demands of charity.

Such narrow-mindedness in matters of ethics (especially in secular circles) has resulted in the evolution of an attitude which is directly opposed to the one mentioned above, namely, that of the so-called *"situation-ethics."* Here the individual is guided only by the duties and demands present in a given situation, refusing to admit the unconditional applicability of universal laws. The extreme reaction against the law, manifested in situation-ethics, may be traced to a failure to make clear-cut distinctions between immutable and changeable positive laws.

It is true that the positive human laws, under certain circumstances, must give way to the call of the moment. There is full agreement on this point between Catholic theologians and the proponents of situation-ethics. The reason for this lies in the fact that the positive human laws are not made in view of the unusual situation and, consequently, do not exclude a different course of action in exceptional cases. But under no circumstances can the call of the moment be in explicit opposition to the natural moral law rooted in man's nature by God's own design, because God cannot contradict Himself.

This false type of situation-ethics tends to open the way to laxity. Ernst Michel, one of the most radical proponents of situation-ethics, holds the opinion that divorce followed by remarriage could be permitted in cases of a declining love and signs of incompatibility between the spouses. This is just another way of saying that under certain conditions the law of fidelity and indissolubility of marriage should not oppose a new union.

On the other hand, Catholic teaching regarding the call of the moment is quite *courageous in its higher demands*. The Christian, open to the call of grace and the need of the moment, may not content himself with the bare minimum requirements of the law. As every individual embodies human existence in a singular and often amazingly rich incarnation, so will each person fulfill the general human obligations in keeping with his own potentials. God has favored us with precious and unique gifts of nature and grace and, in consequence, expects a rich harvest in view of these gifts ("talents" in the biblical sense).

As true Christians we are all obliged to help our neighbor on his way to God. Yet in the case of a St. Paul, God, could in full justice, expect an all-consuming zeal after he had converted from a persecutor of the Church to the apostle of the gentiles. While no Christian may lose himself in mundane affairs, nevertheless, not all are bound to imitate St. Francis in his radical detachment from the world which rendered such convincing proof of the transcendence of spiritual joys. All followers of Christ have the obligation of a wholehearted forgiveness towards their enemies, but all are not expected to imitate the heroism of St. John Gualbert who, like a brother, received his enemy into his own household. Likewise, every truly Christian spouse shall, as far as possible, follow St. Paul's exhortation (cf. I Cor. 7:29) and preserve a virginal heart which signifies a mutual, pure love directed toward God. This, however, does not impose on married people the heroic sacrifice of Brother Klaus who asked his dearly beloved wife, and mother of his nine children, to permit him to lead a hermit's life for the love of Christ.

Even if we are not called to imitate the exalted virtues of the saints, *we are still far from mere "cases" lost in the crowd. God has called each one of us by our intimately personal name.* He is constantly providing each of us with countless opportunities to prove ourselves in the special circumstances of our lives. To each of us He is giving His particular calling and duty in relation to the welfare of mankind and the community of the redeemed.

St. Paul draws a fitting comparison between the diversity of vocations and the complexity of the human organism, dependent on many members with highly specialized and vital functions. "If the body were all eye, how could it hear? If the body were all ear, how could it smell? But, in fact, God appointed each limb and organ to its own place in the body, as He chose" (I Cor. 12:17 ff.). A similar relationship exists in the Communion of Saints to which St. Paul refers as "the body of Christ." It is the duty of each Christian to recognize and fulfill, with a joyful and grateful heart, his calling and mission in life. Thus will he work in the best interests of all. In the mind of St. Paul, the call and the opportunity of the moment is the individual's challenge for his special and unique contribution in the *solidarity of salvation in Christ.* We shall best understand the call and the opportunity of the moment, if unlike the proponents of situation-ethics, we are not bent on insisting on our individual rights or "the development of our personality," but are always ready to utilize our gifts and talents in the best interests of the community.

This should answer, at least in part, the all-important question: How shall I recognize the will of God in each particular situation?* Exceedingly great is the honor implied in Christ's invitation to contribute our personal share to the redemption of the world and the extension of His kingdom on earth. In God's design there is a special task and vocation for each of us. Similarly, each epoch has its own particular mission and calling in God's redemptive plan. In the final analysis, the natural laws implanted in our nature and the ordinances of lawful authority are gifts and blessings from the hand of God. *Their true nature can be comprehended only in a filial attitude of gratitude.* This truth finds fitting expression in the words of St. Augustine: "Love, and then do what you will." These words do not advocate a license for transgressing the law because true charity presupposes a loving attention and responsiveness to the merciful design of God, particularly an openness to the needs of our neighbor. This generous and grateful charity will allow us to participate in the transfiguring power of divine love and enable us to act with inner assurance in all the difficult situations of life.

4. The Unity of Laws in Christian Life

Christian life is endangered if morality is seen as a multiplicity of unrelated laws. The more deeply we penetrate into the knowledge and love of Christ, the more fully we shall become aware of the truly marvelous unity of the Christian way of life, which really embraces a "life in Christ," a grateful use of the God-given talents and graces,

---

* This topic will receive further discussion in another context (virtue of prudence and the gifts of the Holy Spirit, Chapter III, paragraph I).

a loving responsiveness to the plans of God, and an intimate dialogue of love.

In the eternal law of divine wisdom there is perfect harmony between the natural law, the law of grace, the legitimate demands of human authority, and the duties and obligations of the *Kairos* (the need of the moment). Our Lord's utter obedience in His self-sacrificing life, Passion, and death, strikingly manifests the law of divine love. This law of God's wisdom is given to us by faith through the teaching and guiding authority of the Church. Through the powerful operations of the Holy Spirit it can become for us a law of life in Christ Jesus. The Holy Spirit is charity and at the same time He is the bond of unity. If in filial, reciprocating love we try to fulfill the mission inherent in divine charity, the Holy Spirit, who grants us "the life in Christ Jesus" (Rom. 8:2), will Himself bring this divine life to its full perfection in us. The more we grow into Christ, the more our life will gain in interior and exterior unity.

In the growing awareness of our personal responsibility of filial response to God's call, we ought to make definite and conscious efforts to integrate our entire life into the great law of charity. A few examples will illustrate this truth.

a. The Law of Sunday Mass

There are a number of faulty attitudes regarding the obligation to attend Mass on Sunday, as some of the following statements indicate. "This law of Sunday Mass is only a positive law of the Church and, consequently, a merely juridically binding law. Therefore, this precept is fulfilled by attending a whole Mass unless excused by illness or urgent duties. True, all unbecoming activities during the sacrifice of the Mass are out of place. However, one's interior recollection and prayer cannot be subject to the external law of the Church." Such an attitude of mere exterior compliance separates this law from its very root and meaning and deprives the spiritual life of all unity and efficacy.

In the vital unity of the "Law of the Spirit of Life" (Rom. 8:2), the participation in Sunday Mass is much more than an exterior performance. The baptized, as a vital member of God's holy people and a descendant of the "priestly race" (Ex. 19:6; Apoc. 1:6, 5:10), ought to consider his participation in the celebration of the sacrifice of the New Covenant his greatest privilege and most sacred duty. By the special character conferred on our souls through baptism and confirmation, we have received Christ's personal call and invitation. This commandment of the Church requires no more than that which the graces of God's Spirit has written in our souls in letters of fiery language. In order to insure the community celebration of this great mystery of God's love by all the faithful, the Church has indeed issued this precept as a reminder to those tardy and slothful in fulfilling Christ's command to celebrate His greatest act of love ("Do this in commemoration of Me!"). Therefore, it should be our chief concern to participate worthily in this Holy Sacrifice celebrated by the Church. It should be our first concern *to keep our souls in grace as the living, vital members of God's holy people* "in spirit and in truth" (John 4:24). Furthermore, our attendance should be marked by the greatest joy and closest attention so that our singing and praying might become worthy expressions of gratitude for the undeserved gift of our membership in the community of God's holy people. Seen in this light, Sunday Mass, the participation in the banquet of love, will become a sincere manifestation of our friendship with Christ and an evident proof that we are no longer under the law but "under grace" (Rom. 6:14).

If then, despite all earnest effort and good will our attendance at Sunday Mass is marked by distractions, there is still reason to believe that Christ and His Church will be satisfied with our good intention. Even when such distractions have been partially voluntary, there exists no obligation under law to attend another Mass. *Yet, in all such cases a serious effort towards improvement should be made.*

It would be even more regrettable if the Christian performed his Sunday obligation "without a wedding garment" (in the disgrace of mortal sin), without contrition and sincere concern for his unfortunate state of soul.

Those Christians, who failed to pay attention to the sacred mysteries because they talked in front of the Church or engaged in other time-wasting activities during Mass, have not even fulfilled the external law of the Church and would do better to stay away from Sunday Mass because their behavior is a source of scandal to others. Such Christians not only place themselves "under the law" like servants, but outside the law as confirmed anarchists.

On the other hand, a mother prevented from attending Sunday Mass because her sick child requires care, but who nevertheless unites herself with the community of the faithful in the celebration of Mass, is far from violating the law. She is rather proving herself a true participant in the Holy Sacrifice with a full share in all its fruits. Her services at the bedside of her sick child are turned into an "adoration of God in the spirit and in truth," due to her readiness and her desire to participate in the sacrifice of Christ while following the call of the moment.

b. The Law of Friday Abstinence

It is evident that the precept of Friday abstinence, by its very nature, is less compelling than the law which demands our attendance at Sunday Mass. Consequently, a mere mechanical obedience and external performance of the Friday abstinence will prove less detrimental to Christian life. Yet, it should be remembered that the basic law of life inherent in the Christian vocation to sanctity demands our wholehearted effort to enter more fully into the true spirit of the law regarding Friday abstinence. This shall make the Christian cognizant of his duty to follow Our Lord, in His Way of the Cross, in wholehearted readiness for sacrifice even if dispensed from the external observance of this precept.

A working man, who eats meat on Friday because he is forced to bring his lunch to his place of work, but who abstains from smoking in grateful remembrance of the sufferings of Christ, has fully grasped the Church's intention in the abstinence regulation. His life has unity and meaning because it is oriented towards charity.

It is understood that meat could be eaten on Friday without any scrupulosity if meat were served unintentionally by a Protestant host or hostess. The situation would be quite different, however, if meat were served intentionally with an obvious contempt for the Catholic faith.

If it should happen that your brother's wife, forgetful of Friday, would serve meat, it would be an act of charity to partake of it without any comment. This would indeed be better than causing embarrassment by a refusal to eat the meat. However, the situation would be different if your brother were lax in observing the commandments of the Church. Under such circumstances, the refusal to partake of the meat might serve as an implied brotherly correction. On the other hand, in view of more essential issues at stake, it might be imprudent to attempt a strengthening of your brother's faith precisely with the insistence upon the Friday abstinence.

It should be clear that our attention should not be fixed on a particular aspect of a given law, but rather on the law in its entirety and its relation to charity. Only thus shall we be able to meet the challenge arising from the need and the opportunity of the moment and, at the same time, observe the precepts of the Church in their essential demands. *This will give unity and direction to our lives in agreement with the great commandment of charity.*

c. A Situation: Hour of Grace or Danger to Salvation?

The full recognition of the need and the opportunity of the moment is greatly dependent upon our dispositions. If we are guided by the principles of charity and a sincere interest in the extension of God's kingdom, we shall be in a far better position to interpret the needs of our time than if we are narrowly concerned only with our personal salvation.

The hypothetical case of Barbara will illustrate this truth. Suppose twenty year old Barbara, reared in a good Catholic home and rural community, has her first experience of living in a big city and working in a factory. She readily notices that those vocal and influential in the group are governed neither by faith nor by any respect for the feelings and moral principles of others. At the same time, she also becomes aware that another group of shy and reticent girls with sincere dispositions are annoyed and bothered by the bad elements in the factory. Having been reared in a good Christian environment, Barbara may become perplexed, wondering what course of action she should pursue in consideration of the danger for sin inherent in the deplorable situation. Barbara has to choose between the following alternate courses of action. She may pray and seek the advice of a priest or prudent lay person. She may feel herself inadequate to cope with the situation and, characteristic of the determination of the children of God, resign from her present employment according to the counsel of the gospel: "Seek you first the kingdom of God" (Matt. 6:33), because she realizes that in the face of risking eternal damnation, it would be far better to lose one's eye and thus to enter into the kingdom of heaven, than to lose both eyes (referring to a good income without opposition to the evil) (cf. Matt. 5:29 ff.; 18:8).

On the other hand, if Barbara has always been careful to recognize God's call in the circumstances of her life, she will be able to cope with the present situation showing both alertness and determination. In consideration of the well-intentioned but timid co-workers who unaided would lack the strength to persevere, she might form the nucleus of an upright group brave enough to voice its opinion. Such action is imperative for an improved working environment. But even in the absence of far-reaching effects and obvious improvements in the conduct of their co-workers, the good example of the group gives honor and glory to God, their Creator. In addition, the full acceptance of the challenge inherent in the call of the moment, enriches the life of the Christian and brings him to a fuller understanding of the Law of Christ and to a more sensitive perception of the call of grace.

It is the continuous mission of all Christians to exemplify in their actions the marvelous harmony of the natural and supernatural life by a truly upright disposition and an open eye for the needs of their brethren. This will allow free scope to the operations of the Holy Spirit, enkindling in our hearts the fire of divine love.

2 THE Freedom OF THE CHILDren OF GOD

The nine times repeated "Blessed" of the Sermon on the Mount clearly reveals the happy and joyous character of the New Law. As a law of grace and of love, it is not superimposed from without, but rather it is part of man's nature, as renewed through Christ's redeeming love. For this very reason it is a "perfect law of freedom" (James 1:25). The freedom of the children of God will be ours to the extent that we lovingly accept this law. Even in the natural order, law and freedom are intimately related. This inner relationship between the concept of law and liberty reveals itself in the "law of the Spirit of life" which is the very root of the freedom of the children of God. This law itself can only be understood and fulfilled in the supernatural freedom of the loving child of God.

SYNOPSIS OF CHAPTER TWO

(1) Both the freedom of the children of God and the New Law are the fruits of Christ's self-sacrificing love on the cross, granted to us as the beginning of our participation in the glory of His resurrection. (2) Consequently, the freedom of the children of God presupposes a renunciation of the old man and his works. (3) Since charity is the fulness of the New Law, its chief manifestation or fruit is a self-sacrificing love of neighbor. True freedom expands in direct proportion to the purity of our intention and love. (4) This freedom should manifest itself in all our dealings with creatures in every aspect of life, since the entire creation yearns and groans for "the freedom that comes with the glory of the children of God" (Rom. 8:21). (5) A renewal of society based on the principles of the freedom of the children of God, is opposed to man's self-glorifying concept and can only be accomplished in true meekness. (6) The freedom of the children of God, the fruit of Christ's obedience unto death, finds fitting response in both our obedience and the Christ-like exercise of authority. (7 & 8) In the final analysis, the development of the Christian's liberty as well as the dangers and obstacles to human freedom are to be evaluated in their relationship to the freedom of the children of God.

Section I. "The Freedom Wherewith Christ has made Us Free"

"The freedom wherewith Christ has made us free" (Gal. 4:31) is totally different from the freedom for which the children of this world are fighting. Nevertheless, the freedom of the children of God confirms and protects all the important aspects and values of our natural freedom, such as the freedom from tyranny, the integrity of will power, and the natural moral freedom for choosing the good.

The Christian greatly values *freedom from foreign bondage and degrading tyranny* because human servitude is opposed to both the dignity of man and the glory of our heavenly Father and in addition may threaten the development of moral freedom.

The Christian realizes the great importance of a *firm determination of will.* A person entangled in evil, who pursues his wicked designs with a bitter tenacity and an admirable firmness of will, may at times put to shame the weak-willed and slothful Christian. However, such a person is not a truly free man but a slave to sin, because the latter has gained such far-reaching control over him and his most valuable power of choice, his will. "Everyone who commits sin is the slave of sin" (John 8:34). Hell is the very abyss of slavery where man is neither in possession of his powers nor able to love or rejoice.

Moral freedom cannot be measured by the available energy of will power but rather by the soul's ability to choose freely in favor of the good and to reject the evil. Nevertheless, once the choice has been made, the measure and degree of will power exercised in the act enhances and augments moral freedom.

The freedom of the children of God is incomparably more precious than the personal freedom from political tyranny and disgraceful subjection. It greatly transcends even the importance of moral freedom, which is essential for our ethical and religious life. The freedom of the children of God is a most precious treasure, a totally undeserved and gratuitous gift from God. In its perfection this freedom is the closest participation in the blessed freedom of the Triune God Himself.

The liberty of the children of God is the fruit of Christ's

glorious victory. This freedom will be ours to the degree that we imitate Christ. "If the Son sets you free, you will indeed be free" (John 8:36). "He has conquered the powers of slavery; He has set us free from the law of sin and the snares of death" (Rom. 8:2). Christ's perfect obedience on the cross and His exaltation in the resurrection reveal the true nature of freedom and the disgrace of the slavery of sin.

The first Adam refused to place his God-given existence into the hands of his Creator and acted according to his own arbitrary will. Blinded by pride, he resented God's commandment as an infringement of his own freedom because he sought liberty in self-will. But at the very moment of his own self-exaltation, man lost not only the delights of paradise but also God's intimate friendship and the participation in the blessed freedom of God. In the final analysis, unredeemed man shows himself self-centered and self-seeking. In the transgression of the law he openly opposes God's will and looks for his own security. Even in the fulfillment of the law he seeks his own independence instead of surrendering himself to God's will and good pleasure.

Christ truly could say of Himself that He never sought His own will and glory, but only the will and glorification of the Father (cf. John: 8:28 ff.; 4:34; 5:30; 6:28 ff.). He rendered the greatest proof of His unselfish dedication to both His heavenly Father and all mankind by His self-sacrifice on the cross (cf. John 8:28).

By His loving obedience unto the death of the cross, Christ broke the fetters by which man had chained himself through his own volition according to his selfish desires and inclinations instead of complying with the will and designs of a benevolent God.

The glorified risen Savior, living in the radiant love of the Blessed Trinity, bestows together with the gifts of the Holy

Spirit also the special characteristics of the true children of God, namely, a constant awareness and grateful acceptance of our total dependence on God which disposes our soul to a trusting, childlike self-surrender, a life of intimate love and union. "Where the Spirit of the Lord is, there is freedom" (II Cor. 3:17).

The freedom of the children of God is already a beginning and a foretaste of our glorified state in heaven where "with faces unveiled we shall behold the Lord's glory from splendor to splendor; such is the influence of the Lord who is the Spirit" (II Cor. 3:18). Our transfiguration in heaven will fully manifest our deliverance from all selfishness and pride, and proclaim the inestimable honor of a life lived solely for God's glory. This is the work of the Holy Spirit, the personal gift of our risen Savior, for it is through Christ's self-sacrifice on the cross and His glorious resurrection that we have received the power "to become the children of God" (John 1:12).

We, the adopted children of God, cry out in the Holy Spirit: "Abba, Father!" (Rom. 8:15, Gal. 4:6). In filial, childlike prayer we become detached from the enslaving desires of our lower nature which inclines us to live in accordance with the dictates of our arbitrary will. In imitation of the example of God's well-beloved Son, we gratefully acknowledge God as the supreme author of our being and reciprocate His infinite love by a confident, unconditional self-surrender. The first Adam incurred disaster for the whole human race by his attempt to emancipate himself from God's sovereignty. Christ's loving obedience on the cross disclosed the pattern of the new life according to which man should acknowledge his indebtedness to the wise, beneficent and loving will of God. Man should respond by a total gift of self. This is the victory of life.

Section II. Freedom through the New Law

1. Deadly "Freedom" and Liberating "Dying"

The first Adam tried to exempt himself from obedience to God and His law. The serpent had whispered into his ears: "You shall not die. For God knows that in whatever day you shall eat thereof, your eyes shall be opened; and you shall be as Gods" (Gen. 3:4-5). Since man desired to be free like God Himself, he had to reckon with God's threat: "For in whatever day you shall eat of it, you shall die" (Gen. 2:17). Death, the penalty of sin, is overwhelming evidence that every attempt of the creature to live outside God's law, bears the marks of death and dissolution (cf. Rom. 8:13).

On the other hand, Christ's redemptive death on the cross earned for us the fulness of life. Christ has become the fount of life and the source of new freedom for all His followers in view of His complete and wholehearted acceptance of the will of His heavenly Father. Through Christ's loving obedience unto death, the powers of sin have been conquered. Only through the grace of Christ and our humble readiness to a similar obedience can we fully regain the freedom of the children of God. This, of course, involves a painful dying and a continuous mortification of the old man who tends to seek freedom in self-will.

In baptism we have placed ourselves on principle under the Law of Christ, and His own loving obedience. "We were buried in death with Him by means of baptism . . . because we are dead to sin" (Rom. 6:4). Consequently, it would be illogical for the baptized to continue the old manner of life "obeying its lusts" (Rom. 6:12). This would mean subjection to a completely foreign law of servitude from which the baptized has been freed: "Thus you too must consider yourselves dead to sin, but alive to God in Christ Jesus" (Rom. 6:11).

Our readiness to die to the old manner of life is the prerequisite for the life, resurrection and blessed freedom of the children of God as implied in the nature of baptism. By the divine regeneration, symbolized and effected by baptism, we are made participants in the death and resurrection of Christ (cf. Rom. 6:5). *The freedom of the children of God is ours to the extent that our life conforms with the New Law.* This requires a constant struggle against "the works of the flesh" (Gal. 5:19), as long as man is living in this world, tempted from within and without. And yet the essence and keynote of the New Law is not found in the struggle against sin but rather in a childlike relationship to God's benevolent will and law.

2. "Free of the Accusing Law and yet not Lawless"

The above heading is an important statement in the Paulinian teaching on freedom. As long as man remains self-centered and unwilling to deny himself even when confronted with the gracious will of God, he will experience the divine law as a hard yoke and a burdensome restraint and, at times, a challenge for violation. The man who considers law a limitation to his freedom, will by necessity begin to calculate how far he may go without becoming a "transgressor." Thus he will live on the borderland of sin. Logically, such an attitude will tend to produce "the works of the flesh," such as uncharitableness and the numerous kinds of immorality (Gal. 5:19).

The intrinsic poison of all vice is pride or a vain desire for self-glorification which tends to misuse the very laws of God by making them subservient to self-justification. This dangerous inclination asserts itself in man's desire to appear perfect before God on the merit of his own achievements.

Such a self-righteous person may also try to continue "the works of the flesh" and justify his unsanctioned behavior under the cloak of a falsely interpreted liberty. Thus the freedom of the children of God is threatened by a self-glorifying concept of freedom which does not have its root and orientation in the "Thou" of God and neighbor but rather in man's own warped ego. Therefore, the apostle of the gentiles warns: "You were called to be free men; only do not turn your freedom into license for your lower nature, but be servants to one another in love" (Gal. 5:13).

Consequently, the Christian must be relentless in the struggle against the "works of the flesh." The saving and redeeming factor in the combat, however, does not lie merely in a defensive attitude, in the concentration on prohibitions, but rather in our total conversion to the grace of Christ, to the loving will of God. "For sin shall not have dominion over you, since you are not subjects of law but of grace" (Rom. 6:14). Neither are we slaves but children of God, provided we "are led by the Spirit of God" (Rom. 8:14). "If you are led by the Spirit, you are not under the law" (Gal. 5:18).

In the total surrender to "the life-giving law of the Spirit in Christ Jesus" (Rom. 8:2), we shall become liberated from external subjection under precepts and the censure of the restraining law. The fruits of our good works in the power of Christ are the prerequisites for keeping subdued the old man with his unruly tendencies. "But the harvest of the Spirit is love, joy, peace, patience, kindness, goodness, fidelity, gentleness, and self-control. There is no law dealing with such things as these. And those who belong to Christ Jesus have crucified the lower nature with its passions and desires" (Gal. 5:22 ff.).

St. Paul's bold teaching on liberty is evidently rooted in

the powerful newness of the gospel and a firm belief in the strength and abilities of man when touched by grace. For this present life, however, the new doctrine about man's freedom demands both a valiant struggle against the revolts of a warped and selfish nature, as well as a discerning attitude for the camouflages of a false freedom.

3. Purification—The Way to New Freedom

The terms "self-denial" and "mortification," employed by Holy Scripture, are interpreted by the mystics and ascetics as a process of losing or emptying oneself, or as a road of purification, marked in its progress by the dark night of the senses and of the spirit. Our relationship with God and His law will constantly be endangered by our selfishness and vainglory, unless we have passed through the school of the crucified Savior and have begun to taste the consolations of an intimate union with God. Self-seeking man is always inclined to credit God's gifts to himself, even on the occasion of success in the apostolate or joy in prayer, gratuitously granted as a small drop from God's ocean of bliss. While God in His goodness and mercy graciously assists us in the process of detachment through opposition, failure, and desolation of spirit, we are inclined to seek consolation in earthly things and pleasures. This, likewise, indicates our tendency to live according to our own will and desire.

Our unpurified ego experiences an extreme darkness, close to annihilation, when we begin to abandon ourselves unreservedly to God's providence and guidance and without undue evasion accept the trials sent by God for our purification. However, our true self, renewed and assured in Christ, will realize with an ever increasing certainty that in the renunciation of our self-will and self-seeking we are throwing ourselves into the merciful arms of God, there to be liberated from all self-delusion and egocentricity. The road of purification will gradually become a road of illumination and union. Slowly but irresistibly, God will accustom the soul to an intimate union and the blessed freedom of wholehearted surrender. The things that bring joy and consolation to man renewed by grace, cause fear and trembling to the old man. Close intimacy with God becomes a painfully purifying and consuming fire for the soul still attached to sin, because it brings to naught the creature's self-centeredness.

"Blessed are those who mourn." Indeed blessed are we if we can renounce all self-will and all consolations sought for in undue activism, as an escape from the painfully purifying fire of divine love. There is a blessing inherent in all salutary grief and in all forms of self-denial and renunciation, provided they lead us to the freedom of the children of God.

Section III. The Renunciation of Liberties and Privileges in the Service of Our Neighbor

St. Paul equates a considerate and unselfish love in the service of our neighbor with the sure triumph over a false and enslaving kind of freedom. "In love serve one another" (Gal. 5:13). St. Peter, in a similar warning against the subterfuges of a deceitful freedom, adds the following explicit direction: "Honor all men, love all the brothers" (I Peter 2:17).

Christ, who in His self-sacrificing love for us carried the burden of our sins and, like a slave, delivered Himself for our sake, shows us the way to true freedom. While living in the blessed freedom of the divinity, He nevertheless willed to become our servant. Through Him we have been liberated from the threatening legalism of a selfish existence, marked by the consequences of original sin. Hence we should willingly adopt Christ's law as our guide. This law is the love which Christ has shown for us and which we are to reflect in our dealings with our neighbor; "Help bear one another's burdens, and so you will fulfill the Law of Christ" (Gal. 6:2). If we are of the mind of Christ (cf. Phil. 2:5) and gratefully accept God's dispensations by imitating His example in wholehearted service of our neighbor, then only shall we abide in Him and remain in "His Law" and truly participate in His own freedom (I Cor. 9:21).

St. Paul in his own life gives ample testimony of the true essence of Christian liberty: "Am I not free? Am I not an apostle?" (I Cor. 9:1).

In the interest of evangelizing, St. Paul even renounced his personal right to financial support from the Christian communities (I Cor. 9:12 ff.). Through the labor of his own hands as a tent-maker, St. Paul provided the daily sustenance for himself and his co-workers, and this in spite of exceedingly great apostolic labors. He went to extremes in the renunciation of personal rights and his own freedom. He, who in all his preaching energetically defended the right of exemption from the ritual law, nevertheless subjected himself to the innumerable regulations, customs and habits of the Jews. He did this out of sheer consideration for the Christians of Jewish descent. He showed the same concern for timely adaptations regarding all nations, in whatever seemed good and conducive for the spread of the gospel truth. *I became all things to all men, by all means to win over some of them*" (I Cor. 9:22). "Independent though I am of all men, I make myself everybody's slave to win over as many as possible" (I Cor. 9:19).

St. Paul could not expect the actual renunciation of all personal rights from every convert, but he nevertheless asked for a similar attitude from all his followers who wished to safeguard the freedom of the children of God. His many letters to the newly formed Christian communities abound in phrases expressing his sincere solicitude to lead the faithful to a true conception of Christian liberty.

In the Christian community of Rome, some of the members stronger in the faith used their privilege of exemption from the Jewish food restrictions in a manner that was insulting to those who adhered to the old customs. They, thereby, disturbed the community spirit and hindered the spread of the gospel. When St. Paul intervened, he admitted that in reality these stronger ones in the faith were free from the Jewish food regulations, but he nevertheless deplored their selfish use of this freedom. "None of us lives for himself, and none dies for himself. If we live, we live for the Lord, and if we die, we die for the Lord" (Rom. 14:7-8) "If then your brother is upset because of what you eat, no longer do you act according to the demands of love. Do not by your eating bring disaster to a man for whom Christ died!" (Rom. 14:15).

In the community of Corinth, some reputedly broadminded and enlightened Christians openly ate of the meat previously offered in the temples of idols without regard for the possibility of serious scandal to their weaker brethren. Their reasoning seemed logical because the idols were nonexistent, and hence the meat offered really remained the gift of the one and only God. Nonetheless, the way in which they took advantage of their true insight and liberty was selfish because they disregarded the dilemma of the weaker Christians who somehow still counted on the existence of idols. This presented a temptation for the weaker members in the faith likewise to partake of the meat—but with a bad conscience—since to some degree they were influenced by the ulterior but subconscious motive of securing the favor of their former "gods." Therefore, St. Paul exhorts these Christians who had failed to examine their freedom in the light of the law of charity: "Take care lest this right of yours should become a stumbling block to weaklings. Suppose, for example, someone sees you, a man of knowledge, reclining at table in an idol's temple. Might not his conscience, since it is weak, be encouraged to eat food offered in idol worship?" (I Cor. 8:9 ff.). The Christian who is truly free acts in a different manner: "Therefore, never will I eat meat, if food leads to my brother's sinning, lest I should be the cause of my brother's sin" (I Cor. 8:13).

In our daily lives we are constantly confronted with problems of a similar nature more or less consequential to the spread of the faith. All our actions must be examined and weighed in the light of the present situation and its effects on our brethren; whether it be our conduct at work, or our manner and means of recreation, or the position we take in matters of politics, fashions, dance, and friendship (to mention just a few).

Consider the hypothetical case of a pious and well-respected woman, with a mature and discreet taste in art, who repeatedly attends movies which in her opinion were censured undeservedly by the Church. Such a person is forgetful of the fact that others, less discreet, might be encouraged by her example to frequent objectionable and even condemned movies. Although she is entitled to her personal opinion, her actions will be in conformity with the principles of Christian freedom only if she is guided by a delicate consideration for the salvation of the weaker brethren. For the same reason, a mother of a family should rather stop the subscription to certain types of magazines if she feels obliged to prevent her children from reading them because of their unfavorable influence.

Our love of neighbor and our thoughtful consideration for his salvation should serve not only as a criterion for the best implementation of Christian freedom, but more so as its deepest motive. Essentially, Christian freedom as the gift of Christ, who lived, suffered, and died solely for the honor and glory of the Father and our salvation, is the key-element of our existence. Guided by it, we shall no longer live for our own selfish and narrow interests, but rather for God and for our neighbor. Until we have learned to measure all our actions by the criterion of love, we shall remain prisoners to the old manner of existence which is doomed to death.

Section IV. Creation's Participation in the Freedom of the Children of God

1. Man's Solidarity with Creation

The freedom of the children of God infinitely transcends all natural comprehension. This freedom neither requires the extinction of the passions nor does it imply a charter for licentiousness. Its true nature reveals itself neither in contempt for material things nor in an escape into the purely spiritual realms, nor even in the concentration of all our energies towards the mastery of this earth. The Buddhist monk who despises all created things for the sake of entering into the nirvana—an existence without the least desires —is as far removed from the blessed freedom of the children of God as the contemporary man living in a society possessed by a spirit of technical adventure which extols atomic progress above human dignity, prayer, and holiness of life. It should be remembered that, *although this freedom is essentially the gift of the Holy Spirit and implies an entirely new relationship to the heart of God, it nevertheless profoundly affects and enters into all our relationships with the world.*

With the precious gift of liberty, patterned after God's own freedom, man received the Creator's mandate to subject the earth and rule over it in God's name (cf. Gen. 1:27 ff.). According to God's plan, man was destined to develop his most precious powers of liberty in the faithful fulfillment of this commission. However, through sin man attempted to fashion his own destiny independently of God instead of entering into God's loving design. With man's refusal to pay homage to God in a genuine attitude of reverence and dependence, he incurred not only the loss of his exalted dignity of freedom, but drew the entire creation into the disaster of his enslaving pride (cf. Rom. 8:20).

God has not only entrusted the visible creation to man's immediate dominion, but has made him the center and focal point of this world. Hence, creation in its own way shares in man's destiny and in his servitude to sin, with the disastrous consequences of pain, death, and dissolution.

Therefore, if man recaptures the freedom of the children of God and abides by it, not only he himself, but the entire creation will experience the liberation from servitude.

2. Man's Solidarity with His Environment

Holy Scripture presents convincing proof that the liberty of the children of God is not expected to blossom in the spiritual realm only, but is meant to pervade man's entire existence including his body and physical environment. In distress as well as in hope there is a close and intimate relationship not only between man's physical and spiritual powers but similarly between man and his whole environment. Consequently, man in possession of the precious gift of Redemption and living within its exigencies, should create such an imprint on the rest of creation so that it will also feel the beginning of liberation from the "servitude of sin."

We are fully aware that until Christ's second coming (the Parousia), it shall be impossible for us to create a perfect world, an absolute reflection of the sublime liberty of the children of God because of the resistance of those who place themselves in the service of the "potentates and powers of this dark world" (Eph. 6:12) and consequently intensify the servitude of perdition. Another reason for failure is the fact that Christians are often remiss in their mission to manifest the full glory of their spiritual freedom. On the other hand, this gift of freedom of the children of God which enables us to center our entire life in God, including our social and political obligations and responsibilities, also implies a blessed renewal for the rest of creation. *St. Francis,* in his "Canticle of the Sun" and his intimate communion with nature, gave proof of the full development of this precious gift of freedom overflowing to the entire visible creation.

However, *we should not be content with the spontaneous effects of our inner freedom on the environment.* With a keen sense of responsibility to the world at large and with due consideration for the security of our own freedom, we should try to play an active part in the control of environmental factors. In consequence of the intimate relationship which exists not only between man's body and soul but also between man and his immediate surroundings, the development of man's liberty is essentially dependent on the fulfillment of this obligation to the rest of creation. We should take to heart "the yearning of all creation for the manifestation of the freedom of the children of God" not only for our sake, but for the honor and glory of God, our Creator and Redeemer. The opposite attitude would show our failure to comprehend fully the true nature of this freedom and our rightful place in life.

The gospel truth about the freedom of the children of God must find expression in all our dealings and relationships with all created things. This is one of the basic rules for the so-called *"pastoral care of the environment"* which is an excellent form of the lay apostolate. The care and concern for our own salvation and that of our neighbor will be futile and fruitless unless we pay attention to the environment. This is in conformity with God's all-embracing dominion and the true nature of man.

Man's interpersonal relationships in his daily life and activities greatly influence and shape his physical surroundings. Man's environment, including economics, engineering, housing, fashion, food, etc., is a reflection of man's own spirit and character, and in turn leaves its imprint on man's personality.

An essential distinction between Christianity and Marxism lies in Christianity's teaching about the preeminence of the liberty of the children of God and the importance of our person-to-person relationships above all other influences from the material, impersonal world. Marxism considers the material world, especially in matters of economics, the determining foundation for the entire cultural, moral, and religious consciousness of man, in fact the only determining factor for the history of mankind.

By our repeated and unwavering emphasis on both the importance of the reciprocal relationship between man and his environment and man's responsibility to the entire order of creation, we Catholics distinguish ourselves from those currents in Protestant circles which try to restrict the domain of Christian freedom to "the purely interior" and thereby tend to abandon creation to the "principalities and powers of darkness" (Eph. 6:12).

Moral freedom, the precious prerequisite for the complete unfolding of the blessed freedom of the children of God, may under certain circumstances be greatly endangered by the limitations imposed by man's immediate and remote environment. Once we have fully grasped the true concept of the liberty of the children of God, the threat of an unfavorable environment ought to rouse us to a concentrated and united effort to oppose the increasing influence of the spirit of collectivism in the shaping of our environment.

3. The Freedom of the Children of God and the Technological Environment

Today's important task of controlling our environment depends largely on our attitude towards technology and the natural sciences. Man's progress in these fields is in harmony with the Creator's injunction: "Fill the earth and subdue it" (Gen. 1:28). The fact that the world is frightened by the explosions of H-bombs and the appearance of artificial moons is no reason for a condemnation of electronic engineering or modern inventions. The deciding factor is the intention and purpose in their utilization. Here again, St. Paul's words are applicable: "*All things belong to you, and you to Christ*" (I Cor. 3:22-23). They contain the real secret for true world improvement. Like Christ, who in all things sought the honor and glory of the Father, we too ought to use all possible opportunities for the welfare and salvation of mankind. It is unbelievable that Christians would exploit the energy enclosed in atoms for the destruction of entire cities. Service to mankind must always be the primary purpose of all inventions.

Christians share the responsibility for appreciating and utilizing the blessings of modern inventions. Today's media of thought transmission, such as movies, press, radio, television, as well as our technical industry, may under certain circumstances prove to be a hazard to man's natural freedom and his religious responsiveness. The degree of our personal and practical responsibility in these spheres determines whether they will be an asset or a liability in relation to our supernatural freedom.

For example, today's industrial mass production is opening up innumerable avenues of economical and cultural treasures to a large segment of people, while formerly these were reserved for a small group. Yet a materialistic pseudo-religion, in the question of a standard of living, tends to create a real danger for the freedom and dignity of man by means of the very things which are good and desirable in themselves. Christians in responsible positions for world management should oppose such trends by utilizing the modern achievements to make genuine progress in human existence, thereby upholding inner freedom and an exemplary simplicity. The economically favored classes of society should not raise their standard of living to such a degree that they scandalize those who scarcely possess the bare necessities of life and the basic means for raising a family.

In the true spirit of solidarity and with a sincere detachment from the things of this world, the Christians in technically advanced countries with comparatively high standards of living ought to give assistance to the less privileged countries. If this generous help is offered without the least attempt towards subordination, it is an eloquent manifestation of the freedom of the children of God. Such is the doctrine taught by Pope John XXIII in *Mater et Magistra* and *Pacem in Terris*.

In all our efforts to imprint on our surroundings the mark of Christianity, it should be evident that the spirit of charity and the freedom of the children of God are intimately united and in a certain sense represent an extension of the Incarnation of the Word of God in this world. In following the example of Christ who came to serve in order to save us, the Christian likewise shall accomplish his exalted mission as "ruler" over the visible creation only through an unselfish service. The highest degree of Christian freedom will blossom in an atmosphere of selfless charity towards our neighbor and in a climate of consuming zeal for the glory of God, the Creator and Redeemer of all things.

Section V. "Blessed Are the Meek for They Shall Possess the Land"

Meekness, in Scripture language, is a witness of the freedom of the children of God. It arises from the self-possessed powers of kindness, from the heart which is free from all perverted self-love. It enables us to accomplish our allotted task of extending to our environment the freedom of the children of God.

When the Samaritans had refused hospitality to Jesus because He was on His way to Jerusalem, the city which they detested, St. James and St. John, full of indignation said: "Lord, do you want us to order fire to drop from the sky and consume them?" Jesus severely rebuked their vengeful disposition by responding: "You do not know of what manner of spirit you are" (Luke 9:54-55). The apostles reacted in a similar manner at the sight of Judas's treacherous kiss: "Lord, shall we strike with the sword?" (Luke 22:49). At that very moment impetuous Peter already had cut off the ear of the High Priest's servant. Jesus, however, rebuked him saying: "Put your sword back into its place. All those who have recourse to the sword will perish by the sword." (Matt. 26:52).

It is not by force and violence, but by patience and benevolence, as exemplified by Christ, that we can announce to the world the liberating power of Christ's love. Whenever Christians violently espouse the cause of Christ, either in well-meaning efforts or in attempts to seize positions of power, they prove to be traitors to the true freedom of the children of God. It is only in patient endurance and in complete renunciation of all violence that we can possess and save our own soul (Luke 12:19). But above all, only by unselfish kindness can we lift the curse of selfishness and pride from the rest of creation.

For the present time, until Christ's second coming, His words are applicable to the Church, His Bride: "The Son of Man did not come into the world to be served, but to serve" (Matt. 20:28). "I am in your midst as he who serves" (Luke 22:27). These same words found a faithful echo in the deliberations of the Second Vatican Council. Whoever attempts to gain undue influence and power for the Church of Christ, really clouds her exalted mission of announcing the supreme dominion of God. Unfortunately Church history gives ample evidence of such scandalous conduct. There is the example of the Crusaders who placed at the feet of Innocent III the conquered and ransacked city of Constantinople under the title of a "Latin Empire." This act certainly brought discredit and disrepute to religion and the position of the papacy.

True unselfishness, the inner freedom from all desires to rule and domineer, is the Alpha and Omega of the "pastoral care of the environment," which is the great lay apostolate of our time. Only in this way shall the earthly domains of God's kingdom become "our portion." This is God's own paradox, though incomprehensible to the earthly minded; the more self-seeking we are, the more we shall fail to find our true selves and, in addition, shall lose the dominion over the things of this earth as desired and planned by God. On the other hand, the more forgetful of self we become in true imitation of Christ's meekness, the more we shall abound in joy and radiate this inner freedom to our environment.

When St. Paul refers to the world as the "promise made to Abraham and his posterity" (Rom. 4:13), we are reminded of Christ's own promise in the beatitudes, to give us the earth as our "possession." The close and intimate relationship between meekness and faith is emphasized by the fact that Christ proclaimed both as prerequisites for the "possession of the earth." For it was not through law that "Abraham and his posterity were given the promise that the world should be his inheritance, but through the righteousness that came from faith" (Rom. 4:13). Liberation from our selfishness and self-centeredness is not accomplished by particular acts nor by the mere fulfillment of the external law, but by *faith* which chiefly manifests itself in a complete surrender to God in a spirit of *boundless confidence.* Only by this total self-surrender to God in faith and loving trust, shall we be freed from that enslaving self-seeking which even enters into our apostolic activities and our observance of the law. Only thus shall we acknowledge law as the expression of God's benevolence.

We must abide by the Law of Christ in its entirety when dealing with men and the established order of creation. We may not, in our interpersonal relationships, neglect the laws of psychology and sociology. We shall achieve true inner freedom, which is intimately united with meekness and total renunciation of all force and self-will, by an unreserved dedication to God and His cause. Neither the arbitrary, lawless man who is "the slave of corruption" (II Pet. 2:19) nor the man who shelters himself behind the dead letter of the law, exerts a truly liberating influence on others.

The yearning of creation towards the revelation of the freedom of the children of God will be satisfied only by a willing response to God's invitation in every concrete situation of our life. Men with warped attitudes towards law are unable to make a positive contribution to the liberating dominion of God because they are unwilling to abandon themselves to God and His love.

Section VI. Obedience to Human Authority

The freedom of the children of God is a totally undeserved grace. It is founded on a loving obedience to God and manifests itself in thoughtful consideration for the welfare of others, especially when not hemmed in by legal restrictions. Yet what about obedience to lawful authority? Is obedience a necessary virtue for the free child of God? Can the true spirit of freedom unfold itself in an atmosphere of subordination and obedience? In order to fully clarify these questions, we should exclude two extreme positions towards obedience:

(a) Disobedience to lawful, God-ordained authority is not the expression of the true liberty of the children of God; but, on the contrary, is proof of a haughty revolt of the old man.

(b) There is a manner of both commanding and obeying which is entirely incompatible with the nature and development of the freedom of the children of God. In man's present imperfect state, subordination to human authority is a necessary prerequisite for the freedom of the children of God. Both the one commanding and the one obeying must be aware of their obligation to promote true freedom. He who fully comprehends the deep significance of the call to freedom will not be interested in methods and systems aiming at external conformity and mechanical performance.

An example from the time of the Inquisition may illustrate this point. Dostoevski paints a picture of the chief Inquisitor as the irreligious type of a superior who is fault-finding even with Our Lord for placing such unlimited confidence in His disciples. In his opinion, it would have been far better to discipline them under a strict regime of law instead of encouraging them to use their initiative and sense of responsibility in the pursuit of the good.

Subordinates who are afraid to use their own initiative may reveal a similar disposition rooted in excessive scrupulosity and lack of self-confidence. To some extent this attitude is impersonated by the otherwise respectable priest who fulfills all his duties prescribed by the Code of Canon Law with pedantic precision, but in the care of souls lacks initiative. He "anticipates" his breviary prayers as far as the law permits. He adheres to his strict regime even in days of serious illness when warned by his physician to spare his failing strength. All entreaties, and even the assurances from his doctor to consider himself free from law evoke the obstinate response: "All this is simply not applicable to my case. For the past forty years I have learned that I am unable to draw the line, if I should allow myself the smallest mitigation." Despite the laudable good will, such dispositions are not in harmony with Christian faith and liberty. It would be far better in such circumstances to renounce all undue reliance on self and confidently enjoy the God-given freedom. This would produce not only greater joy and fervor in the recitation of the breviary, but also would result in a keen awareness of the call and opportunity of the moment. Very often these rigid attitudes are the outcome of early training and teaching which placed such un-

due though well-intentioned emphasis on outward conformity and obedience while disregarding the virtue of
freedom.

A similar inflexibility in the observance of regulations
and prohibitions may be encountered among lay people,
although it is at times less characterized by a self-sacrificing
attitude. Many truly pious souls lack leisure time for
prayerful meditation and the exercise of fraternal charity,
because they have burdened themselves with a multiplicity
of self-imposed prayer obligations.

*The cultivation of a spirit of obedience in conformity
with the principles of Christian freedom will of necessity
lead to its joyful exercise with an ever increasing awareness
and appreciation of its genuine value.* Such obedience has
its foundation in the firm conviction that all authority,
vested in human agents, comes from God. It is of paramount importance for the growing child that all parental
regulations and all instructions of educators reflect this
truth. On the other hand, it is a real calamity for the spirit
of obedience if parents and educators by their insincerity
and despotism destroy the child's confidence both in them
and in the merits of the command. This danger is especially
grave if the perplexed adolescent has no one to whom he
can turn for guidance and counsel regarding the true inner
meaning of obedience. A mere slavish submission to an
evidently unwise command is as incompatible with Christian freedom as open rebellion.

It should be understood that obedience must be rendered
even in the face of imperfect commands issued by legitimate
authority, provided their execution does not interfere with
other important duties, and that there is nothing sinful in
the command. Early childhood experiences, education, and
self-discipline towards a truly animated obedience are the
determining factors for achieving a harmonious develop-

ment of our natural and supernatural freedom. Both he who commands as well as he who obeys should try to recognize the spiritual value of obedience in each particular command. Since the New Law of the children of God is essentially a "perfect law of freedom" (James 1:25), it is of primary importance to understand the implications of each command. Even a servant is expected to reflect on his master's command if he desires to carry out the commission in conformity with his master's intentions. How much more should the children of God try to enter into the genuine beauty and deep significance of God's designs by a ready response of obedience. This is applicable to situations in which God transmits His will through human agents. Loving solicitude toward fostering an understanding of regulations is of paramount importance if obedience to human agents is to contribute to the freedom of the children of God. Only thus shall human authority reflect the authority and love of our heavenly Father. Those in positions of authority should aid their subjects toward this exalted goal by their very manner of issuing commands and by revealing the reasons for their directions and ordinances whenever possible.

Occasionally we have to conform to a particular ordinance or precept for which we perceive no plausible explanation in spite of all our sincere efforts and good will. This is consistent with our present state of imperfection. Under such circumstances our readiness to obey may mean a decided triumph over our perverted self-will and pride, and consequently, an increase in the true liberty of the children of God. This, however, is no reason for advocating a meaningless or "blind" obedience or a mere mechanical conformity.

St. Ignatius who coined the expression "blind obedience" did not intend it to denote a senseless compliance but a humble readiness to obey willingly and wholeheartedly, if under certain circumstances the underlying reasons for the commands are obscure. However, after so much confusion and misinterpretation of this particular phrase, it would be far better to avoid its use when in reality we mean an "open-eyed" obedience in view of the significance of the command.

Unconscious or at least thoughtless submissiveness to collective mass-opinion or the will of a dictator is really blind and senseless. Persons who have been accustomed to mere mechanical obedience in the home and to a similar soulless participation in the traditional rural activities of the parish without any initiative of their own, will in a short time transfer their thoughtless kind of obedience in the direction of the tide of mass-opinion. This danger is especially grave in cases of change of residence and/or work from rural surroundings to city life and especially to a factory atmosphere. The manner of obeying remains unchanged. Time, however, will show the devastating influence of such submissiveness in the character development of the individual when he surrenders under the influence of the compelling forces of the spirit of collectivism.

In connection with environmental influences, it should be pointed out, however, that moral standards and laudable customs in a community are not sufficient in themselves to insure the implementation of Christian principles. In an epoch witnessing such concentrated forces towards evil, Christians must be equipped to achieve a fuller realization of their true freedom. Only then will their obedience distinguish itself from the spirit of collectivism and their united efforts overcome the deleterious effects of mass-opinion.

The dignity of the free child of God presupposes a joyful, loving obedience, ready to fulfill not only the obligations of a command, but to entertain and express sincere and unaffected charity towards the persons in authority. If we recognize the superior as the messenger of God's will in our behalf, we shall readily render him genuine and respectful love.

Christian obedience to human authority should be given with a wise discrimination, but this is not to be confused with uncharitable criticism of superiors, rooted in obstinacy rather than in a sincere concern for God's kingdom. Under certain circumstances, a mature Christian may find himself in a position which requires an honest expression of criticism to his superior. Consider St. Paul's behavior to St. Peter when he "resisted him to his face because he was in the wrong" (Gal. 2:11). This was on the occasion when St. Peter, in undue concern for the Christians of Hebrew descent, required unnecessary conformity of the converts from paganism. This created obstacles and hardships for missionary activity. Yet before expressing any criticism or disapproval, both the importance of the matter and our personal responsibility to discuss it should be carefully evaluated. In addition, following St. Paul's example, all criticism must be expressed in a spirit of charity and true apostolic zeal. *Uncharitable criticizing, especially if done behind the superior's back, is diametrically opposed to both obedience and the freedom of the children of God.* In addition, such behavior presents a threat to the good spirit in a community, especially if it is done in the presence of immature persons. The situation is quite different if questionable regulations are submitted to persons of mature judgment with due respect and in a spirit of submission. Under certain circumstances, this may even be necessary.

Superiors have a serious responsibility for *moderation in their commands,* because human nature has definite limitations in the degree of moral energy and endurance. Consequently, in his disregard for rules of prudence, a superior may seriously interfere with the development of a dynamic spirit of freedom and a joyful sense of responsibility and achievement. This in turn may hinder the subjects from an alert responsiveness to the call and opportunity of the moment.

Parents who literally smother their child with commands and admonitions thereby make it extremely difficult or impossible for him to become alert to his many opportunities for good, such as displaying loving attention and consideration for his parents and siblings. The results are similar when an adult's attention becomes rigidly fixed on a multiplicity of individual laws and regulations. The objection that the road of perfection consists in a willing subordination to many rules and statutes, regulating religious life to the minutest detail, is answered by the truly great rules of religious orders which distinguish themselves by a wise minimum of regulations. In addition, such regulations are specifically prepared and intended for people with a special calling to a particular rule or constitution. No one will question the benefits accruing from a good daily schedule because it channels our best energies. However, overemphasis on human regulations and a false absolutism are doomed to block the most precious energies of our freedom.

Human ordinances deter men from possible irregularities and disorders. On the other hand, man's nature demands a certain amount of liberty for the exercise of his will power. This is necessary for the full expansion of man's initiative, so vital for community welfare.

It would be misleading to regard obedience to human regulations and laws only in relation to its contribution to personality development. Personality in the sense of a self-glorifying, warped ego leaves no room for the freedom of the children of God and the obedience which it requires. There is no reason for questioning the importance of personality improvement in the sense of utilizing our God-given talents; yet, there is danger in placing the emphasis on self-improvement. Since obedience is of paramount importance for the welfare of the community, even unreasonable commands may under certain circumstances be binding in conscience, especially if their transgression may prove harmful by affecting the community spirit.

Section VII. The Development of Moral Freedom

1. Mental Health and Holiness

Repeated misinterpretations of the slogan "a healthy soul in a healthy body" has led to the belief that mental-spiritual health is dependent on physical well-being. This fallacy has been disproved by the lives of truly great men and women. A contemporary physician declared: "There are countless healthy souls in ailing bodies, and truly afflicted souls in healthy bodies." To an even greater extent is holiness independent of physical health. Tauler and St. Hildegard of Bingen are of the opinion that God does not require a healthy body for His abode, or as St. Paul puts it, virtue becomes manifest in weakness.

The difficulty becomes even greater if we wish to determine the true relationship between *holiness and mental health*, or relevant to the present topic, between supernatural freedom and the natural moral freedom of man. It is true that the freedom of the children of God is not an expansion of our natural freedom but a purely supernatural gift of heaven. Yet both the supernatural in general, as well as the freedom of the children of God in particular, are closely related to and dependent on the nature of man. *This is a reality with far-reaching influence not only for the development of our spiritual life but for the entire creation.* Since interior freedom is one of the most precious and distinguishing gifts of the human personality, deeply pervading and affecting man's entire existence, its repression or destruction will likewise interfere with the development of the freedom of the children of God. The latter, however, is not simply synonymous with a normal functioning of will power.

To illustrate this concept, let us take the rather extreme but still plausible situation of a person on the verge of mental illness and fully aware of his predicament who does all in his power to preserve his mental balance. At the same time he resigns himself fully to God's divine will and providence. His sentiments are expressed in the following prayer: "Dear God, I accept from Your hands cheerfully and willingly whatever may please You, even mental illness itself." This confident surrender to God's holy will represents the highest summit of Christian freedom despite the impairment of will power. Such an extreme possibility should not mislead us; the perfect development of the freedom of the children of God aims at both the preservation and/or improvement of mental health and interior freedom.

Under normal circumstances, growth in the supernatural freedom of God's children will likewise mean an expansion of our natural freedom. Conversely, it is true that an increase in the powers of our natural freedom in itself does not imply an increase in the freedom of the children of God, but rather is its precious prerequisite.

2. Freedom and Heredity

Hereditary factors in personality structure strongly influence both the expression and the boundaries of the individual's moral freedom. However, the genetic endowment, far from signifying a restriction and limitation, provides the basis for special talents and abilities. Even our personal limitations may prove a challenge, if we not only accept them in a spirit of humility but as far as possible forestall their ill effects while centering our attention on the positive aspects of our heredity. Such wholehearted acceptance of God's will convincingly manifests our moral freedom.

Human freedom in both the natural and the supernatural order always represents an endowment and an obligation. If we not only recognize and utilize all the potentials of our freedom but bravely face and reduce the dangers threatening its development, we shall gradually increase the scope of our liberty. Capitalizing on the favorable aspects of our natural endowment will not only expand the boundaries of our moral and spiritual freedom, but will permit a wholehearted concentration on the improvement of our environment. This in turn will benefit countless fellowmen towards attaining greater freedom.

3. Freedom and Environment

Our discussions have emphasized the mutual relationship of our supernatural freedom and environment. A few concrete examples and important principles shall illustrate that environment implies more of a challenge than a danger to our natural and supernatural freedom. Environment plays an equal and perhaps even more important role in the development of moral freedom than heredity because it is environment that provides the setting in which the freedom of the children of God is to unfold.

The erroneous opinion that the extent and the measure of our moral freedom are definitely fixed by our hereditary endowment is disproved in the case of a young man with an excellent hereditary background who gradually becomes the slave of his lower passions in a demoralized environment. Similarly, there are children with definite genetic limitations who blossom under the motherly solicitude and pedagogic ingenuity of religious women. Did not Don Bosco change crowds of neglected and depraved boys into respectable citizens, exemplary parents, renowned missionary priests, and even bishops?

Brother Albert from Poland (who died during World War I), the divinely favored founder of the masculine and feminine branch of the Albertines, went to such extremes in his daring and courageous charity that he took night lodgings in the wretched abodes of thieves and bandits. Inspired by a lively faith, he saw in the most demoralized criminals the "disfigured image of Christ," which he hopefully tried to restore by means of his unsurmountable confidence and selfless charity. He made heroic disciples of Christ and servants of the poor from the very people who were labeled as hopeless rabble. Yet, in addition to his extravagant optimism of confident faith and love, he had a remarkable, intuitive knowledge of environmental influence.* He did not start his mission by preaching relentless moral sermons to the tramps, thieves, and bandits with whom he took lodging; he began by improving their miserable shelters. He sang, played, and dramatized with them. He invited them to work with him. In short, he left nothing undone to improve their environment, but always with their cooperation. His success was so spectacular that very soon

* His life, like that of St. Francis of Assisi, was a penetrating accusation against the many abuses in our Christian society. He plainly foretold that the world cannot be saved from Communism unless, for a majority of people, the environmental conditions are improved.

the elite, the self-centered, and the "pious" people of society could not withhold their astonished admiration although they had originally considered him a fool.†

Such tremendous changes in a perverted environment could only be accomplished by true disciples of Christ in full possession of the freedom of the children of God. Who else could even have dared to attempt it? Yet it should be remembered that these reformers did not simply rely on the irresistible powers of a kind heart; they assisted their brethren by reducing the environmental hazards which threatened to destroy their spiritual freedom.

If we wish to preserve and expand our own freedom and that of our fellowman, we must possess the courage to abide by our convictions and at times withdraw from the crowds, from the senseless mass-hysteria of the press and movies, and the din of amusement. In our era of unlimited mass propaganda it is of vital importance that we ask ourselves whether we are unduly influenced by the opinion of acquaintances and by the actions of others? It would be advantageous for our own salvation and that of our neighbor if we could break away from comparing and competing with the crowd and the rest of men. *We would then be able to act on Christian principles and thereby become the champions of a sound public opinion and a healthier mode of life.*

Only a person brave enough to support a good cause either alone or in cooperation with others will be able to withstand and oppose the opinion of the crowd. At the opportune time he will fearlessly express his convictions in the favor of a worthwhile cause even in the absence of applause or patronage from others.

It should, of course, be recognized that in individual

† M. Winowska, *Das verhoente Antlitz—Das Leben des Bruders Albert,* Salzburg: Otto Müller Verlag.

circumstances the milieu is more an asset and a blessing than a painful burden and a difficult task. Our freedom will expand in direct proportion to our sincere gratitude for the good spirit and protecting order of the community. In assuming our share of community responsibilities, we will not only express our appreciation for the benefits received but also increase the measure of our own freedom and that of others.

4. Our Passions in the Service of Freedom

Although our passions in themselves were meant to be controlled and utilized in the service of the good, some passions, such as anger, inordinate desire, involuntary attachment, fear, anxiety, joy, and sorrow, may become forces in the service of evil. *In the absence of passions, human freedom and existence would be colorless and monotonous and bare of all charm and vigor.* What prospects does a person have in later life whose impulses of self-will and self-assertion were crushed systematically from earliest childhood and in whom every initiative and ingenuity was suppressed or criticized, while a soulless conformity and compliance or "good behavior" is praised and rewarded as the highest ideal of conduct? Such a "good" person will manifest a deplorable lack of initiative for the rest of his life.

It is quite evident that the interior control of the emotions or passions is essential for the full liberty of the interior decision. Yet, we may not overlook the fact that human freedom is deprived of vitality and vigor if the impelling force of the passions or emotions is inadequate or lacking.

Christ, the perfection of humanity, showed Himself to be a man of great passions. The gospels tell us of His anger in the face of malice and hypocrisy, His exultation over the heavenly Father's predilection and condescending love for the poor and little ones, His profound compassion for the suffering, and His fond attachment to His disciples. Yet all His emotions found their unity and fulfillment in the most perfect harmony of His charity for His heavenly Father and all mankind.

We human beings need a lifetime of struggle and effort in order to achieve a perfect or even satisfactory control over our passions so that, purified and harmonized, they may prove their power in the service of the good. *Uncontrolled passions are dangerous enemies of human freedom.* In extreme cases an antecedent passion (aroused instantaneously by external circumstances excluding premeditation) may lessen or even destroy interior freedom on account of its violent and sudden nature. It would be wrong, however, simply to dispense the person from moral responsibility by capitalizing on such an extreme possibility. The degree of moral freedom and responsibility may not be judged only by external appearances based on individual actions. Freedom also implies a responsibility for watchfulness and control over our passions. Such control cannot be accomplished by a mere defensive attitude. The emotions must be profitably directed to the good. Only if we are truly passionate in enhancing God's interests and responsive to the beauty and loveliness of creation shall we be able to preserve ourselves from the consuming fire of the lower passions. Only true Christian sorrow for sin will ward off the gloomy sadness over the loss of earthly possessions. Only he who is brave enough to oppose evil by a just anger will avoid the dissipation of his emotions in useless revolt.

Section VIII. Freedom—Its Obstacles and Dangers

Heredity, environment, and the emotions (or passions), frequently constitute serious hindrances and threats to our moral freedom. Nevertheless, an undue emphasis on their negative aspects and influences with a consequent flight or defensive attitude, may breed both narrow-mindedness and barriers to true liberty. Such an attitude based on a false orientation is bound to impair man's spiritual freedom.

On the other hand, there are certain *enslaving habits, culpable ignorance, carelessness, and the various forms of addiction,* which by their very nature constitute serious threats to our moral and spiritual freedom. *Psychopathic or sociopathic personality disorders* likewise delimit the boundaries of true spiritual freedom to the extent of personality involvement and disorganization. In all these difficulties, as long as sin is excluded, there is good reason to believe that: "For those who love God, all things work out for their good." (Rom. 8:28)

1. Negligence and Ignorance

Inadvertence and non-culpable ignorance may in particular cases exclude moral responsibility. Take for example the person who fails to keep the Friday abstinence because he is not aware that it is Friday when he eats meat. It is evident that there is no free decision and consequently, no sinful action.

On the other hand, *culpable, habitual inattention to moral truths and obligations* seriously lessens man's freedom in moral decisions. *Ignorance in moral and religious matters is not conducive to a firmly rooted joyful freedom.* Unawareness of moral values and of the beauty of Christian law reduces the power of moral motives and the force and energy of will power.

2. *The Force of Habit*

Desirable habits tend to increase the ease and firmness of our free decisions in favor of the good. They are the prerequisites for practical expertness in virtue. By the same token, it is true that a thoughtless and routine performance of duties is indicative of a delimited moral freedom.

Bad habits which carry the deadly weight of previous free decisions lessen moral freedom but do not exclude culpability as long as the free will persists in its evil decisions.

If with true contrition and sincere resolution a bad habit is repudiated by a free act of the will, an inadvertent relapse into a previously established sinful habit may be free of moral guilt. Thus, it may happen that a person who had developed the bad habit of profaning God's holy name may occasionally revert to blasphemy despite his sincere determination to refrain from using God's name in vain. The mere fact that such a relapse evokes immediate contrition clearly indicates that the free will had no part in the act.

3. *Freedom and Addiction*

All forms of addiction are serious threats to moral freedom. A person's enslavement to alcohol, for example, reduces his power of resistance also in other aspects of his moral life. Undoubtedly, some persons unduly dependent on smoking are perfectly lovable personalities; yet it should be remembered that the intemperate use of nicotine tends to impair the energy and free determination of the will in a general way. Man, because of the essential relationship existing between his physical and spiritual faculties, reacts in his totality in matters of moral freedom.

Opiates and other narcotic drugs are only permitted for strictly medical purposes. Nature's gifts, although these may be good in themselves (as for example, the various stimulants, alcohol, nicotine, and the manifold forms of recreational activities and amusements such as dancing, sports and television), should be used according to the words of St. Paul: *"I am free to do what I will, but I may not become enslaved"* (I Cor. 6:12).

4. Mental Illness and Sociopathic Disorders

(a) *Psychogenic mental disorders,* such as schizophrenia, manic depressive psychoses, involutional melancholia, and paranoid states, completely destroy man's moral freedom. In view of the increasing hope for successful treatment and recovery from mental illness, relatives of the mentally ill have a serious moral obligation to secure the advice and help of a psychiatric specialist whenever there is hope for recovery or improvement.

(b) *Sociopathic or psychopathic personality disorders* distinguish themselves from psychoses (mental disorders), in that the sociopath is aware of his abnormal state as revealed in his desires, impulses, and temperament. This personality disorder lies in the wide zone between mental health and mental illness. Consequently, moral freedom has not been completely destroyed in all the aspects of personality. Despite the fact that the predispositions of this serious disorder are rooted in hereditary factors, the degree of personality involvement greatly depends on environmental influences and personal utilization of the remaining moral freedom. It is not enough to condone and excuse the psychopath's behavior. Real understanding and a genuine charity in dealing with sociopathic personalities may prove to be marvelously therapeutic.

(c) A number of psychic disorders, formerly grouped as inherited disturbances of the inner harmony of the personality, are classified as *neuroses, or psycho-neuroses*. From the standpoint of heredity it is an accepted fact that basically they are not (or at least not predominantly) rooted in hereditary factors. Very often they can be traced to very unfavorable family relationships, characterized by undue strictness and lack of affection. The early years of life are particularly decisive in this regard. Excessive psychic demands very often lead to a failure of the integrative functions of the ego, even without hereditary predispositions. Neuroses are born of the feeling of isolation and helplessness especially in those people who possess a sensitive nature and yearn for personal fulfillment in life. This aspect of failure in personality integration is expressed by C. G. Jung when he defines neurosis as "a sorrow of a soul who has failed to find its real meaning." We may define it as a sorrow of a soul who in its inmost depths has not stopped to seek its true purpose in life. *

Research into the nature and types of neuroses has clearly indicated that due to previous personal fault or the guilt of others, human freedom and consequently also moral responsibility are greatly reduced or even absent.

5. "For Those Who Love God, All Things Turn Into Blessings"

Every human being is obliged to recognize his particular gifts and talents so that he may utilize and develop them

---

* A more detailed discussion on the topic of neurosis will be found in the chapter dealing with conscience as discussed under the heading of "Scrupulosity."

towards the attainment of his full measure of freedom in the service of the good. We should try to face ourselves as we are. We should not even try to hide our moral defects and deficiencies. We should be able to see and accept our own shadow. Although the majority of people do not suffer from neurotic disorders, nevertheless, they are burdened by some type of hereditary deficiency or predisposition. We shall run the risk of wasting and even forfeiting the right to our natural and most precious supernatural freedom if we become enslaved by our passions or if we fail to resolve our difficulties in the spirit of a lively faith.

All psychic inadequacies and neurotic tendencies which tend to reduce moral freedom are real crosses for both the victim and his fellowmen. If we willingly and serenely accept the things which cannot be changed, and patiently endeavor to heal what can be healed, we are following in the footsteps of our suffering Lord and shall achieve freedom in the ever-growing conformity with Christ.

3 GOD AND THE HEART OF MAN

In a highly venerated book of Confucius we read an expression closely akin to the gospel message: "If you wish to rule the world, try to do so first of all in your community; if you wish to govern your community, learn to manage your own family; if you wish to direct your family, control your will; if you wish to be master of your will, regulate your heart."

In all our efforts for true world improvement, which is essential for the peace of our soul and the sincerity of our witness for Christ, we must always remember that *God is not satisfied with anything less than our heart. Our share in the renewal of the world and our contribution to the creation of a new heaven and a new earth will be in direct proportion to our renewed good will and generous efforts, shown in the sincerity of our renewal by grace.*

Genuine Christian life is under the radiant influence of

Christ's beatitude: "Blessed are the singlehearted, for they will see God" (Matt. 5:8). It is the Christian's privilege to experience the joy of the New Law, that will become for him "a perfect law of freedom" (James 1:25). The scriptural meaning of "heart" is twofold. It connotes conscience or the very core of our being, where the voice of God's love is perceived (Part One). At the same time, it signifies the *dispositions* and *sentiments* of man as the "thoughts of the heart," namely, the intentions and innermost motives of our actions which essentially determine the value of our response to God's call (Part Two).

PART ONE

Conscience

The *New Law*, by its very essence, is a law of charity. The Holy Spirit Himself, who is Love personified, has inscribed this law in our hearts. The New Law is in harmony with the freedom of the children of God which enables us to respond freely and joyously to the invitation of God's love. In the present discussion we are concerned with the question: How does man's heart encounter God's invitation and law, and what are the necessary *attributes of conscience* which enable it to receive God's message and appeal in true docility, effecting a loving response of man's entire being?

A thorough elucidation of the true meaning of conscience is especially important because the term is used frequently in everyday language. Nobody would like to be labeled as being "unscrupulous" or "without conscience." All kinds of decisions are made in the name and under the patronage of conscience.

1. Conscience is the interior man, the entire man. 2. A comparison between the conscience of the believer and that of the agnostic will give us a glimpse of the innermost core of man. 3. Man is able to arrive at a true and deep understanding of himself only through the voice of his conscience, audible in the very depth of his being. 4. Man will find and assert his true self only to the extent of the purity of his intention. This purity manifests itself in a complete detachment from all pride and selfishness, an essential disposition of the heart for a willing response to God's invitation. 5. Perfect responsiveness to God's will and good pleasure is the determining factor in all our relationships to human authority as ordained by God. Authority and conscience are two closely related concepts. 6. The pure heart—the conscience, perfectly attuned to God's voice—is the most essential prerequisite for the virtue of prudence. 7. Under certain circumstances, the rules of prudence will aid the doubtful conscience. 8. A detailed exposition of the manifold problems of scrupulosity is intended to deepen the insight into the nature of a right conscience and to forestall the dangers of an erroneous conscience.

Section I. The Interior Man Is the Whole Man

A comparison of the wide variety of conscience-manifestations in different individuals may help to clarify the true nature and essence of conscience.

Take for example the person who spends his time and fortune for the protection and well-being of animals. The wellspring of his actions lies in his inner motives, expressed in his own words: "I feel obliged in conscience to do all in my power to protect animals because they are God's creatures." Another person may manifest a similar devotion for the establishment of a true and lasting world peace through the suppression of the spirit of aggressiveness and national- ism, because he has witnessed the horrors of the last war with all its terrible outbursts of hatred and cruelty. What are the inner motives, urging the convinced advocate of birth control to travel to India and Japan, in order to sell his false theory of artificial and unethical family limitation? If questioned about his motives he undoubtedly would try to assure you that it is his conscience which urges him. Even the untiring instigators of world revolutions do not hesitate to label their devastating activities an affair and is- sue of conscience. What credence do they deserve?

Shall we believe every one's assurance that he is acting under the dictates of his conscience? Very often people de- ceive themselves as to their own motives. However, the fact remains that conscience may manifest itself in a variety of ways. What are the common denominators and distinguish- ing features and differences in the manifestations of con- science?

1. *Common Core and Dynamics of Conscience*

All those who feel themselves impelled to act according to the dictates of their conscience, do so because of the attrac- tion to a value which they have perceived and accepted in the depths of their hearts. The value itself may be a false value, *yet all will agree that the good which is recognized must be loved and pursued.* Everyone with a sensitive con- science is aware that his conscience is not just a mere in- tellectual perception. Although it may be difficult to relate the inner experiences transpiring in the depth of the soul at the moment of committing sin, the fact remains that man realizes with unmistakable clarity that a deliberate desire and act opposed to the good, clearly recognized, causes a deeply penetrating laceration at the inner core of his being.

In his letter to the Romans, St. Paul gives a vivid description of the dreadful dissension in man's heart which arises from the fact that the lower self "raises war against the dispositions of conscience" despite a clear and joyful recognition of the revealed good "according to the inner man" (Rom. 7:22-24).

The full disaster of our death-doomed existence reveals itself in the violent conflict between the lower sensual nature and the higher aspirations of our soul, if climaxed by man's free decision in favor of the "alien law in his members" and against the liberating law of God despite the irresistible forces of his higher faculties in their ceaseless yearning after the good. This interior disruption of man's essential unity signifies a real "death" and shakes the very foundations of man's existence, similar to physical death in the rending asunder of man's soul and body. In fact, this dissension between cognition and volition in man's final decision to repudiate a clearly recognized value, has more of the qualities of death than physical dying. The solidarity of man's soul and body in the oneness of the person is far surpassed by the soul's essential integrity through the unity of the powers of the intellect and will. This essential harmony is destroyed in the act of sinning. The powers of the intellect and will are so intimately united in man's soul that their *dissension in the sinful act,* whether in desire, decision, or action contrary to the better judgment of reason, shakes the soul's very foundations.

It would be erroneous to believe that by nature man's will experiences equal attraction to both good and evil. Man's will is not ambivalent. Consequently, it must experience evil as self-destructive and opposed to its true nature, because the spiritual faculty of the will, like the entire man, is essentially directed towards the good. In addition, man's will is bound to seek the good by reason of its essential and irrevocable association with the innermost core of the soul. In the experience of conscience, the person is summoned and challenged in the totality of his being. Basically, the powers of the intellect and will are cognizant of their essential kinship to the good and, consequently, are aware of the dangers inherent in evil. In view of the soul's unity and wholeness, the powers of the intellect and will are conscious of the piercing conflict arising from the opposition to the good as perceived by the soul. The very foundations of the soul tremble and shake when the will turns away from the bright light of truth. The soul is shaken to its innermost depths where "the spark of the soul" (in the words of the medieval mystics) is enkindled by the ocean of divine light and fire. *In short, it is the heart or the whole man who yearns after unity between the intellectual and volitional powers of the soul.*

It is through the inner unity of the powers of the intellect and will in the very core of the soul—"the spark of the soul" —that *man's soul itself is a profound and marvelous image of the Blessed Trinity,* wherein the three divine Persons subsist in one essence and the whole essence is in each Person. The Father, in His infinite truth and love, gives Himself totally to the Son; and the Son, with all the gifts He has received from the Father, is the perfect response to the Father in the love of the Holy Spirit. What the Father knows and loves, the Son and the Holy Spirit love likewise. Man's soul, in its inmost depths, is a perfect reflection of God's own image, both in the order of nature and even more so in the order of grace. For this very reason the unquenchable craving for unity in the intellect and will is an intrinsic and essential quality in man's heart. When the mind is illumined by the light of truth and convinced of the true good, man's innermost heart, with its essential spiritual desire for unity and oneness, is able to present to the will the good conceived as man's true and personal good and thereby awaken and strengthen the conviction that his happiness is guaranteed only if his faculties are harmoniously directed towards the good.

Man's persistent craving after inner unity between knowledge and desire is an authentic manifestation of the soul's likeness to God's own image. Similarly, the estrangement of the will from the true light of our spiritual knowledge and the consequent surrender to the mirage of illusory values— perceived as a contradiction in the very depth of the soul— manifests a shocking defilement of the image of God in the creature.

2. The Differential Elements in Expressions of Conscience

Although there is general agreement on the basic principle that a clearly comprehended value must be pursued, there are, nevertheless, considerable differences in the manner in which conscience expresses itself in particular individuals. What are the underlying factors for such a variation? The answer to this question will re-emphasize the primary importance of the intention or the heart of man as the expression of his deepest essence.

(a) *There are legitimate differences in the manner and mode in which conscience manifests itself in individual souls.* This is based on the natural and supernatural endowments or talents which they have received.

For example, it is possible that a person sincerely concerned for the welfare of animals becomes aware of "the groaning of creation" when he is confronted with gross mistreatment of God's creatures. His natural response is to protect them and to influence others to act in like manner for the greater honor and glory of God. However, the building of extravagant homes for the care of cats and dogs, in cities where thousands of people are housed in the most miserable shelters, would not only be an injustice to the poor but also a sign of a wrong conscience. Another manifestation of conscience is the unparalleled ardor in promoting the cause of peace and mutual understanding which is indeed a refreshing reassurance for all who have witnessed the horrors of World War II and realize the frightening threat of nuclear war. Yet, regardless of high ideals for world peace no one may sacrifice his moral and religious convictions and his true freedom from tyranny. This is a basic requirement to safeguard our conscience and, at the same time, to promote the cause of peace and harmony among nations. *Each man's conscientious fulfillment of his special obligation in the pursuit of his particular vocation will effectively contribute to the increasing recognition and implementation of moral principles in community and world affairs.*

(b) While all those who sincerely claim to follow the dictates of their conscience agree that the good has to be loved and pursued in a given situation, they are often of divided opinion on the question of what constitutes "the good." It may happen that two persons in the same situation have separate but, at the same time, complementary duties. Yet if two mutually exclusive or even contradictory actions are justified by an appeal to conscience, it is obvious that one of the persons is prompted by an erroneous conscience.

Let us consider the following situations. Two young married people are convinced of their moral obligation to ren-

der adequate proof of a joyous acceptance of their procrea-
tive duties, while another conscientious couple under the
pressure of existing circumstances feel unable to raise more
than two children, and consequently follow the dictates of
their conscience by adhering to the principle that one's obligation towards procreation is subject to God's gifts. And
what about Mr. Thompson who, with ample funds and a
host of propaganda agents, travels as far as Japan in order
to acquaint the inhabitants with the newest methods of
birth control and the horror-inspiring practices of abortion?
What is our reaction if he also justifies his actions by appealing to his conscience? The fact is that we do not know
Mr. Thompson and consequently may not judge him as a
person. Yet it is evident that the decisions of his conscience
are erroneous. What is the underlying cause? It may partly
be the fault of his environment. Perhaps he was reared in a
completely irreligious and materialistic milieu where the
refusal to accept the burden of the married state was the
accepted attitude. It also is likely that Mr. Thompson grew
up in an environment which dealt superficially with the
vital problems of life and judged community and world
affairs from the standpoint of expediency. In addition to
environmental influences, Mr. Thompson may have failed
to become acquainted with the moral-religious issues of life.
Under these circumstances he may try to rationalize, saying that his campaign for family limitation not only contributes to the solution of the population problems in Japan
but also helps to alleviate political tension in the world at
large. Incidentally, laudable motives may be mixed with
evident erroneous ideas. In short, it should be remembered
that others share in the guilt of the dangerously false ideas
which he spreads under the pretense of conscience. Conversely, the toleration and promotion of his devastating

propaganda by legitimate authorities may further contribute to the faulty formation of the consciences of innumerable people.

Frequently, wrong decisions or judgments of conscience are the result of distorted principles. These may be the outcome of repeated violations of conscience, because the individual has failed to act in agreement with the dictates of his conscience. Furthermore, a false evaluation of a particular situation may similarly result in a wrong decision.

Take for example the case of a married woman who feels justified in conscience to refuse her husband the conjugal act because she believes that he is a confirmed adulterer. To some extent her false decision of conscience may be due to instigations and rash judgments from relatives and friends, or they may be caused by her own unforgiving disposition which she has fostered by her deplorable lack of charity in thoughts and words. Yet it may be that the external circumstances of the case may be so complicated that she is free of guilt in this particular condemnation of her husband.

This should prove the point that in difficult situations it is possible to make a false decision of conscience without any personal guilt. Because of this decision, the person feels a definite obligation to act in agreement with such a subjectively certain conscience. Despite a personal error in such a decision, conscience has not been violated because the person acted on his honest, though erroneous opinion. The will and heart pursued the good and the true. Therefore, the will, despite an error in judgment, has followed the light of reason.

At other times, man may fail in his duty to ascertain the full truth of a situation before reaching a decision. He may disregard the warnings from the depth of his soul which caution him to search for the true good with increased diligence and sincerity. The inherent laxity points to a certain callousness and defilement of man's heart, namely, his conscience. It reveals the shallowness of the particular conscience.

Furthermore, we should realize that an indiscriminate absorption of the false doctrines of mass-opinion and propaganda have greatly contributed to man's spiritual superficiality. Depth and clarity of conscience are the distinguishing features of the mature and integrated personality which set him apart from the man following the crowd who is tossed on the waves of public opinion. *Personal responsibility in conscience is diametrically opposed to collective prejudices.*

We may not forget the reverse of this truth; namely, that the individual conscience, in its endeavor for inner harmony in opposition to the spirit of collectivism, is greatly dependent on the ethical and moral standards and ideals of his community. A superficial and indiscriminate conformity to laws and customs of the environment is proof that the particular conscience has failed to achieve authentic maturity and watchfulness.

Section II. A Parallel Between the Conscience of the Believer and the Non-believer

It is quite possible that a so-called "unbeliever," who is sincere in his quest for the truth and the good, may have achieved a greater vigilance of conscience than some of the faithful. In fact, the formalism of some Christians regarding moral truths as well as their indifference, apathy, and blindness in strategic situations, is a source of scandal when compared to the ready and open responsiveness of some non-Christians in the hour of need. Such behavior obscures the essence of conscience. The following discussion, however, is not intended to compare the conscience of a superficial, formalistic Christian with that of an open-minded, alert non-Christian. This approach might be harmful because it tends to obscure the sublimity of the truly Christian conscience as well as the utter distress of the conscience which is devoid of faith.

Very often the decisions of conscience in both the believer and unbeliever are in agreement on particular aspects of morality. Under such circumstances they both have the same obligation to follow the dictates of their conscience. This fact provides a basis for common understanding and collaboration between Christians and non-Christians in our modern, pluralistic society. Nevertheless, we need a clear conception of the basic differences characterizing the conscience of the believer and the agnostic in order to achieve closer cooperation and collaboration with unbelievers without endangering our own convictions. The chief object of this discussion is to clarify the true nature of conscience.

1. The Conscience of the Believer

We try to list here some advantages or merits of the conscience rooted in faith.

In the first place, conscience enlightened by faith knows God's loving will, the foundation of moral "ought." *The conscience based on faith is not guided by a dead principle but knows itself confronted with the loving, personal God.* This fact points to the personal dignity of the man whom God addresses personally through the appeal of conscience. It also admonishes man to acknowledge his utter dependence on God by way of humble adoration and acceptance of God's holy will. The conscience of the believer is fully aware of the truth that it is not the highest court of appeal. Furthermore, it is cognizant of the sublime dignity inherent in the intimately personal manner in which God's supreme holiness makes His appeal.

Secondly, *faith,* although not supplying the immediate answer to all the individual questions and problems of our daily life, *grants us assurance and security by providing the fundamental principles applicable to the vital issues of life.* This gives a sense of direction to all our endeavors and strivings. Faith presents the things of this earth in the light of God's own wisdom.

Thirdly, through the infallible teaching of the Church, faith provides more than authoritative statements regarding basic Christian truths. The Church's doctrine offers more than helpful directions in the crucial problems of life. It is the foundation for an intimate, *interior communion of the faithful.* The example of saintly lives in a Christian community greatly contributes to the proper formation of the individual conscience and aids in the application of basic truths and principles in particular situations. Conscience, thereby, remains preserved from the emptiness and sterility of a dead formalism. Man not only lives in solidarity with the good, but also shares in the evil consequences of the sins of his fellowmen.

Very often individual members fail to receive the encouraging example expected in a Christian community because the leaven of faith is lacking in man's immediate environment. This causes a weakening of the bonds of unity. Faith is essentially a grace from above and is reflected in the faithful conscience which is ready to render a loving and prompt response to each personal call from God. Without the experience of faith as expressed in the united liturgical celebrations and in wholehearted collaboration for the welfare of each individual member, the Christian community falls short of its obligation to provide a milieu which exerts a favorable influence in the formation of conscience. Although faith renders the individual conscience sensitive to its obligations to counteract erroneous collective opinions, the Christian needs support and good example from the community because unaided and isolated he may succumb to the dangers of the malicious spirit of collectivism and the consolidated powers of evil.

2. The Conscience of the Unbeliever

In comparing the conscience of a believer and that of an agnostic, the term unbeliever should be clarified. It would be misleading to think of the "unbeliever" as one who by his sincere search for the truth possesses the dispositions of a believer. The term unbeliever in the present context signifies one confirmed in his denial of a personal God and opposed to the search for truth. The conscience of the unbeliever suffers from the following ailments:

(a) *The moral principles of the agnostic are void of the decisive motivation arising from the known or recognized will of a personal God.* The agnostic fails to acknowledge his basic responsibilities to a personal God and consequently considers himself confronted only with impersonal principles. Devoid of the sense of responsibility to a personal "Thou," the unbeliever is guided by his own willfulness and the impersonal circumstances of his life. Unquestionably, the monitor of his conscience still voices the imperative "ought" in moral decisions but the obligation is not supported by the weight of God's holiness and supremacy. To a certain extent the unbeliever may realize and accept the claims of conscience in decisions between good and evil, and between loyalty and disloyalty; yet he is isolated and lonely in his decisions of conscience because he is confronted by selfish and ignoble motives which are unworthy of the personal dignity of a man challenged by the good.

(b) *Strictly speaking, the unbeliever in the proper sense of the word is not touched by the decisive demands appealing to conscience through the summons of divine love.* He lacks the sense of obligation to Him from whose bounty he has received all things. He is not confronting a personal "Thou" who is extending to him an intimate, personal and loving appeal. Consequently, his individual responses of conscience to particular values are unable to break the solitude of his isolated self. The available sense of obligation or attraction to the good in the conscience of the unbeliever is deprived of the genuine brightness and blessed ardor which characterize the conscience of the believer.

(c) Since God is the author and summit of all values, it is inevitable that the conscience of the unbeliever, blinded towards God the Supreme Value, shall gradually reveal a *lack of responsibility to particular values.* Man's estrangement from God reduces his appreciation of moral truths and values.

(d) It is possible that the unbeliever may claim to live in closer agreement with his personal conviction than his Christian fellow citizen because he is entirely dependent on the voice of his conscience. Yet, he is deceiving himself because without the imperceptible influences of his Christian environment he would unconsciously have become the *victim of erroneous collective opinions in the harmful solidarity of the masses.*

The sociological theory of conscience, endorsed by Emile Durkheim and others, which merely views conscience as a practical adaptation to the changing circumstances of life, is in reality no more than the description of a man who deceives himself in thinking that he lives by the dictates of his conscience while in reality he hopelessly follows the shallow maxims and slogans of his environment.

(e) The foregoing descriptions of conscience provide evidence that moral goodness is equivalent to pliability and readiness of the will to follow the clearly recognized good. This presupposes a humble and ready will. In the event that man should fail to surrender himself to the loving designs of a personal God in a *proud attempt to deny God's sovereignty,* his self-glorification reaches a frightening and an alarming degree. Such an egotistic attitude excludes an interior readiness and openness for the light of moral truths, especially if these run counter to man's pride and sloth.

We must therefore conclude that the outstanding disposition which characterizes unbelief is a blunting and obstinacy of conscience. Conversely, a conscience alert and sensitive to the important moral demands and values has, in the true sense of the word, all the indications which set it apart from the conscience of the unbeliever.

3. *The Conscience Wavering Between Faith and Unbelief*

In our daily encounter with people we meet those who are neither faithful Christians nor confirmed unbelievers. There is, for example, the so-called "faithful," one who attends church services and religiously recites his creed but fails to implement his religious principles in daily life as bidden by the unmistakable admonitions of his conscience. He rather follows the shallow opinions and superficial slogans of the crowds. On the other hand, there is the "believer" who through repeated violations of his conscience has become accustomed to act in contradiction to the demands of faith. At a time of serious temptation or mass-apostasy, the dangerous similarity of his life with that of the non-believer shall manifest itself in its frightening and devastating reality.

On the other hand, it is true that some "unbelievers" may be living according to the dictates of their conscience without an explicit awareness that God Himself is calling them through the summons in their hearts. When analyzing such a situation we recognize that long before these persons begin to accept God as their Creator and Lord they have been fostering the dispositions characteristic of believers, namely, a sincere readiness to recognize and pursue the good. While external appearances may be deceiving, many so-called unbelievers by their keen moral perception and ready obedience to the dictates of conscience, are in closer harmony with the community of the faithful than those Christians who despite their apparent righteousness succumb to the tides of unbelief and superficial attitudes of the day.

A rather surprising phenomenon appears in the morally over-exact agnostic who, following his apostasy, puts his Christian neighbors to shame by his truly exemplary life and outstanding works of mercy. The possibility exists that his "apostasy" is in reality a protest against the evident lack of faith in his Christian surroundings and an expression of his deeply rooted yearning for the genuine dedication of a lively faith. This usually manifests itself in his entire attitude and disposition of conscience. It is also possible that his self-evident moral endeavors are subconscious pretenses which arise from his disturbed conscience whereby he justifies his defection from the faith. By its very nature, such external rectitude of behavior is diametrically opposed to the demands of conscience and conforms more or less with Emile Durkheim's description of a "successful or unsuccessful adaptation" to the community. Such a moral life—unlike that of the conscientious believer—does not flow forth from the heart and core of his being.

Section III. Called by Our Personal Name

We have seen that conscience is a vital reality protecting man's inner unity and totality. The summons of conscience pierce and penetrate the very depth of man's soul. This explains why any true understanding of self must take its orientation from the voice of God in the innermost recesses of the soul. The more man lives in agreement with the dictates of his conscience, the more surely and inevitably will he become aware of God's special and intimate interest in him as a person. *The crystal pure conscience, the alert and receptive heart, perceives all things in the light of God's loving designs.*

Ultimately, beyond the voice of conscience there is the majesty of God. This adds weight and importance to the obligations of conscience. It likewise reveals the sublime dignity of man whom God addresses in such a personal manner. The unbeliever's pride may attempt to interpret the "ought" contained in the challenge of conscience as an abstract principle, in order to safeguard his personal prestige. Yet we Christians are fully aware of our intimate encounter with God which is the foundation of our personal transcendence over the spirit of collective opinion and our liberation from the solitude of a selfish existence. God's dealings with us are characterized by utmost sincerity and earnestness. *He asks for the innermost core of our being, aglow with dedication and ardor. We are fully aware that His admonitions are life-giving, if followed with childlike docility.* We are likewise cognizant of the fact that any disobedience or evasion of His urgent summons signifies a real death and a rending asunder of the essential unity and integrity of the person. Whether the unbeliever or the man lacking in personal convictions and moral principles is cognizant or not of his own tragedy, it remains undeniable that man's escape from the demands of conscience causes a mortal wound in the core of his innermost being.

Even the sinner bears witness to the fact that life without orientation and obedience to the summons of God is unbearable. Only obedience to God's call can restore the spiritual integrity lost through insubordination. Holy Scripture gives testimony of this truth in the account of Cain's wickedness. The Yahwist author says that God Himself warned Cain that his heart was afflicted with envy: "Why are you angry and why are you downcast? If you do well, will you not be accepted?" (Gen. 4:6-7). After Cain committed his horrible sin, God asked him: "Where is your brother Abel?" (Gen. 4:9). At this moment Cain's tortured conscience was still in contact with God. Cain's alienation from God, apparent in his deliberate flight from His Creator's face, ostensibly manifested that his conscience was unable to escape the quest and call of God. This is poignantly expressed in his own words: "You are driving me today from the soil; and from Your face I shall be hidden. And I shall be a fugitive and a wanderer on the earth" (Gen. 4:14). If God had not "appointed a sign for Cain" (Gen. 4:15), he would have been unable to survive as a fugitive before the face of the Almighty. Man's refusal of God's appeal causes a mortal wound because the creature's existence is dependent on God's life-giving communication with man. His entire life is a gift of God's love. This explains why man can find his true self only in a perfect readiness to listen and to respond to the summons of God.

Does the foregoing discussion imply that God's admonition through the voice of conscience is a personal address?

Is conscience really and truly the voice of God? The answer is both a qualified "yes" and a qualified "no"!

God deigns to give private revelations and direct inspirations only in rare and special cases. Nevertheless, He is in closest personal contact with each soul by the direct interventions of grace. In general, God does not speak to us directly. He has endowed us with natural capacities which help us to recognize His holy will. Furthermore, we are assisted by morally significant and valuable communities and institutions such as the family, social, religious, and civic groups and especially the teaching authority of the Church. Yet, in addition, God counts on our personal endeavors and desires a full utilization of our spiritual faculties so that we may arrive at a clear value-perception in all the morally significant situations of our life.

God speaks to our hearts through Holy Scripture, the doctrines of His Church, the order in creation, and all the individual circumstances of our personal lives. Through the gifts of nature and grace, God grants us an adequate understanding of our moral obligations relevant to our salvation.

It is important to remember that *God's dealings with us are deeply personal, although He may transmit His message through the mediation of creatures.* His appeal is always a deeply personal and intimate encounter. By means of His grace He Himself "opens my ear that I may hear" (Is. 50:6). Conscience is the "organ" through which God establishes contact with man's heart.

However, not every decision of conscience should be considered an explicit expression of God's will. We should do our best to become attuned and receptive to every appeal from God. We must open our hearts in order to perceive God's voice. Our tendency towards superficiality and our unwillingness to listen are partially responsible for our imperfect understanding of God's will. In addition to personal neglect and the unfortunate circumstances of our environment, our conscience may be clouded by unfavorable genetic tendencies.

If, *without our fault*, we should arrive at a wrong decision of conscience, God in His supreme goodness will accept our sincere desire to know and perform His loving designs. Despite such erroneous judgment, we are still in conformity with God's will and docile to the true light of His truth. On the contrary, a lack of genuine effort to become acquainted with God's holy will points to insincerity and perversity of the heart, which increases our egocentricity and estrangement from God.

With sublime profundity and remarkable simplicity St. Augustine clothed the above truth in the concise imperative: *"Love and do whatever you wish."* He thereby affirmed that we shall attain a marvelous and inevitable certainty in the discernment of God's will provided our heart is pure and steadfast in the pursuit of the good. God in His goodness accepts our sincere desire and efforts in spite of an occasional error in judgment. A faulty orientation of conscience in matters of essential moral demands is generally indicative of the fact that charity is still weak and unenlightened. The certitude and rectitude of the decisions of our conscience will increase in proportion to the purity of our charity.

Section IV. Blessed Are the Pure of Heart

Conscience in its deepest essence is the central core and focal point of man's integrity, of the inner unity and harmony of his life. Man's true value or worthlessness may be judged by the nature of his conscience and its manifestations in the practical situations of his life. Purity of conscience is the shield and safeguard for an enlightened comprehension of the things pertaining to God and the good. The chief aim of the following discussion is to point up the outstanding qualities of the pure heart or untroubled conscience. This picture will be painted against the dismal background of the wounded and defiled conscience.

1. The Defiled Heart of Man

Because of repeated and unrepented violations of moral principles, conscience as the spiritual disposition of man may react either by a warping of self into a *diabolical unity of darkness* or by a complete loss of all spiritual powers and moral consistency. The result is the "split conscience."

(a) *Unity of satanic darkening:* Conscience is the soul's fundamental craving for inner unity and harmony in the pursuit of the good. When man's conduct fails to harmonize with his moral insight, a penetrating, fatal abyss is created between the basic powers of the soul. This pernicious discord can only be bridged by sincere contrition—the soul's ardent appeal to the divine Physician for cure and restoration. Conscience, the heart of man, torn asunder by the discord of sin, cries in agonizing torment for healing and redemption in the unity of light. *If man's pride prevents him from a humble admission of guilt and a sincere acknowledgment of the previously violated moral law, there is grave danger that the unsatisfied basic yearnings of the human heart for inner harmony may lead to disaster because the soul, torn asunder by guilt, no longer seeks its unity in the true light but in the darkness of a perverted will.*

The initial attempt of such a conscience is to forget the guilt incurred. "Pride insinuated to my memory: 'It is impossible that you have acted thus!' Consequently, my mem-

ory weakened to the point of denying the act" (Nietzsche).
Thus, unrepented guilt is buried in the dark recesses of the
subconscious and unconscious mind, where repressed, it
may effect its most sinister powers.

A further step of pride consists in the denial of the perversion of the act itself. As a result of man's unwillingness
to follow the dictates of the remaining moral perceptions
and decisions, the soul's vision becomes more and more engrossed in the evil motives of his perverted desires. If, in
spite of this refusal to acknowledge one's guilt, the monitor
in the depth of conscience keeps reproaching, conscience
will try to escape from the unbearable tortures by means
of many pretexts and evasions. The proud man will no
longer "face himself in constant defilement" (Max Scheler).
Therefore, conscience will declare darkness as light, and
condemn light as darkness. Man's arbitrary will and unruly desires gradually force their arbitrary dictates on his
intellectual powers.

In this perverted state, the soul's unity between intellect
and will becomes re-established, but in a dark and sinister
manner. Christ alluded to such a soul when He said:
"Therefore, if the light that is in you is darkness, how great
must be your darkness!" (Matt. 6:23; Luke 11:34 ff.). But,
is there really a restoration of the soul's unity? To all appearances, man's heart no longer seems torn asunder. However, completely cut off from God's kingdom of light it is
utterly defiled and polluted. Hence, it is no longer capable
of experiencing God and the good in a beneficial and efficacious manner. The soul's reasoning powers are attempting to escape from the face of the Lord. *This is the dark
picture of man's heart estranged from God.*

Naturally, such a perversion is gradual and insidious in
its process. Even the most obstinate and persistent attempts to deceive oneself are slow in stifling the sublime

yearnings of the human heart. The passionate efforts of the wicked in carrying out their infamous designs and their tenacity in advancing their dangerous propaganda are but poorly disguised attempts to drown the reproaches of their guilty consciences. Due to the heart's irresistible inclination towards the good, the sinner vainly endeavors to hush God's inviting voice, by a desperate flight into ever increasing depths of darkness.

Men whose conscience reacts in the described manner usually are inclined towards totality in all their actions. They are truly endowed with the qualities for sainthood, provided they would possess humility.

(b) *The split conscience:* In contradistinction to those confirmed in their evil obstinacy, there are the weak and flaccid types of personalities. *Theoretically, these persons acknowledge the good, but their actions belie what they confess.* They start out with minor but frequently repeated and unrepented violations of conscience. Such souls gradually and insidiously become accustomed to act in contradiction to what they recognize and acknowledge as good. This marks the beginning of the formation of the "split soul" in which moral insight and desires become diametrically opposed to each other, so that eventually the pain of the gaping wound in the inmost heart becomes numbed to complete moral insensibility. The light of truth, although not quite extinct in the intellect, has lost its brightness, its ardor, and its motivating power over the will. In the true sense of the word, the heart—the unifying center of the soul—is dead.

Such a disruption of the soul's innate integrity markedly affects and reduces its moral perception and appreciation which consequently is rendered increasingly misty and formalistic. This is an inevitable outcome because man's intellect is able to tolerate the sight of the good only to the extent that his heart is inclined to embrace it.

2. "The Pure Heart"

By way of contrast, the preceding dismal picture of the darkened and "split" conscience throws light on the significance of the pure heart. Yet the full splendor and the genuine treasures of a pure heart become manifest to us only in the light of God's own promises.

Our Savior's pledge to the "clean of heart" is epitomized in His emphatic pronouncement: "They shall see God" (Matt. 5:8). This explicit promise, like the rest of the beatitudes, has reference to the state of perfection and final consummation which this present life is meant to nurture to its fullest maturity. We shall be able to attain a "face-to-face" vision of God only after our complete cooperation with God's gifts and graces in the various trials and tribulations of our earthly existence—and perhaps after a final purification in purgatory. God is the personification of a gratuitous, self-surrendering, infinitely pure and holy love. The splendor of this love is such that we are able to experience its heavenly bliss only to the measure of our own transformation into a completely selfless love, wholly open and surrendered to God. Yet already in the present life we can attain a certain foretaste of the blessed revelations of the elect, provided our heart is pure and singleminded.

Since we live in an evil and perverted world, and at the same time are more or less weighed down by personal guilt and sin, we have to put forth considerable effort and perseverance in order to purify our heart—our conscience. The first and most indispensable step in the purgation of the heart consists in the humble avowal of our own imperfection. "Who can say 'I have made my heart clean, I am cleansed of my sin'?" (Prov. 20:9; cf. I John 1:9). Both the humility epitomized in the first beatitude ("Blessed are the poor in spirit") and the salutary sorrow of the second beatitude are basic prerequisites for purity of heart. Furthermore, the process of purification implies a continuous self-denial and a persistent effort on our part. The sincere desire for perfect purity of heart requires an unceasing struggle against all inordinate self-love. Nevertheless, it should be remembered that a mere negative approach in overcoming our inborn selfishness is inadequate for a complete purification of our heart. *The pure heart is a heart filled to overflowing with genuine love for God and neighbor.**

Our hearts shall be cleansed provided they are open to God's saving influence. God's word, revealed to us in the teachings of the Church and in the inspirations of the Holy Spirit, possesses a truly purifying power because it is love-inspired. The ready and willing acceptance of the divine will effects its redeeming power by penetrating as a healing balm to the very core of the soul where it clarifies the intellect and strengthens the will in the inmost recesses of our being, in "the spark of the soul." This is another way of expressing the well-known truth: that our moral and religious knowledge is able to effect a genuine rectification of conscience only if we are willing to render the obedience demanded by conscience.

God's benevolent will, made known to us by His word, purifies our intellect, our will, and our heart if it is received in filial gratitude. Christ expresses this truth when addressing His disciples who had willingly received His message: "You are already clean because of the word I have spoken

---

* An important aspect of this truth will be discussed in connection with the loving disposition and the pure intention.

to you" (John 15:3).† A clear comprehension of God's loving designs will fully purify our hearts to the extent that we make our life a love-union with Christ, who is the fountain of all truth and goodness. Therefore Our Lord admonishes: "Abide in Me, and I in you" (John 15:4). If we remain united with Christ in wholehearted acceptance of His Word as revealed in every invitation of grace and in our heart's inclination towards the good, He will lead us to an ever increasing purity of heart through our good works which are done in loving conformity to His good pleasure. "I am the real vine, and My Father is the vine dresser, He prunes away any branch of mine that bears no fruit, and cleans any branch that does bear fruit, that it may bear more abundant fruit" (John 15:1 ff. 7).

The word of God as the expression of His most unselfish love for men possesses purifying power over docile hearts. On the other hand, it holds true that *increasing purity of heart disposes us towards a deeper and more blessed penetration of God and His loving will.* "Holding the mystery of faith in a pure conscience" (I Tim. 3:9) we shall preserve its full luminous beauty and purity. The blessed realization of God's charity and loving designs, perceived in the mystery of faith, is a foretaste of the perfect revelation in the unveiled glory of love as expressed in the beatitude "They shall see God." In our present existence, we can assiduously strive for purity of heart, and humbly pray: "A pure heart create for me, O God, and a steadfast spirit renew within me" (Ps. 50:12).

In the liturgy of the Mass, before announcing the glad tidings of the gospel, the priest implores God to cleanse his heart and lips so that he may worthily proclaim God's holy

---

† This statement of Our Lord expresses a loving invitation to meditate frequently on the "word of God" in Holy Scripture.

word. Similarly, it behooves us to pray that God may cleanse our hearts by His message so that our lives may become a testimony of its purifying influence and power.

Section V. Conscience and Authority

Conscience by its nature is oriented towards *God's supreme authority*. It is subject to Him. From Him it receives its light and its security. The clear revelation of God's benevolent will and our appropriate loving response in obedience tend to enlighten and clarify our conscience. Likewise, it is true that God's authority directly appeals to our conscience. This means that He does not subject us to external measures of coercion. Force is needed only for the wicked and unenlightened, thereby to safeguard common order and morality.

Through the medium of conscience God addresses each of us in a unique and personal manner as His free children. In conscience we experience the obliging power of His revelations. In the depth of our spiritual being we become aware of our total dependence on God's loving will. Significantly applicable are the words of Holy Scripture: "I will allure her; I will lead her into the desert and speak to her heart" (Osee 2:14).

In view of these truths, the well attuned conscience is completely aware of its dependence on God's authority. On the other hand, if we were to consider *human authority* as superfluous we would thereby reveal a complete misconception of both the nature of conscience and the authority of God.

Concerning the formation of conscience and our attitude towards God's benevolent will, we are greatly indebted to human institutions, particularly the *authority of the Church.* Under existing circumstances, while still living in the midst of a perverse and corrupted world, the protection from civil authority is sorely needed both to safeguard the consciences of the good and to suppress the violence of the wicked. Obedience to civil authority is an obligation of conscience whenever lawful authority issues commands in God's name, that is, in agreement with God's will (cf. Rom. 13:5 where St. Paul applies the above maxim to the tax-law).

Aided by God's revelation and guided by the teaching authority of the Church, we are expected to reach that maturity of conscience which permits us to scrutinize the demands of civil authority by the standards of an enlightened conscience, because our obedience to human authority should be an obedience of conscience which in the final analysis is directed towards God. Consequently, all obedience must be in conformity with God's law. An endeavor towards mere external subjection to the justified commands of civil authority without due regard for conscience would jeopardize our true spirit of freedom. It would signify an attempt to withdraw a certain domain of human actions from the dictates of conscience and consequently from the authority of God. Obedience to human authority is not only in harmony with our personal dignity but, at the same time, a worthy holocaust to God, provided it is rendered with a sincere conscience. This fact justifies and even obliges us to examine the regulations of human authority in a spirit of faith to assure ourselves of their agreement with God's law. This is not synonymous with adverse criticizing and finding fault with human authority; it rather reveals an alert conscience that seeks to render a worthy obedience.

Obviously the interdependence between conscience and authority are reciprocal in nature. If human authority wishes to lead its subjects in a manner worthy of man's dig-

nity, *it must issue commands in full accord with conscience.*
This means that in true conscientiousness it must issue laws
and regulations in keeping with God's commandments and
in ways that appeal to and protect the conscience of those
of good will and thereby aid them to a fuller development
of their sense of personal responsibility.

The formation of a truly enlightened and alert conscience in keeping with the true dignity of the free children
of God is the primary aim of both the home-training in the
Christian family and the exercise of ecclesiastical authority.
Any training which is in conflict with these noble objectives
may achieve short-lived outward conformity and subjection, but offers no worthwhile contribution to the education and development of God's free children. It is doomed
to ultimate ruin because it has failed to rectify *man's heart.*

Section VI. Conscience and Prudence

The foregoing discussion affirms the point that a positive
emphasis on conscience in Christian moral teaching is far
from the so-called "subjectivism" which on the claims of the
"venture of conscience" violates the most sacred laws regardless of the consequences of these actions. The well
formed and pure conscience is truly single-minded and
attuned to listening when personal caprice does not enter
into its decisions. Thus we are enabled to carry out God's
will in the most perfect manner. (Prudence is the virtue
which directs the conscientious man in the correct interpretation of God's holy will so that in special and difficult
circumstances he is able to share a *prudent risk* in order to
arrive at a *presumptive solution.)*

doubt
involved

1. *The Relationship Between Prudence and Conscience*

The noble object of prudence is to assist man in the recognition of God's voice in due consideration of all the attending circumstances. Thereby the decision of conscience becomes a command of prudence which in its final analysis is the explicit consent to God's special mission for man. The following discussion aims towards clarifying the relationship of prudence to conscience in consideration of both the culpably erroneous and non-culpably erroneous decisions of conscience.

The sound judgment of conscience is essentially the fruit of the virtue of prudence. On the other hand, the decision of prudence depends greatly on the motivating power of an unsullied heart.

The culpably erroneous decision of conscience does not arise from prudence. In the full sense of the word, such a "decision" is really not even a decision of the innermost conscience which in its making was either consciously violated or ignored. The culpable violation of God's holy will has always indicated an attempt of conscience to escape from the face of the Lord. When conscience is completely turned away from God's face, it will give way to the "prudence of the flesh" which knows no respect for God's will but is guided by the wicked designs of a perverted heart.

The non-culpably erroneous conscience decisions are made under the full influence of the basic orientation of the particular conscience. To some extent even the virtue of prudence enters into such a decision. The sincere effort to know God's will and to comply with it reveals itself in man's basic orientation of reverence towards God's order and an openness to the need of the present moment. Yet, man's failure to act in full accord with God's loving will in a given situation reveals that the virtue of prudence has not been sufficiently perfected. Lack of knowledge might be the underlying reason for such inefficacy of prudence. The chief reasons for this inadequate knowledge may be traced to an environment which fails to provide the necessary moral experience of a good life. Furthermore, the situation may be complicated by the absence of the necessary powers of perception or inadequate foresight.

Lack of prudence may have its root in the very *bluntness of conscience*. A sensitive, tender conscience will inevitably perceive the need for circumspection or prudent advice from others. Conversely, one who frequently violates conscience without subsequent sorrow for sin will gradually show the signs of a "split existence" in which conscience weakens to the point of failing to recognize the truth. This may result in a complete disregard for fundamental principles and significant circumstances. Such a conscience, even in spite of momentary efforts of good will, is not equipped to face the reality of a difficult decision but becomes submerged in superficial, earthly reflections.

In its fullest meaning, prudence requires charity—an overflowing measure of love for the good. The "worldly wise and prudent" manifest unusual skill and power in the attainment of their wicked aims which they pursue with a passionate tenacity. In a parallel manner, the pure heart, inflamed by ardent charity of God, possesses the essential prerequisites for a clear perception of God's will. Accordingly, the pure conscience is able to choose the best means and form the most appropriate resolutions. St. Thomas declares: "The disposition of conscience moves and directs prudence" (*S.Th.* 11, II q, 47, a 6). The distortion of the native disposition of conscience is accompanied by a simultaneous clouding and dulling of the vigilant eye of prudence. With the clouding of conscience, prudence loses its clear vision of God's will as revealed by the teachings of the Church and implied in the need of the present moment. Our awareness of the decline of prudence, as evidenced by decisions opposed to the good, should sound the serious warning: "Bring order into your heart, purify your conscience!"

2. The Chief Objectives of the Virtue of Prudence

The virtue of prudence is oriented towards man's actions. It presupposes the gift of wisdom, man's familiarity with things divine. Because this present life is a period of probation, charity towards God requires positive action in behalf of God's kingdom on earth. In other words, the gift of wisdom demands both the virtue of prudence and the consummating gift of counsel.

The gift of *heavenly wisdom,* the most sublime of all gifts and the perfection of charity, gives us a taste for heavenly things. This gift of the Holy Spirit helps us to discern all things in the sublime light of faith. It fills our souls with joy and delight by means of the very things pertaining to God's pleasure.

The Christian virtue of prudence is not chiefly concerned with self-perfection or a self-conscious rectitude of behavior. Prudence, which directs the active efforts of charity, is "not self-seeking" (I Cor. 15:3), but rather is concerned with the true welfare of one's neighbor and the common good of God's children.

A sincere devotion to God's cause does not consist chiefly nor primarily in external activity. God's kingdom takes possession of our hearts through interior grace and charity. Nevertheless, this interior splendor will inevitably tend towards external manifestation, even in this present life of action and probation, so that on the day of Our Lord's second coming the full magnificence of His glory may become manifest in our body.

Even in this life of exile the kingdom of God has become a visible reality, because God has created a visible world in which He desires to manifest the kingdom of His love through Christ. If the testimony of our good works is to lead men to glorify God (Matt. 5:16), then our actions must be in complete harmony with the established order of God's kingdom. Our lives must be the true expression of the inner glory of grace. Thereby God's supreme order in the world and in His Church will become manifest. This explains the interdependence of prudence and a truly full interior life of grace, based on the three theological virtues.

Whoever is lacking in consuming zeal for the things of God is also wanting in the virtue of prudence. It is also true that, whoever fails in prudence in important matters for the manifestation and extension of God's kingdom on earth, proves himself imprudent because his heart does not possess an all-embracing zeal and love for God and His kingdom.

Thus it is evident that the virtue of prudence is more than right reason dictating the kind of action to be taken. It shows prudence to be a means of recollecting man's inner powers in the regulation of external activity.

It is a matter of prudence to appraise one's personal abilities in the light of the Law of Christ and the needs of the present hour. The truly prudent man must have an open eye for the deep and hidden realities of life. Calmly and discreetly he must seek counsel within his own soul, and if necessary ask for guidance and advice from prudent fellowmen. If someone foolishly despises the counsel of his neighbor, he thereby displays lack of prudence, because his pride prevents him from recognizing the limitations of his unaided intellect.

It would be even more imprudent to consider the Church's pronouncements in relation to the vital issues of our times as restrictions to the exercise of one's prudence. It must be remembered, however, that the directions of the Church are not intended to dispense the individual Christian from exercising the faculty of his own prudence, but rather to provide the basic prerequisites and true vantage points conducive to prudent decisions and evaluations in the light of special circumstances. The Church can provide no more than general guidelines of conduct. Each Christian has the obligation to determine the ways and means of cooperating according to individual talents and special opportunities.

The more steep and rugged the path leading to the heights of perfection, the more we are in need of the virtue of prudence. The Holy Spirit Himself will support our personal endeavors to nurture this virtue by means of His precious gift of counsel. Although the Church through her laws does at times indicate the fatal borderline of mortal sin which is not to be digressed, she nevertheless continuously challenges her children to strive for the very heights of virtue while yet providing the greatest possible freedom for each soul. Every genuine Christian, in due consideration of his special gifts and graces and the particular circumstances of his life, will try to aim beyond the mere minimum of the basic obligations inherent in his state of life. Thus the kingdom of God will achieve its powerful unity in the diversity of gifts and its riches in the perfection of every man's special talents and abilities.

3. The Nurture of the Virtue of Prudence

The virtue of prudence which is essentially oriented toward God's kingdom is an undeserved grace, the fruit of wisdom, the most sublime of all the gifts of the Holy Spirit. This virtue is infused in the soul and matures together with charity. Therefore, St. Paul's words are applicable to all those aiming for prudence: "Make charity your aim" (I Cor. 14:1). Ask for prudence as the highest gift of God!

Although the supernatural effects and inner aptitude of prudence are undeserved gifts of grace, the nurture and full perfection of this virtue require painstaking efforts.

The virtue of prudence demands a constant endeavor to impress on our mind and heart the basic Christian principles. We need a penetrating perception of the essence of things in the light of God's truth and His salvific plans in order to arrive at a true discernment and clear decision regarding the vital issues in our contemporary world. We should develop an openness to God's grace and humbly utilize all opportunities conducive to an increase of our true understanding of the situation. The wise man is always ready to accept counsel and advice from prudent fellowmen.

A person inclined to scrupulosity should learn to be content with the limited moral insight and certitude characteristic of our present imperfect state. He should try to overcome all hesitancy and indecision. On the other hand, the danger of flightiness in both decision and execution can only be corrected by the practice of *circumspection and foresight*. Our course of action should be determined by the criterion of charity, the eternal salvation of souls. We should carefully evaluate both our available powers and every possible obstacle in the execution of our resolutions.

It is especially important to keep in mind that a tender and sensitive conscience or a pure heart, aglow with love for God and neighbor, is the most essential prerequisite for the virtue of prudence. The nurture of charity, conscience, and prudence are most intimately united.

Section VII. The Prudent Risk in Conscience Decisions

Conscience by its very essence is dependent on truth. It demands action in agreement with the truth recognized by the intellect. It requires determined efforts in the quest for truth as regards the laws of God and of the Church as well as the special mission arising from the invitations of grace in the various circumstances of life. Yet there are dubious and difficult situations which defy clarification. It is on such occasions that conscience must at times *venture or risk a decision which nevertheless must always be in agreement with the principles of prudence.*

There is a vital difference between: (1) the uncertain groping of the perplexed conscience; (2) the composed risk of conscience in doubtful or difficult cases relative to legal obligations in which the person is guided by a clear sense for truth and the common rules of prudence; and (3) the collision of opposing duties.

1. The Perplexed Conscience

In difficult and entangled situations conscience may at times become perplexed to such a degree that it is no longer able to perceive a choice of action which is free from guilt. Such is the predicament of the person who sees himself confronted with the alternative of either telling a lie or of sinning against justice and charity by revealing the truth. Either action would be sinful. A sound conscience, however, guided by the principles of prudence, would after careful reflection perceive the unobjectionable possibility of shielding the truth from any disrespectful and uncharitable curiosity without telling a lie. If, on the other hand, a person in the state of perplexity would choose the lie in his sincere attempt to avoid the more serious sin against charity, he would thereby give evidence of his basic good will and morally correct attitude. If in addition he is grieved by his predicament of perceiving no possible alternative which is free from sin, his choice of the "lesser sin" gives evidence of his true love for truth and his conscientiousness.

A person with a perplexed conscience, if taken by surprise, may be free from all guilt provided there is neither neglect nor procrastination in the correction of such an erroneous conscience. Yet this explanation is not sufficient for the solution of doubts in particular instances. The fully mature and responsible Christian, trying to live in conformity with the true liberty of the children of God, needs timely information and practice in the virtue of prudence so that even in dubious and difficult situations he may act prudently and with circumspection. For this very reason moral theologians after much discussion and collaboration have laid down rules of prudence serving as guidelines in prudent ventures in those complicated situations in which an unaided conscience might fail to discern with certitude the true obligations of the law. Although these "rules" are basic principles within the reach of a prudent person's intuition, their formulation remains a difficult task.

2. *Rules of Prudence*

It will suffice to mention only a few of the important rules with adequate illustrations from concrete situations.

a) The principle of possession: *Unless proven otherwise, it may be assumed that the present owner of a property or holder of a right is the legitimate possessor.*

In case of a serious doubt as to the right of property, the present owner is entitled to retain the property in question, if to date he has possessed it with a good conscience (bona fide). Naturally the reverse also holds true: No one has the right to contradict another person's indisputable ownership or right on the basis of a mere doubt. It would be wrong to act arbitrarily in such matters or to start a lawsuit on the basis of mere probabilities.

This same rule is also applicable in those cases where there is doubt as to the existence of a law or its bearing in a particular situation. In such circumstances of direct and persistent doubt, the principle of presumption of right is in favor of the liberty of the subject. This means that we can act virtuously in total disregard of such dubiously existing laws. If, on the other hand, such laws embody the true good in a concrete situation, it would be unwise and consequently wrong to act against it, although their validity may be doubtful.

This rule of prudence is obviously of great significance, for it aids man in keeping alive the sense of personal responsibility and the spirit of true freedom which ventures to meet the need of the moment. If all doubtfully prevailing laws were as binding in conscience as those of undisputed existence, our liberty in seeking the concrete good would be greatly restricted. We could neither meet the special needs of our brethren nor contribute to the extension of God's kingdom in the full use of our God-given talents.

b) *Actions and facts of doubtful existence do not entail any juridical obligation.*

Consider the person who after careful deliberation is doubtful as to whether or not he has committed sin, especially serious or mortal sin. Such a person is not bound by the strict obligations of the law which states that every mortal sin must be confessed. Except in cases of scrupulosity it would be wise, however, and also in keeping with a truly penitential spirit and the heart's desire for purity, to disclose the true state of affairs in the sacrament of penance.

Under no circumstances should such a doubt keep anyone from Holy Communion, especially if there exists no opportunity for confession. Someone in doubt as to the breaking of the eucharistic fast may receive Holy Communion without any scruples.

For good and weighty reasons does St. Alphonsus postulate the opposite opinion regarding those who commit mortal sin habitually. Such persons, if in doubt as to the commission of a mortal sin, should make a decision in their own disfavor, because this is more in keeping with the true state of affairs. This opinion of St. Alphonsus is in no way contradictory to this rule of prudence because past experience excludes practically all doubt in such a situation (cf. the discussion of the fourth rule of prudence).

c) *If an act has been performed or a fact established, it may prudently be presumed that it is valid and correct unless proven otherwise.*

According to ecclesiastical law, a marriage is considered valid unless the contrary is proven, even if the validity of the marriage contract which was performed in the prescribed manner, may subsequently be questioned either on the basis of a possible diriment impediment or a lack of consent.

Similarly, the individual conscience should abide by the above maxim because it is a well-founded and highly commendable rule of prudence. Therefore, a person who habitually makes good confessions should consider his confession valid even in the event of subsequent doubts. In case of misgivings as to the completeness of past confessions, he may presume that his confessions were good. There is no need for him to repeat them.

d) *What takes place ordinarily, or as a rule, may be presumed to have taken place in a particular doubtful instance.*

According to this rule, a person who is accustomed to

131 GOD AND THE HEART OF MAN

prompt and regular payments of wages and debts may assume that he did justice to all concerned even in case of subsequent doubts unless contrary evidence is present. However, a well-grounded doubt as to the clearance of a certain debt, with no indirect evidence to the contrary, demands prompt payment with due consideration of the existing financial circumstances.

This rule could also be applied to the difficult situation cited under (b), according to which the conscientious person, if in doubt as to the commission of mortal sin, may receive Holy Communion without scrupulosity after an act of perfect contrition. The problem of doubt is resolved on this basis that under the given circumstances the commission of mortal sin is something unlikely to occur.

In all these questions the chief concern for the disciple of Christ is not an easy escape from the observance of the law but rather a sincere effort to conform to the established order in God's kingdom. This is the very reason why, in the face of urgent circumstances, the Christian does not wish to be restricted in his freedom by legalistic borderline distinctions of a doubtful nature. He should try to meet the requirements of the universal laws with the same readiness with which he fulfills the demands arising from the particular circumstances of his life which are unaccessible to juridical specifications.

It would be well for both the confessor and the individual Christian, faced with the necessity of risking a conscience decision, to recall the following maxim of St. Alphonsus: "It is an outrage to interpret God's laws with laxity. Yet it is equally detrimental to make the law of Christ an unbearable burden. Too great a rigorism in demanding the difficult closes the road to salvation" (*Theologia Moralis*, lib. I, tract I, n. 82).

Those trying to escape the demands of God's law by comfortably dispensing themselves, may erroneously consider themselves "free." Others, tenaciously adhering to the minutest and even doubtful letter of the law, may even boast of their "obedience." Yet neither one possesses true liberty and a joyful sense of responsibility which is to reveal itself in an openness to both the needs of their neighbor and the exigencies of God's kingdom. Both are lacking in true obedience and prudence and, in addition, they fail to see the deep realities of life.

The truly free and happy child of God is not concerned about the disputed question of "either freedom or the law," but rather about the prudent search for God's will at a given moment and under existing circumstances. It certainly would be wrong to choose the more difficult road for the mere sake of the difficulty when the good cause might be served better by other means. An attitude of undue concern for every doubtful law not only is far from being virtuous but is even a grave danger because it destroys our joy in God's service and stifles the heart's initiative and responsiveness to God's appeal which comes to us in the call of the present moment.

It is evident that a truly doubtful opinion may not be followed *whenever absolute values are at stake, such as the salvation of souls* (our own and that of our neighbor). Under such circumstances the most secure road must be chosen. In keeping with this principle, no one is permitted to expose himself to the near occasion of sin without weighty reasons even though he has the firm resolution to withstand the temptation. The utmost care and vigilance is required if for any reason the near occasion to sin cannot be avoided. For example, it is far better to leave undone a salutary yet unnecessary action if thereby we would give serious scandal to our neighbor. It is well to keep in mind that the rules of prudence are applicable only to situations in which the alternative is between external legal limitations and moral rectitude of behavior.

In the final analysis, it should be remembered that as finite creatures we are unable to heed every minute doubt in the domain of our moral decisions. *Neither does every incipient doubt dispense us from nor bind us to an obligation.* In the domain of moral decisions we cannot achieve absolute certainty except in relation to basic principles. St. Antoninus voices his conviction in the following statement: "It is an expression of a disciplined mind to be satisfied with the degree of security which is in keeping with the particular domain" (*Summa*, P. I, tit. III, Chap. 10). It is a sign of imprudence and lack of mental discipline to dissipate one's mental energy in the solution of doubts relative to minor juridical problems to such an extent that there is left neither time nor energy for concentrating on the important issues of charity and the joyful fulfillment of God's holy will.

3. Conflicting Duties

It may be especially difficult to make the right decisions in situations which *present a number of either apparently or truly conflicting obligations.* This may easily result in a perplexed conscience. The sensitive conscience in such circumstances suffers considerably from the limitations of our human nature and the disorders of a sinful world. There is indeed a crying need for reform and restoration of order which we are unable to accomplish because of our own personal shortcomings and the unfortunate circumstances of the world around us.

We must acknowledge that God, the very source of all goodness, is unable to contradict Himself. Consequently, there can be no question of disobedience to God nor of a disturbance in the moral order, if man in his encounter with so many varying and even conflicting duties is unable to do justice to all, despite his awareness of their indisputable claim. The well-attuned conscience must balance the relative importance of obligations and duties. There are some clear-cut principles for solving a possible conflict of duties. The application of such general norms to particular situations, however, requires considerable prudence.

a) *If a natural moral law conflicts with a mere positive precept, the natural law prevails because it is the higher and more basic law.*

This explains why an act of impurity or insincerity may never be committed in order to conform to a mere human law, no matter how important and just such a human precept may be. If, for example, attendance at the obligatory Sunday Mass could be achieved only by means of a fraud, it would be better to forego the joy of attending the celebration of the divine mysteries than attain participation by means of a lie.

If a seriously ill child in the family is in need of the mother's care and attention, the mother may not go to church, if she thereby neglects the child.

Likewise, if it is probable that the adherence to the law of fast might injure a person's physical health, it would be wrong to fast since reasonable care of one's health is a basic immutable natural law which takes precedence over a changeable precept of the Church.

b) *The higher value or graver matter must be chosen on principle.*

This law of preference, though essentially applicable to our inner dispositions and intentions, must nevertheless as far as possible reveal itself in our actions.

For example, the father of a family who is faced with the alternate choice of endangering the good reputation of

his family or of suffering financial loss, is bound in conscience to safeguard the good name of his family even at
the expense of material disadvantages. He must be ready
to sacrifice a promotion in position or office, if this would
entail a change of residence into a neighborhood in which
faith and religious fervor might be jeopardized.

Although extraordinary difficulties may at times excuse
a person from attendance at Sunday Mass, we are nevertheless obliged to fulfill our Sunday obligation at least occasionally, even at the expense of great sacrifice. The profession and promotion of one's faith should be valued above
any material advantages.

c) *In concrete situations both the urgency of duties and
the gravity of the matter must be weighed.*

Although the inner value of prayer far surpasses that of
earning a living, nevertheless the urgency of physical sustenance is such that at times it takes precedence over the
Sunday obligation. Yet at no time may a comfortable life
and the accumulation of riches be valued above zeal in
prayer and participation in the worship of Sunday Mass.

Section VIII. The Scrupulous Conscience

In order to grasp the full significance and sublime dignity
of conscience as well as the seriousness of our obligation
towards the formation and preservation of this important
function of our practical intellect, we must consider the
manifold manifestations of scrupulosity. The words of St.
Paul: "We carry this treasure in earthen vessels" (II Cor.
4:7) are fully applicable to conscience—the mirror of God's
likeness. Heredity, environment and the freely formed decisions of conscience may all contribute to the formation of
the various forms of scrupulosity.

1. The Momentary Anxiety of Conscience

Although psychiatrists may classify the various forms of scrupulosity as manifestations of mental illness, it nevertheless must be remembered that there are forms of scrupulosity which are part of the normal psychodynamics of personality development. We are referring here not only to the varying degrees of delicacy of conscience but also to the sudden, occasional but nevertheless serious disturbances of conscience.

Cardinal Gerson (1429), the great theologian of the Council of Constantinople, explicitly pointed out that temporary scruples at the beginning of a truly devout life are common and at times even beneficial occurrences. It is not unusual at the time of conversion from a life of superficiality that a person is suddenly overcome by a penetrating and powerful knowledge of God.

This passing "scrupulosity" is merely a stage in the development of a deeper and more humble certitude in the decisions of conscience, provided that this manifestation is understood and utilized properly. A prudent confessor, who guides the soul to the healing depths of conscience and the blessed heights of Christian perfection, will prove to be an invaluable aid in these situations.

Through an exploration of the deep religious significance of such an experience the confessor is in reality treating or healing a neurosis. Every neurosis in its deepest sense is a yearning after a more essential and satisfying conception and realization of life's true meaning. It is questionable, however, whether a momentary anxiety of conscience may be considered a true neurosis although both phenomena have certain things in common.

2. The Neurotically Fixed Scrupulosity

Pathological scrupulosity most often appears in the form of *obsessive-compulsive neuroses and phobias*. Both types usually appear together, but in ways wherein either fear or psychic compulsion predominates.*

In such neurotic disturbances it is not enough to concentrate merely on the unfavorable psychic predispositions or tendencies. It is more important to determine why a neurotic tendency should manifest itself in the moral-religious sphere. (In some individuals the same disorder may appear in the form of claustrophobia, bacteriophobia, or compulsive counting.) Such disorders are more serious than scrupulosity. In every neurosis the deep, unsatisfied, and hidden desires of the human heart for a fuller grasp of its true responsibility to God manifest themselves in a warped and twisted manner. Yet the neurotically scrupulous persons retain a true appreciation of God and their personal responsibilities. The derangement lies in the manner and mode of grasping their personal moral obligations.

The various obsessive, compulsive, anxiety-producing, and neurotic types of scrupulosity may be discussed with special reference to the psychic factors of heredity, in particular, a warped attitude in religious matters. Each particular case must be carefully evaluated in order to determine the real root of the problem. The difficulty may lie in a pathological predisposition or in a faulty religious orientation acquired previously with or without personal culpability.

A distinction should be made between *the more common types of anxiety neurosis* in the religious realm which

* At times there may be a mixture of an obsessive compulsive neurosis and a desire for appearing important in confession by means of all kinds of "scruples." Strictly speaking, this kind of scrupulosity has nothing in common with hysteria.

have their origin in a misinterpretation of God's supremacy with a resulting overemphasis on fear. The cause of such disproportionate fear may be traced to early childhood experiences with an overly strict father in a home atmosphere characterized by undue rigidity or to a school environment dominated by harsh and unrelenting teachers. Furthermore, there is the warping and arrest of personality development in the anxiety neurosis, a disposition which makes the afflicted persons perceive guilt in all conceivable courses of action. Such obsessions are commonly observed in the striving after truthfulness and chastity. In these circumstances the victims of scrupulosity may endlessly repeat the confession of true or possible sins. The continuous anxiety-filled preoccupation with these areas leads to obsessive images which, without volition, may even tend to become gratifying. The afflicted persons are no longer able to perceive the involuntary compulsive nature of these images, which greatly increases their feeling of guilt. They have a tendency to exaggerate the solidarity of responsibility. Some scrupulous persons concentrate all their energies and undivided attention on the observance of particular regulations such as the law of abstinence from food before the reception of Holy Communion or on the validity of their previous confessions. *This type of scrupulosity, directed towards the letter of the law, is referred to as compulsion neurosis.* Another manifestation of neurosis is *the morbid striving after absolute perfection* and completely unrealistic goals which, coupled with a denial of man's imperfect state, produces untold sufferings to the victims. Mention should be made of that kind of *scrupulosity in which compensatory mechanisms are employed in* unconscious or subconscious attempts to arm oneself against failure in certain moral aspects as, for example, charity to God and neighbor. This is the so-called compensation scrupulosity.

Holy Scripture gives a good illustration of this in the person of the Pharisee who scrupulously "paid a ten per cent tax on mint and anise and cummin" (Matt. 23:23) but who nevertheless callously and superficially passed by the misery of his fellowman.

In our dealings with such scrupulous persons and in our own approach to personal problems, we must remember that we are dealing with manifestations of illness in which nothing can be accomplished by a mere intellectual approach.

The first and most decisive step towards recovery for the scrupulous person is a ready and willing acceptance of the inevitable aspects of his illness. This does not exclude the use of all reasonable means for cure. Since every neurosis has its own history and, in a certain sense, represents a sincere yearning of the human heart towards fuller self-realization, a wise and prudent friend is essential for the correct interpretation of this desire for the deep realities of life. It is a priceless service to lead a scrupulous person to a kind confessor. In more serious cases the help of a physician or psychiatrist may be required.

It is a definite step in the right direction when, with the aid of his confessor or psychiatrist, the patient begins to *distinguish between true manifestations of conscience and the mere anxieties of obsessions and compulsions.* Intrinsically, the stricken person is still aware of the vital differences between the two. A more conscious acknowledgment of this truth will help him to see his scruples in the right perspective. Although conscience and its manifestations represent the heart of man, scruples should be treated like foreign bodies. A sense of humor is an invaluable asset towards detachment from scruples. Blessed indeed is the Christian who is able to laugh at everything which is not sin, including his own scruples. It should be understood, however, that no fun may be made of the manifestations of scruples in our neighbor. A person is on the road to recovery as soon as he is able to view his own scruples with a sense of humor.

It is of paramount importance that scrupulous persons have recourse to the consoling truths of our holy religion, recalling that they are glad news, tidings of the merciful, all-surmounting love of God towards man in his wounded state. "It is not the healthy who need a physician but they who are sick" (Matt. 9:12). Persons thus afflicted should try their utmost to rid themselves of this constricting infirmity. They should make the best use of confession by avoiding all unnecessary back-tracking and brooding. Under no circumstances may they make the sixth commandment the focal point of their self-examination. A scrupulous person who hitherto in his examinations of conscience has concentrated on this aspect of morality, should direct all energies to the perfection of charity by a constant readiness for service in sincere kindness and friendliness. This alone can bring about a total restoration of freedom. There is great need for a complete re-orientation towards true personal piety and a warm encounter with God, a new perception of the spiritual life in the light of God's charity rather than concentration on burdensome external duties.

The afflicted persons deserve our genuine understanding and kindness. We are dealing here with well-intentioned but disturbed persons who are greatly in need of our undivided charity.

This topic deserves detailed elaboration because scrupulous persons are very often the victims of an uncharitable surrounding. A thorough understanding of the true state of affairs is the best guarantee against personal blunder. At the same time, it tends to make us more kind and sympathetic in our dealings with the afflicted. Above all, it should aid us in the education of the young and in every interpersonal relationship in order to avoid sowing the seeds of scrupulosity.

PART TWO

Interior Dispositions and Motives

The previous expositions on prudence and conscience stressed the significance of our actions and our conduct in the shaping of the visible world, because God's kingdom itself is a visible reality. Nevertheless it would be an unfortunate distortion of God's kingdom and the true essence of Christian morality, if we were to identify Christian morality with external endeavors and achievements. God's kingdom, "the kingdom of grace and charity," is primarily a dominion over hearts. If this kingdom, as a true and firmly established leavening agent, were permitted to govern and penetrate all our impulses, it would prove itself an irresistible force in our own transformation and that of the whole world.

Faith, hope, and charity, the decisive powers in God's kingdom, by their very nature require an external expression in action thereby affecting every aspect of our daily lives in testimony of their renewed vigor in a new world. Despite this fact, faith, hope, and charity are essentially dispositions of the heart. They are the echoes in man's soul of "the thoughts of the heart of God" as revealed through Christ.

Meditation on the innermost motives of the human heart is both essential and salutary in our dealings with God, for our spiritual life is endangered if it is governed by mere external activities and norms. This truth is rooted in man's spiritual nature and has been proven by history. Christ's

142

sharp condemnation of the externalism of the Pharisees can be applied to Christians of all times and nations.

Section I. Nature and Significance of Sentiments and Dispositions

In view of the very nature of conscience and in keeping with the language of Holy Scripture, we have referred to conscience as the "heart" of man. Yet the term "heart" in scriptural language also connotes the entire realm of sentiments, dispositions, and attitudes which in reality are but conditions or aspects of conscience. We shall keep our conscience clean and unsullied only if our interior dispositions and attitudes are in harmony and order. This point has been emphasized in connection with Christ's beatitude addressed to the "clean heart." Here we shall analyze the meaning of the following terms: basic orientation, basic attitudes, dispositions, and motives. This exploration should lead us to a fuller realization of their importance in our Christian life.

1. Basic Orientation and Attitudes

Man's life is deeply affected by all his decisions and intentions in the choice between good and evil as well as by his habitual *basic orientation to the key issues of life*. This fundamental orientation gives a special imprint to each individual thought, word, and deed. The good gains in significance if it arises from a final and decisive basic orientation. The occasional involuntary evil action loses its venom if the heart is basically oriented towards the good.

We are all aware of the difficulties encountered and the efforts required in order to orient towards God all our thoughts, words, and actions. We likewise observe that those who have turned away from the faith do not thereby relinquish all the nobler impulses of their heart. A basic orientation of the soul becomes a basic attitude when it completely animates the entire man with all his desires, inclinations, and aspirations.

2. The Good and Evil in the Treasury of the Heart

The individual *impulses and inclinations of the heart* play an important role in the realm of our moral endeavors, especially in harmonizing everything with our basic orientation. They reveal to what extent our general good resolutions are effective in producing not only particular acts and actions but a true change of heart. Even involuntary sentiments and inclinations of the heart, which are morally indifferent as such, are important indications of the true state of our hearts.

The good thoughts, impulses, and desires which naturally and spontaneously arise from the depth of our soul are true indications of the accumulated riches of the heart. In addition to our basic orientation, all our good thoughts, words, and deeds necessarily increase in our hearts "the store of good things" (Matt. 12:35).

The same truths apply to the heart's perverted basic orientation and individual evil sentiments, dispositions, words, and actions. They are the expressions of a wicked heart and constitute the heart's "store of evil things" unless washed away by sincere contrition and atonement. Our divine Master Himself commented on this deplorable state of soul by saying: "A good man dispenses what is good from the good things stored in his heart, and a wicked man dispenses what is wicked from his store of wicked things. After all, a man's speech is but the overflow of his heart" (Luke 6:45; cf. Matt. 12:34). Although these words particularly refer to man's basic orientation in a decisive resolution, they likewise allude to man's whole frame of mind with all its manifestations.

3. Sentiments and Dispositions of the Heart

Man's free will is called into action whenever good or evil impulses make themselves felt in his heart. If not confirmed by the will they remain mere tendencies or inclinations. Through the assent of the will they become true sentiments and dispositions of the heart.

The moral significance of spontaneous inclinations or impulses of the heart greatly depends on their harmony or disagreement with the basic orientation of the soul. The incipient and partially involuntary impulses and sentiments, which are in full accord with the soul's good basic orientation, are to some extent its true fruits. Consequently, no special act of the will is needed in order to absorb them into the basic orientation unless opposed by contradictory sentiments. A comparatively minimal degree of advertence is required in order to confirm such favorable sentiments when compared with those which are in opposition to a good but weak basic orientation of the soul.

At the time of conversion the soul's basic orientation does not possess sufficient depth to effect a perfect purification of the heart. Moreover, the obstacles of perverted inclinations may remain even in spite of a good basic orientation. Under such circumstances, the essential purification of the heart is accomplished by *a deliberate attempt to foster favorable sentiments and good dispositions* rather than by a negative approach which tends towards the eradication of perverse ones.

Unruly tendencies and inclinations will inevitably assert themselves until virtuous sentiments have permeated all the thoughts and aspirations of our hearts. Consequently, the careful nurture of worthy sentiments and dispositions is of paramount importance in our moral life.

4. "Thoughts of the Heart"

Since inclinations and sentiments of the heart, especially those which have been consciously affirmed by the will, do arise from the "treasury" of the human heart, Holy Scripture refers to them as "the thoughts of the heart." In fact, they are infallible guides to man's true state of heart, namely, his interior attitudes and dispositions. They are the impulses or pulse-beats of the heart because they bear the imprint of the *kind of charity* which fills the heart.

Man's heart is the center of charity. If it is void of genuine love of God, neighbor, and self, it becomes filled with a warped self-love and perverted desires. Sentiments of the heart are more than impersonal reflections, cool deliberations, and cold decisions of the will. They are "kernels" of thought steeped in feelings, that is to say, they are enveloped in the soul's individual and characteristic way of loving and striving. Sentiments are thoughts of the heart which of necessity gravitate towards the object of love. "Where your treasure is, there too your heart is bound to be" (Matt. 6:21).

Although not all sentiments of the heart are direct impulses of love, they are nevertheless deeply rooted in the very nature and mode of loving. Sentiments as "thoughts of the heart" are not to be confused with mere moods, or with elated, depressed, or anxious states and feelings of a psychosomatic nature which are usually devoid of thought. The latter vague feelings are neither true dispositions nor genuine sentiments and inclinations. On the other hand, the joyful excitement and delight experienced in the presence of a beloved person, the grief occasioned by the sins of the world, humble contrition, and sincere concern for others are true expressions of interior dispositions. Thus we see that dispositions, in contradistinction to mere emotional states, are goal-directed like reasoning and will power, in fact, even more so than cool deliberations and purposeful willing.

5. Sentiments and Dispositions as Responses to Value

Whereas reasoning tends toward comprehension, decision aims toward realization, and striving gravitates toward possession, sentiments and dispositions are simply the heart's response to value. The relative moral value of a de-

cision depends on the harmony of the particular value-
response in relation to the entire hierarchy of values.

Heartfelt joy in the beautiful and the good as well as sorrow for sin are both fitting responses and therefore constitute morally positive sentiments. On the other hand,
envy and sadness over our fellowman's achievement are
psychologically and morally negative responses. In such
cases the person fails to acknowledge the accomplishments
and the intrinsic worth of the other person. If such sentiments are nurtured they will become the predominant mental attitude or disposition of the heart. Envy, a psychologically negative sentiment, tries to negate the good in one's
neighbor because it is perceived as an obstacle to personal
advancement. Thus, undue and selfish desires go hand in
hand with blindness to value and with a violation of the
order of values.

Sentiments and dispositions gain in significance and
depth if they are responses not only to impersonal values
but to *persons*. Man's true sentiments and interior dispositions reveal themselves in the heart's reactions towards the
worth or unworthiness of the "thou." Authentic love of
neighbor may at times manifest itself in heartfelt grief over
his sins.

In order to fathom the significance of man's response to
the value of his neighbor we must take into consideration
the depth of the response as well as its direction to his
deeply personal qualities. Our heart and our imagination
may be stirred more tangibly by a passionate, romantic
carnal love, or by an impetuous enthusiasm for a movie
star or sports champion, than by a deep love and admiration for the purity of soul or the spirit of sacrifice exemplified in the life of a particular saint. In reality, the latter
sentiments and dispositions are more truly directed towards

the genuine worth of our neighbor and, at the same time, are authentic expressions of the depth of our own spirituality.

The dominant sentiments and dispositions of the heart not only reveal our basic attitude and orientation, but further indicate either the depth or superficiality of the person. Interior dispositions and attitudes to value are superficial if they fail to touch deep and lofty values or if they produce but faint responses to higher values. Sentiments and dispositions are capable of rousing the innermost depths of the heart if it is fully surrendered to sublime values.

Comparing the sentiments and emotions of some Christians and non-Christians, it may at times appear that the non-Christian is touched more effectively by an unselfish charity for his neighbor and is imbued with true humility in the face of sublime values. Nevertheless, an authentically Christian value-response to God is basically superior to any mere natural and sensual affection for men. The saint, the perfect Christian, responds to God not only with a measured degree of the will but with the full intensity and ardor of his intentions, sentiments, and dispositions of the heart.

Individual differences further reveal themselves in the predominant sentiments of the heart in relation to value. The heart may respond either with a positive and joyful acceptance of the good or an angry rejection of negative values. Although a sincere love of God calls for a deep hatred for evil, it would nevertheless be wrong for a perfect lover of God to concentrate all his efforts on hatred of sin. Heredity, environment, and education contribute their share to the dominant disposition of the heart. These lay the foundation for a happy and joyful as well as a bitter, frightened, and timid disposition. Zeal for God's kingdom may manifest itself in a variety of ways in keeping with the individual's endowments. The predominant sentiments may be grief over the sins and evils of the world or hatred for the intrigues of the devil. If these negative sentiments and dispositions fill the soul, all joy and spontaneity in the good becomes extinguished. In some instances these negative sentiments of hatred and rejection of the evil, although appropriate in themselves, may be the expression of an unconscious resentment in consequence of a personal inability to embrace the good. The predominant sentiments and interior dispositions of the true lover of God are those of complete surrender to the good and all positive values.

Heaven is the unreserved surrender to the blessed sentiments and dispositions of charity, joy, exaltation, and gratitude. Hell is the wretched condition of the utterly "scorched" heart. Satan, who aims at blackening all that is beautiful and sublime, is incapable of rendering a positive response to the good. His sentiments and dispositions are totally negative. His warped self-love, his pride, and his insatiable desire for selfish happiness can give vent only to hatred, envy, and rage.

6. Sentiments, Dispositions, and Motives

Sentiments are primarily indeliberate utterances of the heart, "the thoughts of the heart." They represent an encounter with the world of value and with the "thou" of our neighbor, and consequently, involve an experience in the very depth of the heart.

Sentiments and dispositions may, although not of necessity, become motives when they provoke action or at least a resolve for action. Such movements of the heart may be genuine even if they fail to produce action. For example, an unselfish delight in the good works of one's fellowman and a loving admiration for the virtues of the saints may move the heart deeply without directly nor necessarily leading to action. Nevertheless, unpremeditated and non-purposive sentiments, if they are deep and lasting, will most effectively contribute to "the treasury of the heart" from where they predetermine the true possibilities for future motives and actions.

In addition to those sentiments and dispositions which are true value responses, there are those sentiments which are insincere and inefficacious because they do not grow into motives for action. In the parable of the good Samaritan we read: "and he was touched with compassion." We cannot imagine that the story would continue by saying: "and he passed by." The two fanatics of the law, who unheedingly had gone their way, either did not feel compassion in their barren hearts or at least gave no heed to the sentiment of mercy. On the other hand, the good Samaritan showed sincere sympathy with the wounded person. His heart was touched and he immediately and spontaneously responded with mercy and compassion. The charitable thoughts in his heart became the motives or moving-power for his kind actions in behalf of the unfortunate person.

In like manner, as there are sentiments and dispositions of the heart which do not directly lead to action, there are also motives which do not (or at least not directly) arise from true sentiments. For instance, charitable works for ulterior motives of esteem before men or a promotion in office or position, amount to no more than external acts of charity, void of supernatural motivation. In reality, such actions do reveal negative "sentiments" such as egocentricity and gross selfishness.

Almsgiving as a possible insurance against the pains in purgatory or for a greater degree of glory in heaven lacks the directness of a true sentiment for its motivation. Consequently, the good action arising from such an incentive or intention receives its value from the remote sentiment and disposition of desire for eternal reward and fear of punishment. If true compassion for the neighbor's misery fails to enter into such an action, either in the form of a sentiment or a motive, the good work of almsgiving remains weak and calculated because it does not arise directly from the heart or from the kindly disposition of charity or the sentiment of compassion. Hence, such an action cannot exert the power of enriching man's heart which the works of charity accomplish because they flow directly from the heartfelt sentiments of love and sympathy. We should bear in mind that secondary motives may enter into all our actions (cf. subsequent Chapters). The more diverse and comprehensive the motives, the greater will be their moving or motivating power for action.

Section II. God Searches the Depth of Our Heart

In the eyes of men, deeds count. God likewise expects the touchstone of our good actions. *Yet, in God's sight the value of our external actions is measured by the degree of charity which motivates them.* God searches the depths of our hearts, that is, our interior dispositions.

There is no point in being justified before men and in parading our external good works (cf. Luke 16:15). God accepts neither our prayers nor even our sacrifices if our heart is not open to Him in complete sincerity (Matt. 15:8; Mark 7:6). This knowledge should prevent us from attempting to please God by a mere external service. Our interior dispositions which motivate our actions must be pure because "we do not curry favor with men, we seek only the favor with God" (I Thes. 2:4).

The foremost desires of God's heart are genuine sentiments and sincere dispositions of love. We begin to fulfill the first and great commandment when we love God with *"all our heart"* (Matt. 22:37; Mark 12:33). This means that our heart must be filled to overflowing with true sentiments of charity towards God. Only thus shall "all the powers" of our soul be called into action for the kingdom of God. Unless we give to God our very hearts, our sentiments, we shall be unable to surrender to Him all the powers of our soul because without "heart" they are paralyzed. God judges our actions on the basis of the sentiments and dispositions which provoke them. The great commandment of charity not only embraces all other commandments of the New Law, but according to God's plan, is a prerequisite for the observance of all other precepts. This new and great commandment is a law written into our inmost heart.

"God searches our heart" means that His gaze penetrates to the very depths of its basic orientation and attitude; it denotes His cognizance of all the sentiments and motives underlying our actions. Yet, the heart's basic orientation and genuine sentiments form the most essential aspect and very root of our motives.

All our interior acts, strivings, desires, motives, and resolutions arise from the basic orientation of the soul. Resolutions, on the other hand, aid interior dispositions to materialize in external actions. Resolutions and actions receive their merit and value from the interior dispositions and motives which produced them.

In the Sermon on the Mount Christ extolled the value of interior dispositions and all actions. Both the teaching of the New Testament and that of the Prophets in the

Old Law loudly proclaim the truth that the decisive factor in God's eyes is the "heart" of man (man's sentiments, dispositions, and interior acts), even aside from the fact that all external activity arises therefrom. "I declare unto you: Anyone who glances at a woman with a lustful intention has already committed adultery with her in his heart" (Matt. 5:28).

If mere external considerations prevent a person from committing an evil action, he is still guilty of sin through his perverse desires even though the action was not performed. Yet it is important that the external sinful action was prevented because each evil deed increases the moral disorder in the world and further entangles man's heart in the derangement of sin.

If a person merely desists from perpetrating a crime because, in the final analysis, his heart shrank from the hideousness of the act, he thereby reveals himself still capable of some good dispositions. This recoiling from evil is the beginning of conversion. Consequently, we do not wish to deny the importance of exterior acts by emphasizing the fact that God searches the heart.

Since God, the searcher of hearts, is the final judge of our dispositions, we should more carefully examine our inclinations, dispositions, and motives; for they are the roots of all action. The true state of the heart is revealed by our deeds and their underlying motives. "Out of the heart proceed evil thoughts and therefrom all evil deeds" (Matt. 15:18). The heart is both the root and the tree which determine the kind of fruit. "There is no such thing as a good tree producing worthless fruit, nor a worthless tree producing good fruit. For each tree is known by its own fruit: you do not gather figs from thistles, and you do not pick grapes from brambles. A good man produces good from the store of good things stored in his heart and a wicked man dispenses what is wicked from his store of wicked things. After all, a man's speech is but the overflow of his heart" (Luke 6:43 ff.).

The good must be deeply rooted in the dispositions of our heart so that it may bring forth abundant fruit. The devil is constantly waiting to steal the good seed before it begins to take root in our hearts (cf. Luke 8:12). Exaggerated worldly cares and love for deceptive riches suppress the word of God in our heart. The soul, completely captivated by earthly enterprises and cares, with no time for loving meditation on the word of God, will gradually stifle the good seed and consequently remain barren (cf. Luke 8:14). This is the reason for Our Lord's admonition to refrain from burdening and defiling the sanctuary of our hearts with worldly cares and dissipations (cf. Luke 21:34).

He who receives the word of God in a truly good and pure heart—filled with sincere dispositions—will bring forth "fruit in patience" (Luke 8:15). This should encourage us not to seek the transitory success of individual good actions. Only unceasing patience in nurturing deep and sincere dispositions will insure the hundredfold harvest. The great model and exemplar in this work is the Mother of Our Lord, who in a pure and loving heart kept and pondered without ceasing all His words and actions (cf. Luke 2:19, 51).

"God, who can read men's minds, . . . purified their hearts by faith" (Acts 15:8-9). He Himself pours out His love into hearts, on condition that the Word of God is received with a willing acceptance. Faith can purify our heart only when we surrender ourselves completely to its sway. The charity of God will bring forth abundant fruit only in those hearts which are sincere and open to good.

God purifies our heart in faith, hope and charity. Only

when they are transformed by God's almighty power of charity, will our hearts incline fully to the "thoughts of His heart." These "thoughts" will receive their efficacious power from the soul's genuine harmony with grace in faith, hope, and charity. God purifies the heart by taking undisputed possession of it.

Section III. Christ Reveals the Innermost Thoughts of the Heart

The truths of faith in which Christ reveals Himself are keys to our own innermost dispositions. The aged Simeon prophetically announced to the Mother of Christ the true mark of the dawn of the messianic time: "This Child is destined to be a sign . . . so that the secret thoughts of many a heart shall be laid bare" (Luke 2:34 ff.). Holy Scripture repeatedly alludes to the blindness of heart as the cause of a lack of faith and a misinterpretation of the word of God (cf. Matt. 13:15; Mark 3:5; 6:52). Blindness of perception, and lack of comprehension and acceptance of the glad tidings of the gospel have their deepest roots in the hardening of hearts (cf. John 12:40), which refers to the basic orientation as well as to the sum total of our sentiments, attitudes and interior dispositions.

It is the heart with its sentiments and interior dispositions which determines the acceptance or refusal of faith, because "the faith that leads to righteousness is in the heart" (Rom. 10:9). The indisputable claim of the bountiful and all-consuming love of God has been manifested to us in the majestic person of Christ. The test of our complete surrender and loyalty to God will reveal itself in our attitude towards Christ, because He is the Incarnation of the Father's Word of Love.

The great separation of hearts, begun with the first coming of Christ, will be consummated in the second coming of Our Lord in judgment when He will "bring to light the secrets now hidden in darkness, and disclose the intentions of men's hearts" (I Cor. 4:5). Christ is "the parting of the way" for all men. This "parting of the way" is essentially the parting of hearts.

Without Christ's coming into the world, the abysmal wickedness of a deicide and the outrage of blasphemies against Christ and the Holy Spirit would never have been perpetrated (cf. John 15:22-24). Yet at the same time men would never have been capable to the exalted degree of charity and purity of heart manifest in true imitation of the crucified Savior. Thus the boundless powers of the human heart reveal themselves in good deeds as well as in the commission of sin.

Therefore, "the parting of the way" of the heart means an irrevocable obduracy for the wicked, and a continuous process of purification for the good. Even the apostles, who generously followed Our Lord's invitation, on various occasions revealed an astonishing lack of purity of heart and a gross attachment to the false expectations of a messianic kingdom. This was especially evident at the first prediction of Our Lord's Passion and in the days of His bitter Passion and death. Their hearts were bent solely on their own glory and the power of a great temporal kingdom. Our Lord had to rebuke the two disciples on their way to Emmaus: "How dull you are! How slow to understand when it comes to believing anything the prophets have said!" (Luke 24:25). Their worldly sentiments and attitudes acted like lead, hampering their faith. Despite this fact their hearts were truly willing. Therefore, they became enkindled by the boundless, all-consuming charity of Christ's heart: "Were not our inmost hearts on fire, as He spoke to us by the way, explaining to us the Scriptures?" (Luke 24:32).

Section IV. The Conversion of the Heart

St. Mark the Evangelist gives the following report of Christ's first public appearance: "Jesus returned to Galilee proclaiming the Gospel of God: 'The time has come; the kingdom of God is upon you. Convert and believe the Gospel'" (Mark 1:14-15). According to the exact translation of the Greek text, "change of heart" or "change of disposition" comes closest to the meaning of "conversion." The word for conversion, used by Our Lord in the Aramaic language, is synonymous with "returning home!" Both shades of meaning correspond perfectly because a return to God is accomplished through *a conversion of the heart towards God*. This inclination of the heart towards God *represents a profound transformation of our interior dispositions and motives.*

God Himself announced the glad tidings of the heart's conversion. We receive the necessary grace for a complete change of heart, or conversion, through the power of God's kingdom in the full revelation of God's incomprehensible love. God's revelation of His own secrets of love will necessarily enkindle our charity, for the fire of divine charity is a purifying and all-consuming flame.

Man's spiritual experience of Christ's captivating and irresistible love is not in itself sufficient to effect a complete change of heart. His unredeemed heart is not even able to comprehend God's plans and to respond to them without God's efficacious grace. Therefore, God Himself transforms our hearts by His grace, making them receptive to love. This important work is predicted by the prophet for the consummation of time: "I will sprinkle clean water upon you to cleanse you from all your impurities, . . . I will give you a new heart and place a new spirit within you, taking from your bodies your stony hearts and giving you natural hearts. I will put My spirit within you and make you live by My statutes, careful to observe My decrees" (Ez. 36:25-26).

In His redemptive work, Christ has fulfilled this prophecy. By the grace of the Holy Spirit, abiding within man, the heart of the Christian is essentially oriented towards the love of God. The New Law, God's redemptive grace, and the sacraments announce the glad tidings of the love of the heart of God and the transformation of our own hearts according to the likeness of God's heart. The proclamation of this consoling truth should be for us an urgent exhortation: *Since you are enabled to love with a new heart, foster truly new, pure and holy dispositions.* "Be of the same mind as Christ Jesus" (Phil. 2:5). We can imitate Christ's dispositions because "Christ dwells through faith in our hearts" (Eph. 3:17).

The work of God's grace is a constant invitation to conversion until all our aspirations and endeavors, all our desires, thoughts and intentions are fully oriented towards God. If we are able to withstand all perverse desires and, in addition, foster the sublime dispositions of Christ by means of a loving meditation on His redemptive work, we shall, even in the midst of the struggle, "rejoice in the peace of Christ in our hearts" (Col. 3:15).

Section V. Disposition—Responsibility— Success

Human folly may corrupt the most precious and delicate truth and may misinterpret the most sublime teaching.

Thus it has happened that, in the course of time, the *Christian teaching on dispositions,* this central core of moral teaching, was disfigured and *misrepresented.*

A despondent pessimism which sees only sin and disorder in the world around us may try to confine the kingdom of God to the *"purely interior"* realm of the heart. In this theory, no importance is placed on good order in the visible world. Exterior actions in behalf of God's kingdom are despised as immaterial. The only thing esteemed important in this false theory of ethics is the interior disposition. The proponents of the misinterpreted "ethics of disposition" seem unaware of the fact that a disposition cannot be genuine and sincere unless it brings forth good fruits. If someone sincerely loves the kingdom of God and its progress, he cannot be indifferent as to his actions, whether they are in harmony with God's will or out of harmony and thereby contributing to the dominion of the devil.

Sincere dispositions prove themselves in a sincere quest for truth and God's will. A pure intention is the best guarantee for a prudent decision in difficult situations.

On the other hand, Christian teaching on the importance of interior dispositions is diametrically opposed to the *ethics of the purely external law* which disregards both the meaningful fulfillment of the law and the genuine dispositions of the heart. The true concept of interior dispositions takes the idea of law more seriously than the external ethics of the law. Furthermore, it aims at a fuller comprehension of the New Law which is intrinsically a law of love.

The prominent role assigned to interior dispositions in Christian moral teaching is similarly opposed to the misleading emphasis placed by the proponents of *"situation ethics"* which insists on the exclusive importance of interior dispositions and the exercise of freedom while disregarding the fundamental natural laws because they seem contrary to a particular notion of freedom.

A Christian philosophy of interior dispositions, which is in harmony with the laws of a benevolent God, is ever mindful of the fact that God sees the intentions of the heart; and that the true and sincere dispositions of the heart must prove themselves in the conscientious and loving fulfillment of God's will. "He who has My commandments and keeps them, he it is who loves Me" (John 14:21). The more solidly established are the dispositions of kindness, joy, and peace, the more the heart of the disciple of Christ will be capable of loving the commandments of God, and of grasping their deepest significance and their application to the innumerable situations in his life.

Christian moral teaching on the subject of interior dispositions has nothing in common with that superficial type of *"ethics of success"* (utilitarianism) which appraises the individual by an external and sometimes questionable type of success. Even the best intentions are no guarantee for success. Failure may be occasioned by lack of intelligence, prudence, health, financial resources, or favorable circumstances. Man may suffer considerably from such reverses, especially if they are more than temporal failures, affecting the well-being of his neighbor. No one sincerely interested in the glory of God and the good of his neighbor can be indifferent about his contribution to either. From the very beginning of our undertakings, we should conform our will to the dispensations and designs of God's holy will in regard to the time and manner of success. God has permitted Christ to suffer on the cross in apparent failure. Yet this external apparent failure of Christ was the beginning of the stupendous "success" of salvation which on the day of Christ's second coming will be revealed to the entire world.

Interior dispositions are synonymous with *value-responses*. The pure and sincere heart is cognizant of God and His holy will; it is open and receptive to the world of values. The proper response of the heart to value is one which by its very essence stirs man's entire being, both his understanding and will. Such a value-response and such a comprehensive disposition manifest an authentically Christian spirit of responsibility. The ethics of interior disposition is genuine only if it proves itself in action as the ethics of responsibility.

Section VI. The Dominant Motives for Moral Actions

The previous sections dealt with dispositions as the motivating power for actions. The chief prerequisite for good interior dispositions is the right kind of motivation. Furthermore, we have seen our obligation to survey the motives of our actions and to purify them more and more. The dominant motives in our spiritual life are: (1) love of God, (2) reward and punishment, (3) social considerations.

1. Love of God

The most noble and sublime motive for all our actions is the charity of God, the love which God has shown us and poured out into our hearts.

If we are animated by the dispositions of true love and penetrate "with the thoughts of our heart" ever deeper into God's marvelous condescensions of charity, God's very charity will become for us the motivating power for all our actions: "The charity of Christ urges us" (II Cor. 5:14). The charity of Christ itself is poured forth into our hearts by the Holy Spirit. This charity transforms us into the image of Christ, and consequently urges us to live according to His Spirit and dispositions: if Christ died for all, then those who by His death have received life "may live no longer for themselves, but for Him who died for them and rose again" (II Cor. 5:15).

"It is now no longer I that live, but Christ lives in me. And the life that I now live in the flesh, I live in the faith of the Son of God, who loved me and gave Himself up for me" (Gal. 2:20). If this truth penetrates our inmost being and motivates us "to walk in love," then we are indeed "imitators of God, as very dear children" (Eph. 5:1 ff.). God has proven His eternal love by way of His incomprehensible mercy as "He has sent His only-begotten Son into the world that we may live through Him" (I John 4:9).

God's own love is the true motive for our love. Consequently, the initiative of love does not come from us but rather from God: "In this is the love, not that we have loved God, but that He has first loved us, and sent His Son as a propitiation for our sins" (I John 4:10). Our love is the response to the impelling power of God's love which *urges towards a fitting expression of our charity in action.*

St. John the Evangelist draws the logical conclusion in regard to God's wonderful works of love in our behalf. He urges us to give God not only the dispositions of a grateful love but to prove our love of God in charitable dispositions and actions for the welfare of our neighbor. "Beloved, if God has so loved us, we also ought to love one another" (I John 4:11). Consequently, God's marvelous works of charity are the motives for our charitable deeds. True love of God and neighbor which proves itself both in dispositions and deeds is "the fulness of the law."

It is not the abstract, invisible love of God but rather the

touching and heart-warming manifestations of the dominion of His love which constitutes the direct motive for
our loving response to God. His marvelous works lead us
to the blessed realization that God, in His eternal Trinity
and undivided Unity, is the essential personification of
charity. In the final analysis, *it is the benevolent love of
God which incites our response of filial love.*

The sacraments, the efficacious signs of God's wonderful works of love, produce in us a certain kinship to the
charity of God. In view of this new interior likeness with
Christ, the incentive of divine charity impels our hearts in
a new and undeserved freedom to become true imitators
of Christ's own love. Both Christ's historical redemptive
deeds and His continuing saving acts in the sacraments appeal to man for a commitment from within and without
in a truly Christ-like life. Our understanding of this truth
and our response to this appeal are synonymous with *making Christ's wondrous deeds of salvation the motives for all
our actions.*

The apostles frequently admonished the early Christians
to recall the wonderful effects of the sacraments: "You
have been washed clean, now you have been sanctified,
now you have been justified in the name of the Lord Jesus, by the Spirit of the God we serve" (I Cor. 6:11). This
exhortation implies a compelling motive for breaking with
sin and living in the fulness of the new life. Since we
are children of light by God's undeserved grace, we should
prove it in our actions (cf. Eph. 5:8; I Thes. 5:5; Rom.
13:12). Through the sacrament of baptism, Christ has
made us participants in the power and glory of His
death and resurrection. This sublime truth should be a
powerful incentive to overcome the perversities of our
lower nature and to live in the newness of a victorious life
in witness to Christ's glorious resurrection.

The entire salvific plan, including God's innumerable graces and the celebration of the sacraments which make Christ's actions present to us here and now, are constant urgings to a life of wholehearted response to the love we have received from God. *In short, the law of grace indelibly engraved in our hearts by the Holy Spirit should become the conscious and powerful incentive for our actions.*

2. *The Motives of Reward and Punishment*

It would be servile and unworthy of the children of God to make fear of punishment or expectation of reward the mainspring of their actions. Yet it would be just as unrealistic to ignore the motive of fear of punishment unless a perfectly purified love has completely transformed the heart.

An example may illustrate this. A married Catholic man, involved in an illicit love-affair, rejects the well-meant warning of his friend with the rejoinder: "The threat of eternal punishment and the promise of reward have no effect on me. If I want to do what is good, I shall do it for its own sake." Such an attitude betrays utter foolishness. If this person faced the facts, he would realize that his heart is filled with inordinate self-love and passionate, shameful desires. Therefore, he is in great need of compelling motives, capable of changing his interior dispositions and external actions. Pride is blinding his mind so that he neither recognizes nor faces the sinfulness of his behavior which is rooted in base selfishness, the very opposite of love. He is acting on motives far below the dignity of a Christian and certainly more ignoble than the motive of fear of eternal punishment which he claims is below his dignity. His failure to admit his guilt makes him both unworthy and incapable of receiving the grace of conversion. The vivid realization of the true nature of sin and the wretched condition of his soul should arouse in him a salutary fear of God and a true turning away from sin. Man, under the influence of passion, is blinded to sublime truths because he is cut off from God's illuminating grace. Only "the clean of heart," filled with unselfish charity, are truly receptive to the good (cf. Matt. 5:8).

While living in sin, man remains subject to sin and its evil desires. Fear of the Lord is the beginning of wisdom and the first step and motive-power for the good. There is a vast difference between the servile fear of the sinner at the beginning of conversion, and the genuine fear of God found in the perfect Christian. St. Augustine refers to the latter as the "chaste fear." He compares the two kinds of fear by drawing a parallel between two married women. The one woman, guilty of infidelity, has every reason to be afraid of her husband's justified anger on his return home. The other wife, completely devoted and dedicated to her husband, is worried for him while he is absent; but once he is at home, she knows only one fear, namely, that of displeasing him. The motive of fear in Christian living should become a "chaste fear" and a fearful love. Eventually, the motive of fear will cease because it will fuse into the love of God. The motives of fear and hope will become elevated and dignified through their association with the sublime motive of charity.

Man, while living under the influence of a warped self-love, tends to be self-seeking even in his expectations of God's promises because he conceives them as a temporal type of recompense. *Man remains egocentric in the performance of the good as long as he aims at personal reward and satisfaction.* With progress in virtue his longing for heaven becomes a more ardent and powerful incentive for virtue. He begins to realize more clearly that heaven consists in a perfectly blessed love-union with God.

There is neither virtue nor merit in the mere expectation of temporal reward or in the fear of temporal punishment. Nevertheless, such motives may have moral significance in connection with motives of a higher order. An example may illustrate this.

A physician speaking to a priest made the following statement: "If I were in your position, I would give different incentives to people. I would offer them more powerful motives for avoiding evil and performing the good than your most beautiful sermons. I would explain to young people how inevitably their frivolous love-affairs and their misuse of the conjugal act lead to dire consequences, such as sexual frigidity in the wife and various forms of neuroses in both partners. The presentation of these simple and powerful motives, in your sermons, in the confessional and in pre-marital instructions, would be more successful than all your preaching."

What is the attitude of Christian ethics to such motives? It would be unreasonable and undesirable to keep the faithful uninformed about the findings of medicine and depth-psychology on the mere proposition that the Christian should use only the purest and highest spiritual motives. Therapeutic reasons and incentives may often effect a decided moral improvement. Yet we should not be content with such motives.

To abstain from external acts of impurity merely for hygienic reasons does not constitute the virtue of purity in interior dispositions and intentions. If married people refuse to accept the burden of parenthood and disdain God's laws, but nevertheless refrain from unethical means of birth control out of fear for its evil consequences such as frigidity and neuroses, they are far from practicing virtue. "God knows the heart" means that in God's sight motives are decisive and that all intentions which do not center in Him are worthless in His eyes. Only he who has recognized and accepted the genuine value of chastity and who in deep reverence for the mystery of virginity and matrimony refrains from interior and exterior acts against chastity is truly chaste. Chaste are the married people who despite great difficulties and temptations sincerely strive to make their conjugal relations a worthy expression of reciprocal love and service to God. They act on the motives of a genuine appreciation of the great value of chastity, mutual charity, and sincere love of God.

To make this affirmation is not to question the validity of the motives postulated by medicine and psychology. *These natural facts, which may serve as incentives to good, prove that according to God's wise plans sin carries its own poison within itself.* Evil brings misery while virtue enriches and gladdens the soul. Therefore, it would be wrong to ignore and despise the lower incentives. A higher motive does not gain by isolating itself from related motives. The latter may increase the higher motive's efficacy and influence over the will. Consequently, thoughts of temporal punishment or reward may enter into our actions as secondary motives. It is dangerous to despise such ordinary incentives because this attitude may imperceptibly lead into the disorders of sin. On the other hand, it is important that the lower motives be directed and animated by the higher ones.

3. Social Considerations

Man is by nature a social being and consequently dependent on social institutions. His actions are motivated or influenced either consciously or unconsciously by social considerations. It is, therefore, important to determine man's awareness, understanding, and evaluation of the various social forces, so that he may not become a blind victim to public opinion.

It is unquestionable that the majority of men are greatly influenced by the *social heritage of their environment*. A milieu with high moral standards is a great blessing for the individual, particularly, if he develops deep interior convictions in his acclimatization to a particular environment. In a depraved atmosphere, the individual runs the risk of personal ruin if he does not resist its evil influences.

This consideration implies a very significant motive for the morally mature person. The Christian is obliged to uphold morality and to improve public opinion in due consideration for those not yet confirmed in virtue. *All our actions should contribute to an atmosphere conducive to spiritual growth and maturity for the young and inexperienced.* Thereby, the merely natural and social considerations will be integrated into the Christian *motive of the solidarity of salvation in the Christianization of society.* This is a noble motive of charity towards God and neighbor. For the same reason, the Christian should abide by the rules and customs of his particular society in all things not sinful, so that he may exert the most far-reaching positive influence on his contemporary society.

This truth also applies to our *personal reputation*. An undue quest for the applause of men is unsound and dangerous because it tends to produce a warped personality and a slave of public opinion. True interest for our good name is safeguarded if we see our good reputation and that of our neighbor in the light of God's glory and our exalted vocation in the apostolate.

Section VII. The Leitmotif or Ideal of Life

Our previous discussion has shown the hierarchy of motives in our moral-religious strivings as well as the coordi-

nation of particular ideals and motives under a lofty dominant ideal. This ideal of life or leitmotif imparts its sublime
beauty and nobility to the more egocentric motives on the
lower level of consciousness. It is important for our moral
life that the motives of our actions, although distinct and
diversified, should not be isolated in an unrelated coexist-
ence; in fact, *their very force and efficacy is derived from
their integration. The "bundle of motives" should be united
into a leading idea, a "leitmotif."*

This dominant ideal which combines and coordinates
the more lowly and ordinary motives must not only express
a true value appreciation but must also be keyed to the
spiritual maturity and religious dispositions of the person.
The *leitmotif* of the beginner in the spiritual life will rarely
possess the mature characteristics expressed in the ideal
of life adopted by the adult person who has faced and
managed the storms and vicissitudes of life.

The adventurous desires of a vivacious young man will
determine the feeling-tones of his religious *leitmotif.* An
ardent temperament may accomplish great things for the
extension of God's kingdom through a total dedication to
the cause of Christ. He will strengthen the good in his own
heart and in his environment and hasten the defeat of
Satan's kingdom. A person greatly concerned for his good
name and reputation could choose the motto: "My actions
may not bring any discredit to God and His Church" or "I
shall prove myself worthy of the grace and dignity bestowed on me by God." A person of a grateful temperament might choose the *leitmotif:* "What shall I render to
the Lord for all He has done for me?"

The following ideal might be suitable for young girls:
"In imitation of Mary, I will keep Christ's words in a lov-
ing heart" or "Like Mary, I will become a loving friend of
Christ and a devoted servant of my neighbor." A loving

young bride may choose the motto: "God is the center of all my love." Many saints in all their actions were animated by the sublime motive: "All for the greater honor and glory of God." The apostolic zeal of others expressed itself in a dominant ideal such as: "To save souls," "To reclaim or recruit souls for the love of God," "To save souls from the dark loneliness of hell." These ideals of life, although good in themselves, are not equally suited to the need of each person.

Recently, several hundred young seminarians and religious were questioned about their main purpose in choosing the religious life. Despite considerable variations of motives this investigation revealed that the *leitmotif* of the young generation is animated by a joyful dedication to God's kingdom and a readiness for service. The thought of personal salvation in the priestly or religious state was hardly mentioned as the guiding motive. It entered only as a subordinate motive. At times the *leitmotif* consciously admitted and expressed in words is in reality not the central or chief motive. There are many who are unconsciously guided by an entirely different motive than the one consciously admitted. It also is possible that the hidden *leitmotif* may be one of resentment such as: "I hope I shall never become like this particular person."

Section VIII. The Renewal of the Good Intention

The renewal of the good intention, frequently discussed by spiritual writers, is essentially the same as the cultivation of the *leitmotif*. There are several important conclusions which can be deduced from the considerations of the *leitmotif*.

1. The good intention should become the deeply personal expression of the soul. This means that *each person should renew the good intention in the manner most appealing to his interior dispositions.* There is no need for using identical formulas. A noble and soul-stirring *leitmotif* gradually reveals new depths and beauty.

The leitmotif could be expressed in a deeply personal way according to the dispositions of the soul and the occasions of grace. At the Eucharistic celebration the heart may overflow with protestations of gratitude while at other times it may petition God's assistance in special hardships and trials. The leitmotif may express sincere sorrow for sin and an ardent desire for reparation. It may implore God's grace in the face of situations in which the soul encounters difficulty with the virtue of brotherly love. Although the soul's relationship with God should be spontaneous, it might be well to indicate here some formulations of the leitmotif, such as: "All for You my Jesus"; "What shall I render to the Lord for all He has done for me?"; "I am sincerely sorry for my sins and promise henceforth to give You joy"; "It is the Lord Himself who appeals to my charity through the needs of my neighbor."

Regarding the renewal of the good intention or leitmotif, we should be more concerned with fervor than with frequency. The sincerity and devotion of the renewal and its integration into the "bundle of motives" remains the most essential aspect of progress. The more the good intention permeates the soul's strivings and endeavors, the more will its renewal produce the desired and lasting effects on one's entire life both in interior dispositions and external actions. The good intention will pervade one's entire life to the extent of the soul's perception and awareness of its inner value. A motive which is deeply perceived will more readily be retained in one's memory. Hence, its *frequent renewal* is of great importance since any idea which remains dormant will gradually lose its effectiveness.

Section IX. *Education Versus Training*

The previous discussion on law and the freedom of the children of God deepened our understanding of the basic Christian truths relevant to education. The fundamental moral truths on dispositions, motives and actions gave us a clear concept regarding the nature of true education and the pitfalls to be avoided in dealing with youth. Education distinguishes itself from training in its appeal to a personal conscience. On the other hand, conscience, the center and core of our human existence, derives its sincerity and purity from the rectitude of our interior dispositions and motives. The sublime goal of education is the proper formation of conscience.

We can train animals through the incentive of reward and punishment in constantly repeated performances. In addition, there are definite limitations in the training of animals unless they are endowed with a pronounced confidence in man and certain instinctive attachments. Our dominion over animals would be greatly increased if they could sense in us the perfect freedom of the children of God.

Education must be on a higher level than the best of training. On the whole, the motive of reward and punishment should have a limited place in education. The recognition of the innermost value of a good deed is more important than any material reward. The repetition of good deeds results in the formation of desirable habits which are of considerable importance in the life of the individual. *Yet, the most important factor in education is the child's gradual awakening to a joyful perception of the good, the adoption of a loving, kind, sincere and impartial disposition, and the selection of worthwhile motives which are appropriate to the stage of the religious development of the young.*

In the formation of character, the exercise of will power and the acquisition of desirable habits are of great importance. However, the decisive factor in all education is the purification of interior dispositions, which requires not only a complete surveillance and nurture of motives but a wholehearted assimilation and imitation of Christ's own sublime sentiments and dispositions.

4 THE SOUL'S INTIMATE encounter WITH GOD

Law, the expression of God's benevolent will (Chapter I); the freedom of the children of God as the beginning of our participation in the blessed life and freedom of God (Chapter II); conscience as the "organ" enabling us to perceive God's benevolent will, the interior dispositions of the heart and the incentives for actions (Chapter III) lead us to the blessed realization that our life is rooted in God. We owe our existence and all our faculties to God's benevolent love, because He deigned to call us by name. We shall meet God's expectations only if we respond to His invitation with loving obedience. Meditations on the three theological virtues, as well as the moral virtues which they inspire, will lead us to a keen perception of the nature of our encounter with God as a loving response, as a heart-to-heart dialogue.

SYNOPSIS OF CHAPTER FOUR

Faith reveals to us the treasures of God's innermost secrets. Genuine Christian faith embraces the heart (Section I).

Through the theological virtue of hope, God promises us the riches of His love and makes us seek Him with every fiber of our hearts. We are securely on the road to God when our hearts are completely free from earthly entanglements and are filled with the expectations of God's promises (Section II).

The divine virtue of charity disposes our hearts to an intimate heart-to-heart dialogue with God. This virtue is the beginning and pledge of our own blessed participation in the dialogue of love existing from all eternity between the Father and the Son in the ardor of the Holy Spirit (Section III).

PART ONE

Faith

SYNOPSIS OF PART ONE

Faith is "the beginning of man's salvation." It is also "the foundation and root of all justification" (Council of Trent). It liberates the soul from an enslaving selfishness. (1) In the light of faith we begin to realize that our entire existence must center in the life-giving word of God, in God's self-revelation. (2) By faith we open our intellect, heart, and will to the saving influences of divine grace. (3) Faith is a loyal response to God's word which demands the external manifestations of our convictions before men. (4) Faith is the belief in the communion of the Church, namely, the communion of the faithful. (5) Faith is a gratuitous gift from the Word of God. Faith possesses not only a transforming power for the heart, but manifests itself in good works. (6) Faith has redeemed us from the snares of a sinful world. Yet, faith, far from being synonymous with a cowardly withdrawal from the world, signifies an obligation and, at the same time, a powerful force to renew the face of the earth. (7) Like the mustard seed, faith should constantly increase both in our hearts and in the world at large.

Section I. The Word of God

1. The Word of God Is a Gratuitous Gift

Supernatural faith is far from being a purely private affair of the heart or the result of intellectual speculations. It is the purely gratuitous gift of God's grace. Faith confronts us with the "Thou" of God, with His very truth and His personal claim on our soul. Hence it is diametrically opposed to all self-glorification and self-centered isolation. The Word of God, in reality, is a gracious appeal to the soul although our lower self may consider it as a stern demand. God's condescending love manifests itself by inviting men to an intimate participation in His own truth and love.

Faith is the gratuitous gift of God. Man's basic and most decisive attitude to God's Word should be a complete renunciation of all egocentricity and false trust in self. In the encounter with the Word of God, the first beatitude is realized: "Blessed are the poor in spirit" (Matt. 5:3), that is, "those bending in humility" (according to the verbal translation from the Greek text). They are the little ones in the full awareness of their poverty. It is these who accept the glad tidings of the kingdom of God. "I thank You, Father, Lord of heaven and earth, for hiding these things from the learned and wise, and revealing

them to the simple. Yes, Father, such was Your choice"
(Matt. 11:25-26).

In faith the all-holy God condescendingly reveals the
innermost secrets of His truths to us. He, likewise, manifests Himself to us in His eternal Word, the very expression
of all the riches of His love. "No one knows the Son except
the Father; nor does anyone know the Father except the
Son" (Matt. 11:27). The joy-giving dialogue between God
the Father and the Son in the love of the Holy Spirit is completely beyond our finite human comprehension. It is an
undeserved grace of faith that the Father deigns to give us
a foretaste of this most sublime mystery through the mediation of His Son, the Word Incarnate. Faith gives us a faint
inkling of our share in the life of the Triune God. The truths
of faith are revealed only to those to whom the Son
wishes to reveal them (cf. Matt. 11:27).

2. *The Word of God Is a Matter of Life and Death*

The Word of God is meant for all people. But why do not all
men receive it? In response to this question Christ gives us
two answers.

In the first place, faith is pure grace. "No one can
come to Me unless the Father draw him" (John 6:44).
"Everyone who has listened to the Father and learned
from him comes to Me" (John 6:45).

Secondly, he who refuses to accept the Word of God
thereby manifests his pride. The proud man is unable to
believe because he fails to acknowledge God and His dominion over him. "How can you believe as long as you
receive glory from one another and do not seek the glory
which is from the only God?" (John 5:44). Christ, the
Word of the Father, lives entirely in and through the Fa-

ther. He delights in His origin from the Father. Therefore, He does not seek His own glory before men (cf. John 5:41). He does not come in His own name, but in the name of His Father (cf. John 5:43). Whoever comes in his own name, or seeks his own glory, might be accepted by the proud and mighty of this earth because he conforms to their standards. The message of Christ, the Word of the Father, is in complete contradiction to the inclinations of the proud man. The world and its self-sufficiency has received its sharpest condemnation through its refusal to accept the Word of God, the light of the world. Men whose works are evil, love the darkness more than the light (cf. John 3:18 ff.).

The Word of God likewise contains a condemnation of the vainglorious strivings of the "old man" in us. God's loving invitation is unacceptable to the proud man because he is slow to relinquish his own selfish desires. He is scandalized at the debasement of the cross, the utter humility of Christ, and God's all-embracing demands on him. If, on the other hand, man awakens to the Word of God and is willing to admit his complete dependence on Him, he will come to the realization that the Word of God means eternal life for him. "He who hears My Word and believes Him who sent Me, has life everlasting" (John 5:24; 3:15, 6:40). "He who believes in Me has life everlasting" (John 6:47). "Now this is everlasting life, that they may know You, the only true God and Him whom You have sent, Jesus Christ" (John 17:3).

In our humble subjection to the Word of God, we renounce the deadly temptation to seek the source and fulness of life in ourselves. Faith makes us receptive to truth and bestows supernatural life, because the Word of God is essentially a life-giving Word. The Father sent His Son into the world in order to bring us true life and salvation. (The primary objects of faith are the Father who gave His only-begotten Son, and Jesus Christ who died for us and rose from the dead so that we, too, may participate in His own life)

3. The Word of God Is One with His Salvific Acts

God's Word which is identical with God's wonderful works of salvation is our very source of light and salvation. We firmly believe in Christ, the Word of the Father, and in His message. Above all, we believe in the wonderful, salvific deeds of God's love: in Christ's death and resurrection. In the light of faith, we see the Word of God and the redeeming actions of Christ as one and the same. The redemptive works of Christ are the most powerful and emphatic words of God, the most luminous revelations of His innermost secrets.

The identity of God's words with His deeds is emphatically pronounced in the administration of the sacraments. The sacraments are efficacious signs, or effective words of divine love which awaken and increase our faith. They assure the faithful heart that Christ's redemptive words are spoken in their behalf and that they effect here and now what they indicate. The sacraments, as efficacious words of God, are part of our faith in the redemptive works of Christ, namely the incarnation, the death, resurrection, and second coming of Our Lord. (cf. I Tim. 3:16).

The mere hearing of God's revelations does not profit us. When God in His loving condescension addresses man personally, He brings about a renewal of man's heart, intellect, and will so that he may become receptive in the manner of a disciple of Christ (cf. Is. 50:4). God's words and the redemptive deeds of Christ transcend time and space when, by the grace of faith, they become present

here and now in the individual soul through the powerful
action of God.

Section II. The Response of Man's Heart, Intellect, and Will

The Word of God, who has appeared to us in person, is
the Word of the Father. His message as well as His redemptive deeds demand a personal response, a total conversion of our entire being towards Him. This truth finds
fitting expression in the intimate associations of faith with
the reception of the sacraments. "He who believes and is
baptized shall be saved" (Mark 16:16). Through the reception of baptism, administered in the name of Our Lord
Jesus Christ, the Christian indicates his firm belief in Christ
and declares his wholehearted submission and surrender
to God's loving dominion.

The liturgical celebration of the sacraments constitutes
the most emphatic manifestation of our faith, because in
the sacraments the Word of God reaches us directly and
efficaciously. All the sacraments are outward signs accomplishing what they indicate. This is clearly illustrated
in baptism, which is a solemn acceptance and profession
of faith, as well as in the Eucharist when we adoringly
proclaim: "O great mystery of faith." In faith and in the
reception of the sacraments, we are given a new life. The
appropriate response to such graces is a total surrender to
God.

We acknowledge Jesus Christ, the Word of the Father,
and His redemptive work; namely, His death, resurrection, ascension, and second coming. Our profession of
faith is significant only if it involves our entire being "our
whole soul, all our mind, and heart." In faith we give our

intellectual assent to all the words and deeds of our salvation, that is, all the truths which God in His infinite love has deigned to reveal to us. Therefore, faith becomes an illuminating light for our intellect. Since the intellectual acceptance of truth is an acknowledgment of God's supreme and benevolent will, our response of faith should involve all our faculties: our intellect, heart, and will. If God deigns to reveal His truths to us in such a loving and personal manner, then our trusting acceptance of God's words can only be accomplished in an attitude of ready and willing acceptance of His grace.

Holy Scripture refers to the purifying action of faith in our heart (cf. Acts 15:9; and John 15:3). The term "heart" in biblical language implies the very center and totality of our being. Consequently, purity of heart is synonymous with the purity and integrity of man's entire being, particularly his intellect and will. Faith can produce its purifying effect only if it penetrates the innermost powers of the soul.

A mere intellectual acceptance of the Christian truths with a simultaneous estrangement from God through wilful attachment to mortal sin, is indicative of a faith which is in reality "dead." Faith can exert its vivifying power only if the sinner is sincere in the acknowledgment and repentance of his sins in the light of faith. A "dead" faith signifies both a denial and a violation of the love-inspired revelations of God which are meant to bestow light, life, and love. On the other hand, a "dead" faith does not exclude the possibility of conversion. While the sinner still believes in the truths of faith, he basically condemns his own sins, and confirms the judgment of faith over himself and his deeds.

Man's most serious sins are those which destroy faith and thereby cut him off from all claims to salvation, namely, the sins of heresy, unbelief, apostasy, and wilful doubts in matters of faith.

Heresy is the conscious denial of a revealed truth, pronounced as such by the Church (dogma). The Greek designation of heresy implies an "autonomous selection"; it refers to the proud man's self sufficiency in selecting the truths of faith which he desires or understands with his limited mental powers.

The adherents to religious denominations, denying some of the truths revealed by God and taught by the Church, are objectively followers of heretical sects. This pronouncement does not accuse the individual members of such denominations of being guilty of heresy. All men outside the Church, without guilt on their part and rightly disposed to revealed truths, belong to the communion of the faithful by the very fact of their sincere faith.

The sin of unbelief is committed by those who refuse to accept Christ and His teaching when effectively confronted with Christian truths. This sin assumes its greatest proportions when a well informed baptized Christian turns his back on Christianity. This is referred to as apostasy.

The virtue of faith is endangered not only by the full-fledged sins of heresy and unbelief but by every voluntary scepticism or doubt in matters of faith. The sceptic appoints himself judge over the Word of God. In the last analysis, pride and the perversion of the heart through inordinate desires are at the root of all heresy, unbelief, and scepticism.

Many Christians erroneously accuse themselves in confession of sins of doubt in matters of faith whereas the substance of their accusations amounts to no more than temptations and compulsive thoughts against the faith. These disturbances do not destroy a firm and sincere belief. The most important weapon in such temptations is prayer, which is in essence a true confession of faith. Compulsive thoughts are best overcome by patience and a calm resignation.

Doubts in matters of faith, arising from lack of knowledge in religious truths, are not sinful, provided the heart is ready to submit to the decisions of the teaching authority of God and His Church. Lack of knowledge in important religious matters is sinful only to the extent that such ignorance is rooted in contempt of truth or culpable sloth.

Our wholehearted acceptance of truth reveals itself best in a zeal for knowledge in religious matters. It is the Christian's duty to become fully acquainted with the truth and splendor of God's revelation. However, a true deepening of faith requires more than intellectual investigation and study. The truth of faith must be accepted and contemplated by a truly loving heart. This is especially imperative in today's superficial and unbelieving world, where knowledge of religious truth prepares us to be "always ready with an answer" (I Pet. 3:15), in order to gain others for the faith.

Section III. Response in Disposition and Word

"With the heart a man believes unto justice, and with the mouth profession of faith is made unto salvation" (Rom. 10:10).

The Word of God is in our very midst; He has made His abode with us. The Word of the Father has addressed Himself to us in the most simple and touching language and with the most powerful deeds of love. It is by the very power of God's grace that we are enabled to utter our response of faith from the very bottom of our hearts. "The word is near to you, in your mouth and in your heart" (Deut. 30:14; Rom 10:8).

It is not sufficient merely to respond in words to such a Word as was transmitted to us by God in the glad tidings of salvation, nor is it becoming for us to hold back our response unspoken in the depths of our hearts. It is but natural that our wholehearted assent to truth with intellect, heart, and will is followed by an external profession of faith. "For if you confess with your mouth that Jesus is the Lord, and believe in your heart that God has raised Him from the dead, you shall be saved" (Rom. 10:9).

The saving truth, that the risen Christ is the Lord and Redeemer of mankind, takes full possession of our souls in faith. Regarding these astonishing and great truths of faith we may recall the words of Scripture: "Out of the abundance of the heart the mouth speaks" (Matt. 12:34). Our psychological needs and endowments as well as the very nature and object of faith demand an external profession of faith. In faith we acknowledge the glorified risen Savior as the Lord of both the invisible and visible creation. Faith is genuine and true only if it is actualized in external manifestations. Failure to profess our faith under the pretext that religion is a "private affair" would mean a denial of Christ. "Everyone who acknowledges Me before men, I also will acknowledge him before My Father in heaven. But whoever disowns Me before men, I in turn will disown him before My Father in heaven" (Matt. 10:32-33).

We have received the holy and exalted mission to proclaim our faith in word and in deed whenever this is demanded for God's glory and the good of our neighbor. Under no circumstances may we ever deny our faith. There is nothing, including the most horrible tortures, which could ever permit us to deny it—even for appearances' sake. The denial of faith is one of the most grievous sins. The pretext of preserving our faith in the interior of our heart does not justify an outward denial.

It is quite legitimate, however, to protect ourselves from persecutors of the faith. We also may evade or refuse to answer unauthorized questions regarding our convictions. "Do not give to dogs what is holy, neither cast your pearls before swine" (Matt. 7:6). Care must be taken to avoid the appearances of wrongdoing before the weaker brethren who might construe an evasive answer to unauthorized questioners as inconstancy or a denial of the faith.

If a non-Catholic has arrived at the full realization of the truth of the Catholic faith, he is obliged to act according to his interior convictions and embrace the Catholic faith. Family obligations and other serious considerations might, of course, permit or even necessitate the temporary postponement of making public this decisive step.

Section IV. The Response of Faith in the Community of the Faithful

Christ who in His resurrection and ascension proved Himself to be the Lord of all creation gave His apostles the solemn command: "All power in heaven and on earth has been given to Me. Go, therefore, and make disciples of all nations, baptizing them in the name of the Father, and of the Son, and of the Holy Spirit, teaching them to observe all that I have commanded you; and behold, I am with you all days, even unto the consummation of the world" (Matt. 28:18 ff.). This does not imply a mere transmission of His teaching authority to the Church. Rather, Christ Himself, the Lord and Bridegroom of the Church, remains intimately united with her. In order that the Church may abide by the truth, Christ remains always present within her through the Paraclete whom He Himself has sent. The Church is "the pillar and mainstay of the truth" (I Tim. 3:15). We, the faithful, "are built upon the foundation of the apostles" (Eph. 2:20). The Church as the guardian and messenger of the Word of God has received the promise: "The gates of hell shall not prevail against it" (Matt. 16:18), "the sure foundation of God stands firm" (II Tim. 2:19).

Our acceptance of faith in the belief in Our Lord Jesus Christ necessarily demands our unshaken faith in the holy, apostolic, and Catholic Church, the appointed messenger of truth. The Church transmits to us the deposit of faith. In the reception of the sacraments, the Christian gives his most important and exalted testimony of faith.

In *baptism* we gratefully acknowledge the Triune God: the heavenly Father who accepts us into the Church as His beloved children, Our Lord Jesus Christ, the head of the Church who imprints His image on our souls, and the Holy Spirit who teaches the Church and disposes our hearts for the worthy reception of His truth.

In the celebration of the *Eucharist,* the Church announces Christ's redeeming death and resurrection "until, He comes" (I Cor. 11:26). She announces the redeeming action of Christ in His death as an event which is lifted out of the confinement of one time and made present here and now. Through the Church's celebration of holy Mass and Communion, Christ, who died for all of us, gives the assurance of faith that "all His love is meant for each of us." Our hymns of praise rendered in unison are effective proofs of faith, pleasing unto God because they are the adoring demonstrations of His well beloved bride, the Church.

In the sacrament of *penance,* the confessor and the penitent join in giving praise to God's justice and mercy. In the absolution, the priest transmits to the penitent God's personal message that his sins are forgiven him. The penitent's humble confession of his sins becomes an expression of his confidence in the redeeming power of Christ. The Church transmits to the faithful the message of reconciliation and in return receives the penitent's expression of faith and confidence in the justice and mercy of God.

Since *matrimony* is a sacrament, it cannot be received without the Church or her consent. The Church, the bride of Christ, announces this "great mystery" as a mystery of faith and salvation. As members of the Church and in the presence of the Church, the bride and groom become the priestly instruments of grace for each other. In matrimony, the contracting parties give their mutual consent in the presence of the Church. They thereby pronounce their faith in the communion of charity in Christ and in the Church and their own sacramental participation in this mystery.

The acknowledgment of faith in and with the Church is at the same time a participation in the Church's mission to spread the gospel truths to all nations and people. A beautiful and inspiring community celebration of the sacred liturgy is a clear and effective profession of faith. It is also an invitation to those lingering "on the wayside." United in heart and voice, while praising God in jubilant songs and prayers, the faithful are made ready to profess their faith in the various circumstances of their daily lives.

Nothing is more detrimental to the respect due to our holy religion than a mere routine mechanical performance of the Sunday obligation or an unbecoming behavior at its liturgical celebration. Take the case of a Catholic girl who took her open minded non-Catholic fiance to the Christmas midnight Mass. After the celebration, he declared that at no time would he attend another Catholic Church service because the men failed to participate in the

divine mysteries and behaved like disrespectful unbelievers, discussing things which would be unbecoming for
Christians even outside the church walls. One may ponder
about the possible beneficial influences on this good Protestant man, if he had witnessed a sincere expression of faith
and fervor in community singing and praying.

The relationship of our faith to the Church does not only
find its external expression in the celebration of the sacred
liturgy but it is such a vital reality that a separation from
her would seriously endanger our faith. There is no salutary faith or even salvation outside the Church. This statement should be understood correctly. It is not meant to
exclude the sincere non-Catholic Christian from the community of the Church. It rather indicates the intimate
bonds existing between faith and salvation relevant to the
communion of all believers in Christ. It unites all sincere
believers into the one holy, apostolic and Catholic Church.
All Christian truths which non-Catholics possess are their
precious inheritance from the Catholic Church. It was in
the bosom of the Catholic Church that the fundamental
truths of Christianity were written under the guidance of
the Holy Spirit and preserved in the books of the New
Testament. Without the Church, the gospel of salvation
would never have reached the non-Catholic Christians. The
willing response of faith from the well prepared hearts of
pious Protestant Christians includes the sincere will to
belong to the true Church of Christ and to profess their
faith accordingly.

The demonstration of sincere faith and devotion in good
Protestant congregations, offering their homage in songs
and prayers, is pleasing to God. Christ is in their midst by
the action of His efficacious grace. God is pleased with such
a community not because it is a community separated from
the true Church (since the separation itself is displeasing

to Him) but rather because of their sincere dispositions to accept and profess the faith of the true Church.

In view of our many separated brethren, we Catholics should ask ourselves: Are we making visible to them the true Church as the exalted sign of faith and charity through our truly Christian lives and our adoration of God in spirit and in truth and especially by our shining example of Christian charity? Or, to what extent are we responsible for their separation from the true Church?

We should understand that a Protestant Christian, who has come to the realization that his Church does not possess the pristine faith, is obliged to embrace the true Church of which his interior acceptance of the truth has made him an actual member.

It should be clear, however, that a person having been raised in the Catholic faith can not apostasize from the true Church without sinning grievously and without "suffering shipwreck in faith." Such a fatal step is the result of previous infidelities and insincerities of conscience (cf. I Tim. 1:19). The case of apostasy from Catholicism is quite different from the return of a sincere Protestant from a false doctrine (cf. Vat. Council I). Those returning to the true Church are led by the grace of God. On the contrary, God cannot lead anybody astray into heresy or separation from the truth. Yet should a non-Catholic join the Catholic Church without sincere convictions or for unworthy reasons, his case would be comparable to that of the apostasizing Catholic.

Every true Christian should have at heart the unity of Christians in the one, holy, apostolic and Catholic Church. This desire for unity should be fostered by fervent prayer and mutual charity.

Section V. The Response of Faith in Our External Conduct

God has manifested to us the secrets of His heart both in word and in deed. In His wonderful deeds of salvation He has revealed His truths and His love for us. The objects of our faith are primarily the redemptive deeds of Christ's death and resurrection. Since faith is rooted in God's manifestations of love, our faith must be a response in disposition, word, and in action.

The central core of the glad tidings of the gospel is the advent of God's kingdom, the mild and loving dominion of God. The profession of faith requires more than empty words or formulas. It demands a sincere acceptance of God's dominion. "Not everyone who says 'Lord, Lord' shall enter the kingdom of heaven" (Matt. 7:21). The dignity and blessedness of our faith consists in the privilege of being the adopted children of the heavenly Father, the Creator of all things, who in His Son Jesus Christ has manifested the dominion of His love. Our assent to Him in faith is synonymous with our consent to His holy will. Thus faith becomes the root of our moral determination against all self-sufficiency in conduct, a determination for a willing surrender to the dominion of God which claims all our powers.

Quite significantly, St. Paul the Apostle refers to faith not so much as a "hearing of the Word of God" but rather an "obeying of the gospel" (Rom. 10:16). Salutary "hearing" is possible only in an "obedience to faith" (Rom. 1:5; cf. 16:19; II Cor. 10:5 ff.).

Our submission to faith will necessarily produce "the works of faith" (I Thes. 1:3). These embrace more than mere outward conformity to the dictates of faith. They demand that all our conduct be in conformity with our religious convictions.

We have received supernatural life by the free gift of faith rather than by our personal merit (cf. Gal. 3:11; Heb. 10:38). Our actions, unless inspired by faith, do not possess any supernatural value, because they are cut off from God's eternal truths. Just as we possess supernatural life through the grace of faith, so must all our actions and endeavors be vitalized by faith. "Faith, unless it has works, is dead in itself" (James 2:17-20).

A life which is inspired by truly Christian principles is the most powerful witness to our faith. Living by faith will enable us to penetrate ever deeper into the mysteries of our salvation. The truths of salvation can exercise their liberating power only to the extent that we submit to faith or "abide in the Word of Christ" (John 8:31). Without the external profession of our religious convictions we are jeopardizing our faith because in this present life we are dependent on external activity and because faith is, in its essence, a response to God's Word in thought, word, and action. Our Lord Himself emphasized this very intimate relationship: "Whoever has the will to do the will of God shall know whether My teaching comes from My Father or is merely My own" (John 7:17).

A faith which does not "work through charity" (Gal. 5:6) is a dead faith. Only a willing faith, animated and inspired by true charity, can prepare our hearts for the truths of salvation and effect our true justification.

Every sin, but especially mortal sin, is an actual denial of the very faith which the Christian professes with his lips. There is greater offense in the sin of the Christian who knowingly transgresses God's law than in the trespasses of those who through no fault of their own are shut off from the light of faith. If the Christian adheres to the truths of his holy religion despite the shame and embarrassment occasioned by his offenses, his sins lose the venom which characterizes the offenses of the apostate who forsakes his belief in the futile attempt to escape the judgment and condemnation of his faith. The sinner's adherence to faith implies an admission of his guilt and an acknowledgment of God's wisdom as expressed in His commands.

Section VI. The Answer of Faith in Our Daily Life

Faith overthrows all worldly standards and criteria. Christians, like their Lord and Master, "are not of the world" (John 17:14). The world, steeped in darkness, resists the light of faith "because men's works are evil" (John 3:19). The true Christian is in open contradiction to the world which is full of "pride, the lust of the flesh and the pride of life."

Despite this fact, *faith is far from being synonymous with flight from the world* into "the realms of the purely interior." "The sinful world," for which Christ refused to pray, does not signify the world created by God. This expression rather has reference to the perverse and pretentious manner of living which is in conflict with God's plans. It is through the Word of the Father that the full splendor of the world's creation and redemption is manifested to us. The rich treasures of faith impel us to shape this world according to the sublime principles and standards of God's truth. This is the essential message expressed in Christ's farewell address before His bitter Passion: "Father, sanctify them in truth. As you have sent Me into the world, so I also have sent them into the world. And for them I sanctify Myself, that they also may be sanctified in truth" (John 17:17 ff.). *Faith, in a certain sense, is a consecration for the great task of regaining the world for God.* It is a consecration which has been earned for the world through the redemptive works of Christ.

Christ's sovereignty is not confined to the interior realms of the soul but extends to the entire world. Christ desires to make everything resound to the greater honor and glory of the Father. In a similar manner, our faith must prove itself in a true zeal for the Christianization of the world. The light of faith enables us to behold the bold outlines of the "new world." The spirit of faith provides the courage to strive zealously for the desired renewal of the world in our rapidly changing society. The salvific deeds of our holy faith imply a commitment to impregnate all human institutions with a distinctive Christian orientation.

In the final analysis, it is impossible for us to preserve and increase the life of faith if we restrict it to the interior realms of our hearts while the various forms of public life such as economics, politics, and public opinion are influenced by atheistic and immoral communication media. Satan will not prevail against our faith if, with full awareness of these dangers, we do our utmost to effect, through a concerted effort, a complete Christianization of the environment. *If we fail to subordinate everything to the law of faith, then our external profession of faith will not withstand a godless and unbelieving world.*

Our united and zealous endeavor to imprint on our surroundings the seal of a lively faith will prove most effective in strengthening and protecting our own faith and that of our weaker brethren. For this purpose we should assiduously renew our fervor by a constant reflection on the truths of our holy religion. If faith is wanting in depth and fervor, our external activity will lose its unction and will become contaminated by "the spirit of this world."

Section VII. Growth in Faith

Faith is comparable to a mustard seed planted in our hearts at baptism and nurtured unfailingly by God's bountiful grace. Faith supplies the clarity of mind necessary for a successful journey to heaven. Faith is strengthened and sustained through the Church's ministry of teaching, guiding and sanctifying souls. The examples of the saints, the dispensations of divine Providence and especially the unfailing guidance of the Holy Spirit aim unceasingly towards the perfection of faith. A true increase in faith requires an unreserved dedication and total surrender of the heart because faith alone provides the all-embracing truths appealing to every power of our soul.

Charity is the supreme consummation of faith. Each increase in charity also brings with it an increase in faith. Faith and charity are animated in us through the gifts of the Holy Spirit. *The gift of understanding* enables us to penetrate into the inner meaning of revealed truths. This gift is the completion and perfection of divine love, namely a faith active in love (cf. Gal. 5:6). *The gift of knowledge* provides a supernatural, penetrating light by which man is able to perceive the credibility and acceptability of revealed truth. It enables man to see creatures in their proper perspective. This gift is the basis for an enlightened faith. It guards us from overcredulity and uncritical approval of private revelations.

Since faith in its deepest essence is undeserved grace, we should constantly pray: "Lord, increase our faith."

PART TWO

Hope

The virtue of hope has already entered into our explanations on motivation in Christian living. Hope, like faith and charity, pervades the entire Christian life. For this very reason, it is impossible to treat any aspect of Christian living without reference to hope. Christian morality is a grateful testimony to the rich treasures of grace in the hopeful expectation of their final fulfillment.

SYNOPSIS OF PART TWO

In this present discussion we are dealing with hope as the key to the boundless riches of God's charity inclining our hearts to genuine love of God and neighbor.

Hope is an enlightening revelation of God's love and a powerful bond of union with Him. (1) This reveals itself in the distinctive marks of Christian hope when compared with the empty expectations of an earthly paradise. (2) Holy fear itself, the companion of Christian hope, is part of God's pressing invitation for total conversion to Him. (3) The transpierced heart of Christ, the compassionate heart of Mary, and the sacrament of God's merciful love are chief pledges of our hope. (4) Christian hope is not confined to selfish concerns for personal salvation but centers in the full consummation of the world's salvation on that final day of Christ's second coming.

Section I. Charity—The Motivation and Perfection of Hope

God Himself is the author of all Christian hope. He unfolds to us the rich treasures of His heart. He calls us to participation in the blessed love-union of the Triune God. *Through His promises and their partial fulfillment He constantly inspires our soul with hope and charity* in the pursuit of perfection. Christian hope is rooted in Christ who for love of us came down from heaven.

The true nature and sublimity of Christian hope will reveal itself further in a parallel between it and the misleading doctrine of Marxism which today is ensnaring great multitudes of people. This analogy is made not for the sake of controversy but rather for reasons of sincere self-examination. It is profitable to get an insight into our own secret mundane expectations and hopes which are likely to mar the genuine picture of Christian hope and predispose us to the snares of this false gospel of a pseudo-humanism.

Communism distinguishes itself by a denial of God's loving providence. Karl Marx's theory is a heartless "dialectic" of revolutionary developments resulting from class conflicts and contradictions. History, according to the Communist Manifesto, is but "a series of class conflicts." This belief forms their basic law for future progress. The danger of such a doctrine lies in the denial of all human hope. Karl Marx has promised the proletariat a paradise in an utterly classless society. His fantastic expectations bear the undeniable traces of the deep-seated yearnings of the human heart for charity, peace, and unity.

Karl Marx's theory of an earthly paradise does not admit the providence and solicitude of a personal God. *It parts from Christian teaching in the ways and means of fulfilling man's hopes and expectations.* If human history advances only through successive contradictions and tensions, then the expectations of a peaceful existence must lie beyond this present time and its momentum.

The object of Christian hope is the eternal kingdom of divine charity, a charity which surpasses all human comprehension (cf. Heb. 11:1). *The aim and means of Christian hope is charity.* This is clearly epitomized in the Sermon on the Mount.

"Blessed are the poor in spirit" (Matt. 5:3). Christ had come to preach the gospel to the poor (cf. Luke 4:18). But He did not promise them a paradise of earthly treasures. His serious warning: "Woe upon you" (Luke 6:24; James 5:1 ff.), was pronounced for the rich. The "blessed" of Our Lord's first beatitude was not intended for the demanding proletariat, consumed by hateful jealousy towards the more favored classes of society. The beatitude was addressed to the poor, who in full awareness of God's gratuitous and transcendent gifts, seek the priceless treasures of God's kingdom. "For such is the kingdom of heaven," namely the full possession of charity, the incipient foretaste of heaven—beginning even in this present life.

"Blessed are those who mourn; they shall be comforted" (Matt. 5:5). Blessed are the poor and contrite of heart (cf. Luke 4:18). Marxism points to the road of "progressive deterioration" of ever increasing depths of misery in a "classless" paradise for the working people, because such extreme pauperization is able to create the measure of bitterness required for a revolution. Our Lord pledged the fulness of His peace and consolation to those sorrowful for all sin and injustice. Bitterness of heart has received no promise from Our Lord. Poverty and grief contribute to our spiritual welfare only to the extent that they inflame our hearts with true compassion for the needy and with a genuine sorrow for our sins.

Class hatred is not the criterion for world improvement. Only the spirit of charity is able to renew the face of the earth. Christ said: *"Blessed are the meek, for they shall possess the earth"* (Matt. 5:4). Our goal indicates the means. Meekness, the interior power of kindness and the renunciation of all violence and vengeance, is the distinctive mark of Christian hope in the midst of the present struggle for the establishment of God's kingdom. The virtue of hope is foreign to those Christians whose only concern is their own salvation while they abandon the world to the impious and subservient. In reality, they share in the guilt of those who work for social justice with an outspoken contempt for spiritual values. Only the meek, whom Christ has promised the possession of the earth, are capable of the wholehearted dedication needed in the establishment of God's mild kingdom of peace.

Although the true disciple of Christ may discern a shadow of Christian teaching in the Communistic accusations about social injustice, he nevertheless is grieved more by sin and its malice than by social abuses. His compassion embraces all men who do not conform to God's ideal of justice. His "hunger and thirst" is directed towards the justice of God in the full assurance that they will be satisfied (Matt. 5:6). But since according to God's plans, charity is to rule in all things, Christian hope demands our cooperation in the sphere of social justice. The Christian, far from subscribing to the merciless law of a constantly increasing opposition between rich and poor, rather does all in his power to reduce the existing tensions by a true spirit of Christian charity and compassion because his own life is under the influence of God's merciful and compassionate love (cf. Matt. 5:7). The final epoch of human history does not begin with the bloody revolution and dictatorship of the lower classes. It already had its beginning in the painful death of the Just One on the cross. *"Blessed are they who suffer persecution for justice' sake,* for theirs is the kingdom of heaven" (Matt. 5:10). The bitter anguish and suffering of the poor and oppressed gains supernatural value and glory if it is borne for Christ's sake; for thus it becomes the pledge for eternal reward and victory which is promised to those who suffer reproach and persecution for and with Christ (cf. Matt. 5:10 ff.).

Material success and socio-economic progress do not count in God's sight. God is charity. The promise of His vision is for *the clean heart,* filled to overflowing with selfless charity for God and neighbor because God Himself is charity. The clean of heart will behold Him in this present life as in a mirror and see Him face to face in heaven's blessedness (cf. I Cor. 13:12).

Dialectical materialism considers all endeavors towards a peaceful distribution of earthly goods as an obstacle to its promised advent of a classless society. It promises victory to hatred and hostility arising from past injuries. The Christian should realize that there can be no easy-going compromise between the kingdom of light and the kingdom of darkness. Christian hope calls for a radical and decisive attitude and action in the struggle against sin and the prince of darkness. In this conflict charity alone will prove victorious. Charity alone is able to touch responsive hearts and win them back for God's kingdom of peace. *"Blessed are the peacemakers,* for they shall be called the children of God" (Matt. 5:9).

Ruthless materialism derives its greatest strength and efficacy from the solidarity of suffering, hatred, and strife. Christian hope lives in the liberating solidarity of Him who in infinite love gave Himself as a ransom for all mankind. Karl Marx has promised an earthly paradise to all the afflicted and oppressed. Christ has prepared for us a heavenly kingdom beyond this mortal life. *The foundations of His kingdom, namely, charity, peace, and the solidarity of hope,* are a beginning reality in this present life. We confidently turn our gaze to the perfection and consummation of all human history because God is its final cause. Contrary to

Karl Marx's ideology, the father of all action is not hatred but rather God, who is love (cf. I John 4:16). In the final analysis *it will be love which rules in all things.* The love of God has indeed entered this world. God has created this world out of infinite love and nothing can efface the traces of this love. In this time of salvation, God has erected the great sign of reconciliation: "God so loved the world that He gave His only-begotten Son" (John 3:16 ff.).

The Christian of today is aware of the presence of a stern dialectic of conflicting class interests and differences which tend to alienate men from one another. Yet he resists the rising tides of collectivism. He believes in the Law of Christ who by precept and personal example has taught an all embracing love for men, including His own persecutors. Christ's law of love is the prerequisite of all Christian hope. The example of reciprocal love among Christ's disciples is the sure sign that the kingdom of God has appeared among us (cf. John 13:35).

Section II. Hope, Fear, and Charity

Hope transports us beyond our own narrow horizons. Christian hope embraces more than self-perfection. *It aims at the victory of divine love in our own hearts and in the world at large,* the eternal communion of charity in God.

God's manifold promises open our selfish hearts to charity. In hope we begin to love God, even though this love is still rooted in self-interest. A deeper knowledge of God's promises leads us to a confident surrender to God's bounty. *Hope prepares the way for divine charity.* The first invitation of hope, comprehensible to our earth-bound hearts, is Our Lord's invitation: "Come to Me, all you who labor and are burdened, and I will give you rest" (Matt.

11:28). With increasing purity and intensity of hope in the accomplishment of our goal, we shall respond to God's invitation, "Taste and see how good the Lord is" (Ps. 33:9). Imperfect hope tends towards charity. The perfection of hope is rooted in charity, in a charity which "hopes all things" (I Cor. 13:7). Christian hope can exercise its truly vivifying and purifying power through Christ's indwelling in our hearts through charity.

Unless hope is rooted in charity it is ineffective. Without fear of God, hope tends towards presumption, while a fear-centered religion results in scrupulosity or even in despair. *The virtue of hope is completely destroyed by presumption, by doubt in God's mercy, and by despair,* even though hope without charity remains a possible seed for an effective desire for charity.

The ineffective hope of the sinner turns into presumption when he believes that God will grant him heaven despite his failure to love Him and that He will offer him forgiveness without contrition and penance, and grant him the reward of charity without worthy fruits of penance from a devoted heart. *Presumption* is, therefore, not only a sin against one's salvation but above all, a sin against the holiness of God who despises sin and rejects the proud sinner.

If the sinner, so to speak, *"takes a chance" on God's mercy and forgiveness while he unduly delays his conversion,* his "hope" borders on presumption and remains utterly ineffective.

Despair is the gravest sin against the virtue of hope and the promise of an all-merciful God. Next to hatred, it embodies the greatest offense against God's charity. Despair insinuates that sin exceeds God's merciful love.

Confident hope, coupled with *fear of God,* steers safely off the road of presumption and despair. *The fear of the Lord is an inherent quality of the theological virtue of hope.*

It purifies and strengthens hope. It is founded on the warnings of the all-holy, infinitely lovable God. The paternal charity of God tells us that nothing impure is allowed to enter heaven (cf. Is. 66:24; Apoc. 22:15). The person absorbed in earthly things and overconfident in his virtue is in need of God's threats of punishment. If holy fear fails to arouse the lazy and wicked servant, then God's promises are of no avail to him either. Without fear, he is unable to grasp the meaning of charity of God as the objective of all hope. He is unable to embrace it with all his heart. The more fully we realize that God's threats, like His promises, are expressions of His infinite charity, the more we shall "work out our salvation with fear and trembling" (Phil. 2:12), and our hope will become purified and strengthened and we will be directed to the Lord "who of His good pleasure works in us both the will and the performance" (Phil. 2:13).

Holy fear and hope are the protection of charity, while the latter is still imperfect and earth-bound. But the center of all things is charity. Without charity, hope is null and void. *If hope does not tend towards charity, it is completely futile and empty.* We are firm in hope because "Christ Jesus has laid hold of us" (Phil. 3:12). But in the fear of God's sanctity and in the consciousness of our own weakness, we acknowledge that we are imperfect and far from the goal (cf. Phil. 3:13). Thus "forgetting what is behind, I strain forward to what is before, I press on toward the goal, to the prize of God's heavenly call in Christ Jesus" (Phil. 3:13 ff.).

Christian hope is animated by fear and charity because it is inspired by the all-holy and amiable God. Fear becomes purified and turns into holy joy with a fuller comprehension of God's holiness and charity. Only "in hope were we saved" (Rom. 8:24). Furthermore, we are saved only as far as we cling to hope in charity. Hope, which derives its glory from charity, provides an inexhaustible *fountain of joy*. "Rejoice in hope" (Rom. 12:12), even in the midst of tribulations and afflictions. Christ is our hope and unending glory (cf. Col. 127; I Tim. 1:1). He is our salvation and our beatitude provided He abides in us.

Section III. The Hope Producing Signs of God's Mercy

Christian hope is firmly rooted in God's infinite compassion and mercy. "His mercy is from generation to generation" (Luke 1:50). *God's promises stir our keenest desires for happiness and love. Through the revelation of His mercy, He strengthens our confidence* which is the essential characteristic of Christian hope. God's marvelous works of salvation through Jesus Christ are the perfect expression of His compassionate love. "All the paths of the Lord are kindness and constancy toward those who keep His covenant and His decrees" (Ps. 24:10). "I extol you, give thanks to the Lord, for He is good; for His kindness endures forever" (Ps. 117:29). Even the damned in hell have to admit the unfailing mercy of God in their behalf.

Three symbols of God's mercy have a special appeal to us: the heart of Jesus; Mary, the Mother of Mercy; and the sacrament of mercy. On May 15, 1956, *Pope Pius XII*, in his encyclical on the devotion to the Sacred Heart of Jesus, pointed out the fact that all words and pictures of the Old Testament which portray the intimate and fatherly compassion of God as well as the salvific deeds and revelations in the New Testament concerning the loving compassion of

God, have found their most fitting expression and fulfillment in the Sacred Heart of Jesus. God's merciful compassion overflows in the Sacred Heart of Jesus.

"In the veneration of the Sacred Heart of Jesus, the Christian in communion with the Church pays tribute to this sign and symbol of salvation which reveals the extremes of divine love through the incarnate Word of God" (*Ibid.*). The Word of the Father became incarnate out of pure love and compassion. In Christ has "appeared the goodness and kindness of God our Savior" (Tit. 3:4). "The Son does not shrink from calling men His brothers" (Heb. 2:11). "Therefore, because His children have blood and flesh in common, He in like manner partook of these. That is why He should in every respect become like His brothers, that He might become a merciful and faithful high priest in matters pertaining to God and so expiate the sins of the people" (Heb. 2:14-17).

Our Lord repeatedly expressed the overflowing measure of His compassion for us. The parable of the Prodigal Son and the Good Shepherd are striking examples. Jesus shed tears over Jerusalem as a mother would weep over her own child (cf. Matt. 23:37). *The most emphatic revelation of His love is His own heart transpierced on the cross.* "Therefore, His heart was open, that we through the visible wound may become aware of the invisible wound of His love" (St. Bonaventure: *The Mysterious Vine*, Chapter III). Recent Popes have repeatedly admonished us to place our confidence in this sign of salvation. The Sacred Heart is our hope and salvation (cf. Pius XII, Encycl. on the Sacred Heart Devotion). The transfigured wounds of Christ and especially of His glorified heart are indeed divine pledges of the consummation of all our hopes in Christ.

Next to the Sacred Heart devotion, the veneration of the

motherly heart of Mary is a powerful sign of God's mercy. "And a great sign appeared in heaven: a woman clothed with the sun, and the moon was under her feet, and upon her head a crown of twelve stars" (Apoc. 12:1). These words apply in an intuitive synthesis to both the Church as the new people of God and to the Mother of the Redeemer. Indeed, the Johannine Gospel presents a moving image of the Mother standing beneath the cross of her only Son, where in the midst of her heart's anguish she opens her maternal heart to welcome the beloved disciple and in him all mankind as her adopted children (cf. John 19:26 ff.). The Mother of Jesus is the prototype of the Church who suffers travail for our sake until Christ is formed in us (cf. Gal. 4:9). Mary and the Church are likewise signs of victory and of the coming of God's kingdom in this present exile because their love, like that of Christ, manifests itself in suffering. Mary's crucified and risen Son is already "caught up to God and to His throne" (Apoc. 12:5) and with Him, also Mary, His Mother. He is the first fruit of victory and the pledge of our ultimate sharing in His own glory which is reserved for all true children of Mary.

God is always inclined to mercy and compassion even without Mary's intercession. *Yet, in Mary, He has given us the most perfect proof of His boundless goodness and condescension. Her motherly heart inspires perfect confidence in the merciful heart of God.* Mary, the humble handmaid of the Lord, has truly been exalted by God's infinite majesty. She gives testimony to the fact that God "exalts the lowly" (Luke 1:52). "The other sign" in heaven, Satan with seven heads and seven crowns which he had appropriated to himself in his arrogant pride (cf. Apoc. 12:3), is a warning that God "has scattered the proud in the conceit of their heart" (Luke 1:51). The proud angel who had refused to serve, came from heaven as lightning together with one third of the "stars of heaven" (Apoc. 12:4; Luke 10:18).

We are not assured of victory by our own strength, nor are we promised access to heaven through our own merit. If in God's providence we are to work out our salvation, we are nevertheless completely dependent on God for the grace of final perseverance which is a gratuitous gift from Him. We should confidently implore this grace from His abundant mercy. The *Church* discharges her sublime duty as merciful Mother in the *sacrament of penance* which is in the fullest sense the sacrament of God's merciful love. This sacrament announces to the sinner that God is willing to forgive if in all humility he implores His grace. For all those living in the misery of sin, the sacrament of penance is God's summons and invitation to return to the heart of God.

Section IV. The Expectation of the Fulness of Salvation

Christian hope enlarges the heart. It dispels all narrow concern for personal salvation. It points to the great day of the Lord when the plenitude of God's mercy will become manifest to every nation. On that day both our body and soul will be glorified in the magnificence of Christ's own glory in the choirs of the elect.

We expect our salvation in the ark of the new covenant, in the community of the Church. We are all one in the solidarity of hope for the fulness of our salvation. In the heavenly Jerusalem, we shall unceasingly praise the charity and mercy of the Triune God.

Our gaze turns heavenward to the "new heaven and new earth," the supreme realization of all desires. *Christian hope*

is all-embracing, excluding nothing which God has made.
It does indeed free the heart from the entanglements of
creatures, from all vain attachments and false expectations.
Christians place their trust neither in perishable possessions
nor earthly power and success (cf. I Tim. 6:17). They are
willing to share in the sufferings of Our Lord in order to
become glorified with Him (cf. I Pet. 5:9 ff.). Christ has
not promised an earthly paradise. Yet, *Christian hope, in
spite of its "other worldliness," does not encourage an idle
complacency in the face of misery and injustice.* Christian
hope provides confidence in man's endeavors for world improvement. It gives us the assurance that our sincere efforts
and our patient suffering and striving for world improvement will not be in vain. The good begun will find its completion even in an unexpected and at times sublime manner. Those who unselfishly love and unite their hope with
the yearnings and expectations of all creation will begin to
understand that "for those who love God all things work
together unto good" (Rom. 8:28).

The virtue of hope does not foster a complacent egoism.
The solidarity of our salvation with the fulfillment of the
hopes and expectations of all creation broadens our perspec-
tives. Although God expects a full measure of personal cooperation with His freely bestowed gifts and graces, He
likewise counts on our share in the work towards the salvation of the whole world. Our united efforts towards the
establishment of peace and order are the most appropriate
expressions of Christian hope and the surest means of salvation for our weaker brethren.

Our hope is directed to the eternal kingdom of charity.
We shall reach our destiny only in the true solidarity of
hope, for salvation is promised to those who in true concern and charity for others bear witness to God's supreme
power.

208

PART THREE

Charity

"Love, therefore, is the fulfillment of the law" (Rom. 13:10).
Charity is not just one commandment among the rest of the
commandments nor one virtue among other virtues, but
"the bond of perfection" (Col. 3:14). Without charity, life
becomes meaningless and valueless for eternal life. Charity
imparts true splendor to all things. An adequate comprehension of charity requires the fervor of the Seraphims. Natural
man is incapable of grasping the full depths of divine charity. God Himself had to enunciate His personal charity to
us. He sent His angels and prophets as messengers and as
solicitors for our reciprocal love. Even more than this, the
consubstantial Word of the Father became incarnate. We
have seen the glory of the only-begotten Son of the Father
full of grace and truth (cf. John 1:14). Christ's salvific
deeds and words revealed the inexhaustible treasures of
divine love intended to enkindle the whole earth (cf. Luke
12:49). The tongues of charity are more eloquent than
those of angels. The fire of charity does not enkindle only
the heavenly spirits with the ardor of divine love. Even
we, poor mortals, may "comprehend what is the breadth
and length and height and depth of the love of Christ
which surpasses knowledge, in order that we may be filled
unto all the fulness of God" (Eph. 3:18-19). The fire of
God's charity, the Holy Spirit, will establish us firmly in
charity in the consummation of perfect union with Christ.

SYNOPSIS OF PART THREE

(1) Loving God with all the powers of the heart; (2)
loving the Lord with all one's soul; (3) loving God with
every power of the soul in compliance with the command-

ment to be perfect as the heavenly Father; (4) the gradual fulfillment of such a far reaching command; (5) the personal and intimate nature of God's call to the fellowship of charity enabling us to love God with every power of the soul; (6) the transforming power of charity in family and social relationships, with its consummation in love of enemies; (7) the noble mission of charity in leading souls to God; (8) earthly goods and possessions in the service of charity.

Section I. With All Your Heart

God, who chose Israel and made a singular covenant of predilection with His people, thus describes the response of love which He expects from all His children: "Hear, O Israel! The Lord is our God, the Lord alone! Therefore, you shall love the Lord, your God, with all your heart, and with all your soul, and with all your strength. Take to heart these words which I enjoin on you today. Drill them into your children. Speak them at home and abroad, whether you are busy or at rest. Bind them at your wrist as a sign and let them be a pendant at your forehead. Write them on the doorposts of your houses and on your gates" (Deut. 6:4-9; 11:18 ff.).

The pious Israelites understood these directions literally. They carried the cherished words with them. They wrote them on their doorposts and kissed the scrolls on which this blessed commandment was written. Frequently and lovingly, they repeated these cherished words to their descendants. The most pious of the Old Testament people never forgot that *this commandment was to be written into their very hearts.*

God's covenant with Israel, which the prophets compared to the marriage contract, is also a genuine prototype of the new covenant of charity. It is in this covenant that God had opened all the treasures of His heart. Christ, raised on the cross, fulfilled the Scripture prophecy: "With age-old love I have loved you; so I have kept My mercy toward you" (Jer. 31:3; cf. John 12:32). The transpierced heart of Jesus is convincing evidence of the inestimable riches of grace and charity in God's loving heart. This heart gave its last drop of blood as an *undeniable proof of a love with "all the powers of the heart."* Christ has transmitted to us God's innermost secrets of love.

We commemorate this charity "from the rising of the sun, even to its setting" (Mal. 1:11) in the Mass and in the sacraments where we are confronted with the fulness of Christ's charity. In them, we have a re-presentation of all the truths and deeds of salvation according to Christ's own words: "I am the way, and the truth, and the life. No one comes to the Father but through Me" (John 14:6). "The heart of Jesus is the gate to the heart of God" (Pius XII, Encycl. on the Sacred Heart Devotion). Christ is not only the most perfect expression of God's personal love for us but we are given a "new heart" through His salvific deeds and the action of His Spirit (cf. Jer. 31:33). If we die to sin and rise to a new life with Christ, we are assured of a place at the heart of God, "in heaven," the kingdom of charity. Thus God revealed "the overflowing riches of His grace in kindness towards us in Christ Jesus" (Eph. 2:5-7). The charity of the Sacred Heart is a reflection of the heavenly Father's own love for us.

The charity of God not only fills our heart to overflowing, but enlarges its capacity for an ever greater share in divine love. The grace of the Holy Spirit not only stirs the inmost powers of the human heart but bestows the undeserved grace of the divine virtue of charity whereby *we are ena-*

bled to reciprocate God's love with His very own love while nevertheless this charity is all our own.

"God has first loved us" (I John 4:10; 4:19). It is not that we have chosen Him but rather that He has chosen us as His disciples (cf. John 15:16). Christ had chosen to treat us as friends by revealing to us the innermost secrets of His Father (cf. John 15:15). The words and actions of Christ "are revelations of God's heart inciting us to a constantly increasing fervor in the pursuit of spiritual values" (Gregory the Great). Through the sacrifice of the cross, Christ gave the greatest proof of love for His friends (cf. John 15:13). The transpierced heart of Christ is the most unmistakable proof of His all exceeding love of friendship. The sacramental renewal of His death and resurrection joined with the grace of the Holy Spirit is the most personal pledge of boundless love to each participant (cf. John 13:1). The message of the commandment inscribed in our heart is: "You shall love the Lord, your God, with all your heart."

Section II. With All Your Soul

The Talmud, the Jewish commentary to Holy Scripture, relates a touching account regarding the full meaning of the phrase "Love the Lord with all your soul."

When the famous scribe, Rabbi Akiba, was martyred he repeated the words of Deut. 6:4 ff.: "Hear Israel. . . ." When he came to the words: "Love the Lord, your God with all your heart," his disciples approached him saying: "Master it is enough!" His answer was: "All my life long, I was concerned about these words: 'with all your soul,' wondering when God would permit me to render my soul (that is my life) as a pledge of my desire. And now, when the opportunity is presenting itself, should I not seize it?"

Christ has given His life as a definite proof of His love for the Father and us. "Father, into Your hands I commend My spirit" (Luke 23:46). God has given us our soul and our life. He has bestowed on us the principle of divine life. Our natural life is a symbol and pledge of eternal life in and through Him. God, therefore, has a special claim to our whole life and to "all our soul" as a perfect proof of charity. He not only has an undisputed right over our physical life as His absolute property, but He also expects us to preserve our life and refrain from any autonomous disposition over it. Our life should be dedicated to God, be it in a long term service or in a swift martyrdom.

In baptism "we have been baptized into His death" (Rom. 6:4). The sacrament of anointing the sick builds on baptism and brings to fulfillment our dying with Christ. In a gracious and impressive manner we are encouraged to render proof of our sincere love for God in a confident surrender of our soul. *The loving assent to God's will in death and in the readiness for martyrdom are indeed the greatest proof of our wholehearted love.* "Love is as strong as death, jealousy is hard as hell; the lamps thereof are lamps of fire and flames. . . . If a man shall give all the substance of his house for love, he shall despise it as nothing" (Cant. of Cant. 8:6-7). Jesus demanded this charity and made it the New Law for His disciples both by word and deed, in life and in death. Whoever tries to save his life shall lose it; and whoever loses it shall preserve it (cf. Luke 17:33; John 12:25).

The Fathers of the Church considered *virginity* akin to martyrdom and in a certain sense a substitute for it, as the most beautiful testimony of the undivided and unreserved answer of charity in response to God's wonderful love and condescension. Only a heart overflowing with charity in an unreserved dedication to God can fully grasp and fulfill

the exalted Christian vocation of virginity. The renunciation of the treasures of this world, of marriage, and of family, has a tremendous impact on the life and soul of man.
This renunciation is not so much a limitation but rather a
"gain for the soul," experienced fully by those who dedi-
cate themselves entirely to God.

However, the commandment to love God with one's
whole soul does not apply only to those living in virginity.
Christians in the married state of life should be united in
charity and offer God their whole soul and all their powers,
not in spite of the love for spouse or despite family cares,
but *in* and *through* this charity and devotion for others.
Thereby all our actions in the care and solicitude for our
neighbor, in the love of husband and wife, of friends and
acquaintances, and in the appreciation of nature, will become fitting expressions of a wholehearted love for Him
who delivered Himself as a ransom for us.

The full manifestation of our loving surrender to God
will reveal itself at the moment of death. Only in the victory
of the abounding charity of Christ having died for love of
us and having risen from the dead and glorified with the
Father (cf. Rom. 8:34), may we exclaim with the Apostle:
"I am sure that neither death, nor life, nor angels, nor principalities, nor things present, nor things to come, nor powers, nor height, nor depth, nor any other creature will be
able to separate us from the love of God which is in Christ
Jesus Our Lord" (Rom. 8:35-38 ff.).

Section III. Perfect as the Heavenly Father

In the Old Testament formulation of the commandment of
charity we are given the loftiest of goals in God's own in-

vitation, namely, "to love God with our whole heart, our whole soul and all our powers." While this exalted aim is far above man's finite powers, the exhortation to "be perfect, even as your heavenly Father is perfect" (Matt. 5:48), is still more astounding and almost frightening in its challenge.

This truly New Testament commandment is in sharpest contrast to the motive of reward and punishment espoused by the Pharisees and to a Stoic and purely humanistic ethics of self-perfection. Christ's beatitudes direct us to the pinnacle of His moral teaching. He clearly addressed His "blessed" to the poor and humble, to those afflicted by sorrow, to the pure of heart, and the patient sufferers of persecution (cf. Matt. 5:2-10). He asked for a sincere charity in all sentiments, thoughts, words, and deeds (cf. Matt. 5:20 ff.); and for a complete renunciation of all ill will and violence through a loving solicitude for the welfare of our fellowmen (cf. Matt. 5:23-26). He exhorted His followers to relinquish not only their most cherished possessions but even their very eyes and members of their body if these should become occasions of sin (cf. Matt. 5:29 ff.). Christ asked for an unconditional chastity, truthfulness and fidelity (cf. Matt. 5:28; 32-37), and, above all, for an unselfish charity to our neighbor which manifests itself in love of enemies (cf. Matt. 5:38-47). All this is summed up by Our Lord in His astonishing injunction: "Be perfect as your heavenly Father is perfect" (Matt. 5:48).

Our heavenly Father who makes His sun rise on the good and the evil (cf. Matt. 5:45), and who has given His only-begotten Son for all men's salvation and has sent us the spirit of charity, wants us to be His true imitators in perfect love. Our perfection in compliance with the great commandment of the Lord implies a resolute renunciation of all egocentricity, an irrevocable giving of self to God and neighbor. "To be perfect as the heavenly Father" means a life *in, through,* and *for* the love of God, because "God is charity" (I John 4:8-16).

Yet despite the honor inherent in such a sublime ideal, the loftiness of the challenge may be frightening to human nature. Is such a challenge a reason for faintheartedness?

To the objection that this sublime ideal of perfection is beyond the capacity of natural man and in direct opposition to his sinful nature, we may point out that *such a summons is inherent in the grace of the New Testament.* Yet it can only be fully understood in the light of Christ's redeeming death on the cross and the consequent renewal of man through the action of Christ and the Holy Spirit. This exalted task is God's all surpassing gift of charity.

Furthermore, an adequate explanation of the true meaning of such a lofty challenge should obviate any danger of faintheartedness. The great commandment is not so much concerned about a strictly obliging *"Erfüllungsgebot"* * or *a commandment which must be fulfilled at all times;* its frightening challenge lies in its nature as a *"Zielgebot."* * *The latter aims not so much at the fulfilment of some minimum requirement but sets up a goal to be achieved.*

A commandment, which strictly obliges towards a minimum requirement of law, binds at all times and under all circumstances and consequently must be unreservedly obeyed by all men. Examples of such commandments are: "Thou shalt not lie," "Thou shalt not steal." There is no alternative in such unchangeable commandments. Their transgression is always sinful unless there is insufficient reflection and consent of the will.

On the other hand, *a goal-setting commandment* points

---

* Since the existing terminology: "prohibitive or negative and positive or commanding," does not fit into the author's approach, the translator retained the German "Erfüllungsgebot" and "Zielgebot." Their meaning should become apparent from the text.

to a lofty ideal. It does not draw the boundary line between sin and conformity to an obligation, but rather indicates a sublime goal to be achieved. The fulfillment of such an exalted precept may be compared to the arduous task of reaching the summit of a high mountain, which requires not only adequate preparation but also appreciable time, effort, and self-denial.

After this preliminary explanation, we shall consider the detailed prerequisites for obeying the first and great commandment of charity to "imitate the perfection of our heavenly Father."

Section IV. Charity as a Commandment

It cannot be overemphasized that the New Law in its deepest essence is not so much a commandment and an obligation, but rather the gift of charity. This is especially true of the great commandment of charity. It is just this gift of charity which *denotes a deep responsibility*. God's gifts and favors imply an obligation which requires a grateful acknowledgment. God's requests always connote blessings.

(a) As a truly New Testament commandment, the law of charity demands that the baptized Christian, endowed with the light of grace and divine charity, *always abide in charity*. "Abide in My love" (John 15:9). Action presupposes being. To be and remain in charity, however, is synonymous with the deeds of charity. The charity poured into our souls is life. Life, however, cannot continue unless it is able to manifest its activities. The deeds of charity indicate that we are living in charity. Our Lord assures us: "If you keep My commandments, you will abide in My love as I also have kept My Father's commandments, and abide in His love" (John 15:10).

(b) The great commandment of charity urgently demands that the sinner, aided by divine grace, do all in his power to *regain the charity of God.* To remain in the state of sin, in the condition of estrangement from God, is an uninterrupted transgression of the commandment of charity. The sinner has a special obligation to pray for the grace of conversion. In addition, he is required to destroy the idol of selfishness and unreasonable love for creatures so that the charity of God may reign in his heart. The sinner should cleanse his soul by an act of perfect contrition or at least prepare himself for the reception of the sacrament of penance by imperfect contrition so that his renewal in grace may give full sway to the virtue of charity.

(c) The commandment of charity implies an obligation to *meditate on God's boundless charity* because only a constant awareness of God's love is able to incite us to reciprocate such love. We should lovingly meditate on God's wonderful deeds of charity. According to the laws of psychology, frequent meditation or a constant awareness of an exalted good and beauty leads inevitably to the love of benevolence. On the contrary, it is possible to forfeit one's love and affection for a value or for a person through lack of attention. The resulting void will sooner or later be filled by other values. A human automaton, who has no time for prayer, for his Sunday obligation, for hearing the word of God and for meditating on God's wonderful deeds, shuts himself off from the commandment of charity. When lovers have no time for conversation with each other then charity grows cold, resulting in an ultimate alienation, especially at times of difficulties.

(d) The commandment of charity demands more than mere pleasure in God. A sublime piece of art or a great intellectual masterpiece may be the occasion of pleasure and satisfaction. Charity and friendship, however, presuppose *reciprocal dedication.* An intimate love-union between bride and groom presupposes a self-surrender of all the powers of the human heart. Similarly, love of God, in addition to the pleasure in the beloved, demands a total surrender and dedication.

Our unreserved surrender to God presupposes an exceedingly great charity, which nonetheless may be devoid of feelings.

(e) *The charity of God must increase.* It is not sufficient to meet the minimum demands imposed by sharply demarcated laws. Strictly speaking, such an imperfect attitude suffices for the worthy reception of the sacrament of penance, if coupled with true contrition for sin. Nevertheless, this is only the first step in the fulfillment of the first and great commandment. The perfection of charity is a strict responsibility similar to the obligations of God's commandments, although the latter may state more precisely the mere minimum boundary of the law.

Our supernatural calling imposes on us the duty "to be perfect as our heavenly Father." This, however, does not oblige us to choose the most perfect road in all given circumstances. Such an attitude would take for granted a state of perfection at the very outset of our spiritual life. By the rules of prudence, we are bound to *pursue the wisest course of action in all situations.* On the other hand, the real obstacles to perfection are likewise contrary to Christian prudence and the great commandment of charity.

The new convert or beginner in the spiritual life is unable to grasp the full height of Christian perfection to which God has called him. However, his sincere endeavor to do the will of God will bring him closer to his goal. God will lead him by degrees to the perfection of charity through both an increased understanding of his noble calling and a greater readiness to follow it.

(f) *The specific degree of perfection* of the individual soul and the manner of proving an all surpassing love of God depends not only on personal cooperation with grace, but likewise on God's loving generosity which freely endows each person according to His good pleasure. Each Christian, however, is assured of God's call to holiness in the fulfillment of the commandment of charity.

Section V. In the Community of Charity

Charity implies a sharing and a union. "God is charity" (I John 4:8). The Father and His consubstantial Word celebrate their eternal love-union in the charity of the Holy Spirit. God has deigned to reveal to us a faint ray of glory from the profound mystery of the Blessed Trinity. In the charity poured into our hearts by the Holy Spirit, God allows us to participate in His own love, in His intimate life of charity. This gratuitous participation in the love-union of the Blessed Trinity is bestowed on us through Christ and His Church. Mutual charity in human societies is an extension of God's love and may become the means and road to divine love.

1. In the Community of the Church

The love-union between Christ and His Church is so unique and intimate that it far surpasses the noble alliance between spouses. "The wound in the heart of Christ gives rise to His Church intimately united to Christ" (Hymn, Vespers, Feast of the Sacred Heart of Jesus). In Christ, her Head, and in the unceasing activity of the Holy Spirit, the Church has become the all-embracing community of the true lovers of God on their homeward journey to the eternal celebration of the triune charity of God. The militant Church, the communion of those engaged in active striving and yearning for charity, is aware of its close bonds with the triumphant Church in heaven and the suffering Church in purgatory.

The Church is the fruit of Christ's undying charity and the work of the Holy Spirit. At the same time, the charity of God and neighbor in true peace and kindness is the fruit of the Holy Spirit (cf. Gal. 5:22), who is the bond of unity. All supernatural charity is "charity in the Holy Spirit" (Col. 1:8). By His own charity, dwelling in our hearts, the Holy Spirit leads us to eternal life (cf. I John 3:10 ff.). In the Church and through the Church, He gathers us into a kingdom of divine charity, where in Christ we love both God and our fellowman with the same love of charity.

To be chosen and loved by God is synonymous with living in the community of God's own people in never ending, reciprocating love. Our participation in the tremendous charity of Christ is equivalent to our love for the Church and all her members. The Church shall become the true community of charity by means of our true love of Christ and our mutual fraternal charity.

St. Paul preferred to address the Christians: "dearly beloved in God" or "elect of God." Each of us has received a *personal call and invitation from God.* Every individual soul is given a particular name and a personal vocation. At the same time, he is the object of a singular predilection and unique charity of God. In the presence of God and in the community of the Church, man is more than a mere number. The supernatural image of God confers on man true personal dignity. Through God's special charity in Christ and the charity to which we are called, we have become personalized in a truly unique and supernatural manner. In baptism, we have received our adoption into the Church, God's kingdom of divine charity.

The full comprehension of the deep inner meaning of the name, by which God has called us, will initiate a truly personal dialogue of charity which will set us free from an impersonal existence in the masses and raise us to the community of the elect.

God has called each of us by a special love of predilection to the most intimate membership in His Church. Therefore, the full measure of our sublime calling will be achieved only to the extent of our complete cooperation in the development of God's kingdom here on earth. Our sincere desire for community spirit will manifest itself in worthy liturgical worship. From the earliest Christian times, the apostles showed great concern that Church services should retain the true imprint of charity and mutual respect without the marring effect of class distinction (cf. I Cor. 11:17-34; James 2:1-6).

It is a deplorable fact that some parishes fail to exemplify and encourage the true community spirit among their members. The rapid growth of modern cities has brought with it a comparatively speedy expansion of Catholic settlements and parishes. This poses the danger that, in large congregations of 20,000 or more parishioners, the participating members at divine services remain strangers to each other and fail to develop a sense of personal belonging and communal obligation.

In such parishes the eucharisitic celebration lacks the true character of unity and charity. Attendance at the obligatory Sunday Mass tends to be perfunctory and self-centered. For various reasons, the parishioners appear to miss the truth that both salvation and happiness are rooted in the communion of charity. Another undesirable feature of such a parish is the very manner of offering the sacrifice of the Mass: the glad tidings of the gospel remain unannounced; the greeting "The Lord be with you" finds no wholehearted response; the priest's prayers receive no reply of "Amen" from the people. Such congregations are not accustomed to community singing and praying; the administration of the sacraments lacks true solemnity and the vital experience of genuine community feeling. In this type of parish the various Church societies are characterized by narrow, self-centered interests which border on cheap competition and jealousy.

Such parishes, of course, still remain communities within the Church according to the letter of the law, but fail to represent the Church in her true image and tend to become a serious scandal, particularly to the young who are exposed to the present-day spirit of collectivism.

What are the Christian's duties in such a predicament? An escape from such a deplorable situation by moving into another parish would not solve the problem. The selection of a parish and site for a home is quite an important question. But once settled, the Christian ought to do all in his power to cooperate with all men of good will. *A close collaboration with the parish priest would aid in vitalizing the common forms of prayer and worship. Furthermore, the perfection of faith should penetrate beyond the surface of our daily life and should vitalize all our interpersonal relationships in every sphere and unit of society.*

The sacrament of matrimony may be considered a reflection and image of the love-union between Christ and the Church. The charity of God takes root and form in family life. *The Christian family* as the center of true self-sacrificing love will enrich the parish and the whole Church. On the other hand, the Church and the parish will teach family members the true meaning of charity and community spirit when the family and the Church cooperate in true reciprocating charity.

Not only the Church, but every legitimate human society is a means of diffusing supernatural charity. The experience of genuine love is a vital and significant aspect in man's spiritual and emotional development. Divine charity, gratuitously bestowed on man by God, will become a means of enriching the individual as well as the community. Through mutual charity we will glorify our common heavenly Father and aid our neighbor towards a fuller experience of both natural and supernatural charity.

2. Love of God in Love of Neighbor

A true communion of charity is based on an unreserved acceptance of each person. Reciprocal love and community spirit are inseparable entities. Mutual fraternal charity is inseparable from the love of God. Our true solidarity of charity with all men is part of the incomprehensible newness of the gospel messages. Men are able to reciprocate God's boundless love only if their love extends to their fellowmen. True love of God embraces God's children. "If we love God, and keep His commandments, we can be sure of loving God's children" (I John 5:1).

Daily experience confirms the truth based on the mystery of the sonship of God and the communion of all the redeemed. St. John calls our attention to this fact when he says: "If anyone says, 'I love God,' and hates his brother, he is a liar. For how can he who does not love his brother, whom he sees, love God, whom he does not see? And this commandment we have from Him, that he who loves God should love his brother also" (I John 4:20-21). All the charity and kindness, all the understanding and sympathy, which men can bestow on us, are basic prerequisites for a lively and deep comprehension of the truth: "I am personally loved by God." Fraternal charity disposes our own heart as well as the heart of the recipient of our love to an ever greater charity of God.

But the love of neighbor is more than a moral prerequisite for a deeper love of God. Charity, in its sincere manifestations of love of our neighbor, is the surest proof of genuine love for God. *Love of neighbor flows from a union and kinship with God* (cf. I John 4:7 ff.). Because God is charity, no one can be united to Him without loving his fellowmen (cf. I John 4:17). When we are filled with true love of God, we are unable to ignore the needs of our neighbor.

Aware of our predilection as chosen children of God, not on the basis of our own merit but rather in view of divine charity, our compassionate love for our neighbor will surmount all difficulties and survive despite his disgrace and disfigurement by sin. Since we are followers of the Crucified, our compassionate love will seek and aid the defaced and obscured image of God hidden under the misery of sin. The victory of charity has become manifest in the condescension of Christ, in His incarnation and death on the cross. Only genuine charity will bring men to the full realization and acknowledgment of this victory. True love of neighbor will dispel the darkness of sin and will aid in building up the community of charity (cf. John 2:8 ff.).

3. God's Charity, the Measure of Our Love of Neighbor

At the Last Supper, Christ referred to the commandment of charity as His own commandment (cf. John 13:34). It is truly His commandment as the composite of all His individual commands and ordinances (cf. John 15:12-17). This new and unprecedented blessed commandment, which asks

us to love one another as Christ has loved us, has brought
to fulfillment the Old Testament ordinance: "Love your
neighbor as yourself" (Lev. 19:18; Matt. 22:39, etc.).
Thereby the commandment of charity has become in full
truth the "royal law," the charter and proof of our participation in Christ's kingdom of charity (cf. James 2:8). The
observance of this commandment will be a sign of true
discipleship for all the world (cf. John 13:35).

Christ is the very source of this new charity for neighbor.
Enamored by His own love, united in the charity of His
own Heart, transformed by His Spirit, we shall love our
neighbor as Christ loves him.

Therefore, *Christ is the chief motive of our love of neighbor.* In Christ, we are all one body and one spirit as we are
called in one hope of our calling "one Lord, one faith, one
baptism" (Eph. 4:4 ff.; I Cor. 8:6; 12:6). In Christ, we have
God as our common heavenly Father and the Church as
our common Mother. He has given us the heart-warming
example of charity. "The love of Christ impels us" (II Cor.
5:14).

*Christ asks us to measure our love for neighbor against
His own love.* He gave His own life for us (cf. John 15:13).
In a similar manner, our love for Christ will enable us to
spend our life for the welfare of our neighbor (cf. I John
3:16). This readiness for sacrifice will reveal itself in a constant self effacement. "None of us lives to himself, but we
live to the Lord" (Rom. 14:7-8).

The secret of the royal commandment of charity is found
even among pious pagans, unfamiliar with Christian truths
but yet inclined to charity. Hence, the ever-ready charity
for neighbor becomes for them a still hidden but, nevertheless, royal road to the heart of God, the expression of an
effective union with Him. Christ revealed this truth in the
parable of the final judgment. To those who will ask Him:

"Lord, when did we see You hungry and feed You?" He will answer: "I say to you: As long as you did it for one of these, the least of my brethren, you did it for Me" (Matt. 25:37-40). Thus the charity of the truly God-fearing pagans is rooted in the love of God. This charity will be the beginning and the means to a heart-to-heart dialogue with God.

4. Christian Self-Love

The commandment to love our fellowmen "as ourselves" finds its deepest explanation in the "new commandment of the Lord." The true measure of our charity is not a natural love for self, although important as such, but rather God's own charity to us in His obedience unto death, which reveals both the true nature of divine love and the perversity of a narrow self-love.

More than this, enamored and transformed by God's love, we begin to encounter God in the very love of one another, because the same love of charity embraces both God, our fellowmen, and ourselves. This new manner of self-love in Christ, namely, supernatural charity, will be the measure of our love for neighbor. Christian self-love and fraternal charity, namely, the solicitude for our own salvation and that of our neighbor, are united in the charity of our Redeemer. We shall achieve the full measure of genuine self-love only to the extent that we surrender to Christ in perfect fraternal charity.

Only the road of self-denial and self-abnegation leads to authentic Christian self-love. Active charity in the community, the carrying of our neighbor's burdens, is the most basic and fruitful means of acquiring the perfection of charity.

Section VI. Our Neighbor

1. Who Is Our Neighbor?

When the Jewish lawyer asked Our Lord: "Master, what must I do to inherit eternal life?" Jesus answered by way of another question: "What is it that is written in the law?" And he received the right answer: "You shall love the Lord your God with your whole heart, and your whole soul, and your whole strength, and your whole mind, and your neighbor as yourself." Jesus confirmed the answer by saying: "You have answered right, do this, and you shall find life." However, the lawyer continued by asking: "*Who is my neighbor?*"

We should indeed be grateful for this very question because Christ's answer has clarified much doubt on the subject of one's neighbor. In the parable of the Good Samaritan, Our Lord defines in an unforgettable manner the person of our neighbor. The neighbor to the poor, mistreated pilgrim on his way to Jerusalem was, in God's plan, a Jewish priest. The priest, however, "saw him there and passed by on the other side." And the Levite acted in like manner by passing by the injured fellowman. But there was the Samaritan who according to strict Jewish standards was no neighbor but rather a member of a despised and hated race. Yet the response of the Samaritan was one of charity: "He saw him and took pity at the sight; he went up to him and bound up his wounds." His charity went beyond the minimum of rendering first aid. He made himself fully responsible for the victim until completely restored. The Jewish lawyer got the point in Christ's parable: the merciful one proved himself neighbor (cf. Luke 10:25-35).

In the parable of the Good Samaritan, Our Lord clearly indicated that neither nationality nor religion may set limits to our merciful love. We are united by the closest bonds of charity to each soul created in the image and likeness of God and redeemed by the precious blood of Jesus Christ. We all share in the common destiny of an eternal blessed possession of God. Our charity, rooted in God, must embrace all men. We shall prove our unconditional charity by helpful readiness to serve our needy fellowmen, irrespective of their nationality, social status or disposition. *Living in close union with the Sacred Heart of Jesus, we shall recognize our true neighbor in all the circumstances of our life.* Our neighbor's petitions for aid shall be met by a ready response.

2. Unequal Claims on Our Charity

Under ordinary circumstances, our closest neighbors are those related to us by the bonds of blood and affection. This is not in contradiction to the parable of the Good Samaritan. The misery of the poor, wounded fellow-Jew appealed in the first place to the priest of his own religion who certainly was expected to help him. St. Bonaventure fittingly remarks that friends, spouses, parents, and children are united by special bonds of Christian charity. In a certain sense, supernatural charity continues to take human form in a manner comparable to the Incarnation. The order of grace is not unrelated to earthly realities but permeates and elevates every natural value and power.

He who fails against charity to members of his own household is unlikely to accept as brothers in Christ the strangers who are in need. Therefore, the warning of the Apostle: "But if anyone does not take care of his own, and especially of his household, he has denied the faith and is worse than an unbeliever" (I Tim. 5:8). In a similar manner, he desires that the "members of the household of the faith" be the recipients of our special charity, although no one should be excluded (cf. Gal. 6:10).

Christian charity enlarges the heart. It unites all men in the bond of brotherhood in Jesus Christ. *It builds on our innate inclinations of love and affection.* Natural charity in family life and conjugal relationships should surpass all other loves in tenderness, ardor, depth, and sincerity because this natural human love is meant to be an expression and a preparation for a true and all-surpassing Christian charity. *Supernatural charity does not destroy the good and noble in human affections but purifies, deepens, and dignifies it while elevating it into the kingdom of divine charity.*

All charity, including filial and parental devotion, the love of friends and spouses, should be elevated and united into the charity of Christ. This *supernatural quality* will increase the power of charity over the hearts of our fellowmen and bring them closer to Christ. Friendship among Christians is imperfect and deficient if it remains at a purely natural level.

3. Even Our Enemy Is Our Neighbor

The true test of genuine Christian charity is a sincere love of those who are ill-disposed to us—our enemies. *Love of enemies is a special aspect and at the same time one of the most revealing qualities of charity.*

If our love is firmly rooted in the heart of Christ, it will develop into a benign and forgiving type of charity, able to perceive and appreciate the real problems and troubles which beset our neighbor's relations with us. We shall try to understand and overlook our neighbor's external manifestations of bitter suspicion and aversion, his evil gossip and open opposition whereby he is torturing his own soul. All this may be painful and provoking to the "old man" within us. But our heart, renewed in Christ, takes cognizance of the affliction of our neighbor in a very real and tangible way, because we are the unwitting occasion for his spiritual distress, even against our will and without our fault.

Our own happiness and eternal salvation is dependent on love of enemy. The antipathy and aversion emanating from our adversary exerts a dangerous power over our old self. Unless we aid our enemy in a spirit of lively faith we shall eventually be unable to suppress uncharitable thoughts, words and deeds. Therefore, St. Paul warns: "Be not overcome by evil, but overcome evil with good" (Rom. 12:21). Fully aware of the agitation experienced in the soul of the offended, the Apostle admonishes us to settle all disputes before sunset (cf. Eph. 4:26). The most efficacious means towards this end is a genuine love of the other which best expresses itself in sincere prayer.

In the final analysis, the issue in love of enemies is our genuine concern for *our neighbor's welfare and eternal salvation.* Therefore, St. Paul exhorts the early Christians, "If your enemy is hungry, give him food; if he is thirsty, give him drink; for by so doing you will heap coals of fire upon his head" (Rom. 12:20). This is another way of saying: Do your utmost for your neighbor, afflicted with feelings of hostility, anger and resentment against your person and shower on him that overwhelming degree of love and affection which will induce him to reciprocate your charity. The person tortured and dominated by hatred and hostility is in special need of God's blessing and our prayers (cf. Rom. 12:14).

Another consideration regarding love of enemies is *the honor of our heavenly Father and our incorporation into the Mystical Body of Christ.* Christ emphatically pronounced this truth in the Sermon on the Mount and by His personal example. He left an unmistakable proof of His love "because when as yet we were sinners, Christ died for us" (Rom. 5:8-9). Compassionate and merciful love for our opponents is the acid test of our adoption as true children of our heavenly Father, who, with unlimited generosity, embraces even the undeserving. Love of enemies is the distinguishing mark of Christians, setting them apart from "pagans" who are self-seeking in their love, because they favor those from whom they expect advantage and return (cf. Matt. 5:44-48).

The virtue of love of enemies is more than a pious counsel. It is a stern commandment with a strict and urging obligation. This law is a decisive prerequisite for our Christian discipleship. At the same time, the obligation of charity applied to love of enemies takes into consideration our weakness and imperfections. That which God expects of us is in keeping with our capacities and our progress on the road to perfection.

The law of love of enemies imposes the following obligations:

(a) *We must forgive an injustice* before the offender's implicit or explicit request for pardon. Although the guilty party has the greater obligation to make the first attempts towards reconciliation and amendment, the commandment of love of enemies and God's special invitation of grace may appeal to the charity of the innocent party, inviting him to aid the opponent entangled in the mistrust and bitterness of evil thoughts.

It is important to presume the good will and sincere intention of our neighbor unless proven otherwise. History gives evidence that even canonized saints of the Church suffered from mutual misunderstandings and consequent opposition and resistance. But, nevertheless, their charity in presuming mutual, sincere intentions greatly helped to avert the danger of animosity. The principle of ascribing a good intention applies in a special way to our relations with superiors if these have offended us or treated us unfairly. Our forgiveness and sincere charity may never be dependent on the degree of guilt incurred by the offending party. Even obvious injustices must be forgiven.

(b) *True forgiveness implies a complete relinquishing of all thoughts and memories of the wrong endured.* Neither should the injury be the subject of conversation because of the danger of evoking feelings of ill will and aversion. Failure to forget offenses and to cease harboring ill feelings makes forgiveness from the very bottom of the heart almost impossible. Nevertheless, God sees our earnest endeavor to forgive our enemies. But there is lack of a determined will towards forgiveness if the injuries and the wounds inflicted are voluntarily recalled.

(c) The sincere will and endeavor towards forgiveness implies a *readiness to aid the offender* in case of real need. The willingness to give assistance to our adversary in any real distress is a guarantee that we are not overcome by hatred and are on the road to Christian forgiveness.

(d) A further touchstone of our good will and endeavor towards Christian love of enemies is our *unaffected effort to recognize and acclaim the good qualities and accomplishments of those who have offended us.* The first step towards forgiveness is implied in the determined resolution to abstain from detracting comments about those ill-disposed towards us.

(e) We are unable to live in mutual friendship and concord with all men. At times it may even be wise to avoid the company of certain persons because of their difficult disposition and in view of our inability to cope with the situation. But we should at all times meet them with *due respect and courtesy,* especially if "our enemy" is a member of an intimate circle of acquaintances. Therefore, it would be wrong to pass him by without recognition and greeting because it might be construed as a sign of hostility.

Nevertheless, there are special and obvious circumstances which should discourage us from an exchange of courtesies. It would be unwise, for example, for the wife of an adulterer to greet and treat in a friendly manner the crafty and cunning seducer of her husband. She would be bound in justice and charity towards her husband and this unfortunate person to indicate her disapproval. However, in some instances an open and kind exchange of views might accomplish more than stern and accusing looks. This explanation indicates that prudence should guide us in the true estimation of our abilities in the total situation and in the manner of expressing love of enemies.

Section VII. Zeal for Our Neighbor's Salvation

The previous sections on charity fully apply to zeal for souls and its expression in daily life. The concern for the eternal salvation of our neighbor is not just a commandment among other commandments but rather the core of Christian charity; it is the commandment which should motivate every form and expression of Christian charity. Since this point was emphasized in the previous chapters, we are concerned here mainly with a general summary.

The concern for the salvation of souls is not a prerogative restricted to priests. It is, in a very special way, also the obligation of the lay apostle.

(1) Zeal for the salvation of others is a fundamental attitude and basic disposition inherent in the nature of being a

Christian, irrespective of social position, rank, and vocation in life. (2) There are forms of the lay apostolate which are applicable to all Christians, namely, prayer, expiation, good example and admonition. (3) In addition, consideration must be given to the special vocation of the Christian lay apostle in view of the universal priesthood and his special and unique position in the Church and in the world. (4) A distinction must be made between the universal vocation of the lay apostle as a member of the Mystical Body of Christ, and the special obligations implied in the command for Catholic action.

1. Zeal for Souls—A Manifestation of Solidarity with Christ

During a mission in a chiefly non-Catholic district I attempted to discourage a young divorced woman from remarrying and to this end sought the support of her mother. The latter, however, declared: "This is strictly my daughter's own business; she is old enough to decide for herself." To my rejoinder: "It is a question of your daughter's eternal salvation," this Catholic woman who otherwise was faithful to her religious obligations answered spontaneously: "That is strictly the priests' business!"

There is no doubt that priests are especially appointed for the care and direction of those entrusted to them. But despite this, each Christian in his own way has a definite obligation toward the eternal salvation of his neighbor according to his particular means and position in life. It is obvious that in the above-mentioned incident, zeal for her daughter's salvation was doubtlessly the foremost duty of the mother in view of her special vocation. She had the greatest responsibility for her daughter's spiritual welfare since she was the nearest "neighbor" to her daughter.

Following are some of the reasons obliging the Christian to show his zeal for the salvation of his neighbor:

(a) The most convincing reason is the impulse of *divine love* in our own hearts. God in His incomprehensible love and condescension desires to make us participants in His triune charity. In proportion to the growth of this charity, we shall increasingly desire our fellowman's share in God's love and eternal bliss. Divine charity unites us intimately to the heart of God. Consequently, as true lovers of God, we should desire with God's own heart that His love be fully reciprocated by our neighbor and ourselves.

(b) It is the *sacramental likeness with Christ* which makes us an "alter Christus." In *baptism,* as well as in the other sacraments, our soul increasingly receives Christ's imprint. Baptism incorporated us into the Mystical Body of Christ and made us citizens of His priestly kingdom. We witness to our partnership with Christ to the extent of our sincere cooperation with Him towards the establishment of God's reign of love over all men, thereby increasing the charity of God in the heart of our neighbor.

In the sacrament of *confirmation,* we receive the fire of divine charity, the Holy Spirit. If we surrender to Him, we shall understand to an even greater degree that our own salvation and our increase in grace is intimately connected with our zeal for the things of God's kingdom and the salvation of our fellowmen. To the measure of our absolute surrender to Him, we shall increasingly understand that our own salvation and increase in grace is closely allied with our zeal for God's kingdom and the salvation of our neighbor.

The sacrament of *penance* opens our eyes to the guilt and injustice of sin and the resulting detriment to our neighbor's spiritual welfare. The Church communicates to us God's mercy and at the same time, through the mediation of the priest, gives us the salutary injunction to make amends for our faults through increased fervor and zeal for God's kingdom. (See Chapter VII).

Participating in the unbloody renewal of Christ's sacrifice on the cross and united to Him by *Holy Communion,* we receive the ennobling and holy mandate to adopt Christ's sublime dispositions so that in Him and through Him we may devote ourselves to the salvation of our neighbor and the diffusion of His charity in the Christian community.

Our Christian life achieves its final consummation in the sacraments administered to the dying, especially in the anointing of the sick by which, in imitation of Christ, we offer to the heavenly Father our sufferings and eventually our dying for the salvation of our fellowmen.

2. *Chief Implementations of Zeal for Souls*

In union with Christ, the high priest, and as true children of the Church, we are to aid each other by prayer, sacrifice, patient endurance of suffering, mutual help, and good example, so that by word and deed we may achieve an ever-increasing charity of God.

(a) Our prayers will become more pleasing to God as we become less self-centered and more *concerned with the glory of our heavenly Father,* which will be enhanced by the salvation of sinners and an ever-increasing charity in the Church.

The painful realization that so many of God's children still remain in the darkness of idolatry, despite Christ's suffering and death, will be intensified in our prayer in His presence. In imitation of Christ who during His earthly life and for our salvation "offered prayer and entreaty to God with piercing cry and tears" (Heb. 5:7), we shall at the Sacrifice of the Mass entreat God's mercy for the salvation of all men, particularly those dear to us. St. Paul draws a logical conclusion from the blessed truth "that God desires the conversion and salvation of all people" by admonishing "that petition, prayer, entreaty, and thanksgiving should be offered for all mankind" (I Tim. 2:1-4).

The author gratefully recalls an incident illustrating with what spontaneity and inner necessity true prayer opens the heart to the needs of the brethren. In the ensuing flight after the capture of Stalingrad, we arrived completely unarmed with fifteen wounded soldiers at some Russian farmhouses. The good people did all in their power to make our wounded companions comfortable. They even took care of our horses and kept nightwatch for our personal safety. At our parting on the following morning, I could not help but inquire into the motives for such unselfish charity towards perfect strangers. Their answer was a marvelous testimony to their faith and love of neighbor: "We too have our sons on the battlefields," they said, "and hope for their safe return. But how could we expect God's protection for them unless we have pity on you for the sake of your own parents' prayers?"

(b) Following the example of Christ who added to His prayers the supreme sacrifice of His own life, we should mingle with our prayers and supplications the *offering of our hardships and sufferings* in sincere expiation for sin and in imitation of the sublime dispositions of the apostle of the Gentiles who could say to himself: "I rejoice now in the sufferings I bear for your sake, and what is lacking to the sufferings of Christ I supply in my flesh for the benefit of His body which is the Church" (Col. 1:24). "This is why I bear all things for the sake of the elect that they also may obtain the salvation that is in Christ Jesus" (II Tim. 2:10). No doubt, Christ's propitiation for the redemption and salvation of all men was superabundant. Nevertheless, according to His condescending mercy and redemptive plan, He permits us who are united to Him by grace and charity to participate in His own redemptive work through personal expiation and prayer. The most salutary action, in our solicitude for the salvation of a loved one, is the offering of our prayers for supplication joined with voluntary sacrifices and gracefully accepted God-sent sufferings. This is true expiation.

(c) While imploring God's mercy by prayer, voluntary sacrifices, and works of atonement, in behalf of our fellowmen, we may exercise a more immediate and direct influence on them by means of good example and exhortation. Good example is the most effective and, at the same time, most indispensable means of exercising a salutary influence on men. Good example means more than individual exemplary actions, although these may be important in themselves. The most important kind of example is that of the *truly ideal personality*, able to exercise a direct, compelling and captivating influence on others.

By the example of His own life and death, Christ has disclosed and made visible the love of the heavenly Father. He could truly say: "He who sees Me also sees the Father" (John 14:9). Since by the grace of God we have "become conformed to the image of His Son" (Rom. 8:29), we have the cherished privilege and obligation to become more and more a faithful reflection of God's own goodness. Our personality should radiate such genuine kindness, justice, purity, and self-possession that God's ineffable charity will become manifest to all men. We should become living sermons for our fellowmen as indicated by St. Paul: "Be imitators of me, as I am of Christ" (I Cor. 4:16; 11:1). Our example should be the most immediate and most effective recruiting power for the gospel of Christ.

It is a well-known fact that men of today, and young

people in particular, are to a great extent under the conscious or unconscious influence of film and TV stars. This is by no means conducive to fostering genuine goodness and affability. The spell of such unfavorable impressions will best be broken by truly amiable Christian personalities who will remind their fellowmen of Him who is the exemplar and master of all men. Exemplary parents are an invaluable blessing for the growing child who thereby spontaneously and gradually awakens to the perception of God's infinite condescension and benevolence, acknowledging: "How great must be God's love if my own parents are so good and kind."

Good example must be the genuine expression of inner maturity, charity, and kindness towards our neighbor. An obtrusive and studied kind of "setting an example" is repugnant and will provoke contradiction. It is unquestionable that the truly kind and sympathetic personality possesses genuine convincing and recruiting power.

In the final analysis, we ought to act with circumspection in consideration for our weaker brethren. A mother of a young boy told the author that on one occasion she disregarded the ecclesiastical censorship by seeing a condemned movie, while reasonably convinced that it would do her no harm. Through this action she lost the confidence of her seventeen-year old boy, who likewise went to see the particular movie. When being corrected for seeing the forbidden film, he considered his mother's rebuke a form of evident hypocrisy. No explanation was able to restore his former confidence in his mother. We should anticipate the possible consequences of our actions in regard to our neighbor and, therefore, always act with circumspection in the wise use of our God-given freedom. We will fail to become exemplary personalities unless we avoid all scandal in the total conquest of our selfish desires.

(d) Besides the unobtrusive influence of good example there may at times be need for the *encouraging and convincing power of the spoken word*, a very important aspect of human relations whereby men enter into communication and transmit their thoughts, ideas and attitudes.

In the past, when public life and opinion had an essentially Christian orientation, Catholic moral theology placed greatest emphasis on direct personal contact and influence on one's neighbor through instruction, encouragement, and correction, thereby minimizing the power of evil and making the good attractive. Yet, today, when the chief source of shipwreck for the individual is to be traced to a predominantly un-Christian and secular society, the lay apostolate assumes a new and vital role in uniting the efforts of all the good towards shaping man's environment according to truly Christian principles and thereby restraining the tides of irreligious mass opinion.

The important task of the lay apostle to influence and shape public opinion requires more than good will. Constant effort and continuous training are required. All personal endeavors and actions must be carefully scrutinized in order to avoid the repetition of mistakes and to improve techniques. An efficient means for this purpose is the systematic exchange of ideas and experiences as practiced, for example, by the Legion of Mary and the YCW (Young Christian Workers' Organization). A sympathetic perception and awareness of the needs and characteristics of different social groups and individual personalities, as well as an empathic understanding and appreciation of the psychosocial development of each individual, is of paramount importance for success in the lay apostolate. A different approach is required for the person embittered through serious scandal occasioned by so-called practicing Catholics or priests than is needed in dealing with the irreverent cynic who reviles all that is holy because it is opposed to his way of thinking. In larger gatherings it may at times be necessary to openly embarrass a scoffer of religion or a proponent of immoral principles in order to defeat his purpose and to safeguard the good of the group. Yet this negative approach should always be objective without implying dislike or personal offense. A subsequent private interview with such a person might forestall bitterness of heart.

3. Fraternal Correction in the Spirit of Charity

On the whole, we should always try to take a positive attitude toward our neighbor's difficulties. It reveals a deep understanding to penetrate to the real and hidden concern of our neighbor and to use this insight whenever we have to correct his erroneous ideas. Ordinarily, we are lost from the start if we try to contradict him and prove ourselves victorious. More essential than the psychological approach and skill in debating—although important in themselves— is a sympathetic understanding and absolute unselfishness.

It is well to postpone all corrections and admonitions until our excitement and anger have subsided. No good will come from an angry retort or correction. This applies in a very special manner to those engaged in education and in positions which obligate them to admonish and correct the misdemeanor of others. Whoever bears such responsibility should remember that the point at issue is not the correction of every individual fault. If there is no danger of an immediate repetition of the mistake it is wiser to make no point of it and to utilize an opportune occasion for a gentle reminder and admonition.

Immature adolescents are especially vulnerable to continuous corrections. It should be remembered that wine in the process of fermentation needs much time and confidence. Many shortcomings and signs of immaturity will eventually be rectified under favorable conditions. Far-reaching effects could be achieved by providing inspiring ideals for the young rather than by reprimanding each wrongdoing.

Strictly speaking, the obligation for fraternal correction and exhortation exists only if there is a question of serious scandal for a third party or a need for forthright action as the only possible means for converting the sinner. It would be wrong, however, to restrict our charity to these minimum demands of fraternal correction. In the true spirit of Christian charity, mutual regard among friends demands reciprocal encouragement towards progress in virtue, through graciously given admonitions regarding faulty dispositions and imperfections. Any personal constructive influence on our neighbor and any improvement in his spiritual milieu is of far greater significance than repeated corrections.

4. The Special Apostolate of the Laity

The sacrament of ordination sets the priest apart from the rest of the priestly race of God and invests him with sacred powers for the fulfillment of his special mission for the salvation of souls. As Christ's messenger and servant he has been appointed to minister to the faithful through the administration of the sacraments and the preaching of the word of God, and thereby lead them to the "full maturity of Christ." Yet the priest's office in no way minimizes the lay person's responsibility for the extension of God's kingdom. Only their united efforts and genuine cooperation in the fulfillment of their respective vocations will meet the needs of God's kingdom.

The Christian lay person is not a "second class Christian."

According to the dictionary the word "lay" refers to one outside a particular profession or specialty. The ordinary layman is certainly not a specialist in moral theology. But it is in his domain to prove himself expert in the practical aspects of Christian living. In the positive Christian sense, the term "lay" (Greek *Laós*) signifies one who is an active member of God's kingdom "a holy nation, a people that is God's possession" (I Pet. 2:9).

The priest is singled out for a special mission by his ecclesiastical superior. Like Abraham, he is called from his father's house and country and sent into a new territory. The layman, on the other hand, finds his apostolic field in the particular station in life assigned to him by divine Providence.

The apostolate peculiar to the layman should not be confused with "Catholic Action" which will be discussed under a separate heading. The layman's immediate and chief vocation is connected with: (a) the Christianization of family life; (b) his contribution to the economic and social life of contemporary society; (c) his efforts towards the alleviation of the all-embracing need for pastoral sociology in the care of souls.

(a) The Family as a Pastoral Unit

Analogous to ordination, the sacrament of matrimony equips the Christian spouses and parents for their conjugal and parental duties in the family. Their responsibility for souls does not demand a change in position and station of life but rather confers on them an apostolic mission for their own particular sphere of action.

The Christian spouses not only mutually enrich each other by their reciprocal pledge of love and fidelity as they are joined in the chaste wedlock ordained by God as the sanctuary of life and the source of grace and blessings for them; but they also bind themselves indissolubly and irrevocably in an ever-faithful and fruitful charity. In this sacred pledge, the Christian spouses are the true ministers of the sacrament and thereby enter into a life-long "apostolic" alliance.

This sacrament of charity is intended to be a faithful reflection of Christ's own covenant with His Church through the spouses' reciprocal charity and devotion converging in selfless love for their children. As the bride and groom administer the sacrament of matrimony to each other in loyal service to Christ and His Church, they pledge their mutual assistance towards eternal salvation. They are for themselves and their children the most immediate and nearest spiritual advisors. Their apostolic obligations, far from being superimposed, are an integral part of their conjugal love and mutual responsibilities. All that is beautiful, good, joyful, and charitable, all that is difficult and disagreeable in marriage and family life, is part of their life's vocation and God's salvific plan. All is meant to lead them to a fuller realization of God's personal and intimate love.

The spouses are to grow in divine charity through the tenderness, sincerity and ardor of their devotion, as well as through their mutual understanding and reciprocal patience and solicitude. God has created man—both male and female—according to His own image and likeness (cf. Gen. 1:27). God's very essence is charity. Consequently, man, created in the personal likeness of God, is bound to reflect the immense charity and benevolence of His creator. Each person is called to become a true copy and mirror of God's bountiful love, and, in a certain sense, another incarnation of His transcendent charity. Husband and wife are aided through the sacrament of matrimony to come closer to this fond expectation of God. Their mutual charity and magnanimity provide a foretaste of the inexhaustible goodness and mercy of God, which will be fully revealed to us in heaven.

Accordingly, both father and mother are charged with true "priestly" commitments in regard to their children. They are for them the chief messengers of the glad tidings of the gospel by way of an unforgettable example of genuine fatherly and motherly charity which is, at the same time just and kind, devoted and merciful. The parents' attitude toward their children is of paramount importance for the children's concept of God and the resulting relationship and attitude toward their heavenly Father.* The overly strict and narrow-minded father may for a lifetime obscure and distort for his child the true picture of the heavenly Father. Although the scrupulous person may intellectually acknowledge God's goodness, he, nevertheless, subconsciously lives in constant fear and dread of the heavenly Father's tyranny.

Family members meet their spiritual obligations to each other not only through kindness and consideration in daily life but, likewise, through prayer, counsel, timely warnings and a genuine spirit of faith in the various problems and vicissitudes of life.

Parents are the first messengers of divine love for their growing children. They are more than mere preachers and monitors. It is their specific prerogative to transmit to their children God's will as a loving expression of His beneficence. One of the primary objectives of this book is to aid parents toward this worthwhile goal.

Even the most difficult and complex situations of the married state will appear in their true perspective if parents begin to realize that, by reason of the sacrament of matrimony, they assume reciprocal responsibilities for each other's salvation.

* A definite example of this was cited in our discussion on scrupulosity.

Should there be a question of adultery, the innocent party should refrain from showering the unfaithful spouse with self-righteous accusations. A searching self-examination might prove more salutary for both parties. The guiltless one should make concessions beyond the minimum requirements of strict justice, according to which the blameworthy spouse could be refused the privilege of the marital act to which he has lost all right and claim. The chief criterion for action should be the question of the spouse's eternal salvation. Questions like these should be answered: "What effect will my conduct produce on both spouse and children? Which actions might be most conducive to their spiritual well-being?" Such charitable concern and solicitude for others will tend to soothe the injured spouse's turbulent emotions and effect a truly liberating influence.

The life of Paul Rubens' mother presents an exemplary and magnificent testimony of unshaken loyalty in the face of evident infidelity. While her husband, Jan Rubens, was in custody for an illicit love affair with the Princess of Oranien, she not only averted capital punishment for him but even shared the prison cell with her guilty husband. During this time of incarceration, she gave birth to her son, the famous artist. A letter to her husband written shortly after the publication of the scandal is a touching document of Christian charity:

My dear Husband:

. . . regarding the pardon which you implored of me, be assured that I shall gladly offer it to you as often as you desire it, provided you shall love me as before. I desire no other amendment than a love similar to my devotion because this will be able to rectify everything. I am glad that I have received some news concerning you because my heart is perturbed by our separation

*and the constant yearning for your presence. I have
written a letter of petition in your behalf. May God
grant that my intercession for you may have the desired result. . . . Many times each day our little ones
ask God's protection for you so that we may soon be
united again. . . . My dearly beloved husband, this
very moment the mailman delivered your latest letter.
It gives me great joy that you believe in my sincere forgiveness. How could you even suspect me of being so
hard-hearted as not to forgive? It would simply be
impossible to oppress you further while you are in
such great distress and anxiety from which I would like
to save you with my own blood. . . . How could true
love so suddenly give way to hatred? How should I not
be able to forgive so small a debt in comparison with
my own trespasses for which I daily implore our heavenly Father's pardon by the prayer: "as we forgive our
trespassers"? I am living in great anxiety and hope.
Yet, I trust in God's help. I shall confide everything to
Our Lord—imploring Him with all my heart. Likewise,
our children are praying for you and are sending
their love with the fond hope of reunion. Our Lord
knows we desire your return. Written on the first of
April between 12 and 1:00 A.M. Please do not call
yourself "unworthy husband" because all is forgiven.*

Your faithful wife,
Maria Rubens

There are certain situations and circumstances which
make common life simply impossible, such as continued
infidelities, a perverted will of one of the spouses, or any
similar weighty reasons. In the most extreme case, namely,
that of planned seduction of the children by one of the
parents, the only solution is complete separation. But even

under these circumstances, the sacramental bonds persist and the spiritual concern of the Christian spouse must survive the upheavals of separation. Further regulations of their external relationships and the question of possible reconciliation and the resumption of common life are real problems. These can be solved satisfactorily only in view of the spouses' mutual concern for each other's eternal salvation and in consideration of Christ's own love for His Church.

(b) The Realms of Worldly Activities

God's kingdom is not of this world. Proficiency in worldly endeavors and progress in civilization and technology cannot hasten the coming of God's reign. But the kingdom of God has revealed itself in and for this world. This was discussed at great length in the chapter dealing with the freedom of the children of God and the yearning of all creation towards participation in this blessed liberty (Chapter II). The previously stated truths fully apply here, although seen from a different point of view, namely, that of the specific mission of the layman.

In the light of the lay apostolate every province of human endeavor appears in its true perspective. Man's career provides the chief scene for the exercise of his conscious efforts in the implementation of Christian attitudes and principles. On the other hand, man's outlook, aspirations and character are greatly influenced and colored by the world at large and by his particular vocational sphere of activity.

The Christian ought to consecrate his daily activities by means of a good intention and by positive actions which proceed from a sincere disposition. This alone, however, is insufficient. Our ultimate goal in contemporary society, be it in the work-a-day world or in the political, economic, or cultural system, is a sincere acknowledgment of God's undisputed supremacy in every realm of human endeavor and enterprise for the safeguard of Christian life and morality.* The various provinces of human society and the existing social forces must either receive the genuine imprint of Christian ideals or else they will become barriers towards religious truths and retard the life of faith. There is only one alternative—*we shall either be the "salt of the earth" for the entire social structure or be ourselves corrupted.*

Our faithful endeavor to regulate our occupational activities should be in harmony with our supreme aim in life, that is, to live for God's glory and the salvation of others. This very goal is indicated in the two objectives underlying every apostolate and is implied by the twofold aspect of charity expressed in the great commandment. The Christianization of society will facilitate man's efforts to work out his salvation.

It follows that many factors determine an individual's degree of responsibility, even in secular matters. Thus, it is obvious that an able architect in a leading role is in a far better position to promote family living through improved housing projects, than the plain workman, who makes a comparatively limited contribution in the building of particular houses through his conscientious work and helpful suggestions.

Labor and trade unions and, in particular their leaders, exert a far-reaching influence in the socio-economic world within the framework of the existing technological and political advances and in the exploitation of the possibilities of mass psychology. A good example of this is the flexible workweek which produces such significant effects on

* In my two books: *Soziologie der Familie—die Familie und ihre Umwelt* and *Macht und Ohnmacht der Religion—Religionssoziologie als Anruf* (Otto Müller Verlag, Salzburg 1956), I have tried to present substantial evidence for the deep and far-reaching social influences towards good and evil.

family life and divine worship. Each individual employee, technician, capitalist, and common laborer shares the responsibility for epoch-making decisions through his support and membership in such organizations.

The sincerity and reliability of individual workmen, artisans, farmers, and officials add to the fuller realization of a genuine Christian concept of one's vocation which is not conditioned by selfishness but, rather, by a readiness for service to one's own family and the common welfare.

In the past decades, slogans such as: "Art for art's sake," "Pure politics," "Self determination of economics," and the most dangerous of all, "Religion is a private affair," brought about a departmentalization of man and ignored the reciprocal influence between religion and the different realms of society. There existed a deplorable blindness to social conditions. Consequently, our conscience reproaches us the more severely today.

Two shocking historical experiences should serve as eye openers for all those of good will. What was the result of that teaching about the self determination of economics? Early capitalism, which built a tremendous economic system and enormous wealth at the expense of the working man, was unscrupulous enough to employ women and children for more than fourteen hours a day and thereby ruined the physical and moral health of innumerable people. Even more horrifying was the encounter with an autonomous political system. Christians have likewise contributed to that horrifying experiment of Nationalism because they were deluded by the slogan that politics is a private affair and consequently unrelated to religion and morality. The resultant heart-breaking and shocking happenings have deeply affected every family and realm of life.

It is the special vocation of the lay apostle to work towards a more concrete realization of the Christian philoso-

251 THE SOUL'S INTIMATE ENCOUNTER WITH GOD

phy of life in the various social systems, especially in the fulfillment of the particular duties of his vocation.

Thus, for example, it is of paramount importance that the Christian artist be not only a perfect master in his special field with a deep insight into its own inner laws, but that he should likewise possess the ability to make it a worthy expression of a Christian way of life. It is by no means irrelevant for the salvation of souls whether men are presented with authentic Christian art or unworthy religious reproductions. Neither is it immaterial whether we are exposed to an art which is the expression of a spirit of collectivism, of unbounded arrogance, and arbitrary existentialism, or one which is the embodiment of genuine Christian temperance and devout reverence for God, for life, and the dignity of man.

Even dialectic materialism is aware that the various realms of our human existence form but one unity. The adherents of this particular ideology are, therefore, opposed to any expression of art, science and economics which contradicts their own philosophy of life. Catholic teaching on the transcendence of supernatural realities and the interdependence of all earthly domains is in direct opposition to a philosophy which advocates a dependence on economic systems. A clear concept of this difference and the distinction between the duties of the priestly office and the mission of the laity safeguard a greater independence and initiative for the different walks of life than the system of Karl Marx.

The whole realm of worldly affairs is, strictly speaking, the domain of the Christian laity. The teaching authority of the Church considers itself inadequate in socio-economic matters and cultural activities. The Church will interfere only if there is a question of faith and morality. Her positive directions therefore are fundamental and general so that the Christian lay person may use his own initiative, inventions, and abilities for a concrete and relevant realization of the Church's moral teaching. In answer to the repeated complaints of Catholic laymen that the Church's teaching on sociology is given in terms too broad and indefinite, we wish to clarify the Church's teaching position and the laity's responsibility in this particular sphere of action. The *Church's teaching in the moral religious realm must be fully applied and utilized by the lay person in his own specialty.* It is his duty not only to consider the basic principles of morality but also the tenets of his specialty, and the existing possibilities and demands of his particular time and sphere of action.

(c) The Layman and His Apostolic Work for the Environment

The Catholic lay person is not only the "object" and aim of the Church's apostolic endeavor but, as a member of God's holy people, he is also an important *participant in the Church's ministry* for souls through his active cooperation in the liturgy and his personal contribution towards a communal spirit in the celebration of the eucharistic services. In addition, his specific vocation demands his wholehearted endeavors to influence the social structure through direct and indirect efforts for the salvation of his neighbor by means of the re-Christianization of the environment.

In past Christian times the emperors received the Church's blessing and anointing in preparation for their exalted worldly mission. This points to the fact that the people of those days were fully aware of the religious implications connected with the proper execution of civil authority. In a similar manner, the knighting of nobles was a religious ceremony. Christian nobility, the leaders of that time, were to be impressed with their responsibilities in the discharge of their office and their contribution to the social order and the salvation of souls. In our age of democracy and improved educational opportunities for the general public, the responsibility of the Christian laity has become more pronounced. It is the laymen's duty to incorporate the Christian spirit not only into their private lives and vocations but also into all realms of public life.

The foundation of the apostolic work for the environment has been discussed to some extent in relation to the family unit. In a manner analogous to the sacrament of matrimony which bestows a specific mission within the confines of the family, the sacrament of confirmation confers a priestly mandate for active participation in community affairs. Through this sacrament the lay person is both called and anointed for "the battle against the enemies of salvation." St. Thomas Aquinas says that the confirmed has received an official mandate and power "to express in words his faith for Christ." In the spirit of this great doctor of the Church, we add that protestations of faith must not only be in words but also in actions through the shaping of public life by systematic efforts towards influencing public opinion.

In view of his Christian vocation and his particular station in life, the lay person has a special responsibility for the urgently needed pastoral sociology in the care of souls. His place is in the most strategic position—but he is not a subordinate soldier nor an instrument of the clergy. The latter is not expected to give him minute directions but rather a sound foundation of religion. The prerequisites for the lay apostolate are expert knowledge of his particular vocation and a keen perception and an open eye for concrete possibilities towards the realization of Christian principles in his particular vocational sphere. While the teaching authority of the Church is responsible for providing the lay apostle with adequate religious instructions and techniques for the apostolate, the clergy, on the other hand, is dependent on the lay apostle's suggestions regarding problems and difficulties arising from concrete situations in life.

The chief virtues in pastoral sociology, the care of souls, relate to a spirit of responsibility and readiness for service and collaboration. Concern for the environment is essentially an obligation of the Christian community. The comment of Bishop Emanuel Larrain (Chile), made at the Second World Congress of the Lay Apostolate in Rome in October 1957, underscores this point: "The rediscovery of the social and communal character of salvation is one of the great advances in today's life of the Church and her influence on the world. The chief characteristic of the apostolic-minded Christian of today is his outspoken understanding of the mystery of the Christian community. . . . The community spirit has taught man to realize the dependence and interdependence of community life and the liturgy of the Church."

Summing up his thoughts, the Bishop affirmed: "The Christian lay apostle of today is fully aware that the apostolate is not something marginal or supplementary to the Christian life but rather the Christian life itself, if it is fully and truly conceived and lived."

(d) Catholic Action

Today the term "Catholic Action" is often used in its wider sense, denoting all the activities of the lay apostolate. In its specific and intrinsic connotation, however, it refers to an *organized participation of the laity in the apostolate of the hierarchy*. This implies a service of cooperation under the direction of the episcopate. Such is the essential meaning of Catholic Action as presented and developed by Pope

Pius XI. The distinctive mark of Catholic Action is its authorization by the hierarchy which assumes final responsibility for the guidance of its activities. *Catholic Action delegates certain mission privileges to the laity which are not directly implied in the general apostolic vocation of a layman.*

Pope Pius XI's definition of Catholic Action emphasizes its mandate from and supervision by the hierarchy. This official or formal character of Catholic Action is not meant to destroy the lay person's initiative. It represents a co-operative endeavor of the clergy and laity in which the layman seeks the advice and approval from his ecclesiastical superior in regard to effective methods of apostolic procedures in his specific sphere of activity. The final decisions in all Catholic Action rest with the bishop who, in turn, may seek the advice of qualified lay people. Laymen are not mere instruments but co-workers with the hierarchy. This is evident from the fact that individual lay persons are directly charged with the care for souls, as for example, catechists, and pastoral assistants.

Catholic Action, without doubt, can be one of the most extraordinarily effective instruments for apostolic work in the improvement of the environment, if we think in terms of its direct and indirect apostolic endeavors for souls. The basic principles and rules for Catholic Action are a guarantee for concerted action and harmonious collaboration between the clergy and the laity.

The subdivision of Catholic Action into separate units directly responsible for the apostolate of the neighborhood must be distinguished from the "Universal Catholic Action" which originally was organized around the four natural states of life occupied by men, young men, women and young women. Its chief aims are to broaden the religious foundation of Catholics and to influence public opinion.

Pope Pius XII in his address at the Second World Congress of the Lay Apostolate expressly declared that Catholic Action cannot lay claim to a monopoly of the lay apostolate, not even the organized apostolate, much less the apostolate in general. Although Catholic Action by reason of its purpose attempts to select the elite for membership, this does not mean that other organizations are of less value.

Since Catholic Action by its very nature is concerned with apostolic endeavors which are not the specific duties of the laity, we may rightly conclude that the Christian is not automatically bound to join it. This does not exclude the possibility that an individual, for reasons of some special graces and in view of the existing needs of the time, may feel the clear call and desire to follow the invitation of his bishop.

There are individual missions of the lay apostolate which are not embraced by Catholic Action because the latter is a united apostolate. In addition, there are the apostolates of the neighborhood which are so specifically the domain of the lay person that they cannot be incorporated into Catholic Action without ignoring the true nature of the laity and of Catholic Action.

Subdivisions of Catholic Action may have secondary aims and activities, such as cultural, socio-economic, and social service responsibilities. Yet in all these domains, the spiritual direction from the hierarchy is less competent than in direct apostolic work for souls.

Unions, cultural societies, athletic organizations and scientific societies, information centers, etc., are by reason of their nature lay unions with lay responsibilities even if, according to their particular objectives they work for the Christianization of a particular sphere of action. Social welfare agencies and organizations, by reason of their close connection with the care of souls, may become incorporated into Catholic Action, although this is not a requisite for the attainment of their goals.

In the framework of Catholic Action all political parties and their subdivisions must be excluded. Catholic Action may never deteriorate into a political party without losing its very nature, neither can any political party become a subdivision of Catholic Action, even though it may be a Catholic party. Nevertheless, while Catholic Action is essentially non-political, it would be wrong for it to abdicate its right of influencing the formation of the Christian conscience in regard to the socio-economic and political spheres of life.

Similarly, just as the teaching authority of the Church takes position on all the vital questions of culture, economics, and politics, in so far as these concern faith and morality, so should Catholic Action take a stand on these questions.

In conclusion and for the sake of avoiding misunderstandings, it should be pointed out that Pius XII in the above-mentioned address expressly stated that the issue of differentiation between the terms "Lay Apostolate" and "Catholic Action" is still under discussion. If ecclesiastical documents occasionally refer to the "Lay Apostolate" within Catholic Action as the so-called "specific" apostolate and all other forms as the "general" apostolate, this should not be contradictory to the general use of the terms, according to which the activities of Catholic Action are not the chief domain of the laity. Yet the activities within Catholic Action deserve, in a special way, the name of apostolate according to the original meaning of the word which refers to a special commission; because Catholic Action has, in addition to the commission implied in being a Christian, an additional express mandate for this particular work.

Section VIII. The Earthly Gifts in the Service of Charity

God's charity is *all-embracing;* it is His own gratuitous gift to man and implies a sublime mandate. The love of God is genuine only to the extent that we love our neighbor for God's sake. Moreover, both the lover and the beloved must be seen in their total personality. Sincere concern for our fellowman's eternal salvation presupposes positive action toward the alleviation of his physical needs. It is impossible to spend the energies of our soul in the service of the destitute without sharing our material possessions with them. "He who has the goods of this world and sees his brother in need and closes his heart to him, how does the love of God abide in him?" (I John 3:17). All endeavors for the salvation of our brother and all our assurances of imploring God's help for him, appear false and incredible unless we relieve his physical and economic needs within the limits of our means.

The hearts of the underprivileged easily become embittered less by the deprivation of the necessities of life than by the awareness that others, living in superfluity and luxury, are insensible to their needs. "And if a brother or a sister be naked and in want of daily food, and one of you say to them: 'Go in peace, be warmed and filled,' yet you do not give them what is necessary for the body, what does it profit?" (James 2:15-16).

In view of man's essential unity of being, we must remember that his bodily needs are closely interwoven with his spiritual well-being. Lack of true compassion for the needy neighbor is proof that Christians have failed to see their brothers and sisters in the poor and underprivileged. Repeated experiences of injustice and callousness, in regard to the bare necessities of life, prevent the poor from arriving at a perfect perception of God's own goodness. Persons thus harmed by consistent lack of charity are unable to enter into supernatural communion with Christ without the liberating power of brotherly charity. The apostolic nature of generosity to the needy is evident in its dual effect of externalizing the supernatural love and preparing the way for a fuller participation in its experience.

The goods of this earth are the gifts of a universal Father in heaven. They are, therefore, meant to strengthen the fraternal bonds among God's children.

Within the family itself the mutual concern for temporal welfare necessitates a constant expression and deepening of reciprocal charity. Financial independence among family members, in which each member owns and disperses his individual resources, is a definite indication of an increasing family disorganization.

Even beyond the confines of the family circle, men in their respective vocational and social endeavors are dependent on each other for services and remunerations. This social and economic interdependence should strengthen the fraternal bonds between men of various classes. Do we ever acknowledge the contribution from others towards daily living, as for example the peaceful enjoyment of a meal?

We should gladly spend our energies and the goods of this world in the service of charity because these are gratuitous gifts from the goodness of God. Above all, we should endeavor to perform our social and economic duties in the true spirit of justice and charity. Our almsgiving remains controversial, unfruitful, and devoid of respect for human dignity if it is not based on the principles of social justice.

The economic liberalism, postulated by Adam Smith (1790), refused to acknowledge the competence of the norms and ideals of morality in the realm of economic affairs. The proponents of this theory argued that the economic system is dependent solely on the labor market's supply and demand which, in turn, is motivated by a generally understood desire for profit. The practices of early and later Capitalism, built on such a false doctrine, have revealed the horrible consequences of selfishness in the ensuing disorders in both economic and social affairs.

Our firm belief in the God of charity, who has given us our earthly possessions in the manner of a trust, evokes sincere gratitude to Him through thoughtful consideration and charity for our neighbor. Authentic Christian self-love is impossible without a deep and sincere love for one's fellowman.

Our willingness to share our earthly possessions in the service of charity will give us an increased appreciation of them as gifts of our heavenly Father's generosity.

Consequently, it is clear that the Christian's final criterion in economic affairs cannot be based on profit. This does not deny the right to private gain in business, because without it, business cannot survive and flourish. Yet the final purpose of the entire economic structure is the good of society in service, production, and collaboration. Mere calculation for profit and an unbridled boundless desire for wealth creates discord and serious problems in the socioeconomic order. The spirit of charity, on the other hand, will lead to reasonable moderation in the production and use of commodities and to social justice between employer and employees.

The Christian's foremost aims in the social structure are justice and charity. These are more important than economic progress and wealth which the Communists espouse as their goals and as the supportive structure of their relentless system. For the Christian, economic security and the necessary goods of this world are means rather than the end of their striving. Paradise does not consist in earthly riches. *The socio-economic life of the Christian must be marked by the imprint of God's charity.* In all realms of our endeavors we are to give testimony of our complete support and implementation of Christian principles. In the final analysis, it is God and His charity which are at stake in the wise use of earthly possessions.

In an atmosphere of gross selfishness, material possessions assume both a disintegrating force and an enslaving power. There is a great danger in today's selfish world which ignores the beneficent love of our common heavenly Father, that the very gifts of God's charity, intended to express our love for God and fellowman, will be turned into "the mammon of iniquity," a dangerous idol which thwarts our adoration and love of God (cf. Matt. 6:24 ff.).

Avarice and the restless quest for a higher standard of living possess the true characteristics of idolatry (cf. Col. 3:5; Eph. 5:5). The hearts of those who idolize "the standard of living" become impenetrable to the word of God and blind to the needs of their neighbor (cf. Matt. 13:22). Therefore Our Lord warns: "Take heed and guard yourself from all covetousness, for a man's life does not consist in the abundance of his possessions" (Luke 12:15). We can free ourselves from the snares and the servitude of the mammon of iniquity and prepare ourselves for our entrance into the eternal kingdom of charity by the wise use of the treasures of this world in a genuine spirit of charity (cf. Luke 16:9).

The material goods of this earth will direct our attention to the higher treasures of salvation. *Through the deliberate utilization of earthly possessions in the service of charity, we shall free our hearts for an undivided love of God.* Although we are engaged in business transactions like other men, we Christians should aim at a lofty interior detachment (cf. I Cor. 7:30 ff.). Thus we prepare for Our Lord's second coming, and provide ourselves with the burning lamp of charity by perfect trust in divine Providence in all the vicissitudes of our daily existence (cf. Matt. 6:25 ff.).

Christ's prediction of events on the final day of judgment makes the exercise of Christian charity in the use of material goods the decisive mark of true discipleship (cf. Matt. 25:34-46).

The Fathers of the Church have repeatedly emphasized the truth that it is impossible to participate worthily in the great eucharistic sacrifice of charity, which unites us all in a common brotherhood, without loving and honoring Christ in our needy brethren. *The communion of charity around the altar must prove itself in genuine solidarity by means of mutual concern and assistance.*

5 adoring charity

Faith and hope will be turned into the joyful vision and irrevocable possession of God; into the adoring vision of God's holiness; and into the jubilant possession of His love. In the theological virtue of charity we have received "the greatest" of all treasures (I Cor. 13:13), the pledge of eternal happiness. Charity, the theological virtue which alone continues throughout eternity, should even in this present life assume and possess the essential characteristics of the charity of heaven as a jubilant adoration of the all-holy and supremely lovable God. Our true relationship to God is fittingly expressed in the phrases: *adoring charity* and *loving adoration.*

The kingdom of God will be consummated on that final day when "every knee shall bend of those in heaven, on earth and under the earth," and "every tongue shall confess that the Lord Jesus Christ is in the glory of God the Father"

(Phil. 2:10-11). All men will eventually bend their knees,
but, whereas the elect will do it in great rejoicing over the
victory of God's love, the reprobates will consider it their
insufferable punishment to acknowledge Jesus Christ as the
supreme Lord. Love is the criterion underlying the separation of the two groups which will bend their knees. *True
worship of God in loving adoration is the prerogative of the
children of God.* Its core is charity. The love of God's children, adopted in gratuitous and selfless charity, is essentially
an adoring, glorifying, and grateful love.

SYNOPSIS OF CHAPTER FIVE

(1) Through Jesus Christ, God has revealed to us His
name, His holiness and His glory. In Jesus Christ, He has
given us a high priest who is able to render worthy praise
and adoration. (2) God has revealed to us His name and
His holiness and, in addition, He sanctifies us by means of
His sacraments. They unite us interiorly with Christ, our
high priest, so that our adoration of God becomes completely absorbed into His own priestly actions. (3) The
center and climax of all divine worship is the supreme
sacrifice of Christ and of the Church which, at the same
time, is our own sacrifice. (4) The appropriate attitude
for an adoring love in the presence of God is that of humble
readiness for unselfish service towards our fellowmen. (5)
The active works of charity form an important part in divine
worship. (6) In addition to the celebration of the holy
mysteries and the administration of the sacraments, the
chief forms of worship are prayer, the vows and the oath.
(7) The priestly Christian people sanctify the whole of
human existence and, therefore, also man's work-a-day
world and vocation. Sunday Mass, the center of worship,

elevates man's entire life by making it an act of praise to God, his Creator and Redeemer.

Section I. Christ Our High Priest

What is man's contribution to the adoration and glorification of God? Man possesses nothing which is not a gift from God's infinite goodness. Furthermore, by his separation from God through sin, man has become incapable of surrendering himself totally to God in virtue of his own power and merit, although, strictly speaking, he is God's rightful possession.

Man, by his very nature, is a worshiper. His vocation, as a loving adorer, is part of his royal dignity. If man refuses to abandon himself to God, he still remains an adorer, but stripped of royal dignity, he becomes an idolater in the abasing slavery of sin. Man's superstitions, his feverish striving after a higher standard of living, and his impatient desires for an earthly paradise are manifest proofs that he is bound to pay homage to creatures if he fails to adore God. In the first chapter of his letter to the Romans, St. Paul points to the truth that man's vices and aberrations of heart are rooted in the deplorable fact of his refusal to acknowledge himself as an adorer of the true God.

In a similar manner, as man has received his existence from God, so does all his dignity, honor and happiness consist in the joyful surrender of his life to the service and adoration of God.

"The heavens declare the glory of God" (Ps. 18:2). Sinful man fails to understand the full implications of this statement. He shows himself incapable of participating adequately in the song of praise arising from the rest of creation. Man's heart has become hardened by pride and inordinate desires. For this reason, God in His great mercy has revealed anew His infinite glory and given us a new mediator in the person of His only-begotten Son. Our Savior, while on this earth, did not only acknowledge and magnify His heavenly Father's power, wisdom and providence in the beauties and marvels of nature, such as the flowers of the field, the birds of the air and the roaring of the sea, but He proclaimed in a marvelously new manner God's glory in the world and gathered all creation into His own hymn of praise.

1. *Christ's Revelation of Our Divine Adoption*

In Christ and in virtue of His superabundant merits, we are entitled to address the Lord of heaven and earth with the confidence-inspiring and loving title of *"Father."* God's immeasurable greatness has revealed itself in the marvelous condescension of permitting His creatures to address Him by name. God has entered into personal and intimate communion with us through the revelation of the *Name of Jesus* and all other titles referring to Him, such as "Christ" (the "Anointed"), and "Emmanuel" ("God-with-us").

The supremely great God is no longer the anonymous God. He has uttered His divine Word filled with His own glory. In this Word, made flesh and dwelling among us, we have received all grace and salvation, as was indicated by the *Name of "Jesus."* Thereby God has drawn us into close and intimate communion with Himself and has made us the "co-celebrants of His love," according to the expression which Duns Scotus used to indicate the essential meaning of Redemption and Creation.

This sublime and blessed mystery of our salvation has already been revealed to us in the name which God had made known to Moses when He said to him: My name is Yahweh, I am "who am," which is synonymous with the Lord of endless ages, the mighty Helper ready to aid His people (Ex. 3:13 ff.). The mystery of God's name has been disclosed to us in an even more exalted manner in the name of "Jesus" (Savior) and "Emmanuel" (God-with-us). *The most blessed revelation of God's name is contained in the privilege which entitles us to address the Father of Our Lord Jesus Christ as Our Father.*

In His loving colloquy with His heavenly Father, Jesus has both vividly demonstrated and effectively taught the true meaning of God's name in that beautiful prayer called the "Our Father." We are permitted to enter into dialogue with God. Our prayer is a participation in the jubilant exclamation of Jesus: "I praise You, Father, Lord of heaven" (Matt. 11:25; Luke 10:21).

The adoration which God desires above all other things is the confident invocation of His name, the true elevation of our hearts and the united veneration of His paternal goodness, because He is, in all truth, our common father just as Jesus is the salvation of all mankind.

2. Christ, the Revelation of God's Holiness

The all-holy God had been offended through the sins of mankind. He, before whom the Seraphims tremble in the fervor of their ardent charity, is obliged to insist on His own glory before man, the work of His own hand. The prophets repeatedly proclaimed that our God is a jealous God, a God whose unique holiness precludes His tolerance of the unholy claims of falsely imagined deities. The atoning sacrifice offered in our behalf by Jesus Christ, our High Priest, is the supreme revelation of God's infinite holiness.

The all-holy God desired to redeem mankind in a manner

which would be a revelation of His incomprehensible holiness and at the same time be the means of man's salvation. God's outraged holiness and justice demanded an atonement in due proportion to the magnitude of the offenses incurred. God accepted the propitiation of His only-begotten Son whom, in the bounty of His love for men, He gave to redeem the world. The depth and intensity of Christ's expiatory suffering not only give us an understanding of the enormity of man's guilt and the iniquity of sin, but at the same time clearly proclaim the all-consuming holiness of God. At the sight of that supreme paschal sacrifice of the God-man, the earth trembled, the rocks split asunder, and the sun darkened. The heavenly Father allowed the truly awful consequences of sin to work full havoc in the whole being of His divine Son who suffered frightful agony unto the sweating of blood and who, outraged by injustice and spittle, bore the tortures of whip, thorns, and nails. Christ's very soul was plunged into utter desolation. "My God, My God, why have You forsaken Me?" (Matt. 27: 46). This exclamation from the lips of the sinless Lamb of God is undeniable testimony of God's bounden zeal for His own glory.

Yet from the very abyss of anguish created by man's iniquity, Our Lord addressed all mankind in the compassionate words directed to the sorrowful women of Jerusalem: "If in the case of green wood they do these things, what is to happen in the case of the dry?" (Luke 23:31). In Christ's Passion, the unholy heinousness of sin as well as the resplendent glory of God's holiness and justice has been proclaimed. On the day of the last judgment all the world will receive final proof of God's splendor and justice. Then all shall behold, as on the Mountain of Golgotha, although with faces unveiled, the mystery of the all-holy and just God who has prepared salvation for those who honor Him and who cannot but repudiate those who refuse Him loving adoration. This will constitute the terror of the damned that they, too, must bow their knees in honor of God, while with gnashing of teeth they are forced to acknowledge the glory of Our Lord Jesus Christ (cf. Phil. 2:11).

3. Christ, the Revelation of the Glory of His Father

From all eternity, from the beginning of creation, the Son of God has enjoyed all glory with the Father (cf. John 17: 24). He has made visible the glory of His heavenly Father: "He who sees Me also sees the Father" (John 14:9). God's holiness and immense charity have become manifest in the humble appearance of the Son of Man, in His words full of kindness and in His magnificent deeds but, above all, in the bruised and broken body of the Crucified. Its resplendent beauty has become evident in the glorious resurrection of Christ and will fully appear on the last day of His second coming in the glory of His Father to judge all mankind "with great power and majesty" (Matt. 24:30; Luke 9:26).

It was in our behalf that the heavenly Father's voice announced: "I have glorified You, and will glorify You again" (John 12:28). The glory of the Father, voiced from all eternity in His consubstantial Word, was bestowed in full measure on the human nature of Christ. The Incarnate Word uttered His own response in the loving surrender of His life to the Father's will and glory. The Father, in turn, honored His Son by shedding His own splendor on Christ's glorious resurrection and by appointing Him the final judge at the consummation of the world. "Once everything has been brought into subjection to Him, then the Son Himself, in order that God may be everything to everyone, will be brought into subjection to the Father who subjected every-

270

thing to Him in order that God may be all in all" (I Cor. 15:28).

God's revelations are intended for our salvation through Jesus Christ that we may reverently acknowledge His name and pronounce it with loving veneration while rejoicing in His presence. We may wonder whether we sinful creatures are allowed to utter the inexpressible name of God and approach the burning ocean of God's holiness. Are we, simple men, capable of rendering worthy praise and adoration to God?

We are enabled to do all this in Jesus Christ, our high priest and mediator, to whom we are united and made conformable through the sacraments. God has not only given us an external revelation of our heavenly Father's name, holiness, and magnificence, but He has opened our very hearts and has sanctified us so that "through Him, with Him, and in Him, we may offer worthy adoration and praise to the Father in the unity of the Holy Spirit (Canon of the Mass).

"Hallowed be Your Name!" This should be the foremost petition in all our prayers because God Himself has not only revealed His holy and lovable name to us but has also placed us within the radius of the full splendor and glory of His own holiness through the sacraments.

Section II. The Sacraments—the Fountains of Our Sanctification and Salvation

Since worship of God is essentially man's response to God's revelations of His own holiness and glory, God has to give us both the understanding and the inner disposition for the desired response.*

* Cf. my book: *Law of Christ*, Vol. II, pp. 111-204; 269-281.

The basic prerequisite for a faithful and reverent perception of God's glory is a spirit of humility. Enslaved by pride, selfish concerns, and the desire for earthly possessions, man is unable to comprehend God's ineffable holiness and majesty. "Blessed are the poor in spirit" who, in a salutary way, grieve over their own sinfulness (Matt. 5:3 ff.). These poor and lowly ones readily submit to the saving revelations of God's merciful holiness. This is the victory of grace for which God has first to supply the most essential prerequisite, namely, *the grace of a humble faith and a childlike adoring love.*

God has endowed our souls in a marvelous manner for an appropriate response to the revelation of His name, His holiness and His magnificence. The interior disposition required for worthy adoration and worship of God is given to us through those sacraments which imprint on our souls an indelible character (baptism, confirmation, and holy orders) as they *give us participation in the royal priesthood of Christ.*

Through *baptism* we are reborn to a new life and, therefore, we are "living stones, built thereon into a spiritual house, a holy priesthood, to offer spiritual sacrifices acceptable to God through Jesus Christ" (I Pet. 2:5). Those who believe and acknowledge God's revelations "shall be honored" (I Pet. 2:7). God has saved us from the darkness of sin and placed us in the marvelous light of His holiness and glory. God has given us a High Priest who leads the way into the sanctuary of true worship so that our lives may become a song of praise to His name. He has ordained us in Christ to a priestly race. Through baptism we become incorporated into the Mystical Body of Christ. In the important task of our salvation and sanctification we have become "a chosen race, a royal priesthood, a holy nation, a purchased people" (I Pet. 2:9).

As baptized Christians we are privileged and enabled to offer both loving and worthy adoration to God. Baptism entitles us to a place before God's altar and in the choir of the singing, praying, and worshiping community of the faithful. Through our active participation in the sacrifice of the Mass, we gratefully acknowledge our membership in the priestly race of God. By a special grace and an indelible imprint on our soul, baptism obliges us to make our whole life a worthy expression of divine worship.

Similarly, the *sacrament of confirmation* imprints on the soul a special character and imposes the ennobling obligation of the apostolate. It makes the Christian an official witness for Christ in this world. St. Thomas describes this mission as one with "a so-called official power." The Christian's function in public life consists in a personal participation in the establishment and extension of God's kingdom on earth through timely apostolic endeavors in improving man's moral-religious environment. All apostolic endeavors receive their dignity and importance when seen as true acts of divine worship offered to God by the faithful who have been sanctified by the Holy Spirit.

Since the Holy Spirit is the special gift from our glorified risen Savior, we receive in confirmation the "power from on high" to make manifest our risen Lord's glory in the social, vocational and political spheres of life. We should remember that *baptism and confirmation* are indispensable foundations for our participation in divine worship. These sacraments give us a share in the priestly work of Christ which was accomplished on the cross. In view of the sacramental sanctification in baptism and confirmation, the most painful and difficult aspects of our life, such as failures and reverses, should be directed toward divine worship. These acts of atonement are more important than external power, easy victories, or an undisputed position of the Church in public affairs. The cross constantly admonishes us to overcome all the secret temptations of the old man to constantly seek self instead of God.

The *sacrament of ordination* confers on those specially called by God the full participation in the priesthood of Christ, our High Priest. In virtue of the singular powers entrusted to them, the priests are to collaborate with Christ as living instruments in the sanctification of the Christian community and in offering to God sacrifice and praise for and with the people. The ordained priest alone has the power to change bread and wine into the body and blood of Christ. He alone has the power to forgive sins and to anoint the sick. The bishop alone confers the priestly powers in the sacrament of ordination. The object of the priesthood is the sanctification of the entire people of God and, hence, the glorification of God.

The remaining sacraments, although they do not imprint a permanent character on the soul, nevertheless, accomplish in it a special sanctification and transmit an inner ability and, consequently, a particular mission for the worship of God.

Through the *sacrament of matrimony* the spouses are "ordained" and commissioned to sanctify themselves and their children through mutual charity, patience, solicitude, and conjugal chastity and thereby make their family a "miniature church" (St. John Chrysostom). The married life and the entire domain of the family should be a means of worthy adoration of God, the Creator and Redeemer, and thus give testimony before men that family life, the work of the most tender love, is a vital concern for God's honor.

The *sacrament of anointing the sick* is intended to give us the grace to unite our suffering and resignation with the Passion and supreme sacrifice of Christ, so that all pain and anguish may become part of Christ's own oblation as a worship of thanksgiving, praise, and expiation as well as a petition for the salvation of our neighbor. This sacrament of anointing the sick will bring to fulfillment the task entrusted to us in baptism: the Christian is to die to all selfish desires and strivings in order to live and to die solely for God. "For if we live, we live to the Lord, or if we die, we die to the Lord" (Rom. 14:8). The person anointed with the oil of heavenly consolation and spiritual strength receives the pledge of eternal participation in the glory of Christ's resurrection in which both body and soul will share.

The *sacrament of penance* makes us poignantly aware of our obligation towards holiness of life, in virtue of the sacraments which imprint on our soul an indelible mark and in view of our participation in the Eucharist. The soul of the baptized and confirmed Christian carries the spiritual seal of Christ's priesthood. Mortal sin as a revolt against God is in direct contradiction to the royal sonship of God. While his soul has received the indelible imprint for divine worship in spirit and in truth, the sinner debases himself to the enslaving idolatry of self and the devil. He thereby renders himself unable and unworthy to pay God the homage of an adoring love. Even the external good works of the sinner are not meritorious for heaven nor do they possess the intrinsic character of divine worship like the virtuous actions of the children of God. The sinner refuses to pay homage to God. In sacramental confession, we demonstrate our readiness to offer God true adoration and worship. God purifies and absolves us in this sacrament of boundless mercy. Thereby God enables us to rejoin the community of His priestly race in the celebration of the mysteries of salvation and in the reception of Holy Communion.

By their very nature *the sacraments imply a loving adora-*

tion of God. They are fountains of grace and salvation because they enable and obligate us to devote our lives to God's glory. We are to grow in God's grace and charity in order to render Him worthy adoration; we are to devote ourselves to humble and loving adoration of His holiness and to the jubilant praise of His majesty in order to grow in the love of God. The sacraments will become genuine worship and sanctifying encounters with Christ in proportion to our wholehearted devotion to God's cause.

Section III. Our Share in the Sacrifice of Christ and the Church

Christ's supreme sacrifice rendered the greatest possible homage to God the heavenly Father. The eternal covenant of charity between God and redeemed mankind, between Christ and the Church, was sealed and ratified on the cross. In His sacrifice of loving adoration and charity, Christ, our High Priest, chose His Bride, the Church. He entrusted to her the work of gathering into unity all the scattered children of God for loving adoration of their Creator. He desired to establish an adoring and active community of charity in the Church through the renewal of the sacrifice of the cross. As a pledge of His abiding love, Christ has left to His Church the legacy of the holy sacrifice and the sacrament of His perpetual presence.

In the sacrifice of the Mass we become one with Christ in the most perfect adoration of the Father. At the same time, we are united with our brethren in an intimate communion of love. The fruit of Christ's sacrifice is "communion," a sublime union with Christ and all those who are united with Him. This union finds fitting expression in the celebration of a common worship. The unity among Christians means, above all, a common love and worship in and with Christ.

The Holy Eucharist, more than all other sacraments, proclaims the fact that our entire existence is sanctified. Our greatest dignity and honor consists in having a High Priest through whom we may offer ourselves to God in thanksgiving, praise, propitiation and petition. Through Christ, our Redeemer and our High Priest, all barriers of sin are torn down as we truly live in Him.

In Holy Communion, the sacred banquet of love, we encounter Christ in the most tender and intimate embrace. Christ speaks to us through the eloquent language of the sacraments and the inner inspirations of the Holy Spirit. He communicates a personal message to each soul, saying: "All My adoring and self-sacrificing charity in the presence of the Father is meant for you." Yet He speaks to us as members of a community. Our personal encounter with Christ can take place only in the congregation of the faithful, the priestly people of God. In union with Christ we are permitted to address the heavenly Father as *Our* Father. Yet we shall be able to offer fitting praise to our universal Father only in an authentic union of charity with our brethren. In the sacrificial banquet of love we experience the divine paradox: our life will grow more uniquely personal the more fully we enter into the true family spirit of the Christian community; we will become more intimately united with each other in an adoring charity before God the more fully we penetrate into the deep significance of God's universal Fatherhood and the meaning of our personal uniqueness before God.

In the holy sacrifice and in the eucharistic banquet we encounter God's beneficent love: "of His fulness we have all received, grace for grace" (John 1:16). Each grace implies a sacred trust to act according to Christ's own example (cf. John 13:15). The more completely we are conformed to Christ in truly selfless service, the more worthy and efficacious will be our participation in His own sacrifice.

In keeping with our exalted vocation and our common responsibility in striving after perfection, we should try to enter into the sublime intentions of Jesus Christ, our divine High Priest. Thereby, our worship of adoration, praise, and thanksgiving will become the most efficacious means towards sanctification. In community singing and praying we honor our heavenly Father in an authentic spirit of charity which breaks all barriers of personal preferences, social positions, and political affiliations.

Christ's supreme sacrifice, bequeathed to His beloved Church, becomes our very own sacrifice in Holy Mass. Yet our participation is completely dependent on our willingness to enter into Christ's sublime intentions. In a similar manner, as the earthly life of Christ, from His conception to His death, tended towards the final sacrifice on the cross, so must our life be completely under the influence of God's holy will: "Behold I come to do Your will, O God" (Heb. 10:9). We should imitate Christ's own example, who, during His entire life, even unto His supreme sacrifice on the cross, steadfastly pursued His Father's will. In perfect imitation of Christ, our life should take its orientation from the eucharistic celebration at the altar and thereby become an acceptable offering to God in humble adoration and in a loving service of charity. The sacrifice of the Mass is not only the climax of our worship of God but also a grace-laden mission to a life of selfless service to God and neighbor.*

* Such is the teaching of the Fathers of Vatican Council II when, in article 10 of the Liturgy Constitution, they affirm that "the liturgy is the summit toward which the activity of the Church is directed; at the same time it is the fount from which all her power flows. For the aim and object of apos-

Christ's resurrection is the undeniable proof that His sacrifice of atonement was pleasing to His heavenly Father. Christian hope, in the expectation of a final resurrection and consummation in heavenly bliss, demands a consuming zeal for God's honor and glory. In union with Christ and in conformity with His eucharistic intentions, we feel assured of God's gracious acceptance of the sacrifice of our life and death. This shall find its supreme consummation in our own resurrection from the dead.

Section IV. Humility and Adoring Charity

1. The Humility of Christ

In the administration of the sacraments and our active participation in Christ's sacrifice of the Mass, the very law of the imitation of Christ has become imprinted into our hearts with the fiery letters of the Holy Spirit: "Have this mind in you which was also in Christ Jesus, who though He was by nature God, did not consider being equal to God a thing to be clung to, but emptied Himself taking the nature of a slave and being made like unto man. And appearing in the form of man He humbled Himself, becoming obedient to death, even to the death of the cross" (Phil. 2:5-8). The Son of Man divested Himself of all His glory and majesty by His infinite condescension in the incarnation, thereby making Himself subject to all creatures. He can truthfully say: "I am in your midst as He who serves" (Luke 22:27). In the full awareness of His sublime dignity He addressed His disciples: "You call Me Master and Lord, and you say well, for so I am" (John 13:13). It is sig-

---

tolic works is that all who are made sons of God by faith and baptism should come together to praise God in the midst of His Church, to take part in the sacrifice and to eat the Lord's supper."

nificant that the glorified appearance of the risen Lord on the final judgment day will bear the marks of His humble subjection: "Therefore God has also exalted Him and has bestowed upon Him the name that is above every name" (Phil. 2:9).

The true glory and dignity of the Christian as a "chosen member of a priestly race" is based on humility. This explains why humility is the only road whereby we honor God and obtain a personal share in His glory.

2. Humility Is Rooted in "God's Superabundant Charity"

By reason of his inborn pride, man tends to consider humility as the composite of all that is lowly and worthless. Yet Our Lord Himself has revealed to us the true dignity of Christian humility in the mystery of the Incarnation, in His sacrificial death on the cross and in His first beatitude: "Blessed are the poor in spirit."

According to St. Augustine, all humility flows from "the superabundance of God's charity." *In the Incarnation, God has humbled Himself to the abyss of our nothingness because of His boundless charity.* Humility is the royal road and the daring venture of the invincible love of God which drew the Son of Man from the highest throne of heaven to this vale of tears. Christ's humility condescended to the poorest and lowliest of men. It led the way to the pinnacle of Golgotha, to the very climax of the most unselfish charity, without the fear of losing anything.

The attitude of humility disposes our heart for the worthy reception of God's graces and condescending charity. A basic prerequisite for sharing in God's blessings is an openness of heart based on sincere humility. God has favored us by His love and has enabled us through humility to participate in the interior life of the Blessed Trinity. This sublime life is continued in Christ's sacrifice and is to be proclaimed to the world through our personal participation in the sacrifice of the Church.

God is gratuitous charity. From all eternity, the father, in the abundance of His own love, gives Himself to the Son. Both Father and Son give themselves mutually in an intimacy and abundance of love which is the person of the Holy Spirit. God yearns to give Himself to His creatures, neither from a want in charity nor from a lack of happiness, but rather from the eternal blissful abundance of the charity which Father and Son celebrate in the unity of the Holy Spirit. God resists the proud by the very nature of His holiness and majesty. Our Lady fittingly proclaims this truth. Mary, the humble handmaid of the Lord, who had received an overflowing measure of His grace, jubilantly sings: "He has scattered the proud in the conceit of their heart. He has put down the mighty from their thrones and has exalted the lowly" (Luke 1:51-52). The same principle is expressed in Our Lord's brief but impressive words: "Whoever humbles himself shall be exalted" (Matt. 23:12).

3. Humility in Giving and Receiving

Humility frees us from the chains of false self-love and self-sufficiency. It turns our eyes to the things which are truly great and lovable. Above all, humility prepares our heart for a *grateful and graceful acceptance of God's gifts.* Out of our own resources we are poor in charity. We are utterly dependent on the charity which we have received.

The creature's humility consists in a humble acknowledgment of his complete dependence on God. All that we are and possess is a gratuitous gift from the Creator. The greatest and most undeserved gift of God is our divine sonship.

In view of this fact, our *prayers of petition and thanksgiving* should become true *expressions of humility*. The more we have received from God's charity the easier it will be for us to acknowledge with unbounded gratitude and rejoicing everything as a gift of God's generosity: "We give You thanks for Your great glory."

God desires to enrich our souls by means of His condescending charity in order to make us participants in His divine humility. Christ's humility is not based on a lack, but rather on an abundance of charity. Truly great charity is the gratuitous gift of divine bounty, which, in turn, obliges the recipient to a still greater humility, thus making him capable of a self-effacing charity. A truly great and unselfish humility is rooted in a sublime charity. It is characteristic of charity to become enriched through selfless giving. Humility is the power which makes us truly free for perfect adoration of God and unselfish service to God's children. It thereby disposes our hearts for a constant growth in charity.

The humble person reverently opens his heart to everything supernatural and sublime and thereby grows in likeness to it. The proud man, in an attempt to exalt himself, constantly looks down on those below him to emphasize his own supremacy and thereby sinks into ever greater depths of spiritual poverty. The proud man never loses sight of himself whether he prays or is engaged in almsgiving. His actions always aim towards self-glorification. He wants to make himself important. Charity, on the other hand, is essentially a selfless giving. Only a complete forgetting of self in all charitable deeds makes the giver grow in the very charity which he diffuses. This is the meaning of Our Lord's words: "He who loves his life, loses it; and he who hates his life in this world, keeps it unto life everlasting" (John 12:25). Our Lord emphasized this same lesson, not only in words, but above all by His own sacrifice on the cross. His unselfish love must become the law of our own interior life. In true conformity with Jesus Christ, our High Priest, we ought to render due homage to God and a selfless service to our fellowmen in order to participate fully in God's boundless riches of charity.

4. True Dignity in Serving

Humility derives its efficacy and beauty from charity. Genuine charity makes us see and acknowledge the good qualities in others even if these should be embarrassing to our pride. The proud person, on the other hand, lives in a constant anxiety about being placed in the shadow by the excellence of others. Pride may even see a threat to personal glory in the special gifts and graces of one's neighbor. Man's genuine dignity as a creature is jeopardized by his proud assertion: "I will not serve."

Reverent charity, the queen of all virtues, begets humility. The humble man rejoices in his total dependence on God as well as in his neighbor's graces and merits. Humility is completely dedicated to God's glory and the service of others. Only a truly humble and adoring love of God makes us comprehend the length, breadth, height and depth of God's condescension and of our own stupendous exaltation by God. The joyful awareness of God's ennobling charity gives us the strength for selfless service.

Humility derives its genuine dignity from charity because without charity all service is synonymous with servitude. Even divine worship may degenerate into a form of slavery if it is not carried out in the state of grace and in the spirit of sincere humility and charity. Without charity all service loses its charm and beauty.

Charity enables the humble soul to render a gracious and

joyful response to God's special invitations. It would indeed
be a hidden form of pride to disdain God's lofty challenge
instead of placing all trust and confidence in His all-sufficing charity and power. Humility is always ready to accept
and carry out God's special missions. It is faithful in little
things and trusts in divine grace if God should demand the
more difficult; it is ready if He invites the soul to follow Him
on the steep and narrow road leading to the heights of perfection. God's special gifts and graces tend to make the
humble soul aware of its own nothingness: "He who
is mighty has done great things for me, and holy is His
name" (Luke 1:49). As a royal race and a priestly people
of God, we have been called to the most exalted and joyful
service through humility.

5. *Humility Is Truthfulness*

Humility is truth. This principle points out our true relationship to God, that is, a respectful attitude of friendship
and a loving dependence on His power. Our misery is so
profound that despite our good will and sincere efforts, it
constantly endangers the virtue of humility and hence jeopardizes our exalted dignity and our adoring charity for God.
In this present life of exile, humility is subject to temptations
and hence remains imperfect. It is of the essence of this virtue to recognize the real and possible dangers of pride. The
person actively engaged in acquiring humility will try to
overlook the shortcomings of his brethren because of the
realization of his own weakness. Thus he will escape the
temptation of exalting himself above others. The humble
man will acknowledge God's gratuitous gifts with great
gratitude and joy. He shall see these as loans or talents entrusted to him for God's glory rather than as means for
personal enjoyment. The grateful acknowledgment of our

God-given dignity is an essential element in Christian humility. Yet this knowledge must be accompanied by a sincere rejoicing in the excellent qualities of our neighbor. Sincere joy in the virtues and the success of others is pleasing to God especially if it is accompanied by sentiments of grateful praise to the Author of all good gifts. Such an attitude of gratitude further inclines the humble to render glory to God and a loving service to his neighbor who is in need of his help.

The sincere disposition of humility in one's dealings with God and fellowmen gradually renders the soul completely unbiased in regard to personal merits. Consequently, humility is the prerequisite for a true self-love which really is a love of self in God. In heaven, when our humility will find its consummation in an adoring love of God, we shall rejoice in all perfection whether found in ourselves or in our neighbor, because in heaven all things will be possessed and enjoyed in God.

Humility, likewise, is truthfulness in action. It would be contradictory to acknowledge ourselves before God as poor sinners and unworthy of grace, if we did not possess the firm determination to submit ourselves to God and His plans. It is of the essence of an adoring love of God to love His divine will regardless of the mode and manner in which it reveals itself. Humility enables us to acknowledge and adore God's permissive will even in the most disagreeable circumstances of our life. An ardent avowal of our sinfulness before God is impossible if, at the same time, we resent even the slightest contempt on the part of our neighbor. He, who is able to accept humiliations in the sincere acknowledgment of the truth that he receives more honor from God than he deserves, will be able to imitate our crucified Savior who prayed for His enemies.

The humble person gladly relinquishes undeserved honors. He does not abuse when he is abused; he does not boast; he does not prefer himself; he does not bear a grudge, because his life is ruled by charity (cf. I Cor. 13). Wherever there is charity, that precious gift of God's condescending goodness, we also find humility. Conversely, authentic humility is found only when charity has taken full possession of the heart.

Christian humility is the fruit of the charity of Christ who, in abject humility, became obedient to the death of the cross for our sake. Christ's own charity towards us carries the distinguishing mark of humility. St. Augustine exclaims: "The most glorious road is charity, but only the humble are able to tread it."

Section V. Worship of God in Active Charity

Our previous discussions on Christian living and the New Law have pointed out the close relationship between genuine love of God and authentic love of neighbor. Sunday after Sunday we participate in the most profound expression of divine worship, which the Mystical Body of Christ offers while assembled around God's altar. It should be emphasized that the works of charity in daily living are, in their deepest essence, genuine forms of divine worship. This applies to all acts of mutual love and helpfulness in our interpersonal relationships with family members, friends, and those encountered in our apostolic endeavors.

God is glorified in a special manner by Christian unity and harmony. Christian concord bears witness to the mystery of charity which is celebrated in the sacraments and in the eucharistic sacrifice. This is the mystery of God's own charity in the bosom of the Blessed Trinity, which was revealed to us by Christ and in which we participate through grace. In the high-priestly prayer before His death, Christ prayed for His Church, symbolized in the congregation of His apostles: "However, I do not pray for them alone; I also pray for those who through their preaching will believe in Me. All are to be one; just as You, Father, are in Me and I am in You, so they, too, are to be one in Us. The world must come to believe that I am Your ambassador. The glory You have bestowed on Me I have bestowed on them, that they may be one as We are one, I in them and You in Me. Thus their oneness will be perfected. The world must come to acknowledge that I am Your ambassador, and that You love them as You love Me" (John 17:20-23).

The sacerdotal dignity and consecration of God's holy people is a blessed participation in the love-union of the Triune God. Only to the extent of our mutual cooperation and collaboration in daily life can we convince the world of God's abiding love and Christ's redemptive deeds. This solidarity in grace will manifest itself in mutual love and harmony.

An extremely painful wound in the Mystical Body of Christ is the lack of unity and harmony in Christendom. Each Christian should be distressed by the discord of separation which also greatly impedes missionary work and activities in pagan countries. We ought to do all in our power to resolve the difficulties of disunion by our united prayers and by great charity toward our separated brethren. We should try to make the Church a more perfect City of God wherein all Christians are to find, in full truth, their Father's house, providing genuine charity and a worthy celebration of the divine mysteries. We ought to do away with all detracting formalism at divine worship. A mere routine, mechanical performance in our pious practices will prove to be a scandal to our separated brethren. Although in questions of doctrine we may not relinquish the least fragment of truth, we ought to meet our separated brethren with the greatest possible charity as instructed by Christ Himself: "By this will all men know that you are My disciples, if you have love for one another" (John 13:35).

At no time should we overemphasize the differences arising from historical developments which are unrelated to basic principles of faith. An important prerequisite for our mutual collaboration towards unity is a thorough understanding of Christian doctrine. It is deplorable for Catholics to try to impose on their separated brethren certain beliefs and practices which are not founded on dogma.

An example may illustrate this point. It was on the occasion of blessing a mixed marriage that the bride who was not a Catholic confided to me: "I would have joined your faith a long time ago if it were not for the teaching that Latin is the exclusive language in which Holy Mass can be celebrated." The answer I gave this woman was: "Your feelings on this point are quite legitimate but I hope you do not consider me a bad Catholic if I agree with you. There are many priests and even Church dignitaries who are confirmed in their belief that the use of Latin in the liturgy is unfavorable for a wholehearted participation by the faithful who are unfamiliar with this language." Years later this same woman converted to Catholicism despite her reservations regarding mere externals in religious practices. In this respect the Second Vatican Council has made favorable decisions.

Section VI. Forms of Worship

By his very nature man is an adorer. The Christian should aim to respond to this natural disposition and supernatural calling towards "a worship in spirit and in truth" (John 4:23ff.). This requires a piety which disposes the soul towards a total self-surrender to God. This piety finds its expression in: (a) prayer, (b) vows, and (c) under rare circumstances, oaths.

1. Prayer

Prayer is a dialogue with God, a communion in word and charity. It is the expression of our union with Christ and our adoption as children of God. True prayer is expressed in the name of Christ and the charity of the Holy Spirit. It is the glorification of God's holy name—the name of our heavenly Father and Our Lord Jesus Christ. In prayer we place our entire trust in God and show our readiness to relinquish for God's sake all that we are and possess.

(a) Communion in Word and Charity

God has called us by our personal name. He has inscribed on our souls the magnificence of His grace and the mark of His consecration. He Himself lives within us. Grace has made us vital members of the Mystical Body of Christ and participants in the divine nature. We have been accepted into the blessed dialogue between the Father, the Son, and the Holy Spirit. This sublime calling has been revealed to us in the significant and deeply mysterious words of Christ: "He who loves Me will be loved by My Father, and I will love him and manifest Myself to him . . . and We will come to him and make Our abode with him" (John 14:21-23).

Prayer, in a certain sense, is the necessary and natural expression of our intimate and personal union *with* God and *in* God. Every truly personal communion, by its very nature, tends to express itself in language and in acts of charity. Even the love-union of the Triune God is an alliance of love eternally spoken in the Word and breathed forth in love. The fact that we ourselves are enveloped in God's own eternal dialogue of love finds its most fitting expression in prayer, in the mutual loving discourse with God. God speaks to our soul. He opens our ears that we may hear in the manner of disciples and children of God. His divine operations of grace are words full of love and tenderness which place the divine imprint on our life. He Himself enables us to speak to Him in response to His own invitation: "And because you are sons, God has sent the Spirit of His Son into your hearts, crying, 'Abba, Father'" (Gal. 4:6).

Prayer, aided by grace, makes us realize the deep significance of our divine adoption. Our response to God's boundless charity is the surrender of our heart, the answer of filial, grateful love. We address God as "Our Father!" This prayer contains all the blessedness which Christ, Our Lord, enclosed in it when He exclaimed: "Father, glorify Your name" (John 12:28). This name contains all the charity which God has bestowed on us through Jesus Christ. Yet this prayer also manifests the immense holiness and dignity of God which Jesus Christ has revealed to us on the tree of the cross. Therefore, our divine Master adds the phrase: "Who art in heaven." God is the Unique, the Supreme, and Holy One before whom the Seraphims tremble in reverent awe. The disciples whom the Lord had taught to pray recalled the words of the Old Testament preacher: "Be not hasty in your utterance and let not your heart be quick to make a promise in God's presence. God is in heaven and you are on earth" (Eccl. 5:1).

Encouraged by sacred precepts and divine institution we recite the "Our Father" before Holy Communion as the eucharistic grace before the banquet of love. The phrase: "Our Father who art in heaven!" expresses both a jubilant charity and the most humble adoration. The reverent remembrance that God is the God of heaven does not detract anything from the confidence-inspiring name "Abba," "Our Father." The greater our reverence before the all-holy God, the more keen shall be our joy in the realization that He is "our" Father and that we are His children. The attitude of reverence and confidence, adoration and charity, makes our prayers truly pleasing before God and gives us a foretaste of heaven's joy.

Prayer is meant to be a heart-to-heart colloquy in humble and joyful love, the expression of a union sealed by charity and expressed in the spoken word. Hence, under no circumstances may prayer deteriorate into formalism. Christ has taught us the "Our Father" as the perfect description of our union with God. He has given us in this prayer the great themes of our dialogue with God and, at the same time, a formula for community prayer. But it was not Christ's primary intention to give us a definite prayer formula but, rather, general directions regarding the manner and content of our dialogue with God. If the primary aim of Christ's teaching on prayer had been the insistence on an inflexible formula, the Holy Spirit would have prevented the evangelists from recording the "Our Father" in different words while yet retaining the same meaning (cf. Matt. 6:9 ff.; Luke 11:2 ff.).

Formal prayers are important and even necessary for community prayer in divine worship and in the family. We need the sublime prayers taught by Christ, the Church, and the saints, so that through them we may learn how to pray. Yet, under no circumstances, may our personal prayers be confined to the mere recitation of routine prayer formulas. Our community prayers, as well as our private prayers, will become truly living and worthy expressions of our sentiments only when we practice authentic interior prayer. The meaningless and mechanical recital of prayer formulas does not even deserve the name of prayer. Standard prayers should be an expression of our own attitude of adoration, praise, thanksgiving, and petition, or they should at least give us an incentive and inspiration towards a personal encounter with God in interior prayer. This should be the goal and ideal in all spiritual training of children beginning with early childhood.

It is a deplorable fact that even in convents prayer-life may deteriorate into the mere recitation of fixed formulas. The vocation to the religious life is, in its essence, a special calling to a life of union in prayer and charity. Consequently, it is understandable that a girl after entering the convent will feel frustrated if she is expected to recite the daily rosary and breviary in Latin, a language completely unfamiliar to her. Under such circumstances she should not question her own religious vocation but, rather, choose another religious community where good prayer formulas are in use.

Our Lord uttered this serious warning: "But, in praying, do not multiply words as the Gentiles do" (Matt. 6:7). It is typical of superstitious men to have recourse to unintelligible phrases because they place their trust in the magic power of words and formulas. *Black magic* is the sad and ugly caricature of true worship which is meant to be an adoration in "spirit and in truth" (John 4:23 ff.). Sincere believers—and such are found even among pagans—take heed to perceive God's message in the interior of their hearts. *Superstitious men, on the other hand, resort to ridiculous means* in their inordinate desire to discover the secrets of the future. Popular superstitions, remnants from ancient paganism, induce superficial men to regulate their actions by omens and forecasts instead of using the word of God as a signpost for their actions. The superstitious person tries to soothe the dark powers of fate by fixed formulas and mysterious exercises. Instead of being a confident response to God's personal communications, his life is influenced by unreasonable fears of spooks and phantoms. Our orientation to prayer should be truly Christian and thereby distinguish itself from both the old and new forms of paganism. *Genuine personal encounter with God at prayer, both liturgical and private, is the best protection for the faith in the dangers arising from superstitious beliefs and from the fear of the devil and all witchcraft.**

Each adorer of the true God should be solicitous to fight against today's gross forms of superstitions. This is part of our mission towards the Christianization of the world and the coming of God's kingdom.

(b) Honoring the Name of God

We pray "in the name of Jesus." In this name the heavenly Father has revealed His very personal and intimate love for us. There is no other name assuring us of salvation.

There is an intimate connection between the revelation of the holy name of Jesus and that of God, our Father. It is in union with Jesus that we dare to address the all-holy God as "Our Father." In the name of Jesus we confidently speak to the Father because we know that our prayers, united to His petitions, will penetrate the heavens as a pleasing homage. "Our Lord gave a great hope to all His disciples who confide in these words: 'I go to the Father'" (Commentary of St. Augustine to John 14:10).

Whatever we ask from the Father in the name of Jesus will be granted to us (cf. John 16:23). *Prayer in the name of Jesus is equivalent to living in a grace permeated union*

---

* Completely opposed to prayer are maledictions and the wicked attempts to get in direct touch with the devil.

with Him. This means that we put all our trust in Him and that we pray only for the things which are in agreement with His loving will. We pray in the name of Jesus, not only when following His instructions to address God as "Our Father," but also when we petition according to His intentions and the inspirations of the Holy Spirit. St. Cyprian of Carthage expresses this truth in the following manner: "Our prayers to God the Father should bear an unmistakable resemblance to the words of His only-begotten Son so that the Father may recognize them as such."

Our whole life will be a witness to the fact that we "pray in the name of Jesus." The Son of God, the eternal Word of the Father who reveals the Father's boundless glory and amiability, surrendered Himself to the Father in a perfect response of love. This sublime answer of love is expressed in Christ's own words: "Father . . . not My will but Your will be done" (Luke 22:42). "Father into Your hands I commend My spirit" (Luke 23:46). *In Christ's loving obedience to the Father, Jesus revealed to us His true essence and name.* We, in turn, shall keep holy the name of "Jesus" and the name of our heavenly "Father" when our actions fully conform to the words: "Your will be done on earth as it is in heaven."

Our weakness and inclination to evil ought to inspire us to pray frequently: "Forgive us our trespasses as we forgive those who trespass against us." Our sorrow for sin, our confidence in God's boundless mercy, as well as our readiness to forgive others, are pleasing confessions of faith in the power of the holy name of God and our Redeemer Jesus Christ.

Blasphemy is an outrageous affront to God's dignity expressed in words, thoughts, or acts intended as an insult to God or His saints. Cursing, if done deliberately, is one of the most serious offenses against God. The habit of *mis-*

using the holy name of God is a direct contradiction to authentic prayer. Far worse is the use of holy names in violent and sinful emotions of impatience, anger, rage, hatred, and fury. The unfortunate person who displays his anger with scornful utterances of holy names should make a sincere effort to rid himself of this bad habit because of the danger of becoming a blasphemer. The confirmed blasphemer who fails to make an honest attempt to stop cursing makes himself incapable of true prayer. How could such a person in all sincerity say: "Hallowed be Your name?" Family members who pray together will thereby mutually aid each other in overcoming the detestable habits of offending God's holy name.

(c) Prayer in Communion with the Saints

Prayer is a constant reminder of the intimate communion existing between all the children of God. We prayerfully address God as *"Our* Father." We are all members in the household of God's elect who pray together to the self-same Father in heaven. Authentic community prayer requires perfect concord in genuine brotherly charity. It is for this reason that Our Lord admonishes us to make peace with our brother, who is angry with us, before approaching the altar to offer our gifts of prayer (cf. Matt. 5:23).

Genuine solidarity in prayer expresses itself both in a confident, loving attention to the saints in heaven and a compassionate intercessory remembrance of the poor sinners. Thereby we acknowledge God's all-embracing dominion. This idea finds fitting expression in the petition: "Thy kingdom come."

Similarly, our prayer-colloquy with the saints and, especially our acts of petition and intercession to our heavenly Mother, redound to the glory of our heavenly Father in praise of Christ's merciful kingship. In addition, our conversation with the saints in heaven is an acknowledgment of the consoling truths expressed in the Creed: "I believe in the communion of saints." Personal communion expresses itself in words as well as in deeds of charity. We are united with those in eternal glory *in* and *through* Jesus Christ.

Prayer for the poor souls in purgatory is both an expression of the belief in the communion of saints and a loving remembrance of our dear departed friends and relatives. While the saints in heaven support our prayers when implored, the needy brethren in purgatory are particularly entitled to our intercessory prayers. While it is quite salutary to pray for the members of the suffering Church (cf. II Macc. 12:44 ff.), it is even more urgent to pray for the members of the Church militant. The poor sinners are in the most dire need for our prayers of petition because they are "our neighbors" in a very special sense.

(d) Prayer in the Frailty of the Flesh

The saying: "Heroes are made, not born," applies likewise to our prayer-life. The art of prayer must be learned and practiced. At times we are too exacting with ourselves in regard to prayer. We expect our prayers to be perfect in concentration and abounding in unalloyed joy. It is well to strive for such an exalted goal; but we should remember that it can be achieved only gradually and to an imperfect degree.

Progress in prayer is closely connected with an increase in faith, hope, and charity, and growth in all the moral virtues. If we correspond faithfully to the graces which we receive in prayer, God shall grant us the ability to pray in a childlike manner. The more sincere, humble, devoted, confident, and persevering we are in prayer, the more truly will our lives bear witness to the efficacy of prayer.

If at certain times in our prayer-life we are discouraged by *aridity* or annoyed by *distractions,* we should examine our conscience as to the underlying causes for such trials. It might well be that our prayer is poor because our heart it attached to earthly things. "Where your treasure is, there, too, your heart is bound to be" (Matt. 6:21). Our thoughts will involuntarily and naturally revert to whatever is dear to us. Annoying distractions may be the expression of physical or mental exhaustion. The only weapon against such an evil is patience, rest and recreation. If we are unable to concentrate in prolonged prayer, we ought to compensate by substituting frequent ejaculations which provide an occasion for giving free scope to our filial feelings toward God.

Distractions may be the expression of our hesitancy to follow the inclinations of our heart in the choice of the prayer form best suited to our spiritual development and the present state of mind. There are times when vocal prayer is very conducive toward progress in our union with God. On the other hand, there are circumstances which dispose the soul to spontaneous outpourings of sentiments of joy, fervor and humility. Our affections may be contained in a single phrase, as was Christ's own: "Yes, Father." It would be mistaken zeal to abide by prayer formulas after they no longer serve their particular purpose.

Our entire life should become a continuous prayer, an interior intimate colloquy with God. Our sentiments of adoration, thanksgiving, and petition should unceasingly ascend to the throne of God. Yet since our hearts are earthbound and weak, we need definite times set aside for prayer. Weekly attendance at Mass in fulfillment of our Sunday obligation is not sufficient, although it should form the center and climax of all our devotions. Man is in need of daily periods of conversation with God if his life is to be a faithful response to God's invitation of grace.

Morning and night prayers, as well as grace before and after meals, are in keeping with common Christian usage although not prescribed by definite commandments. Morning and evening prayers are matter-of-fact forms of politeness of the child of God to his heavenly Father. However, no fixed prayer formulas need to be recited in the morning or evening. Hence, there is no violation of law, charity, or filial politeness if such are omitted. We may use such simple elevations of the heart at the beginning of a new day, as: "The love of God is abiding within me," or we may exclaim: "All for You, O my God." These are pleasing and fruitful prayers. At the end of the day the Christian should not neglect to ask God's pardon for sins and to give thanks for all blessings received. In order to sustain the intimate heart-to-heart conversation with God, the Christian ought to reserve a certain part of the day for prayer. The hour of the day is immaterial.

The practice of saying grace before and after meals is an expression of a true family and community spirit. Community prayer, or prayer in unison, is the expression of authentic "communion" among Christians, particularly at the celebration of the sacrificial banquet, the most sublime mystery of Christian solidarity. The family which fails to sanctify its gathering at mealtime, by omitting grace before and after meals or by failing to use other forms of family prayer, is bound to become worldly and profane also in other aspects of life. Such a family lacks the solidarity and stability which are characteristics of the family possessing sound religious principles.

2. Vows

There is a close relationship between the concept of sacrifice and vow. By means of a vow the true worshiper offers to God a votive offering as an expression of his gratitude, thanksgiving, and praise. This gift is, at the same time, a symbol of our self-oblation. The vow is a deliberate, holy, and strictly binding promise made for the purpose of honoring God.

The most significant forms of vows for the Christian are the *baptismal vows,* the *marriage vows* and the *vows of religious life.*

The solemn pledge of the newly baptized Christian is far more than a mere promise towards the accomplishment of a task. Baptism makes us the "consecrated" property of God. Baptized in the Holy Spirit, we are ordained and destined for a life of divine worship. The baptismal vows represent the soul's grateful response to God's gracious and condescending act wrought in the waters of regeneration. The newly baptized surrenders himself willingly and unreservedly to God as His inalienable possession. He pledges himself to a life which will reflect God's condescending marvels of grace. This explains the transcendence of the new life in Christ which is no longer under law but is lived in Christ as a jubilant hymn of praise to God. Henceforth, the life of the baptized person ought to be a perfect expression of a personal oblation and a total self-surrender. All this is implied in the baptismal vows. The solemn renewal and confirmation of these sacred promises at the time of First Holy Communion and during the yearly celebration of the Easter Vigil and on other special occasions is a pleasing and worthy act of divine worship. Such a renewal impresses our mind with the sublimity of our high mission as God's holy people, endowed with sacerdotal dignity. All other vows in the life of the Christian are, in a certain sense, a consummation of the baptismal vows.

There is great danger that sinful men tend to deny and ignore the supernatural character and sanctity of Christian marriage. They fail to see its essence and consider it merely as a contract between two people and a social institution sanctioned and protected by law. Marriage is a contract in the full sense of the word and with all the rights and duties of interpersonal justice. Yet it is a very special kind of contract by the very fact of its divine institution and blessing by God, the Creator and Redeemer. Marriage is a sacrament or a grace-giving institution which is a means of sanctification for the spouses. It equips them for their sublime mission as cooperators with God. Marriage is a mutual grace-giving bond uniting the partners to God as well as to one another. By their mutual consent of love and fidelity, in the presence of God and the Church, the spouses administer the sacrament to each other. Reciprocal charity, faithfulness, patience, and solicitude will lead the marriage partners ever deeper into an adoring love of God. *Their mutual consent connotes a sacramental word of honor in which the spouses surrender* to each other their services and promise to sanctify their *common life.* Hence, it is significant that our pious ancestors referred to these promises at the altar as the *marriage vows.* The violation of conjugal chastity and fidelity is more than a disobedience, more than just a breach of faith, it is the sacrilegious denial to glorify God in holy charity and chastity. Conjugal chastity, namely, authentic charity and loyalty, are sublime, holy, and "priestly" services and, at the same time, the fulfillment of a vow.

The vows of religious life occupy a special place in Christian thinking. They aim towards a life of sanctity. The person called to this life dedicates himself by these vows to God's special service in virginal chastity, poverty, and obedience. The fulfillment of these promises to God implies a total gift of the most precious goods and the most dynamic powers which man possesses. For this reason, these vows are a very special expression of man's complete self-surrender to God. Self-oblation represents the core and essence of every vow which unites it to the sacrifice of Christ.

Vows differ from mere resolutions by the fact that they are voluntary, deliberate, and explicit acts of divine worship. The object of a vow must always be an act which is pleasing to God and salutary for the one making the promise. The promise contained in the vow must be the more perfect act. Hence, any resolve or promise against the virtue of prudence is not binding. A person is dispensed from a private vow by the mere fact that its fulfillment is opposed to his spiritual progress. In doubtful cases, the confessor is to decide. He may grant a dispensation or substitute another good or salutary action.

In the case of a solemn vow the competent ecclesiastical authority may grant a release from its obligations. However, a sincere self-examination should be made before requesting a dispensation, in order to ascertain whether the promise was in agreement with God's will. No one can be dispensed from the baptismal vows because they are the essential expression of the sacramental sanctification accomplished by God. The marriage vows demand fidelity until death. No earthly power or authority can dissolve a sacramental consummated marriage.

Serious considerations should precede the pledging of a vow. As far as the sacraments of baptism and matrimony are concerned, the Christian ought to meditate on the great blessings contained in these sacraments and the far-reaching promises which they entail. Similarly, the person who plans to make a vow should seriously reflect on the significance of his promise and its acceptability in God's right.

3. *The Oath*

The oath is a solemn invocation of God to bear witness regarding the truth or the fidelity of a promise. The oath is a true veneration of God's name, His truthfulness, and constancy, provided it is made *"in truth, in judgment, and in justice"* (Jer. 4:2). By means of the oath man pledges his will and intention to abide by truth and faithfulness according to God's own name which is the essence of all truth and fidelity. This is done in remembrance of the fact that God Himself has confirmed solemn promises and affirmations by the use of His own name.

In the *declaratory* oath God is called upon to be a witness to our sincerity in knowing and telling the truth. In the *promissory oath,* God, as it were, is made the guarantor of the pledge or promise which is given. A "formal declaration" in certain legal documents takes the place of the oath. Strictly speaking, such a solemn statement is not an oath because it is not intended as an act of religion. It is important, however, as a formal attestation of one's truthfulness.

Perjury, swearing to what is untrue or omitting to do what has been promised under oath, is one of the gravest sins against the virtue of religion. Thoughtless swearing is usually no more than a venial sin if there is no danger of perjury. Oaths which are used as instruments of detraction are gravely sinful. Likewise sinful, and at the same time null and void, are oaths which promise something forbidden by God's law. No oath, not even the oath of allegiance, can oblige us to do something sinful.

Whenever Christians make use of the solemn oath there ought to be no question about their truthfulness in the matter and the sincerity of their intentions: "Let your speech be, 'Yes, yes'; 'No, no'" (Matt. 5:37). Since we are united through faith with Christ who is Truth Himself, and since we are called to bear witness to eternal truth, all our words and declarations ought to have the weight and significance of oaths and thereby glorify God's truthfulness and fidelity before men.

Christ Himself gave proof that oaths may be permissible and even salutary at certain times. He did this in the assembly of the priests and elders in response to the high priest's interrogation regarding His divinity (cf. Matt. 26: 23 ff.). St. Paul's letter to the Hebrews compares God's oaths with the oaths uttered by men, which are "the final settlement of all their disagreements" (Heb. 6:13-17). We should have recourse to the oath only when it is contributory to God's greater honor and glory. Then only shall our solemn testimony be pleasing to God the Father who swore to His Son: "You are a priest forever, according to the order of Melchisedec" (Ps. 109:4), and to our High Priest who by His own death sealed the solemn oath professed before Caiphas.

Section VII. Sunday Observance and Sanctification of Work

We are on our way to the "eternal city of God," where Churches are no longer needed; "For the Lord God almighty and the Lamb are the temple thereof" (Apoc. 21:22). "The throne of God and of the Lamb shall be established in that city, and His servants will minister to Him. . . . Night will be no more, and so they will have no need of the light of lamp or sun, because the Lord will shine on them, and they will reign for ever and ever" (Apoc. 22:3-5). Our entire human existence should become one continuous act of divine worship. In our earthly sojourn we are still in need of

places of worship, definite prayer times and the celebration
of Our Lord's Day because both the world and our own
hearts have not been transfigured as yet, and because sin
and evil abound in the world and are in opposition to God's
glory.

Sunday is the day on which we celebrate the resurrection
of Christ and the anniversary of our own regeneration to a
new life in the sacrament of baptism. The celebration of the
Lord's Day is a decisive factor in our work and our vocation. It makes the latter a pleasing and worthy glorification
of God in union with the sacrifice of Christ.

*Work, in the original design of the Creator, was meant
to be an honorable service to God.* "The Lord God took the
man and placed him in the garden of Eden to till it and to
keep it" (Gen. 2:15). Our true image and likeness of God is
to shine forth in our "dominion over the earth" (Gen. 1:26).
Man's creative work is intended to imprint on the world,
which is God's incontestable dominion, the personal seal of
his own likeness to God. By means of his labor, man is to
earn the rightful title of possession. His labor is meant to
manifest the strength of his charity to his family. Through
labor he is to develop his spiritual and moral powers. However, God gave him the protecting commandment to rest on
the seventh day and pay homage to Him in order that he
might not forget his sublime dignity and final destination.
This day of rest gives man a prospect of the eternal day of
glory with God where there is no evening and no morning
(cf. Gen. 2:2 ff.). For the Christian, Sunday is a preview of
his eternal participation in the resurrection of Our Lord
Jesus Christ, who after the difficult and exalted work of
redemption, consummates everything in the glory of God
the Father.

It should be remembered that work, although it *has retained its dignity even after the fall in Paradise,* now bears

the characteristic of a burden: "In the sweat of your brow you shall eat your bread" (Gen. 3:19). Every man is obliged to toil for the sustenance of his life and the support of the community. "If anyone is unwilling to work, do not let him eat" (II Thes. 3:10). We are to accept our share of work in the spirit of penance and propitiation for sin. Thereby, we also participate in Christ's redemptive work.

Yet God does not want us to be crushed under the burden of labor. In consideration of our weakness He gave us a weekly day of rest. Sunday is God's thoughtful gift to the underprivileged, assuring them of this one day of leisure and relaxation. The observance of Sunday provides a foretaste of an eternal repose and rejoicing in heaven.

Since man's fall in Paradise, *work has taken on the character of a burden because of man's extreme selfishness and lust for power* (cf. Gen. 3:18 ff.). By His willing acceptance of the heavy burden of the cross in atonement for sin, Christ has removed all malediction from the earth and the domain of labor. Consequently, those who resist their liberation from the responsibility of work on Sundays and holy days of obligation in order to celebrate the eucharistic sacrifice remain under the curse of sin. These should heed Christ's serious warning: "What does it profit a man, if he gain the whole world, but suffer the loss of his own soul?" (Matt. 16:26). In the parable of the rich farmer Our Lord showed the futility and eventual curse of work as an end in itself (cf. Luke 12:15 ff.). In his vain endeavors to enlarge his barn the wealthy man was surprised by death which found him empty-handed in good works despite his bulging barns.

Our participation in Christ's sacrifice is a worthy celebration of Our Lord's Day. It transforms the curse of work into a blessing. It places the burden of labor under the law of the imitation of Christ, under the mild yoke of charity

which is the fulfillment of all justice. The Christian community which has fully entered into the inner life of worship,
that makes the Mass an act of corporate worship in the
charity of the Crucified and Risen Lord, is bound to ac-
tualize God's law of social justice and charity in daily life.
The liturgical celebration of Sunday Mass implies a solemn
commitment to transform the work-a-day world by the
spirit of the Lord's Day, the spirit of Christ's victorious
charity.

The obligatory Sunday rest and attendance at Holy Mass
are not primarily matters of law but occasions for rejoicing.
The observance of Sunday does not reduce the productivity
in human affairs and undertakings, but rather contributes
to real progress. Sunday should be far more than a day of
repose. Those who make Sunday a time for indulgence in
pleasures without active participation in the sacrifice of the
Mass fail to find the center of their life in the adoring charity
of God. Their work and vocation remain outside the radius
of God's grace.

In some countries the introduction of a staggered working
week by labor and industry is a downright injustice to
family unity. It deprives the family of the common day of
rest and worship. The staggered working week is the result
of an unscrupulous desire for profit with a total disregard
for the dignity of the workingman, the basic rights of the
family, and the holiness of Our Lord's Day. In cases of real
economic depression the Church may tolerate such a system provided that only a limited number of people are
employed on Sundays. In addition, each Catholic should be
given sufficient time to attend Sunday Mass.

On the other hand, the long weekend, a desirable outcome of industrial progress, permits the workingman to devote more time to his family and to leisure activities. It
enables him to attend to his home or garden or other

recreational activities on Saturday thus providing ample time for divine worship on Sunday. With a certain amount of good will, athletic activities and other public perform-ances could be reduced and regulated on Sundays thereby allowing more time for leisure and prayerful worship. We are fully cognizant of the dangers inherent in a highly com-mercialized "Recreation-Industry" which takes advantage of long weekends to the detriment of true repose and sancti-fication in our Sunday observance.

We are fulfilling the external law regarding Sunday regu-lations if we attend Holy Mass in union with the Christian community and at the same time abstain from all work which is opposed to the character of the Lord's Day. Necessary work, especially acts of charity in behalf of the needy or afflicted, may of course be performed on Sunday. Yet the sincere Christian is not satisfied with the external fulfillment of the law but tries to enter more fully into the true spirit of God's law. Thus will he begin to appreciate the blessed and liberating nature of the law of Sunday ob-servance as a perfect praise to God. The correct observance of the Lord's Day transforms the whole life of the Christian into a continuous and worthy act of worship marked by an ever-increasing personal dignity and freedom.*

* Cf. page 44. Also Vatican Council II, Liturgy Constitution, article 106.

6 THE CHRISTIAN VIRTUES IN RELATION TO CHARITY

Although St. Paul, in masterly fashion, presented the sublime vocation of the Christian life in the light of the glad tidings of God's grace and charity, he did not neglect to emphasize the rest of the virtues. On one occasion he compared the moral virtues with a garment of antiquity which needs the touch of charity to add grace and dignity to its appearance (cf. Col. 3:12-15). Thereby he indicated that charity endows all other virtues with true charm and splendor. Another quotation of St. Paul contains the image of a soldier in battle array: "Stand, then, ready for battle, with the belt of truth about your waist, wearing the breastplate of holiness, and the shoes of preparedness furnished by the gospel of peace. With all this take up the shield of faith, with which you will be enabled to put out all the flaming arrows of the wicked enemy. Finally, take the helmet of salvation and the sword supplied by the Spirit, that is, the sword of God" (Eph. 6:11-17).

Treatises on moral theology by the early Fathers of the Church enumerate not only the three theological virtues of faith, hope and charity, but also the four cardinal virtues: *prudence, justice, temperance* and *fortitude*. This particular arrangement of the moral virtues reveals the influence of Greek thought in early Christian teaching. Holy Scripture contains only one casual reference to the cardinal virtues where the evident intention of the sacred writer appears to be a clear differentiation between a purely worldly ethics and these four virtues as *fruits of heavenly wisdom or charity*. "What is richer than wisdom, which produces all things? . . . and if a man love justice: her labors have great virtues; for she teaches temperance, and prudence, and justice, and fortitude, which are such things as men can have nothing more profitable in life" (Wis. 8:5-7).

Extensive historical research indicates that the so-called "cardinal" virtues of prudence, justice, temperance, and fortitude have played a significant role in Catholic tradition. Yet these same studies also reveal other approaches to the subject of Christian morality. The Christian virtues could just as well be presented according to a Chinese scheme. This system, in its chief emphasis on charity, bears an astonishing resemblance to the pattern of divine revelation. "The portion which heaven has bestowed on the sage is the virtue of *benevolence, justice, courtesy,* and *prudence*. They are all rooted in the heart. They manifest themselves in the radiance of the countenance, in the posture of man, in the whole physique." *

It is immaterial whether we follow the Chinese system, the Occidental pattern, or whether we adhere to an ethical scheme which conceives all the other virtues as particular aspects of the cardinal virtues. However, the virtues of religion and humility should never be subordinated to the

* Cf. *The Law of Christ*, Vol. I, p. 513.

cardinal virtues because of their unique position in revelation.* Unquestionably, every Christian virtue has its supernatural center and pattern in charity. St. Augustine illustrates this with unsurpassed clarity: "Since virtue leads us to the blessed life, I maintain that virtue is nothing other than supreme love for God. For as I understand it, the fourfold virtue is no more than a diversity of the effect of one same love. Thus those four virtues (it would indeed be a blessing if they would be found in the hearts as the words are on the lips of all) I define without any hesitation as follows: *temperance is love* bestowing itself fully and without reserve on the object loved; *fortitude* is love gladly enduring everything for the beloved; *justice* is love serving the beloved alone and therefore ruling others rightly; *prudence* is love wisely discerning the means leading to the beloved amid the obstacles which would bar the way. Yet we have already noted that the object loved is not simply any object indifferently, but God, supreme good, supreme wisdom, supreme peace. We may, with a slight variation, define these virtues in this way: temperance is love serving God totally and without corruption, fortitude is love gladly suffering all for God's sake; justice is love serving God alone and thus ruling all else with reason and right order; prudence is love clearly discerning what is helpful and what is hindrance on the path to God." †

SYNOPSIS OF CHAPTER SIX

(1) The first section of this chapter is devoted to the fundamental *virtue of truthfulness*. This place of emphasis is due to its close relationship with the mystery of charity. Such an arrangement is also in agreement with St. Paul's ap-

---

* These virtues were discussed in the previous chapter.
† *The Law of Christ,* pp. 497-498.

proach, who lists truth as the chief weapon for the champion of charity. (2) Truthfulness requires *sincerity in disposition,* in thought, in word and in deed. All this may be seen in the light of prudence. In addition, "the armor of justice" constitutes the essential internal and external protection for God's kingdom of peace and charity. (3) *Temperance* and *discipline* are the evident expressions of a vigorous charity, thereby preserving and channeling the powers of the heart, the will and emotions towards the good of God's kingdom. (4) Charity subdues and regulates the unruly passions through the virtue of *fortitude or courage.* This enables the soul to persevere faithfully in the struggle against the enemy of salvation by a patient endurance of difficulties for the sake of God's kingdom.

PART ONE

Truth Illumined by Charity

The only escape from the prison of our self-centeredness is communication with the "thou" of our neighbor. The spoken word is the pledge of truthfulness and charity in all our interpersonal relationships. Every word which is not rooted in truth and genuine charity endangers human concord and harmony. Conversely, there can be no authentic charity which is not founded on truth and does not lead to truthfulness.

SYNOPSIS OF PART ONE

(1) The deep mystery of Christ's own sublime truth will enlighten our minds regarding the essential *demands of truthfulness.* (2) This will lead us to an appreciation of the *basic requisites of truthfulness* in our interpersonal dealings.

(3) In the light of genuine charity, we shall recognize the *obligation of secrecy* in the service of truth and the good reputation of our neighbor. (4) *Fidelity* is truthfulness in the pledging and redeeming of promises.

Section I. Christ's Sublime Truth

Christ could say of Himself "I am the truth" (John 14:6). He is the Word which from the beginning was with God (cf. John 1:1). The heavenly Father has "pronounced" all His magnificence, power and charity in Jesus Christ, His own eternal Word. There is nothing in the Father which is not likewise in the Son. "The Father's utterance would indeed be imperfect if His Word were less than Himself. Here (in the Blessed Trinity) we find in its deepest essence those decisive words, Yes, yes and No, no" (St. Augustine). The coequal Word of the Father is "not just any word but the Word uttered by Charity" (St. Thomas Aquinas). God's own Word, eternal Truth in person, is the glad language of charity. It is the Truth which, in an all-surpassing charity, becomes fruitful in the Holy Spirit.

Every truth in the world is but a faint reflection of God's overflowing riches of charity and truthfulness because "All things were made through Him, and without Him was made nothing that has been made" (John 1:3). Man was created not only by the Word of God but also according to the image and likeness of the Blessed Trinity and especially in the image of God's only-begotten Son. Since He is the Truth it follows that we are actually what we ought to be, inasmuch as we are "in the truth." *We remain in the truth only if we are rooted in love.* Truth and charity are inseparable entities. Only a service of charity inspired by love reflects the image of divine truth.

Christ is the messenger of divine truth and charity. He not only bore testimony to the truth by the open declaration of His solemn oath before the High Priest (cf. John 18:19-23), but He likewise gave proof of His love by the shedding of His blood on the cross. If we wish to be His disciples and the messengers of His truth, we, too, must see His truth diffused by the radiance of His love.

Truthfulness is a very basic virtue for all members of the Mystical Body of Christ because Christ, who is Truth Himself, came into the world to give testimony of the truth. "Lay aside falsehood and speak the truth to the neighbor because we are members of one another" (Eph. 4:25). If we wish to be sharers in the Word which endures forever, we are to put away all malice, deceit, pretense, envy and slander (cf. I Pet. 1:25; 2:1). Our unity and concord in genuine truthfulness and charity will be an image of God's own truthfulness and harmony.

We are sanctified in the truth (cf. John 17:17-19). United with Christ we are both privileged and obligated to become *witnesses to the liberating truth of God.* We shall meet the challenge of such a noble calling only if, under all circumstances, we remain in truth and charity. Whoever violates charity cannot give testimony of the divine truth which God's charity breathes forth. We may not impair our glorious testimony of the eternal truth and charity by falsehood or insincerity in our life. No lie may defile the lips of him who desires to sing God's praises as a messenger of His truth, charity, and holiness (cf. Is. 6). "O Lord, who shall sojourn in Your tent? Who shall dwell in Your holy mountain? He who walks blamelessly and does justice; who thinks the truth in his heart and slanders not with his tongue" (Ps. 14:1-3).

Section II. Prerequisites for Truthfulness

We ought to be truthful in our whole being: in our *thoughts,* *words* and *actions.* Our obligation to truthfulness arises from our intimate union with Jesus Christ, eternal Truth Himself. In addition, we owe complete sincerity to the "Spirit of Truth" in view of our gratuitous membership in God's kingdom of truth and charity.

1. Sincerity in Disposition

Our entire being will be without affectation and dissimulation if, true to God's expectations, we are completely responsive to His personal invitations of grace. God has destined each of us for a uniquely personal task. He has endowed us with special talents and gifts of mind, heart and will. His loving invitations of grace correspond to the soul's innermost yearnings and strivings. He has a uniquely personal mission for each of us. If we try to evade God's summons and refuse the graces of the particular moment by retreating behind the minimum requirements of the universal law, we shall fail to meet God's fondest expectations. We are true to ourselves only if we orient our entire life according to God's desires. In addition to the danger of escapism behind the impersonal law, there is the peril of man's unquestioning surrender to mass-propaganda and mass-suggestion which is at the root of his shallow and superficial mode of existence.

2. Truthfulness in Thought

We gain conscious participation in God's own truth by truthful thinking. A humble faith places us within the *radiant light of the gospel truth.* We are to make room for

314

eternal truth in our silent world of thought. Thus we shall constantly deepen our knowledge through the loving contemplation of divine truth. The man versed in worldly wisdom but ignorant of the glad tidings of the gospel truth is unable to enjoy the genuine radiance and beauty of divine truth. If despite his erudition he remains oblivious to the mysteries of salvation and divine charity, he is put to shame by the simple and unlearned man who lovingly meditates on God's revelations. The misdirection of our innate desires for truth into the exclusive shallow channels of technology and the natural sciences is no more than "a delicate and imperceptible introduction of the humiliated children of Adam into the proficiency of lying" (Franz Kafka).

Our reflections on God and His attributes can be sincere and genuine only to the extent of our humble and willing acknowledgement of our dependence on God's truth. Similarly, *we can only achieve true self-knowledge in the light of God's faithfulness and mercy.*

Without true knowledge of God and an awareness of moral truths, all our appearance of knowledge remains mere useless and confusing ballast. We need both wisdom and prudence in order to meditate on truth and to remain in truth. True wisdom has its roots in a loving remembrance of God and all the things pertaining to Him. It implies a reverent interpretation of God's work and words in the light of faith. The light of wisdom discloses God's supreme dominion over all the events of history and His direct or permissive will in even the smallest happenings of our life.*

There is neither a need nor an obligation to know everything, although we never can know enough about God's

---

* This topic has been discussed previously in the sections dealing with conscience and prudence. Here we merely wish to make a general reference to the virtue of prudence as the virtue of truthfulness in relation to the perception and interpretation of individual circumstances which transmit God's will to us.

magnificent works of love. Despite our limitations we should aim to acquire all possible knowledge. However, there is an *inordinate and, at the same time, dangerous desire for knowledge.* Thus, the proud man is not satisfied with the knowledge provided by faith. He refuses to accept divine truths on the basis of God's authority; he himself wishes to penetrate the deepest mysteries of faith and know them as they are known by God alone. Yet, since he is unable to do this by means of his limited powers, he closes his mind to the most blessed truths of faith. The Christian, on the other hand, humbly and patiently desires the light of eternal bliss which will allow him to behold everything in God's light and glory.

Inordinate curiosity seriously interferes with profound reflection and tends to lead us astray from the straight path of truth and from the faithful discharge of our vocational duties. Insatiable curiosity frequently violates charity because it unnecessarily explores and exposes information of a confidential nature. A curious person approaches truth from a wrong angle because he lacks the required reverence for truth which is the foundation of all sincere thinking. The wise and prudent man familiarizes himself with truth in the silent world of his thoughts so that he may recognize God's benevolent will in the various circumstances of his life. His mind is bent on seeing the truths which are of vital concern to him.

3. *Truthfulness in Action*

The truth which makes us free (cf. John 8:32) is the God-given truth which we must not only hear and contemplate in our hearts, but likewise implement in daily living. The only road to a full possession of revealed truths, which is God's own gratuitous gift to us, is the sincere "practice of truth in love" (Eph. 4:15). *We remain in the truth if we perform the works of truth* in perfect unanimity of love (cf. II John 1-3; III 3). The prerequisite for a constantly increasing understanding of the truth is a devoted and loving performance of the works of truth. "He who does the truth comes to the light" (John 3:21). The brave determination to follow the path of truth in the actual situations of life is a decisive resolution of the virtue of prudence.

Our union with Christ, eternal Truth Himself and witness to our truthfulness, presupposes a faithful imitation of Him in the actual pursuance of the good. A serious discrepancy between knowledge of the truth and its acknowledgement in action proves that we are still walking in the darkness and in falsehood (cf. I John 1:7).

Hypocrisy is an irreconcilable contradiction to "the implementation of the truth." It is a conscious dissimulation of the truth in words or deeds and a misleading pretense of virtue and goodness.

The most serious contradiction to sincerity and truthfulness in action is the conscious and deliberate feigning to be what one is not. It is the false assumption of an appearance of virtue and faith. It is a life in contradiction to the convictions of faith and the recognized will of God. Such behavior is proof that men "love and practice deceit," which bars them from the kingdom of truth and charity (Apoc. 22:15).

4. Truthfulness in Word

In the meaning of divine revelation our speech is in harmony with truth if it faithfully reflects the word of God. "We convey the truth in words if our statements are sincere expressions of our innermost thoughts in a particular matter, because men have the right to hear the truth. Known truths should be transmitted in words, and nothing should be contained in our statements which is contrary to our interior convictions" (St. Augustine). Truthfulness brings us closer to the inaccessible truth of God who expressed His own essence in the Word begotten of Him, who shares with Him equal power, magnificence and charity.

The most sublime mystery concerning the eternal Word, begotten by the Father, is the truth that the Son, together with the Father, breathes forth the Holy Spirit who is love in person. *Therefore, our words become true reflections of eternal truth to the extent that they are faithful expressions of charity and, in turn, means for an increase of love.* We sin against truthfulness by a deliberate statement contrary to our knowledge; we also forfeit our likeness to eternal Truth by any revelation of a full or partial truth which violates charity. A lie or a deliberate distortion of the truth is never permitted. Similarly, in view of the Christian's supernatural likeness to Christ, it would be wrong for him to reveal the truth in a manner or under circumstances which would violate or undermine charity.

A deliberate lie in serious matters is grievously sinful because truth is a precious treasure and a vital bond of unity between Christ and all the members of His Mystical Body. At the same time, truthfulness is a testimony of charity. In consideration of our human frailty, we need some guidelines for judging the seriousness of certain violations against the truth.

Lies committed with full deliberation and which, at the same time, greatly offend against charity by causing considerable harm to the good reputation or earthly possessions of our neighbor are by their very nature grievously sinful. Similarly grave are the *lies which are detrimental* to our neighbor if committed through sheer *negligence and carelessness.* On the other hand, so-called "little lies" which lack all previous deliberation and are free from any danger of scandal or harm to others are less serious. This is not meant to minimize the serious nature of all lies as threats to salvation, particularly if they are habitual offenses. Contempt for truth is in itself a mortal sin, because truthfulness is an important attitude of the soul. Careless violations against truth in small and insignificant matters tend inevitably towards insincerity and dishonesty in more serious matters.

A lie of particular malice is slander or calumny. It is a false and malicious defamation of the good name of a person or a community. *Detraction* is an uncharitable and unjust use of information which injures a person's good reputation. No matter in what manner such information may have come to our knowledge, it should always be covered with the mantle of brotherly charity and guarded with considerate and prudent secrecy.*

In order to prevent any possible misunderstanding of the author's strict condemnation of lies, it should be remarked here that *jokes or jocose lies,* of which pious people may accuse themselves in confession, are usually not lies in the full sense of the term, especially when seen in the entire setting of the occasion. Their purpose is to enliven a conversation rather than to mislead anyone. Every sensible person will recognize them as apparent attempts at humor. This is evident in the twinkle of the eye, the smile and the whole manner of presentation. In addition, they usually transmit some sort of truth in a cheerful and amusing manner.

The lies of children in the age group from four to six years do not deserve the name of "lies" because they are simply the product of an overactive imagination. Children at this particular age are unable to distinguish between reality and the products of their phantasy. It is unwise to

* The topic of secrecy will receive more detailed explanation in subsequent paragraphs.

label their fantastic stories as "lies" and to correct and expose the child as a "liar." It is far better to lead the child in an imperceptible and kind manner to the realization of the true state of affairs by referring to such unrealistic fictitious products as "make-believe stories." The parents' personal example of truthfulness, as well as their confidence in the child's sincerity, will gradually lead him to truthfulness in word and deed. Parents ought to acknowledge the child's upright and candid admission of guilt. It is especially important for the child to realize the parents' attitude of sincerity in dealing with him. This alone will convince him that he, in turn, must be sincere if he wants others to place trust and confidence in him.

The lies of certain types of epileptic, psychopathic, hysterical and feeble-minded personalities should be treated in a manner similar to the treatment of children's lies. These lies are symptomatic of an emotional immaturity which simultaneously reveals itself in other aspects of the person's behavior. The only help which we can offer such people is personal kindness, while teaching them the beauty of truthfulness and the ugliness of insincerity and falsehood.

Section III. Truthfulness and Professional Secrecy

The word of God, who is eternal Truth Himself, has transmitted to us the truth which He has received from the Father; because the Son "can do nothing on His own initiative; He can only do what He sees the Father do: for what things soever He does, these the Son also does in like manner" (John 5:19). Yet at no time did Christ reveal His truth indiscriminately to all people and on every occasion. Not all men are able and worthy to receive the blessed fulness and challenge of truth. For this reason, Christ has glorified His heavenly Father for His infinite condescension in revealing His innermost secrets to the poor and little ones rather than to the worldly wise and prudent (cf. Matt. 11:25). Even the apostles received the divine truths gradually as is indicated by Our Lord's words: "Many things yet I have to say to you, but you cannot bear them now" (John 16:12). In imitation of our divine Master we likewise should foster an attitude of reverence for truth: "Do not give to dogs what is holy, neither cast your pearls before swine" (Matt. 7:6).

Discretion in guarding information of a confidential nature from the unscrupulous curiosity of the weak and wicked is necessary in consideration for the sacredness of our own good reputation and that of others and out of respect for truth and the right to privacy. Information of a personal nature may not be misused nor thoughtlessly exposed to human malice and weakness.

A distinction should be made between the *natural, promised,* and the *entrusted* secret. A natural secret is one which obliges the possessor to secrecy in virtue of the natural law of justice and charity. The promised secret is one which binds a person because of a gratuitous promise, even if the nature of the matter confided would not require strict secrecy. Such a promised secret is binding until all reasons for the pledge become null and void. However, a promise to refrain from revealing certain facts does not oblige us to suffer great loss or hardship for the mere sake of such a pledge unless high values are at stake. Every promise needs a sensible interpretation. *The entrusted* or *professional secret* is one confided to another on the implicit or explicit condition that it will be kept hidden. Doctors, nurses and priests in particular have a strict obligation to respect all information of a professional nature. This is indispensable for maintaining an atmosphere of confidence and truthfulness in professional relationships. *Under no condition can the priest be dispensed from keeping secret all information received in confession.* The other secrets, whether natural, promised, or entrusted, oblige the confidant to strict secrecy provided that there are no higher values at stake which would require their revelation, as for example, the welfare and good name of an innocent party.

Every person has a strict right to his own secrets. Therefore, all curious prying into secrets and all unnecessary surrender of confidences is seriously sinful unless it concerns mere trivialities. Professional secrets are to be guarded in a special manner since great goods are at stake (such as charity, confidence, justice, and the good reputation of others).

The usual manner of guarding a secret is by *maintaining strict silence*. This requires that we *refrain from giving any information in word or deed* which could endanger the confidence. Unauthorized questions should be met either by profound silence or an unyielding and firm retort. In situations where a simple refusal to answer a question is likely to cause suspicion and danger to the secret, the only alternative is a reply which veils the truth. This is the only possible choice because we are never justified in telling a lie. This "veiling" of the truth might be referred to as "enigmatical or disguised speech." Moral theologians call it "broad mental reservation."

The response employed in *broad mental reservation* in itself is not in full accord with the scriptural ideal: "Yes, yes, No, no" (Matt. 5:37). Consequently, it is permitted only under certain conditions and in a manner which does not admit a doubt regarding the "dove-like" simplicity and evident sincerity of the speaker—even under the existing circumstances which, by reason of the indiscretion and malice of the curious, force him to answer with the prudence of the serpent (cf. Matt. 10:16). Mental reservation or the use of an expression which has two meanings is only justified because we are living in "a world full of malice." The disciple of Christ uses it only as a last resort in the attempt to safeguard a secret and to refrain from an untruth. *Mental reservation if used under the proper circumstances is truth; if used indiscriminately it will undermine fidelity and lead to untruthfulness and falsehood.*

Mental reservation is permissible only under the following *conditions.* One must have *a proportionate reason* for having recourse to mental reservation. In addition, *the expressions used in mental reservation must have, besides the plain and obvious meaning, also a less obvious or "hidden meaning."* It should never be used for selfish reasons, although it is a licit means for protecting personal secrets. Any sensible person should be able to detect "the hidden or less obvious meaning" in the words and expressions used. The aim of mental reservation is not a deception but rather the veiling of a truth which must be guarded for the sake of charity and justice. The possible misleading of the questioner must be taken into consideration, but he encouraged such an answer by his untimely questioning.

Simple people who are unfamiliar with the teaching on mental reservation recount their actual use of it with the more or less significant statements: "I had to resort to double meaning" (this indeed is close to its essence); "I had to pretend to be stupid" (this also comes close to the truth); "I was obliged to tell a lie." In reality they did not have the slightest intention to lie but simply attempted to find an escape from a difficult situation. A conscious lie is never permitted; but we should remember that *the broad mental reservation has nothing in common with a premeditated lie.* It may happen, however, that in the excitement and stress of the moment one may be unable to find appropriate words for veiling the truth adequately without telling an untruth. The decisive factor in such situations is the good will and the determined effort to be truthful.*

Detraction, scandalmongering and uncharitable critical judgment are in direct opposition to considerate silence and concealment of facts and truths which, if revealed, might endanger the good name and jeopardize the spiritual and temporal welfare of our neighbor. *Faultfinding and uncharitable criticism of superiors* and their regulations are especially sinful because such revelations seriously undermine authority and the respect due to superiors. The most contemptuous and indiscreet use of truth is made by the scandalmonger who by his malicious gossip and the revelation of secrets destroys friendship, confidence, and charity. This disorder is closely related to malicious lies.

However, it is not a matter of idle and sinful gossip if we transmit certain facts in order to safeguard the neighbor's welfare and salvation. Such actions may aid to avert the dangers inherent in false friendships with crafty seducers. The evil and wicked ones have only a conditional right to their good name. In case of conflict, the common good precedes the preservation of the reputation of the wicked.

Not everyone is worthy of praise and honor but *each person is entitled to his good reputation and a certain amount of external prestige in order to live up to the social expectations.*† We should try to imitate God who in His infinite mercy receives the sinner with consideration and respect. This is a basic prerequisite for a genuine interior renewal. In all our words and actions we should zealously

---

* This difficult topic is discussed at great length in one of my other books: *The Law of Christ*, Vol. I, p. 553.
† Cf. Social Considerations, p. 167.

guard our neighbor's reputation. Under no circumstances should we ever undermine his good name with untrue reports or with unnecessary manifestations of his faults and failings. We should foster an obliging and respectful politeness toward our neighbor. This will safely keep us from all errors and faults of the tongue.

Slander, detraction and scandalous gossip seriously violate justice and charity by undermining morality and human concord. Consequently, these sins are grievous by their very nature whenever there is serious matter. Under all circumstances, they are hideous distortions of the truth and offenses against veracity. Truth, of its very essence, is meant to serve charity. Sins of the tongue may be venial in trifling matters or in cases in which forethought and advertence had been lacking. Needless talk about the known faults and failings of others is usually no more than evidence of bad manners unless it is prompted by hatred, contempt, or gross unkindness.

One who has committed either detraction, slander, or malicious gossip is obliged in justice and charity to restore the good name of the injured person by all possible means.

Section IV. Fidelity

Just as veracity guarantees harmony between our words and convictions, so does fidelity assure the redemption of a pledge. Fidelity is truthfulness to the extent that our promises express our intentions and to the degree that our deeds redeem the pledge. Fidelity implies faithfulness not only to the spoken word but to the deepest expression of self.

Fidelity is more than an objective bond, more than a mere fulfillment of an obligation towards the redemption of a pledge; it is primarily a personal responsibility to the "thou"

of our neighbor and the community. Fidelity is an attri-
bute of charity, of self-respect and reverence towards our
neighbor. *Fidelity* is not only a duty which we owe to self
and our good reputation, but it is also a basic *prerequisite
and expression of true community spirit.*

God's own faithfulness and constancy is the very source
and pledge of all human fidelity. He who is called "the
Faithful and True" (Apoc. 19:11) has manifested His
fidelity in Jesus Christ, His only Son. God's loyalty survives
all disloyalty of men. He has renewed His covenant of
everlasting love and fidelity in the death of His own Son
who delivered Himself as a ransom for our sins. Through
the sacraments we gain participation in Christ's own covenant which He has established with His Church. *The sacraments give expression to the law of fidelity which is inscribed in our hearts through our renewal by grace.* We
receive the most sublime revelation of God's superabundant
faithfulness through the grace of conversion and the sacrament of God's merciful forgiveness. His fidelity remains
unwavering during our entire period of probation and
exile. He unceasingly offers His grace of loving forgiveness.
We respond to God's fidelity by our grateful and humble ʼ
reception of the sacrament of penance and our loving participation in the eucharistic sacrifice. Our confrontation
with Christ in the sacraments verifies and enriches our
personal pledge of fidelity which we have rendered at
baptism. Our dealings with our neighbor should be patterned according to God's own faithfulness because all
share His divine life as members of the Mystical Body of
Christ.

The sacrament of matrimony is a grace-giving participation in the faithful charity of Christ for His bride, the
Church. It represents a unique interpersonal union in love
and fidelity. It is an exalted sign and a faithful reflection of

God's fidelity among men. A previous discussion of this topic has pointed out the supernatural character of the *marriage vows* when seen in the radiant light of divine worship (cf. p. 299). Consequently, a betrayal of conjugal love and fidelity is a sacrilegious act against the faithfulness of Christ, who pledged Himself for His Church, as well as a treason to the sacramental bond of marriage (cf. Eph. 5:22 ff.).

God's faithful charity patiently waits for our reciprocating love. Despite our infidelities, He invites us to the closest intimacy of divine friendship. In a similar manner conjugal charity will prove itself more than a mere reward for mutual fidelity. Marital love and fidelity, founded in God, will try to assist the spouse in the dangers of temptation and protect him from ruin. Even in extreme cases of gross infidelity in which he may feel constrained to refuse conjugal relations temporarily or permanently, the faithful spouse nevertheless must remain aware of his personal responsibility of fidelity unto death. He must not only refrain from entering into a civil marriage, but must offer sincere forgiveness and seize every opportunity for reconciliation. Above all, he must feel responsible for praying unceasingly for the eternal salvation of the unfortunate spouse.

The unique nature of the marriage bond should cast its bright ray of glory into the preparatory period of courtship. *In view of conjugal fidelity, the engaged couple may not squander their God-given powers of soul and body in frivolous relationships.* Premarital chastity is the best preparation for a chaste and total gift of self in wedlock. All protestations of love which are not founded on the determined will towards fidelity and constancy are mere forms of duplicity and dishonesty. Even during the time of courtship, while there is no absolute promise of engagement, each word and action hinting towards future marriage should be sincere and trustworthy. The person who is shamelessly unscrupulous in this regard, through effusive, insincere assertions of love, seriously undermines confidence and trust.

There is a decided difference between the early, timid manifestations of love and affection and the beginning signs of a determined will towards fidelity and marriage. The young lover desires to prove his affection by word and deed in the hopeful expectation of a reciprocating love and a devotion worthy of his own love and fidelity. It should be understood that the indissolubility of the marriage bond is based solely on the marriage vows. These are rendered in God's presence and are confirmed through the sacrament. Consequently, even the most sincere will and determination of the engaged couple towards mutual loyalty in no way authorizes or permits the intimacies of conjugal love, ordained by God to be the expression of an irrevocable solidarity.

The love and affection between parents and children assumes a special dignity and holy obligation in the light of the sacrament of matrimony. Only to the extent that fidelity and sincerity are fostered in family life will loyalty and confidence reign in the other domains of life. For this reason it is imperative that the ideals of the unity and indissolubility of the marriage vows be supported by legislation and public opinion. Conversely, it is true that conjugal fidelity will receive its due respect and esteem as the foundation of all social order only to the extent that truthfulness, fidelity and integrity are treasured in public life. It is imperative that parents carefully redeem the promises made to their children if they have fulfilled their respective obligations. Otherwise, the parent-child relationship will be destroyed and the children will be unable to grasp the significance and sublimity of fidelity.

In general, fidelity binds us to a greater extent than truthfulness. This is due to the fact that fidelity, in the fulfillment of a promise, is more essentially dependent on the spiritual values basic for interpersonal relationships and community life than truthfulness in the mere verbal assertion. Failure to redeem a promise may be a venial sin only when the promise is inconsequential or if the promise was neither made nor received in all seriousness.

PART TWO

The Virtue of Justice

St. Paul's description of the Christian's armor mentions both the weapon of truthfulness and "the breastplate of justice" (Eph. 6:14). The latter is an essential prerequisite in our combat with the evil one. Yet the apostle's concept of the "armor of justice" has nothing in common with the rigid shell of selfishness wherein men shield themselves against the evident duties of charity. He who tries to hide behind the outward appearance of justice in order to escape the demands of charity has *failed to comprehend the true meaning of Christian justice*. The noble object of this virtue is to direct our will along the path of righteousness and thereby establish order and harmony in the community and at the same time enable us to stand firm in temptations against justice and charity. Justice is one of the strongest weapons in the conquest of the world for the kingdom of charity. In order to accomplish this, justice must be animated by charity.

SYNOPSIS OF PART TWO

(1) The virtue of Christian justice should be seen in the light of God's own justice as revealed in His just dealings in the work of our redemption. (2) The moral virtue of justice and the juridical order have a direct relationship. Yet the virtue of justice is more embracing than external juridical order. (3) Justice and juridical order are indispensable in this world, full of injustice and malice. (4) In the final analysis, distributive justice is the realization of both justice and charity "in an evil world." (5) Sins against justice demand corresponding restitution. (6) Sins against the fifth commandment are characterized by a special malice. (7) Justice, when seen in its true nature, is far from a rigid coat of armor. It is a charming virtue which embraces the social virtues and graces, such as love for family, patriotism, gratitude, generosity, and politeness.

Section I. The Justice of God and of Men

God's charity is based on His justice; for charity "does not rejoice over wickedness" (I Cor. 13:16). Every sin is an outright refusal to love God and consequently a grave injustice towards Him who is charity and holiness.

God intensely desires our acknowledgment of His supreme right over all creation. This is clearly brought home to us in the injunction imprinted on the tablets of the Covenant: "I, the Lord, your God, am a jealous God" (Ex. 20:5). God is a "consuming fire" of justice (cf. Heb. 12:29). He revealed His unrelenting justice when He hurled the proud angels from the heights of heaven and expelled our first parents from the Garden of Eden. His supreme work of justice became manifest in the great work of redemption through the sacrificial death of His only-begotten Son. The all-holy, just, and merciful God accepted the redemptive sacrifice of His well-beloved Son in atonement for the sins of the world and as an act of homage to His sublime justice and holiness. It is significant that Our Lord, in His high priestly prayer, addressed His heavenly Father as "just Father" (John 17:25). God's boundless kindness and all-holy justice meet in the great work of redemption: "justice and peace shall kiss" (Ps. 84:11).

The glad tidings of conversion are essentially a message of God's charity and mercy. The only way by which the sinner can return to the heart of God is a humble admission of guilt: "Father, I have sinned" (Luke 15:21). The sinner who fails to admit his injustice in the awesome presence of God and who neglects to adore God's holiness and justice in sincere humility will also be unmindful of the boundless mercy of God. On the final judgment day, God will manifest His justice before all mankind; on that day His judgment will mean salvation for all those who, trusting in His mercy, have adored His justice.

Both Holy Scripture and tradition speak of the sinner's transformation into a child of God as the work of God's justice. St. Paul frequently reiterates the truth that *God's justification of the sinner is a work of His mercy* and is dependent on our faith in Jesus Christ: "God manifests His justice at the present time"; for He is "just and justifies any man who puts his faith in Jesus" (Rom. 3:26). A similar thought recurs in St. John, namely, that God will reveal Himself as just and faithful in the remission of sins. "If we acknowledge our sins, God is faithful and just to forgive us our transgressions and to cleanse us from all iniquity" (I John 1:9). After God has redeemed and sanctified us, we are to lead a new life in all justice and holiness. "It is the man who does right, who is righteous as God is righteous" (I John 3:7). "Justice" or "righteousness" here as elsewhere in Holy Scripture is used in its broad meaning, denoting God's own holiness and in man a life according to "the new self, created after the image of God in the justice and holiness that come from truth" (Eph. 4:24).

Man's justice presupposes a sincere admission of guilt and an acknowledgment of utter dependence on God's mercy and gratuitous grace of justification. Therefore, the essence of our new life in "justice and holiness" is humble gratitude and loving homage to God. For this reason the virtue of divine worship forms the core and foundation of all Christian justice. What is all interpersonal integrity without righteousness and justice towards God, our Creator and Redeemer? Men are unable to render justice to each other if they fail to give God the fair tribute of a humble and grateful love. On the other hand, it holds true that men shall make vain efforts to pay fair tribute to God if they undermine the God-ordained order in the world through lack of mutual justice and honesty. Interpersonal justice is pleasing to God only if it conforms to His own sublime standard and ideal. The servant in the gospel for whom his lord had canceled an enormous debt sinned grievously against justice when he tried to extort the last penny from his fellow servant who owed him but a petty sum of money (cf. Matt. 18:23-34). God's work of redemption loudly proclaims both His justice and condescending mercy. In like manner, human justice, in order to be true, must be animated and guided by genuine charity.

Section II. The Virtue of Justice and Juridical Regulation

In the words of St. Thomas, justice consists in *"the firm and constant will to render to every person whatever is his due."* Men's rights are determined in view of their essential equality and individual dispositions, talents, and accomplishments.

Men have an even claim in all those matters in which they are equal, unless such right has been forfeited through their own fault. All men possess equal rights to personal freedom, respect for human dignity, truthfulness, a good reputation, and a living family wage. Each child is entitled to fair educational opportunities. Parents have the primary right and duty to provide an education for their children. This aspect of justice has received considerable emphasis through the United Nations' support for "Human Rights."

Those whom God has favored with special talents and gifts are expected to bring a rich harvest of fruits. St. Paul uses the analogy of the human body, with its various parts and systems, in order to convey the idea that every gift and ability implies a corresponding duty and mission. Each member of the Mystical Body of Christ is worthy of respect if he renders requisite service. In addition, each member of the Mystical Body of Christ deserves the honor inherent in his position or special service (cf. I Cor. 12:12-26). *The same truth applies to all interpersonal relations in the domain of the socio-economic system.*

Justice may be classified according to the rights which it regulates. The demands of justice are well defined and circumscribed in the case of *commutative justice.* The general principles of rectitude in the exchange of goods demand that *the price of a commodity or a service charge should be in agreement with its true value.* Commutative justice regulates all types of *contracts and agreements.* It would be unjust to take advantage of a person's distress and poverty to force him to offer his service or his goods for less than they are worth. Equity, the decisive factor in any contract or bargain, is more important than the mere adherence to the letter of the agreement. The virtue of justice disposes man towards an impartial and fair exchange of commodities and services. It is based on the will towards equity even in the absence of expert knowledge in particular situations. Such an attitude of rectitude presupposes a high degree of unselfishness. Self-seeking is the greatest obstacle to just and equitable treatment.

Social justice requires a deeper insight and higher degree of virtue than commutative justice. Its object is fair and equitable dealings between persons, communities, and social institutions. Social justice is based primarily on natural rights and duties of communities and their members. The chief object of social justice is the *common good*. Social justice embraces both *legal* and *distributive* justice. Legal justice as a moral virtue disposes the heart to seek the common good not only in complying with the demands of the law but in the sincere efforts towards a sound juridical system. Distributive justice is an essential virtue for those in authority insofar as they are responsible for a fair distribution of rights, privileges, and benefits. All members of a democratic society, whether superiors or subjects, should be guided by the demands of distributive justice. It plays an important role in regulating political propaganda, especially at election times when the desire for the common good should triumph over all personal advantages of unworthy partisanship.

Times of economic depressions and general upheavals of law clearly indicate the tremendous impact which the socio-economic and juridical aspects of life exert on man's appreciation of justice and equity. *The object of civil law is the protection and enforcement of the minimum standards of justice.* Social justice aims towards the legislation and enforcement of fair and equitable laws. Yet the virtue of justice is more than a mere conformity to the demands of civil law. The latter neither embraces nor expresses the fulness of justice. Juridical regulations are usually no more than acceptable compromises between the various social groups and the leading parties.

Individual citizens should render justice to each other and their respective communities. They should do this *on their own accord* and *without the external pressure from civil law.* Everyone should employ his earthly possessions and talents in a manner which safeguards the natural rights of others and promotes the common good. Social justice is a necessary moral virtue for both rulers and subjects because of man's social nature.

Social justice regulates man's interpersonal relationships in social domains, such as the family, socio-economic institutions, national and international affairs, as well as in every political, cultural, and social endeavor.

Social justice is not founded merely on equity in business transactions, but on men's innate tendencies as social beings. The ideals and claims of social justice arise from both the nature of man and his social institutions. For this reason, social justice is a natural right. Man's very nature demands a solidarity of interests and responsibilities because the entire human race is one large family under a common Lord and Creator. All earthly goods in the nature of gratuitous gifts from God's generosity imply a social obligation. Individuals as well as nations may not appropriate each others' possessions, rights, or privileges required for a dignified human existence. Social justice demands that man's cooperation and collaboration on a personal, national, and international level may glorify the common God and Creator. These are demands based on man's social nature. In the supernatural realm the virtue of social justice assumes a new dignity and splendor as the distinguishing *family spirit* of the children of God.

The basic prerequisites of social justice are charity and community spirit. It is charity alone which enables us to perceive our neighbor's needs and to respond willingly to his particular rights and just demands. Charity alone is able to move the hearts of the privileged ones of society so that they forego their prerogatives and priorities for the sake of the common good. Charity plays a leading role in averting the threat of class-hatred among the underprivileged of society. It guards against the danger of spiteful arbitrariness in the pursuit of important interests.

Section III. Justice in a World Full of Iniquity

The virtue of justice can unfold itself only in an atmosphere of selfless love. It will manifest itself in just and equitable laws. Even the most solid juridical order will fail to achieve its aims without charity and the moral virtue of justice. Conversely, in the absence of sound juridical regulations the virtue of justice will fail and charity will tend to grow cold. This is expressed in Our Lord's comment on the consummation of the world: "and because iniquity will abound, the charity of many will grow cold" (Matt. 24:12). The term "iniquity" in the above quotation implies, above all, a denial of God's laws. Man's refusal to acknowledge God's just demands is intimately associated with the disorganization of all social order. A faithful observance of God's law guarantees a sincere concern for the observance of juridical regulations. That is why citizens of Christian countries should strive to bring all civil laws in true conformity with God's laws.

The pastoral care of man's environment also embraces the layman's efforts towards just and equitable laws in the socio-economic and political realms. Yet we should not forget that a complete realization of our high ideal is unattainable in this present world. Our continuous endeavor for improvement in the social order is an aspect of the Christian virtue of justice and an expression of zeal for the kingdom of God. Nevertheless, we must face the fact that our testimony of charity and justice is rendered in a world full of injustice. This awareness is a distinguishing mark of the Christian virtue of justice.

1. Peaceful Opposition Against Injustice

In the Sermon on the Mount, Christ expressed a serious warning against the unlawful use of violence to ward off evil: "You have heard it said, 'An eye for an eye,' and 'A tooth for a tooth.' I, on the contrary, declare to you: do not meet evil with evil. No, if someone strikes you on the right cheek, turn to him the other as well. And if a man intends by process of law to rob you of your coat, let him have your cloak as well. And if someone forces you to go one mile with him, go two miles with him" (Matt. 5:38-41). This teaching, although incomprehensible to natural man, should not be misinterpreted. It does not endorse a sluggish indifference to all the injustices in this world. On the contrary, the Christian should employ all the powers of charity in order to overcome evil. Yet such a determined will presupposes a firm desire to remain unconquered by evil (cf. Rom. 12:21). This is an illustration of Christ's way of "fulfilling" the Law. The Christian should be ready to suffer even grievous wrong without yielding to any feeling of revenge or acts of retaliation. The most effective means of overcoming the evil designs of our enemies is a response which is prompted by an unselfish charity (cf. Matt. 5:44). This is the true victory of charity. Prudence should guide us in the various circumstances of our life. The patient endurance of wrong may, at times, bring about a triumph of justice over evil. This is especially true if our actions manifest a benevolent will towards the offender. Genuine charity is the prerequisite for a truly prudent judgment.

Scripture reports an occasion when Our Lord was asked to determine the legality of a claim in regard to an inheritance. Our Lord's answer is quite decisive: "Man, who has appointed Me a judge or arbitrator over you?" (Luke 12:14). Jesus then used this opportunity to condemn all covetousness. The insidious danger in every opposition against injustice and in every lawsuit arises from overemphasis on earthly and transitory goods. The Sermon on the Mount does not imply an unconditional renunciation of our right of self-defense. The words of this Beatitude are but an amplification of the admonition: "Seek first the kingdom of God and His justice" (Matt. 6:33). *It is a serious injustice against God and self to start lawsuits for insignificant matters and thereby jeopardize God's glory and the eternal salvation of souls.*

Legal proceedings are, of course, not wrong in themselves; they become sinful through inordinate attachments to earthly goods and hatred for the opponent. It is a grave injustice against God and self to risk His friendship and the eternal salvation of our neighbor by resorting to lawsuits in trivial matters. In this present world, full of malice, Christians ought to try as far as possible to avoid legal proceedings and should use them only as a last resort. They should always remain conscious of the inherent spiritual dangers in legal involvements.

2. Legal Defense Against Injustice

On the other hand, excessive yielding of personal rights in the face of grave injustice may not only confirm our opponent in evil but endanger others. Hence, the Christian should not hesitate to employ legal proceedings in matters involving the financial security of his family or the welfare of orphans and widows. Provided his intentions are sincere and laudable, the Christian should not shrink from such action because of the unfavorable publicity resulting from court proceedings.

Yet at no time should the Christian exploit law proceedings for personal advantage. The virtue of justice demands a sincere desire to know what is right before resorting to lawsuits (cf. Rules of Prudence p. 128).

Take, for example, the so-called *contestable last will and testament*. For the sake of certainty, civil law guarantees legal protection only to those declarations of dispositions of property which have been executed in the prescribed form and manner. Although the relatives of a deceased person could contest the legality of a "formless" last will and testament, it would be wrong to make use of such a right if the beneficiary is a poor man, who has been reduced to dependence by illness or old age. After careful consideration of all the attending circumstances they should try to settle their dispute without filing a lawsuit.

The Christian should decide questions of "justice" and "right" by the criterion of charity. Although justice does not demand restitution if a person has failed against charity by insisting on his personal right, nevertheless, he should repair the damage resulting from his lack of charity. Our best protection against the snares of an unjust world is a life under the impulse of charity.

3. *Justice in the Rectifying of Injustice*

Our awareness of the abounding iniquity in this world, full of pernicious solidarity with the "prince of evil," demands not only a renunciation of unfair means in opposing injustice but also a support of the juridical system. This demands appropriate punishment for those who are guilty of a serious offense. Although individuals may at times refrain from retaliating against injustice, in keeping with the spirit of the Sermon on the Mount, this norm does not apply to those in authority. It is the State which carries the sword of retributive justice. "He is God's minister, an avenger to inflict punishment on evildoers" (Rom. 13:14). If the State should refrain from punishing the evildoer, it seriously violates justice and fails to safeguard the common good. It is evident that a breadwinner would fail against justice to his family if he submitted to exploitation by his employer. In like manner, it would be unfair of the State to relinquish its right of vindicative justice.

In principle, the State posseses the *explicit right to enforce capital punishment*. Its purpose is to reduce crime and to keep alive the spirit of justice and atonement for serious wrongdoing. Nevertheless, there is no absolute need for capital punishment as long as other types of retribution reduce the incidence of crime. In view of the new law of grace, the State's penal system should take cognizance of the fact that God's justice is always combined with mercy and that God's punishments are intended for man's ultimate good. The decisive factor in the penal system of the State is the manner of enforcing punishment. The treatment of prisoners should at all times be humane and in keeping with human dignity. The prison environment should be conducive to the good of the prisoner rather than to his further deterioration.

In the case of juvenile delinquency there should be more emphasis on preventive than punitive measures. The State should ferret hidden sources of crime and abuses which are tolerated in the socio-economic and cultural life of the people. At times, juvenile delinquents who are brought before the law are less guilty of misdemeanor than those citizens who are responsible for the glorification of crime through various media of communication, such as movies, radio, television, and press. In God's sight the youthful criminal may be less responsible for his misdeeds than those who neglect their serious duty of upholding the norms of public morality. An attitude of undue severity in the exercise of justice may often be traced to the unconscious effort of the "real guilty ones" to soothe their accusing consciences by their loud cry: "Convict the guilty."

The same principle of justice applies to discipline in education and training. At no time may punishment be an aim in itself. Furthermore, it is preferable for education to achieve its objectives without punishment. Parents should refrain from correcting every infraction of the rule. They should use appropriate discipline for the sake of assisting the child in acquiring a firm determination of will, a fair sense of justice, and an appreciation for the need of atonement. All disciplinary measures should aim to meet the unique needs of each child. This should also be the chief objective in giving praise and recognition.

4. The Love of Enemies in an Unjust World

The justice of men is no more than a conscientious striving after equity in the midst of "an unjust world." This truth seems to be ignored by those who, under all circumstances, flatly refuse the right of force. It is unquestionable that we Christians should be aware of the secret supernatural power of opposition in conformity with the principles of the invincible charity proposed by the Sermon on the Mount. All Christians have a serious obligation to work towards peace and harmony among nations. This duty is especially incumbent on those engaged in journalism and politics. Every citizen can contribute to peace by shaping public opinion. What great good could be achieved if all Christians would refrain from uncharitable and hateful criticism of other nations! On the other hand, we should guard ourselves against those nations who, while advocating general disarmament for others, are doing all in their power to keep the fire of war aglow by supporting dangerous revolutionaries. An unconditional condemnation of all warfare would mean a foolish encouragement for all dangerous agitators and disturbers of peace.

War should be the last resort in the attempt to defend inalienable rights and the survival of the State. We cannot be guided by the unrealistic maxim of a complete rejection of warfare because it is our duty to defend peace and justice as long as there is any unjust aggression against a State or Nation. Lovers of peace are bound to fight for justice. "Peace is a work of justice" (Pius XII). In this world of iniquity it is a matter of justice that each State be granted the inalienable right to defend its own liberty and dignity by means of appropriate measures and, in extreme cases, even by force of arms. Such action involves the most overwhelming responsibility on the part of those declaring war and requires utmost conscientiousness in weighing all possible consequences and alternatives. A war would be both ridiculous and unjust if, in the final outcome, it simply added to the already existing misery and injustice. The thought of today's terrifying weapons of warfare firmly convinces the entire human race of the crying need for morally outlawing any aggressor from the very beginning. Today, no discussion of the Christian's attitude toward the problem of war and peace is complete without some reference to the great encyclical *Pacem in Terris* which Pope John XXIII gave to the world as a final legacy of his historic pontificate. In that document he clearly enunciated the duty of individual citizens, State and Federal governments, as well as national and international organizations, to work for good order and a peaceful existence of men in our times. He emphasized the singular importance of love-inspired justice at all levels and in all relationships, as he inspired men all over the world to strive anew with greater earnestness for the attainment of true peace.

Section IV. The Necessity of Laws Governing Private Property

It is significant that the great theologians of the early Christian period and the Middle Ages always referred to the sinfulness of this world whenever the question of regulating private property was brought into focus. In the absence of sin and injustice, civil law could indeed be simplified and law enforcement would become superfluous. Likewise, the regulation of private property would present an entirely different picture. In comparison with Christian sociology, capitalistic Liberalism as well as Communism fail to recognize the true state of affairs in relation to private property. These two systems are based on the false assumption and naive belief that man is perfectly good as soon as he has found the most suitable system of property allocation. Christians, on the contrary, are convinced that any theory of property ownership must take into consideration the fact of the sinfulness of this world.

1. Capitalistic Liberalism

The originators of Liberalism and Capitalism, such as Adam Smith and David Ricardo, regarded the social-economic order exclusively as an affair of economics where considerations of social justice should not interfere. Yet their entire theory, corresponding to the deistic or materialistic image of God, is based on the very naive optimism that man's egotistical "instinct" can achieve maximum results in the socio-economic sphere if left unmolested by both the State and the Church. It would be unfair to the founders and representatives of Capitalism to presume that they sanctioned the extreme exploitation of the workingman in the early and late epochs of Capitalism.

There are several fallacies in Liberalism. One is the failure to understand the absolute necessity of property regulations for the sake of man's own protection in a "world full of inequity." Property laws aim to reduce injustice and sin as far as this is possible. The false philosophy of Liberalism, which refuses to admit that equitable civil laws and the moral virtue of prudence should be the determinants of property right and domestic economy, further adds to human injustice and misery because man's fallen nature tends to seek its own advantage rather than social justice. What else can we expect from "the free play of social forces" than the so-called "wolf-freedom" which makes the underprivileged of society the victims of greed and selfishness.

Past experiences with the deplorable practices of Liberalism have resulted in government regulations intended to correct abuses in the social-economic system. Neo-liberalism admits the necessity of minimum governmental planning and control, but it places less emphasis on the natural rights of the underprivileged of society than does Catholic social teaching.

2. Communism

Communistic propaganda in its dealings with guileless Christians takes advantage of the fact that the early Christians practiced a type of communism based on the spirit of charity. In this connection, it is important to remember that the voluntary "communism" of the early Christian communities had nothing in common with the materialistic Communism of today. The latter uses unrelenting force and violence while the former was the free choice of those impelled by love of God and neighbor. The attempt to justify the ruthless practices of Communism with a reference to the selfless charity of the early Christians or to the voluntary poverty of religious men and women in the Church is a serious pitfall because it confuses "right" and charity, juridical order and freely chosen selfless sharing of personal property. It is indeed an unrealistic optimism which allows materialistic Communism to hope to re-create, by violence and force of pressure from the social-economic system, an earthly paradise comparable to the communion of charity exemplified by the early Christian communities.

Although Marxism loudly protests against the social injustice of Capitalism, it nevertheless fails to believe in the power of sin and the injustice of man's heart. It traces all social disorders in this world to faulty property distribution and regulations. It expects, by means of external regulation of economic production and distribution, to achieve a perfect state of earthly happiness and human innocence in a classless and propertyless society.

3. Christian Principles in the Social-Economic Order

Christian principles relating to the social-economic order and man's right to property are based on a common sense approach to existing realities and on man's essential freedom and sense of responsibility. Neither an excessive public control nor an unbridled liberalism is in conformity with the true nature of man and society. All property regulations and the entire social-economic order should respect man's freedom and, therefore, provide the individual, the family, and the community with opportunities which are essential to the exercise of the virtue of justice and the development of moral responsibility. Civil laws in the social-economic order should guarantee mutual collaboration and act as effective deterrents against all types of injustice and exploitation.

Contrary to communistic propaganda, a society without legal regulations regarding property rights is both unrealistic and unattainable. Furthermore, the right to own private property is not in itself a cause for class-hatred nor is the improvement of the social order (even the abolition of private property) the panacea for all sin and injustice in this world. It is the Christian's task to aim at an economic order which embodies the ideals of social justice. True social reform necessitates a moral renewal.

History provides eloquent proof of social systems which successfully merged individual and collective ownership. There are many legitimate variations in the exercise of man's right to property which are in conformity with the exigencies of man's nature. Property laws must be in agreement with the natural law imprinted in man's heart and must do justice to the social needs of the particular epoch. It is important that they should *acknowledge the fundamental role of the family* as the bearer of all property rights.

It is the duty of the State to amend property laws in order to correct abuses, maintain social justice and mutual concord in the community. "The State may not abrogate the right to private ownership which is a natural law and hence cannot be abolished by men" (Leo XIII: Enc. *Rerum Novarum*, No. 35). "Man's natural right to the possession and the transmission of property by inheritance must be kept intact and inviolate. The State has no power to abrogate it, for man is older than the State. Moreover, the domestic household is antecedent, logically as well as in fact, to the civil community" (Pius XI: Enc. *Quadragesimo Anno*, No. 49).

The Church's emphatic pleas for the right to private and, particularly, family ownership have been prompted by motives other than favoritism to a particular social class. "The Church's defense of individual property is not meant to favor the status quo of the rich or to shield those powerful in the social-economic world against the poor and indigent. Her aim is the exact opposite" (Pius XII: Address, March 22, 1944). The very foundations of both private and public ownership would be jeopardized by such a biased approach to the property right of the privileged class of society. Ownership regulations should safeguard the rights of both the individual citizen and the family group. Thus, they shall insure personal liberty and dignity and allow men to prove their sense of responsibility towards the community.

The distribution of wealth into individual and social property (of legitimate scope) may never obscure the basic truth that all earthly goods are entrusted to us by a common heavenly Father in view of the common good. *Every possession implies a social obligation* and basic responsibility for the rest of the human family.

Man's indisputable social responsibility may under certain circumstances obligate those favored with the superabundance of both capital and natural resources to assist their indigent fellowmen. Regardless of the necessary division of earthly goods into individual possessions, all men, strictly speaking, have an equal claim to the treasures of this earth. For this very reason, the wealthy are bound in justice and charity to aid the poor through job opportunities and material assistance. In the event that the rich fail to share their material possessions with the needy, the poverty-stricken would be entitled to appropriate to themselves whatever is required to sustain their life or maintain their health, because the lesser right to property yields to the greater right to life.

No social-economic system can ever achieve an ideal condition which would automatically forestall every form of injustice. The mere attempt towards such a perfect social order is bound to lead to an extreme control by the State and to coercive measures which are unworthy of free men.

A new social juridical order regarding ownership right must keep the golden mean between the controlled economy of collectivism and the concentration of wealth in the hands of a few. A State-planned economy or a total nationalization of industry and business will suppress private enterprise and personal responsibility. On the other hand, unrestrained liberalism will give free scope to the sordid selfishness of the wealthy and influential. The reconstruction of the social order according to Christian principles aims to cede to each individual a fair measure of personal responsibility in agreement with his position in a democratic structure of society. In the final analysis, the State should provide public assistance only when the family or the local social units are unable to fulfill their natural obligations. The Church proposes the principles of subsidiarity and a functional social order. It was especially Pope Pius XI who insisted on the principle of mutual assistance. In a similar sense, reference is made today to an economic structure organized on a company level in which the single corporations of the industry are federated into an Industry Council. The important principle in all this is the spirit of solidarity, a joyful sense of responsibility, and collaboration of all concerned for the good of all.

348

4. The Social Issue in the Wage System

The industrial revolution, followed by a liberalistic capital-ism, confronted Catholic moral teaching with many social problems which it recognized as far beyond solution through the mere application of the principles governing commutative justice and charitable almsgiving. The burn-ing question of the workingman was at that time, as it is to-day, a *social problem*. There is no doubt that the spirit of charity is basic to the resolution of this important issue. However, impersonal charitable donations without the gen-uine spirit of brotherly love, far from rectifying the de-plorable situation, add further insult to the poor unless such action is combined with the sincere will towards social reform. Genuine brotherly love alone guarantees a sympa-thetic understanding for the needs and demands of men, especially those from another social class. The principles of commutative justice safeguard against injustice from equals which would further accentuate the social issue. The key-note in this vital question of social justice is the complete integration and full recognition of every class, especially that of the wage-earner.

During the course of the industrial revolution, an exclu-sive individualistic concept of property as well as a declin-ing solidarity of interests led to an aggregation of wealth in the hands of a few. At the same time, the wage-earner was completely excluded from private and stock owner-ship.

It was just this withholding of productive goods from the hands of the workingman which, during the widespread economic depression in the past, led to the creation of the *proletariat*. Catholic social teaching and endeavor, as enun-ciated by Pius XI in the Encyclical *Quadragesimo Anno,* and even further by John XXIII in *Mater et Magistra* and

Pacem in Terris, clearly aims towards abolishing the proletariat by granting the wage-earners their rightful place as
a social class in the existing social order. The most important problems in this domain are: fair and equitable
wages; the workingman's share in ownership, management,
and profit; organized labor unions; and workmen's strikes.

(a) Justice in Wages

While not condemning the wage system in itself, recent
Popes, nevertheless, have repeatedly emphasized the principle that work agreements should be tempered in certain re-
spects with partnership arrangements so that "workers and
officials become participants in ownership, or management,
or share in some manner in profits." According to Catholic
social thought, the employment agreement should not be
based merely on the principles of commutative justice because labor cannot be purchased like a commodity. Furthermore, the workingman must be respected as a partner.
Even in employment contracts, the basic principles of commutative justice should be supplemented by social equity
and social respect.

Wages are unjust from the start if they violate commutative justice which demands a fair and equitable remuneration for the work performed. In virtue of this fact, wages
should be commensurate with one's performance. Yet, it is
impossible to determine a just wage on this principle alone.
There is more to the problem of just wages than mere cal-
culations of productivity. Above all, there is the issue of
social justice which poses the vital question: What share in
the "social product" (the outcome of capital and labor)
should be the property of the workingman, the employer,
and the capitalist? This is really the pivotal question underlying the wage issue which can be solved only by the principles and in the spirit of social justice.

The great Popes advocating social justice, from Leo XIII to Paul VI, have repeatedly emphasized that the average diligent laborer is entitled to a family-wage. This means that the wage-earner's share in the profit, accruing from capital and labor, should be equivalent to an income which enables a diligent and thrifty laborer to raise a good-sized family without the need for unnatural birth control. It is a social abuse that the mother of a family should be forced to work outside the home in order to earn the bare necessities of life for the family, if she thereby has to neglect the duties of housekeeping and the rearing of children.

By the same principle of justice, the unmarried working-man is entitled to a family-wage because he should have the opportunity to save sufficient funds for the future when he is ready to marry and raise a family. If individual industries cannot meet this goal, it remains a joint responsibility of society, industry, and the government to allot at least to each married workingman a family-wage in due proportion to the number of dependent children. In cases of large families the payment of an additional sum of money for each child through special "family funds" is in no way equivalent to almsgiving. On the basis of social justice, these families are entitled to society's fair share in their social-economic burdens. In former times when the family unit was a productive community, large families enjoyed economic and social advantages. In our modern industrial society, this situation has been reversed. Today's large families carry the greater economic burden while society reaps the benefits because of increased manpower.

The question of fair remuneration for work performance concerns not only the workingman but also teachers, doctors, nurses, public officials, and other professional groups. However, in all cases, the basic maxims of social justice are applicable. Consequently, it is an injustice for the upper class to live in luxury and opulence while the industrious and honorable people of the lower classes are unable to earn sufficient money to raise an average family.

(b) Partnership in Management

We have seen that the social issue of just wages encompasses far more than the aspect of financial remuneration. The core of the modern social question and at the same time the cause for the wage-earner's embitterment is the one-sided settlement of labor affairs by capital and management. In many countries the employee feels himself excluded from even those aspects of administration which vitally affect his own life and social rights. In recent years, workingmen have achieved some participation in the formulation of policies relating to wages and other items of management through the instrumentality of labor unions and through government policies. At present it seems unreasonable that capital, on the mere basis of ownership or investment, should refuse to grant the wage-earner his rightful share in formulating policies which chiefly affect him. This seems just as illogical as the workingman's attempt to acquire undue management of his employer's property and products.

Strictly speaking, the natural right does not entitle the wage-earner to a clear-cut participation in management problems beyond the wage agreement. Furthermore, it would be unwise to grant new and inexperienced employees such a major share in management. On the other hand, it is in full agreement with the human dignity of the workingman and also in full accord with social justice, that workingmen should have a voice, on general principles, in the operation and overall management in proportion to their contribution to the particular enterprise. *Capital, management, and labor are partners in the industrial undertaking.*

The demand for "joint management" or "co-management" by the workingman on an *industry-wide basis* is accomplished through the medium of labor organizations and industry councils provided these are treated as partners in business. Labor disputes may also be settled through the mediation and arbitration of labor specialists and government officials.

On the local industrial plant level, it would be unwise to solicit support from outside political organizations and trade unions for arbitration in questions pertaining to plant management, because the chief aim is a peaceful partnership between those engaged in the particular enterprise. A joint responsibility in management decisions, safeguarding that degree of co-responsibility for each worker which he deserves in view of his personal contribution to the industry, should contribute to both his personal development and his job satisfaction. Joint management, if carried out within reasonable limits and with due consideration of particular circumstances, should markedly reduce class differences and oppositions. The workingman who feels himself respected as a trustworthy partner in economic endeavors has no inclinations for class-hatred and opposition. He has become emancipated from the proletariat.

In the final analysis, the chief objective in promoting the wage-earner's participation in management problems is the establishment of a sound bond of partnership between capital, management, and labor; a relationship of peaceful cooperation in the sharing of rights and duties. Such an ideal situation will be achieved only gradually. Attention should be called to the decisive pronouncements of Pope Pius XII: "The Church encourages all efforts which, within the framework of the given circumstances, aim to include into the labor contract such constituents of the partnership deed which are designed to improve the workingman's lot" (Address, November 3, 1951). The encyclical *Mater et Magistra*, follows exactly the same line of thinking, in even clearer enunciation of Christian principles.

(c) Share in Ownership and Profit

An equitable distribution of the profits of industry would ultimately result in private ownership among the workingmen. It was the fond expectation of Pope Pius XI "that at least in the future the new abundance of goods would be directed into the broad stream of the working class" (*Quadragesimo Anno*, No. 61). Such a desirable situation would eventually enable an industrious and thrifty workingman to lay aside a modest capital for the financial security of his own family.

It would indeed be a worthwhile achievement if the majority of the wage-earners in all industrialized countries could own their own home and garden. However, the ultimate aim of social justice is the full assimilation of the working class into the structure of society. This objective can only be accomplished if the wage-earner is granted his rightful share in stock ownership or management profit in proportion to his contribution to the industrial enterprise.

Catholic teaching on social issues is fully cognizant of the fact that the full realization of this aim can never be achieved by subjecting all industrial productivity to State ownership and control. However, we should not condemn every attempt at nationalization as gross socialism, especially in cases where the productive property cannot be safely committed to private enterprises. The danger for every class of society lies in the excess of public ownership. The transfer of capitalism into the hands of the State will not eliminate the proletariat, it will rather aggravate the condition through the wage-earner's ultimate dependence on a heartless bureaucracy. Yet, milder forms of socialism which are timely, appropriate, and limited in scale may contribute to the disappearance of the proletariat. Such possibilities may also be seen in the various forms of partnership, bonds, and investments. The Church's teaching can point the way and sound timely warnings against misuses. However, the concrete realization for the most part depends on the social-economic possibilities which require skilled evaluation by specialists in the field.

(d) Strikes

Strikes, or organized cessations of work, are the chief weapons in the hands of labor to attain the employer's assent to certain demands, such as just wages and socially equitable working conditions. Morally, there is no objection to a strike if sincere and peaceful endeavors at settlement of the dispute have failed and if the strike does not add to the social evils. Both the objective and the means of the strike must be in conformity with justice, peace, and the common good. The *lockout,* the reverse of the strike, is the employer's weapon against the workingman, whereby he shuts down his plant and closes the door against them. Such a harsh measure can only be justified in extraordinary and difficult circumstances in which all other measures had been exhausted.

These extreme means to wage industrial conflicts are definitely objectionable if used for political purposes. Only under very rare and extreme circumstances may a *general strike* be initiated, such as to break passive resistance against an unjust and unlawful government. In such an event, the individual employee should ascertain the reason and moral issue of the strike before he follows the summons of the union for cessation of work.

In our modern society the Christian has to join leagues and alliances which are neutral in their philosophy of life (*Weltanschauung*). Nevertheless, he should guard against the danger of being exploited in the attainment of aims which are opposed to faith and social justice.

Section V. Forms of Injustice and Restitution

Any violation of personal right or any refusal to give to another that which is "his due" is by its very nature a serious offense against justice. Even *omissions* in this matter may be grievous violations of both justice and charity if occasioned by lack of responsibility and culpable negligence by those appointed for the administration or protection of the property rights of others. In such instances one is bound in justice to make restitution.

The most common and obvious sins against commutative justice are *cheating* and *fraud, usury* and the *charging of exorbitant prices, unjust damage* to the property of others, and *stealing.*

Cheating and fraud are unjust appropriations of other people's possessions or rights *under the pretense of justice* and mostly under the cover and protection of a contract. Forms of fraud are: the falsifying of documents and breaking of contracts, the use of false weights and measures, unfair and unscrupulous competition, bankruptcy for profit making, income tax violations, and fraudulent claims for public assistance and subsidies. Justice demands full restitution for all damage incurred through cheating and fraud.

The *usurer,* who capitalizes on the need of his neighbor

or a general financial depression by charging exorbitant prices, is guilty of grave injustice.

Unjust damage is a willful act by which one causes property loss to another. It does not arise from a desire to enrich oneself, as is the case with the usurer and the thief, but rather has its roots in sinful negligence, mischievousness, animosity, or revenge. While the degree of injustice is measured by the extent of the loss or damage to property, irrespective of the sinful intention, such uncharitable attitudes increase the gravity of the sin. The one who has caused damage to his neighbor's property without forethought or grave negligence is not bound in strict justice to make restitution although he may incur a legal liability. It is charity, above all, which demands restitution especially if the injured party is a poor person.

Theft is the secret seizure of another's property against his reasonable will. *Robbery* adds the iniquity of violence to the injustice of stealing. The *extortionist* uses threats and intimidations to obtain money or things of value. *Failure to pay a just wage* is an injustice comparable to robbery and extortion. Holy Scripture refers to such an injustice as one which cries out to God (cf. James 5:4). The unethical exploitation of the workingman's need through unfair labor contracts is a form of fraud in which the appearance of right is preserved. There is no question of unjust dealings if, on the other hand, the employer is unable to pay higher wages or if the workingman freely renounces part of his payment.

Various attempts have been made to establish definite criteria for evaluating the *seriousness of the sins of injustice* and the consequent duty of restoration. Great circumspection is needed in such an endeavor lest we might create the false impression that God has fixed an arbitrary boundary line beyond which He does not take seriously the transgressions against His law. *The veniality of sin,* namely its incomplete denial of charity and its mere partial contradiction to the state of grace and friendship with God, *has its roots in man's state of imperfection.* The borderline between mortal and venial sin greatly depends on the degree of religious-moral perfection of the individual. This means that a person who has arrived at an exalted level of spiritual perfection may recognize a minor act of injustice as diametrically opposed to the love of God and neighbor. Consequently, it would be sinful to take advantage of the veniality of sin by saying: "Up to this point I can defraud or damage others without committing a mortal sin." After sins of injustice have been committed, the rules of prudence should be applied in regard to restitution and the strict requirement for confessing the sins. These provide safe guidelines for the average conscience.

The seriousness of any sin of injustice is determined not only by the extent of damage incurred but also by the sinful motives and the foreseeable consequences, such as animosity, suspicion, mistrust, and insincerity. The extent of restitution should be in proportion to the damage and the special needs of the injured party.

As indicated above, it is difficult to determine a strict border line between mortal and venial sin on a mere quantitative basis of the injustice. Nevertheless, with careful circumspection we may give the following guidelines: a theft or fraud in the equivalence of a day's wage requires restitution in conscience. A theft in the value of approximately one hundred dollars could hardly be considered a minor infraction of justice even by the average conscience. A sensitive conscience will sound a warning in any injury regardless of the extent of damage.

Formal cooperation in the evil deeds of others and culpable neglect to avert acts of injustice make us accomplices in the sins of others. *The duty of restitution* is incumbent chiefly on the malefactors, instigators, and perpetrators of evil. If these fail to fulfill their obligation of restitution, the accomplices in sin have to carry the full burden of restitution. Even persons who unknowingly have acquired stolen goods are obliged to return these as soon as they become aware of the rightful owner. Undue postponement of restitution is sinful to the extent that such delay causes disadvantage or loss to the owner. Justice demands that injustice willfully committed be repaired, not only in cases of theft or damage but in every type of injustice, such as slander, seduction, and sins against the life and health of others if these occasioned property loss.

Under certain circumstances the question of restitution may be involved and complicated. If considerable values are at stake, experienced persons should be consulted as to the required restoration. In the event that this fails to clarify the issue, the duty of restitution is not binding in conscience.

Restitution should not be postponed except in certain situations which warrant a delay for serious reasons, such as the loss of one's position and good name, or the danger of legal prosecution and extreme poverty of one's family. However, the owner should be reimbursed at the earliest possible time or else an equivalent value should be donated to the poor.

In every event, the sincere will towards restitution is a basic prerequisite for true conversion. "If the wicked man turns away from his sin and does what is right and just, giving back pledges, restoring stolen goods, living by statutes that bring life, and doing no wrong, he shall surely live, he shall not die. None of the sins he has committed shall be held against him; he has done what is right and just, he shall surely live" (Ez. 33:15-16).

Section VI. Sins Against the Bodily Life

The Christian should duly appreciate his own bodily life and that of his neighbor. Man's life has been placed under the protection of both justice and charity. Our neighbor's life has been entrusted to our special care and solicitude. Our own life is no more than a loan from the Creator. It remains the property of Him who created us: "None of us lives for himself, and none dies for himself. If we live, we live for the Lord, and if we die, we are the Lord's" (Rom. 14:8).

Life may never become our supreme value in this world. It is God's precious gift to us, for the purpose that in agreement with created order, prudence, and charity we might use it in the service of God and our neighbor. Following the example of Our Lord Jesus Christ, we should be willing and ready to lay down our life in the service of our neighbor who is in extreme distress. "It is by this that we know what love is: that Christ laid down His life for us. And we in our turn are bound to lay down our lives for our brothers" (I John 3:16). Yet at no time may we dispose of our life or that of our neighbor in an autonomous and arbitrary manner.

Suicide is a terrible invasion of God's sovereignty over life and death. In Holy Scripture God insists on His supreme right: "I alone, am God . . . It is I who bring both death and life" (Deut. 32:39). Self-destruction violates not only all the cardinal virtues but also the theological virtues of hope and charity. Suicide is a terrible aberration which is diametrically opposed to a well-ordered self-love and the natural instinct of self-preservation. It represents the most grievous immoderation and the very excess of unauthorized behavior. The deliberate taking of one's own life is an insolence towards God, the Creator. It is an expression of desperation and complete inability to cope with the difficulties of life. Nevertheless, we are not entitled to judge the self-killer. Frequently, the underlying cause is a mental disturbance. The alarming increase in the number of suicides should be taken as a serious warning and an indication of widespread social disorder and a deplorable absence of worthwhile aims and orientation in life. It further reveals a shocking decline in reverence for life and charity, as well as an extreme aversion to suffering. In the final analysis, suicide is a revolt against God.

Premeditated murder is a most atrocious crime which cries to heaven for vengeance. It is a grievous sin against charity and a grave injustice against God, society, and our fellowman. A clear distinction should be made between *murder* which is the unlawful killing of a human being with express or implied malice, and manslaughter which is committed in the transport of passion.

The *killing of an unjust aggressor* is neither murder nor manslaughter. It is, rather, a necessary act of self-defense. It is permitted for the sake of warding off danger of death to oneself or another or for the protection of goods equivalent to life, provided there are no other means of adequate self-protection.

Infanticide and *judicial murder* are sins of particular gravity. Judicial murder is an unjust execution of an innocent person by public authority.

Voluntary abortion is murder in the fullest sense of the word because the unborn fruit of the womb is truly a human being with an immortal soul. It is one of the most hideous crimes because it is a question of a mother killing her own utterly defenseless child. It is indeed frivolous to talk about "the mother's right over her own body." At the same time, abortion constitutes a moral attack on the dignity of motherhood. Those participating in the sin of voluntary abortion through advice, instigation, or active collaboration are likewise guilty of murder. The Church denounces voluntary abortion by the penalty of excommunication. This serious ecclesiastical censure excludes the guilty ones from the communion of the faithful until they make themselves worthy of reconciliation through sincere repentance. Abortion is voluntary if it is brought about by deliberate action. It is involuntary and consequently not sinful if it results spontaneously from a number of physiological causes. The term *"criminal"* is used to designate those voluntary abortions which are carried out for motives other than medical.

State legislatures and all those in responsible positions for influencing public opinion or improving social conditions have a serious obligation to shield the life of the unborn child from the heinous crime of voluntary abortion. The number of voluntary or criminal abortions could possibly be reduced by an attitude of sympathy and respect for the human dignity of the unwed mother who bravely shoulders her full responsibility in bearing the consequences of her sin.

The arguments in favor of so-called *"indications"* for the inducing of abortions are evident remnants of a heathen philosophy no matter whether the alleged reasons are: the possibility of congenital or hereditary diseases (of the child), financial hardships of the family, poor health of the mother, or danger to the good reputation of an unwed mother. Similarly unjustifiable are the so-called *therapeutic abortions.* This term refers to the interruption of a pregnancy under the pretense of "therapeutic" indications. We should remember that no physician has the right to pronounce or execute a death sentence on an innocent party even under the pretext of saving the mother's life. He should, rather, do all in his power to save the life of both the mother and child. If despite his professional skill and sincere solicitude he is unable to achieve both objectives, he should remember that God has the final decision over life and death. Today's most experienced gynecologists testify to the fact that through their adamant refusal to interfere with the unborn child's life they have saved not only the lives of innumerable children but also those of many mothers.

Surgical operations which cannot be postponed without danger to the mother's life may be performed even if these might lead indirectly to an abortion. This is different from a direct abortion in which the termination of pregnancy through the destruction of the fetus is primarily and immediately intended. In the former case, every attempt should be made to have the fetus baptized. Under similar circumstances, a pregnant uterus might be removed if there is immediate danger to the mother. However, as far as possible, such an operation should be postponed until the child is at least viable (able to live outside the uterus).

Euthanasia, or mercy killing of incurables, even if these should request such an action, is forbidden for the same reason as the killing of the unborn child. Furthermore, the planned annihilation of cripples and the mentally ill is sinful murder. Every life is worth preserving as long as God deigns to sustain it. Even the miserable existence of the maimed and deformed has a sublime purpose if it awakens the charity and benevolence of others. It would spell the ruin of all human dignity if the utilitarian aspect of man's existence would be the criterion on which his right to life depended.

On the other hand, it is unobjectionable to administer pain-relieving drugs which indirectly or accidentally might hasten death. Although pain relief in the treatment of patients is an important act of charity, the restoration to health and the preservation of life are the physician's chief obligations. In the face of imminent death, the physician should place his skill in the service of the Christian ideal of suffering and dying. Consequently, care should be taken that the patient has the opportunity to receive the *sacrament of anointing the sick* while still fully conscious and able to prepare for his final journey. It is essential to remember that this sacrament produces a twofold effect. One is the spiritual renewal in grace through the divine assistance which aims at our perfect conformity with the will of God in matters of life and death and makes us participants in Christ's redemptive death. The other is the bodily effect which often will aid the patient and "will raise him up" (James 5:15) if such is the good pleasure of God.

Modern therapy poses a number of new moral problems and questions. The possibility of *organ transplantation* has occasioned a discussion and dispute about its ethical implications. The author agrees with a number of eminent theologians that there is neither a denial of God's supreme dominion nor a contradiction to Christian self-love if a person willingly donates a member or an organ of his body, such as an eye or kidney, in order to save the life of another or to help him in great distress, provided there is good reason to expect success. This is based on the reasoning that it is permissible to sacrifice a member or an organ of our own body in order to preserve our health or life. In a similar manner, we may, in the service of charity, expose ourselves to contact with communicable diseases. Consequently, in view of this and in imitation of the example of Christ who sacrificed His own life in our behalf, we may presume that under certain circumstances it would be permissible to donate a part or an organ of our body. It would be wrong, however, to use the term mutilation in this regard since the particular part of the body is not destroyed. On the other hand, it would be unethical and forbidden (and this is stressed by Pius XII) if the State or any other authority would force an innocent person to donate a part of his body for experimental surgery.

Our corporal life is placed under the protection of God's supreme dominion and the charity of our neighbor. Consequently, reasonable care must be taken to protect one's own life and that of others. It is especially important to adhere to traffic regulations and speed limits in order to reduce the number of highway accidents as far as this is possible. Grave carelessness, which endangers human life, is by its very nature grievously sinful. If such thoughtlessness or recklessness causes death, we use the terms *accidental homicide or manslaughter*. It should be remembered, however, that the moral guilt is inherent in the recklessness and therefore is not augmented through the accidental death of the victim, but the fatality impresses more forcibly the guilt incurred and may at times produce an exaggerated guilt feeling. If, on the other hand, the accident could not be avoided, there is no guilt. On the whole, the sharp increase in highway accidents caused by careless and intoxicated drivers should make all traffic violators keenly aware of their guilt. In view of the many serious injuries and fatalities, it is a matter of conscience to abide by all traffic regulations. Furthermore, all incompetent motorists should refrain from driving.

Closely allied to accidental homicide, even somewhat related to murder, is that disposition of mind which out of sheer ill will and selfishness desires the death of others. Similarly sinful is a gross uncharitable behavior, especially between spouses and to aged parents, which may "grieve the injured party to death." Likewise, the person who neglects to feed the hungry or to offer aid in accidents or disasters, sins seriously against the fifth commandment.

Section VII. The Social Virtues

The virtue of justice has nothing in common with a narrow-minded calculation nor with an unkind bargaining for the mere minimum of duty to our neighbor. This becomes strikingly evident in God's own dealings in the justification of the repentant sinner. The essence of the interpersonal virtue of justice is the solicitude for the common good which gains new meaning in the light of our incorporation into the Mystical Body of Christ. This intimate union with Christ should make the Christian aware that his own life's purpose will be achieved only in true solidarity with his fellow members and an unselfish subordination of personal interests for the common welfare. Even quantitative appraisals in the fair exchange of material goods must not overlook the person and his individual contribution. The truly gracious character of justice is indicated by the fact that the social virtues of *devotion for family, patriotism, gratitude, generosity,* and *courtesy* are classified in Catholic moral philosophy as manifestations of justice.

Devotion to one's family is the natural expression of an innate feeling of belonging and of mutual reverence in the keen perception and intuitive knowledge of the sublime mysteries underlying family life. Husband and wife should consider themselves as fellow travelers towards heaven and as partners in the creative love of God. In the presence of the Creator, who is the source of all paternity, parents learn to respect the innate calling and dignity of their children. The child's filial devotion towards his parents is the faithful echo of the parent's mutual respect and their expression of parental authority and love. Reverence should animate both the act of commanding and obeying.

Children are expected to respect their parents, in virtue of their position and their authority from God, even if parents seriously fail in their obligations. In such unfortunate circumstances, the child greatly depends on the Church and various human institutions to provide helpful experiences of true authority. It is this devotion and family spirit which motivates family members towards mutual assistance in all corporal and spiritual needs, even in the face of failure or the disgrace of a loved one.

The nurture of love and devotion in the bosom of the family produces untold blessings for community life. True community spirit, in both the Church and society, is psychologically dependent on an authentic family spirit.

Patriotism is the sincere devotion to the welfare of one's country, based on the feeling of solidarity between men possessing similar obligations and a common heritage. Love for country ennobles the mere judicial relationship between the State and its citizens and elevates this interdependence to the dignity of a truly personal communion. The genuine Christian character of this virtue should prove itself in embracing rather than excluding other people and other nations. Patriotism is the connecting chain between devotion to one's immediate family and the universal brotherhood of man under a common heavenly Father. A sincere patriotism manifests itself in sharing the country's responsibility for order and peace. This will prove itself by willingly contributing to its welfare through the payment of taxes. In extreme cases, it may demand a readiness to defend the country against aggression.

Opposed to patriotism is the behavior of the hardhearted bureaucrat and the unscrupulous lawmaker because they sow seeds of hatred against the State. Similarly guilty is the disinterested citizen who fails to realize his debt of gratitude to his country. A serious offense against patriotism is the misguided patriot's fanatic worship for the racial superiority of his people, which makes him intolerant of other nationalities or races.

Gratitude is a distinctive Christian attitude towards God and all those who transmit His superabundant gifts. The grateful person is humble in the full awareness that he owes all things to God and that he is unable to reciprocate His infinite love and gratitude. He rejoices in the knowledge of His dependence on God and his fellow creatures. The proud person, on the other hand, is ungrateful. He refuses to acknowledge and admit his debt of gratitude to others.

Closely allied to gratitude is the *virtue of generosity*. It is the natural expression of the person who knows himself to be enriched through the gratuitous charity of others. The generous person gives without petty calculation and without impressing the recipient with the magnitude of the gift. Gratitude and generosity know how to make the natural and supernatural gifts of God true expressions of mutual charity. These two virtues are able to ennoble all interpersonal relationships which are regulated by strict justice. "The one who loves, gives gladly and graciously not only what he owes but beyond the mere debt" (Thomas Aquinas: *Summa contra Gentes,* Book 111, Chap. 128).

Courtesy is an important Christian virtue. It is the expression of charity and true kindness and refinement of the heart. It is the habit of treating others with deference and respect. The virtue of courtesy is more than the application of rules of politeness. It despises both affectation and rudeness of manner. Courtesy readily adapts itself to the changing customs and special social circumstances as far as this is conducive to the spirit of reverence and congeniality.

Diametrically opposed to courtesy are flattery and an un-critical support of opinions, as well as the spirit of contradiction and bluntness in expressing the truth.

PART THREE

Temperance

Section I. Discipline and Moderation in the Service of Charity

"Temperance is a selfless self-possession" (Joseph Pieper), or as St. Augustine states more clearly: "It is that charity which keeps itself intact and undefiled for God." The virtue of discipline and moderation is based on the will's genuine orientation towards God. Its specific aim is the control of the concupiscible appetites, especially those basic instincts in man which aim at self-preservation and the continuation of the species. Their reasonable control will safeguard the integrity of man's powers and assure the victory of charity. For the children of Adam, the acquisition of the virtue of moderation and discipline demands a certain degree of self-control, and self-denial. However, all self-conquest should aim towards the possession of God.

Our Lord Jesus Christ, the prototype of humanity, manifested His deeply human feelings and emotions. He greatly rejoiced over the heavenly Father's choice in revealing the mysteries of His heart to the poor and little ones (cf. Luke 10:21). He shed bitter tears of sorrow at the grave of Lazarus (cf. John 11:35). He feelingly complained over the impenitence of Jerusalem and its terrible fate (cf. Luke 13: 34 ff.). His anger swept like a storm over those desecrating the Temple (cf. John 2:12-17). His vehement denouncement of the Pharisees sounded like the roaring of thunder which announced the coming judgment (cf. Matt. 23). His soul was deeply afflicted by the foresight of His bitter Passion (cf. John 12:27). In the Garden of Olives, fear pressed the bloody sweat from the pores of His skin. On the cross He loudly complained about His utter dereliction by His heavenly Father. "Jesus, when He had a mortal body, offered prayers and supplication with piercing cries and tears to Him who was to save Him from death" (Heb. 5:7). According to the ancient Stoic philosophy, Christ might be accused of immoderation in both the depth of His feelings and in the ardor of their expression. His heart was overflowing with fervent love for His heavenly Father and all mankind. The fulness of Christ's charity is a love without limit. All the emotions and desires of Christ's heart have no other measure than a boundless, all-embracing, holy love. They are governed by His supreme charity. They lend their full energy to the efficacy of His love, which they express.

Section II. Difficulties in Achieving Moderation and Discipline

In view of man's evil inclinations and the evident dangers of contagion from a degenerate environment, the virtue of temperance in man assumes certain characteristics which are foreign to the absolutely undefiled emotions in the humanity of Our Lord. Every impulse of His heart was an expression of His infinitely pure and ardent charity. Therefore, His emotions required no discipline or restraint. Our passions, on the other hand, demand a strict guard and surveillance. Our chief efforts, however, should not be directed towards their eradication or suppression; but, rather, towards a wise control which subdues all that is perverse and unruly. The acquisition of the virtue of temperance requires an uncompromising self-conquest. Inordinate pride and selfishness defile man's heart and will. They lead astray the powerful instincts and impulses implanted in his very nature. Purity of heart and affection is the foundation of peace and order in our moral life. The dangers of defilement from inordinate attachments and uncontrolled passions must be averted not only by a close guard over our dispositions and motives but also by a careful subjugation of our instincts and desires. However, a retrospective examination of our passions should not assume such proportions that they would paralyze the soul's powers and receptivity for positive, compelling moral values.

The encounter with our unruly passions will be crowned with final success, provided we make charity our chief aim and supreme rule in life. This shall be elucidated by some illustrations on the subject of chastity. In order to obtain a more comprehensive view of Christian teaching on this particular topic, the present explanations should be supplemented by additional readings on matrimony, family life, chastity, and virginity. The discussion here chiefly aims to show the interdependence of charity and the control of our passions through discipline.

Take for example the person addicted to the practice of self-abuse or *masturbation*. He will derive little benefit from a negative approach directed merely towards the suppression of sexual desires. Isolated conscious attempts towards self-control and surveillance of erotic impulses may, under certain circumstances, tend to fix the person's attention on the process of self-stimulation and thereby precipitate more frequent sexual excitations which simulate an anxiety neurosis. The obsessive or compulsive aspect of this particular disorder becomes further aggravated through self-centered efforts towards control. Many psychologists fittingly refer to this type of self-indulgence as ipsation or self-entangle-ment. Consequently, the liberation from such gross self-gratification requires a simultaneous, determined opposition against all forms of selfishness. Deliberate efforts to live a life of charity are more conducive to victory than a mere negative opposition to sin. Both aspects of discipline are complementary.

Although self-indulgence (masturbation) is a definite sexual perversion, young people troubled in this regard should not be classified as sexual perverts. Some of the suggested physical remedies are: a non-stimulating diet, adequate sleep on a fairly hard bed, conscientious diligence at work, active participation in sports, and planned periods of relaxation.

Homosexuality is the sexual attraction to those of the same sex combined with an unnatural apathy to members of the opposite sex. Temporary enthusiastic friendships among adolescents of the same sex should not be confused with homosexuality. However, such friendships extending into adulthood and marked with definite erotic overtones, indicate serious sexual deviations which tend to make the persons unsuitable for the married state. It is essential to control such perverted sexual impulses, which become more or less fixed through repeated previous violations. It is quite understandable that the majority of States punish homosexual behavior as an infraction of the law. *Exhibitionism* is the sexual deviation which prompts the sex maniac to expose his body, especially the sex organs, to the gaze of others. The *masochist* derives sexual pleasure in experiencing pain while the *sadist* perceives such pleasure through inflicting pain on others. *Bestiality* refers to sexual perversions with animals. In the Old Testament this serious crime was punished by the death penalty (cf. Ex. 22:19). Serious sexual aberrations markedly mar man's relationship with God and his neighbor (cf. Rom. 1:24 ff.). Perverse tendencies do not simply exonerate the sexual deviate, especially if he fails to cooperate in the removal of causative factors.

Therapeutic management greatly depends on the underlying causes and their complications. The root of the problem may be either lack of will-power or excessive indulgence in sensuous pleasures. Self-control must be exercised in the particular area of difficulty. Positive steps towards self-victory include: a firm resolution which should be renewed after each infraction; salutary penances; and, above all, acts of charity. It is undesirable to overemphasize the aspect of voluntary penances, unless hope and self-confidence are strengthened simultaneously. Irrespective of all moral implications, therapy should aim towards a joyful and self-sacrificing charity. In judging the degree of the virtue of discipline and moderation, we should take into consideration the unusual force of the instincts and passions in certain individuals as well as psychic distortions which complicate the process of self-control. Both effort and achievement must be evaluated. Furthermore, the deciding factor in temperance is the liberation and utilization of man's basic powers for the service of charity.

Conjugal chastity is an important aspect of temperance. However, it only deserves the name of a truly Christian virtue in all its pristine beauty and dignity if it expresses due reverence and respect for the selfless love which is the source of human life. "Selflessness" in the context of Christian marriage does not imply a suspicious hesitation to accept the sensual-spiritual pleasures of the love union. The distinguishing feature of chaste wedlock is the spouses' humble acceptance of the passionate pleasures accompanying their mutual love and self-surrender. Autonomous passion, on the other hand, is self-seeking and incapable of an enriching, ennobling, and joyful love experience. The selfish spouse, despite his irreproachable external behavior and self-control, is incapable of satisfactory marital relations or an unselfish possession and surrender. Such a person needs a basic change in attitude before he is able to acquire the virtue of temperance.

The couple's refusal to accept the responsibilities of love and parenthood may arise from selfish desires for pleasure, comfort, and a high standard of living. Unless they change their basic disposition, their selfish desires may prompt them to resort needlessly to the "rhythm theory" and eventually lead them to the violation of God's law. On the other hand, spouses, who are mutually devoted to each other and willing to render their creative service may at times encounter difficulties and failure. Nevertheless, their basic attitude is more in agreement with the virtue of chastity than the righteous complacency of those who need no restrictions on their conjugal rights because there is no possibility of conception.

The sacrament of matrimony is the bond which intimately unites the spouses' reciprocal love, as well as their self-abnegation in the pursuit of temperance, with the self-sacrificing love of Christ to His bride, the Church. Not only the conjugal love-union, expressive of their mutual surrender, but also their willingness for renunciation should reflect Christ's own self-immolation on behalf of His Church.

The spouses' efforts towards moderation and discipline aim at safeguarding the sublime values of matrimony. In a similar manner, the consummate virtue of temperance in conjugal relations is the fruit of the spouses' fundamental disposition to collaborate with the Creator. Conjugal chastity is the fruit of the spouses' reverence for the mystery of life and their vocation. It implies a ready willingness to accept the blessings of children as well as the sorrows of childlessness. It likewise demands mutual charity and a keen solicitude for mutual sanctification.

In this connection we would like to ask: What is the underlying reason for the evident inability of some to adjust to widowhood and involuntary celibacy? Why do certain unmarried people become frustrated, warped or dissipated, while others who have voluntarily embraced the state of celibacy are the most joyful and untiring laborers in God's vineyard? A partial answer may be found in today's widespread and indiscriminate exposure to temptations, through curiosity of the eyes, impure thoughts, obscene literature, improper dress, and indecent entertainment. Yet in the final analysis, the determining factor is the basic attitude. In the one case it is a grudging acceptance of a difficulty, while in the other it is a joyful and passionate embrace of a life of service. Conjugal and virginal chastity, despite their differences in aim and mode of expression, closely resemble each other in their reverence for man's sexual powers and their unselfish devotion to a worthwhile cause. *Reverence and charity* are the two supporting pillars of chastity. They impart true dignity and splendor to all endeavors for moderation and self-discipline.

Similar rules of temperance apply to the enjoyment of food and drink and all other temporal goods. The Christian virtue of temperance must be marked by a sincere endeavor towards moderation, a grateful acceptance of God's gifts, and an unselfish renunciation of all pleasures which impede the exercise of genuine charity and the freedom of the children of God.

According to St. Thomas Aquinas, a perfect self-possession of the powers of the heart and will tends to regulate and channel charity and all man's passions to such an extent that they themselves exert their desires in a manner which is in agreement with reason and in conformity with an exalted happiness. In order to attain this aim, considerable and persistent efforts are needed to overcome the temptations from the devil, the flesh, and the pride of life. Even our humble attempts towards self-control give honor and glory to God. Although charity is the decisive factor in all our efforts, the difficulties encountered may increase the meritoriousness of the acts. Diametrically opposed to the cold norm of duty for duty's sake, postulated by Kant, Catholic moral philosophy sees the highest degree of virtue not in the joyless imperative of duty but in the guiding and impelling power of virtue which facilitates the good.

Just as the sacramental conformity with the Crucified implies a commitment to overcome all that is selfish and perverse, so does the triumphant and joyful nature of virtue indicate the power of the risen Lord.

Section III. Lack of Self-Control and Licentiousness

The subjugation of our unruly passions is but the beginning of virtue. Its consummation consists in the efficacious transformation of the sensuous desires through the powers of charity. Opposed to self-control is lack of discipline which accounts for occasional failings despite basic good will and intention. The undisciplined person easily repents after his relapses. His sins are not occasioned by malice but rather by weakness. Yet this does not eliminate the danger of mortal sin.

Diametrically opposed to the virtue of temperance is the vice of *licentiousness*. The licentious person is bent on satisfying his passions in explicit opposition to good order and the judgment of reason. Far from repenting, he rejoices in his sins. He regrets if opportunities to sin have escaped him. For him the transgression of God's law has become second nature, just as virtue has become habitual for a sincere and fully committed Christian.

Licentiousness achieves its highest degree of malice in the *boasting and applauding of evil* (cf. Rom. 1:32). Today's increasing desire for sensuous pleasures and an alarming degree of approbation, justification, and even glorification of lewdness, adultery, and crime in public life, should rouse the Christian to an active apostolate for improving public opinion in this regard. One of the best means of achieving self-control and of guarding against licentiousness is the humble acknowledgment of sin in the sacrament of penance and a decided resolution to live and uphold a life of temperance and chastity.

PART FOUR

The Virtue of Fortitude

Section I. "Love is Strong as Death"

The virtue of fortitude is that charity which employs the force of the irascible emotion of anger whenever there is need to oppose a threatening injustice. At the same time, this virtue subdues the rebellion of the passions against suffering and death. It controls the emotions of fear and anxiety if these should tend to dissuade us from risking our life for a good cause. In our struggle with the unearthly powers which are mightier than flesh and blood and which St. Paul refers to as the principalities of darkness and the wicked spirits who defile the very air, charity must prove its power by utilizing every energy of the will and each impulse of the passions "to put out the flaming arrows of the wicked enemy" (Eph. 6:16). The Christian virtue of courage has nothing in common with the thoughtlessness and recklessness of the daredevil. Courage without prudence is rashness or presumption. "Courage without justice is an instrument of evil" (Joseph Pieper). Fortitude derives its genuine beauty and value from charity. "If I should yield my body to the flames, but have no love, it profits me nothing" (I Cor. 13:3).

Courage is far from a stoic insensibility to danger, suffering, and death. He who despises and carelessly endangers his earthly life does not possess the Christian virtues of courage or fortitude. Christ is the great hero of bravery who leads the way in the conquest of the world. He willingly sacrificed His own life and carried the full burden of pain and death. Despite the revolt of His human emotions, he accepted the bitter chalice of suffering in the agonizing anticipation of the tortures of both mind and body. The greatest manifestation of Christian fortitude in imitation of Our Lord is *martyrdom,* the generous surrender of life for the sake of faith or charity. Truly applicable are the words of Holy Scripture: "Love is strong as death; jealousy is hard as hell" (Cant. 8:6).

The virtue of fortitude likewise reaches its consummation in the wholehearted resignation of the Christian in his last illness and dying, in the confident surrender of his life to the holy will of God.

Section II. *"Love is Patient"*

Those fighting on behalf of the kingdom of charity may not retaliate the injustice and wickedness of the enemy. Christ's teaching in the Sermon on the Mount extols the victory of *meekness* as the greatest achievement of courage and charity (cf. Matt. 5:38 ff.). It is easier for human nature to give way to the surge of rage and the use of the sword than to bear the trials of continued irritations which require patient and loving endurance. Malice tries to achieve its victories through *violence*. The Christian, on the other hand, possesses his soul in peace (cf. Luke 21:19). The Christian virtue of *patience* opposes injustice by an overwhelming genuine charity towards the offender. "Charity bears all things, endures all things" (I Cor. 13:7).

Patient *perseverance in suffering* and affliction requires perfect self-possession. A truly sublime charity enables us to rejoice in suffering, because through our afflictions we gain participation in the redemptive sufferings of Christ. This aspect of Christian fortitude finds meaningful expression in the words of a patient, who after enduring a painful malady for twenty years, could say: "In the beginning it was difficult; but gradually I began to realize the good fortune of suffering with Christ for others."

Section III. The Gift of Fortitude

A truly great charity, rather than sheer force of will power, is capable of unleashing all the powers of fortitude. St. Peter, who thought himself valiant enough to embrace death with his Master (cf. Matt. 26:35), needed a rebuke when he took recourse to the sword. Only after he had placed all his trust in God, did he receive God's gift of fortitude which caused him to rejoice in the sufferings and ignominy endured for the name of Jesus. The same gifts of the Holy Spirit which perfect charity are likewise needed to consummate the virtue of fortitude. *The gift of the fear of the Lord* turns man into a humble adorer of God, who is fully confident in God's power and help. He who has no other fear except that of offending God, will prove himself valiant and invincible in every temptation.

The gift of fortitude gives the disciple of Christ a joyful courage to undertake great things in the power and strength of God's grace. It makes him remain firm and steadfast in the trials and difficulties of life. It inspires him with constancy in strategic and formidable positions in God's kingdom. Strengthened with the gifts of the Holy Spirit, the Christian is enabled not only to bear the many unavoidable trials and tribulations of life but, supported by his unselfish charity, he is willing to embrace voluntary sufferings and self-denials. In a perfect act of self-surrender to the purifying flames of love, he places himself unreservedly at God's disposal.

Confirmation is frequently called the sacrament of Catholic Action. It makes us full-fledged members of the Church with the commission and power to carry on Christ's work in social action. It gives us an undaunted courage and a persevering constancy to confess our allegiance to Christ. True determination and continued steadfastness in adhering to the law of the Crucified require a great ardor of charity. Therefore, fortitude in the public confession of faith presupposes the gift of wisdom which is the perfection of charity.

7 conversion

The transcendent beauty of the gospel truths and the exalted dignity of Christ's discipleship make our hearts rejoice. "Your law is my delight" (Ps 118:77). Yet at the same time we are frightened by the threatening depths of sin "which excludes us from God's kingdom." We are alarmed by the lofty challenge inherent in this New Law which far exceeds our finite, human powers. The glad tidings of salvation and conversion have deep though different implications for the sinner who squandered God's intimate friendship in mortal sin and the tepid soul languishing over the tedious progress on the road to perfection. The sinner, deprived of sanctifying grace, receives the invitation for the "first conversion" which is a transition from death to life. Likewise, he, who has squandered the grace of his "first conversion," is called to a spiritual restoration and rebirth or a renewal of his first conversion. For the soul living in

God's friendship, the exhortation to conversion is an "imperative of grace" to bring to full fruition God's salvific action begun in baptism.

Christian life should not be viewed under the aspect of minimum requirements of law. The great commandment of charity, "the fulness of law," is a call to perfection. Yet, in view of the consequences of original sin and the temptations from the world as incentives to evil, we are in constant need of conversion.

PART ONE

The Essence of Conversion

The exhortation to conversion is basically a joyful message.

SYNOPSIS OF PART ONE

(1) Man's conversion is God's gratuitous gift. (2) Conversion is the humble and grateful acceptance of the kingdom of God. (3) Man's conversion is marked with a joyful and utter determination in view of its eschatological implications, namely, the separation of the good and wicked at the Last Judgment.

Section I. The Glad Tidings of Conversion

The first scriptural account of Our Lord's preaching is a summons to conversion: "The time of waiting is over; the kingdom of God is close at hand. Change your evil ways; believe in the Good Message" (Mark 1:15; cf. Matt. 4:17). In Aramaic, the word *conversion* signifies a "home-coming." The advent of Christ brought us the fulness of salvation and the urgent appeal to a universal return to the Father's house. God Himself ardently desires the happy moment of our renewal in grace. In Holy Scripture God solemnly declares: "Return, rebellious children, says the Lord, for I am your Master; I will take you home" (Jer. 3:14).

In the parable of the prodigal son, Christ gave us an excellent illustration of man's spiritual conversion. In the utter degradation and disgrace of sin, the youthful spendthrift recalled the benevolent kindness of his father. This remembrance instilled confidence in his tortured soul: "I will quit this place and go to meet my father." In his anxiety to appease the father's expected wrath, he was determined to acknowledge his guilt and implore pardon. Yet the father anticipated his son's self-accusation: "He was still a good way off when his father caught sight of him and, stirred to pity, ran and threw his arms around his neck and kissed him affectionately." In answer to the son's confession the father arranged a great celebration. He gave him the finest robe and put on his hand the ring of reconciliation. The whole house was in an uproar of joy and merry-making (cf. Luke 15:11-32). God has sent His only-begotten Son in order to gather the lost sheep. Christ, the Good Shepherd, rejoices over every sinner who returns to the fold. Similarly, all heaven celebrates each time a sinner does penance (cf. Luke 12:15).

In scriptural language, *conversion* signifies more than moral regeneration. *It implies the establishment of a new and intimate relationship between God and the soul,* redeemed from the disgrace and poverty of sin. The full significance and joy of conversion lies in God's marvelous work of grace. "It is the Lord who calls the dead to life. It is He who touches the heart" (St. Augustine, *Confessions*).

Though the need for conversion is universal, the apostles, in their sermons, made a definite distinction between *the conversion of the unbaptized* and *the repentance of sinners in the Christian community.* For those outside the fold, the gospel truths are truly urgent invitations to enter the Father's house and participate in the marriage feast which Christ celebrates with the Church. When speaking to the baptized who remained faithful to their call, the apostles encouraged them "to be built, as living stones, into a spiritual temple" (I Pet. 2:5), and, in view of their justification, to yield their bodies "to the service of righteousness and a holy life" (Rom. 6:19).

Holy Scripture is quite explicit in emphasizing the preeminence of grace in the work of conversion. This is especially vividly portrayed in the administration of the two *sacraments of conversion,* namely, baptism and penance.

Baptism is the sacrament of the first conversion. The sacrament of penance "is a second liferaft after the shipwreck of sin" (Tertullian on Penance). The decisive elements and conditions for our return to God are a firm *faith in the glad tidings* and a humble acceptance of grace. "Repent and believe the gospel" (Mark 1:15). "He that believes and is baptized will be saved" (Mark 16:16). Whoever possesses the readiness of faith and the humble desire for God's grace shall receive salvation in virtue of this faith and desire (the baptism of desire). The same truth applies to sacramental confession. The Christian, who after his first justification in baptism has revolted against God, shall be reinstated in grace through the sacrament of penance. If there should be no opportunity for confession, an act of perfect contrition will suffice because a sincere charity implies the essential readiness and desire to receive the sacrament of God's mercy.

For those Christians who are in the state of grace, God's salvific action in the sacraments of penance and the Holy Eucharist is a source of abundant graces and a means for "a second conversion" or an explicit re-orientation towards God. Baptism, which according to one of the earliest Fathers of the Church (Justin) is the "bath of conversion," reminds us of our mystical death with Christ (cf. Rom. 6). Conversion, therefore, means a humble and loving response to Christ who confronts us with a singular predilection and charity in order to grant us a full share in the fruits of His bitter Passion and death, and thereby conforms us more fully to His own likeness. *Baptism marks our soul with the fiery character of the Holy Spirit,* which signifies: "sanctified for the Lord." In addition to the special imprint, baptism also confers *the life of grace* and a share in the divine nature. If the recipient of baptism is an adult, all perverse dispositions must be renounced before God's action of grace can be accomplished.

Conversion, according to Holy Scripture, is synonymous with a *rebirth in God* (cf. John 1:12 ff.; 3:36); with a *divine adoption* through a *participation in Christ's Sonship* (cf. Rom. 8:15; Gal. 4:5; Eph. 1:5), and at the same time, the full *freedom of the children of God.* It is an *interior justification through grace,* a truly *"new creation"* (II Cor. 5:17), and *a transition from darkness to light.* All these sublime operations of grace emphasize the great dignity and blessings of conversion.

The reception of the sacraments signifies a personal encounter with Christ, an encounter in which God takes the initiative. Therefore, every religious conversion is essentially a work of God's love, mercy, and power. In other words, every genuine return to God must bear the sacramental imprint of a humble attitude of surrender to the transforming power of God's grace. This openness towards grace is the authentic mark of every religious conversion.

God anticipates the sinner's cooperation by the efficacious action of His grace. In the sacrament of penance, or at least in view of the sacrament, God effects men's change of heart. God's grace in the first conversion is the divine pledge that God will bring to perfection what the sacraments indicate, provided the soul will surrender unreservedly to the guidance of divine grace. The preeminence of grace, which was specifically enunciated by the Council of Trent, far from entitling man to a careless and slothful attitude, rather emphasizes the importance and urgency of the call to conversion and man's obligation towards full cooperation with God's actual grace. *The truth of the transcendence of grace dispels all discouraging thoughts arising from our human misery and weakness.* God will bring to perfection the salutary action initiated by actual grace and marvelously supported and confirmed by the sacramental character and the life of grace, if we surrender ourselves to Him in perfect faith, confidence, and charity. "The God of all grace, who called you into His eternal glory in Christ, will Himself, after your brief suffering, restore, establish, and strengthen you on a firm foundation" (I Pet. 5:10). Despite our human frailty and the temptations from the pride of life, the concupiscence of the eyes and the flesh, our trust in God's efficacious grace will give us the joyous conviction: "Now we know that for those who love God all things work together unto good, for those who, according to His purpose, are saints through His call. For those whom He has foreknown He has also predestined to become conformed to the image of His Son, that He should be the firstborn among many brethren. And those whom He has predestined, them He has also called; and those whom He has called, them He has also justified, and those whom He has justified, them He has also glorified" (Rom. 8:28-30).

The firm foundation of our hope in the mercy of God is Jesus Christ, Our Lord and Redeemer. He is our guide and divine physician on our homeward journey to the Father's house. Christ is the very goal of our conversion. He is the sublime exemplar of perfect love and obedience to the Father. In union with Him we shall celebrate the boundless exultation of God's Triune love.

Thus, every institution for dispensing God's bounty and all interior and external graces are solemn and, at the same time, joy-giving and encouraging invitations to a spiritual renewal. For the person who has lost the supernatural life of grace, it is a summons to the first conversion. For those in God's friendship, it signifies a challenge towards greater perfection through a total surrender to God's boundless love.

In the minds of the apostles, baptism was synonymous with conversion. This was based on their firm conviction that God's abundant gifts of graces demand not only a life free from mortal sin, but a continuous growth in holiness. Therefore, *St. Peter's castigations of the tepid and the licentious are marked with unusual strictness and severity.* "They had once escaped the world's defilements through the knowledge of Our Lord Jesus Christ; yet if they have entangled themselves in these all over again, and are mastered by them, their plight in the end is worse than before. For it were better for them not to have known the way of justice, than having known it, to turn back and abandon the sacred commandments delivered to them! For them the proverb has proved true: 'The dog returns to its own vomit; and, the sow after a wash rolls in the mud again'" (II Pet. 2:20-22). It should be remembered that these harsh accusations were addressed not so much to the weak but to those confirmed in sin and evil. There is no doubt that those reborn of the Holy Spirit and enriched by God's ineffable gifts seriously jeopardize their perseverance in faith and eternal salvation by a relapse into sin. Consequently, every sinner exposes himself to the danger of impenitence and eternal perdition (cf. Heb. 6:4 ff.; I John 5:16 ff.). *The truth that a new conversion after deliberate rejection of divine sonship is possible only because of God's sheer, undeserved grace and mercy, should be an effective deterrent against all sin and disobedience.* God's call to the second conversion is a glad tiding and joyful summons to the soul similar to the first conversion, although differing from the call addressed to pagans still waiting for redemption. The Christian in the state of mortal sin, "which excludes from God's kingdom," should realize the irreconcilable contradiction between his state of soul and his "incorporation into Christ." This poignant awareness of the need for reconciliation is the beginning of the soul's re-orientation to God. The wondrous transformation accomplished by God's grace through the first conversion is a favorite topic in the exhortations of the apostles. The realization of the marvels of grace in conversion should urge the zealous Christian towards progress in virtue and a life in conformity with grace. After illustrating the disgraceful servitude of sin, St. Paul admonishes: "Such were some of you. But you have been through the purifying waters; you have been dedicated to God and justified in the name of Our Lord Jesus Christ, and in the Spirit of Our God" (I Cor. 6:11).

The apostles addressed the most urgent exhortations to those in danger of sin: "Wake up!" (Apoc. 3:2), "Keep awake and sober" (I Thes. 5:6; I Pet. 5:8). The call to a life in accord with the grace of conversion has always been a keynote of the Church's admonitions since early apostolic times. "For you were once darkness, but now you are light in the Lord. Walk, then, as children of light. The effects of the light are every kind of goodness and justice and truth" (Eph. 5:8-9). Holy Scripture describes the infinite marvels of grace wrought in the first conversion in such sublime terms as: a rebirth in the Holy Spirit, a new creation in

Christ, divine adoption, and death and resurrection in Christ. These expressions exhort the Christian to live up to the sublime realities of grace in all their thoughts, intentions, desires, and actions (cf. Eph. 2:1 ff.; 4:20 ff.; etc.). The apostles addressed their admonitions for repentance to all the baptized Christians. The saints give ample testimony of a truly wholehearted response to God's invitations of grace. Despite their continuous striving for perfection, they never considered themselves exempt from the duty of repentance and reconciliation. God's invitation to a continuous renewal of spirit is apt to arouse a deep sense of humility in the humble acknowledgment of both our accomplishments and our repeated failings. The glad tidings of conversion should fill our hearts with a joyful gratitude in view of the exalted aim which God has given us in baptism and the other sacraments and to which He invites us with a uniquely personal charity.

Section II. Conversion and God's Kingdom

Our Lord's appeal for conversion was based on the fact that God's kingdom was close at hand. "Jesus returned to Galilee to preach God's Good Message. This was His theme: 'The kingdom of God is close at hand. Repent and believe the Gospel'" (Mark 1:15). The coming of God's kingdom implies not only an urgent imperative but also the graces required for a change of heart and a return to the true fold. Conversion in its deepest sense is the humble acceptance of God's dominion, implying both a receptive heart and an active inclination towards the universal kingdom established by Christ. The Preface for the Feast of Christ the King refers to God's kingdom as "a kingdom of holiness and grace, a kingdom of justice, love and peace."

Conversion is more than the acknowledgment of a future realm of bliss and glory. *Conversion implies a grateful and willing acceptance of God's dominion in the present interval between the first Pentecost and Christ's second coming.* The future state of happiness is meant for those who unreservedly surrender to God's present dominion.

1. "The Kingdom of Grace and Holiness"

God's kingdom is not the result of human endeavors. It is God's gratuitous gift to men. God is free to dispense His gifts according to His infinite wisdom and charity. Sinful man, who complacently relies on self-acquired rights and virtues, proudly opposes God's sovereignty and makes himself unworthy of grace. God grants His gifts of salvation only to the poor and humble because they alone are conscious of their basic needs and confidently implore God's help. For these, Our Lord's Beatitude holds true: "Blessed are the humble souls, for theirs is the kingdom of heaven" (Matt. 5:3). God's powerful grace becomes an all-consuming fire for the proud. "He has scattered the proud in the conceit of their heart. He has filled the hungry with good things, and the rich He has sent away empty" (Luke 1:51-53).

Man's appropriate response to the infinite condescension of the all-holy God is a childlike simplicity and docility. "Unless you turn and become like little children, you will not enter into the kingdom of heaven" (Matt. 18:3). It is natural for the child to petition and render thanksgiving. The child's entire existence is one of unbounded confidence in his parents' love, and utter dependence on their charity and solicitude. God's kingdom is a completely gratuitous gift of His infinite mercy and charity. Therefore, it can only be attained by those who in childlike sincerity and self-surrender make themselves receptive to God's beneficent action and humbly submit to His all-embracing dominion. *"Whoever does not accept the kingdom of God as a little child will not enter into it"* (Mark 10:15).

The repentant sinner, who sincerely acknowledges his abject poverty and sinfulness, is closer to God's kingdom than the self-righteous and self-complacent "just" man who refuses to acknowledge his indebtedness to God. "A heart contrite and humble, O God, You will not spurn" (Ps. 50:19).

In the efficacious language of the sacraments, God tells us that conversion is a humble assent to His undeserved gifts. The sacraments place our entire life under the pre-eminence of grace. By means of their symbolic language and the words of life, they assure us that God is the principal agent and that all our endeavors derive their fruitfulness from an attitude of grateful appreciation and acceptance of God's divine words and actions. Since we are wholly dependent on God's generosity for the remission of our sins and the justification through grace, the motto of our life can be no other than: "What shall I render to the Lord for all the things He has rendered to me?" (Prayer of the priest immediately after the reception of Holy Communion).

The Preface of the Mass on the Feast of Christ the King refers to God's sovereignty as "a kingdom of grace and holiness." God has sanctified us by means of the sacraments. Sanctification signifies a solemn charge imprinted on the soul which obligates us to a life of sincere dedication to God's honor and glory. In view of man's abject poverty and utter dependence on God's benevolence and powerful grace, we are committed to a life of "justice and holiness."

2. The Kingdom of Truth and Life

Christ, the eternal Word of the Father, has brought the full light of truth to this world. Consequently, faith is the prerequisite for conversion and full incorporation into God's kingdom. Only a childlike faith disposes us to an unqualified confidence in God's word and, consequently, to a clear perception of the light of truth. This enables us to become true torchbearers who diffuse God's light to a dark and sinful world. The object of faith is truth.

The truth, brought to us by Christ, is an intimate participation in the very life of the Triune God. It is a life-giving truth and, consequently, demands a life regulated by its powerful influence. The humble admission of sinfulness is the first step in a return to a Christian life of truthfulness. The important factor in the conversion to faith is not the mere intellectual assent to a particular truth, but the heart's unqualified commitment to a truth which places one's entire life under its transforming and dominating influence and judgment. We pay homage to God's truthfulness and expose the heart's deceitfulness in the humble confession of guilt: "Father, I have sinned" (Luke 15:18).

3. The Kingdom of Justice, Charity, and Peace

The repentant sinner confesses his guilt before the all-holy God, who justifies him in view of the redemptive sufferings of His Son, Jesus Christ. We shall gain participation in the fruits of Christ's redemption if we humbly submit to His Law of reparation. Therefore, the choice fruit of conversion is a humble *readiness to make restitution and atonement.*

Charity is that "higher justice" which Christ announced in His Sermon on the Mount and which, by His personal example, He confirmed as the foundation law of His kingdom. Charity is the distinguishing feature of the children of light. Consequently, it is the very core of conversion. All attributes and effects of charity are distinctive descriptions of the kingdom of God (cf. Chapters IV-VI).

Conversion is the key to God's kingdom on this earth, which in turn is the indispensable prerequisite to our ultimate goal in the eternal kingdom of bliss where, with all the angels and saints, we shall joyfully participate in the life of the Triune God. This future communion of saints is foreshadowed and initiated through the communal life of the Church, the Bride of Christ. The Holy Eucharist is the special bond through which we are enabled to join in the mutual love-union between Christ and His Church till the consummation of the world. This sacrament reminds us that *Christ established His kingdom in this present world through His supreme act of charity in passing through His bitter Passion and death on the cross to the glorious life of His triumphant humanity.* Hence we rejoice in the victory of Christ's love in the resurrection, which is the pledge of our own future glory at the banquet of divine charity.

The Holy Eucharist is the center of all other sacraments. It is particularly closely associated with the sacraments of conversion, baptism and penance. This sacrament of love is the efficacious sign of the unity of Christ's Mystical Body and the reciprocal charity of its members. Therefore, it is evident that conversion aims towards an increase and consummation of charity in mutual concord and collaboration. At the beginning of Lent, the Church prays: "Pour forth upon us, O Lord, the spirit of Your charity, that by Your mercy You may unite those whom You have fed with the one bread from heaven" (Postcommunion Prayers on Friday after Ash Wednesday). In the postcommunion prayer of Easter she asks for the same identical gift of charity.

Mortal sin excludes the baptized from the communion of salvation. Nevertheless, the sinner is not forsaken by the Church who not only announces God's kingdom but, at the same time, is the efficacious sign of the will of God to communicate Himself to us. The Church admonishes, sacrifices, and prays for the sinner's safe return to the Father's house. Through the sacrament of penance she re-admits the lost sheep to Christ's embrace of charity and peace which restores all privileges and rights of true children and heirs. The Church's keen solicitude to reinstate the sinner into the solidarity of the elect is clearly expressed in the ritual for confession: "Return them to the bosom of Your Church . . . Grant, O Lord, that after the remission of their sins they may safely be returned to Your Church from whose solidarity they have strayed through their transgression . . . in order that Your Church may not be debased in some of her members and that Your Flock may not suffer harm. Clothed in Your wedding garments, grant them admission to Your heavenly banquet from which they had been excluded" (Roman Pontifical).

The Old Testament prophecies herald the coming Messiah as "King of Peace." Christ has become the great Mediator between God and man, not by earthly warfare, but rather by His self-sacrificing charity. His peace is far different from an armistice of war which the mighty of this earth try to enforce (cf. John 14:27). Peace of heart and concord in the Christian community are fruits of the Holy Spirit, our risen Savior's precious gift. *A sincere re-orientation and return to God is the basic prerequisite for the fulness of interior peace* (cf. Matt. 9:13; 11:19). Peace is the exclusive prerogative of "men of good will" who are determined to turn away from sin and abide by the will of their heavenly Father. Attachment to sin, on the other hand, is a barrier to God's kingdom (cf. I Cor. 6:10).

4. The Kingdom of God in this World

Christ solemnly declared before Pilate, the judge and representative of the Roman empire, that His kingdom "is not of this world" (John 18:36). Consequently, Christ employed no earthly weapon in rendering testimony to the truth. He opposed and conquered the mighty powers of darkness by an all-surpassing, self-sacrificing charity. From the foundation of His kingdom till His second coming it will suffer violence from the infernal forces of evil (cf. Matt. 11:12; Luke 16:16). God's kingdom, which is synonymous with peace and joy in the Holy Spirit, demands an unrelenting struggle: "I have not come to bring peace but the sword" (Matt. 10:34). Christ's disciple should be aware of the radical opposition which exists between the two opposing sovereignties. The two kingdoms differ not only in their nature but also in the very means of combat. Christ warns us against contagion from the spirit of the world: "Anyone who loves the world is a stranger to the Father's love, because all that is in the world is the lust of the flesh, the lust of the eyes, and the pride of life" (I John 2:15-16).

Peace of heart and concord in the Christian community are the essential qualifications for a successful outcome in the encounter between the powers of darkness and the kingdom of light and truth. Only thus can they drive back the perverse spirit of this world and only thus can they become capable to preserve all fields of life from corruption by the spirit of the world. "Salt is a good thing; but if the salt loses its saltiness, what will you season it with? *Have salt in yourselves; and be at peace with one another*" (Mark 9:49).

The kingdom of God, though not of this world, is still established in the world. Christ's chief aim and purpose in the incarnation was the establishment of His Father's kingdom. He refers to Himself as "the light of the world" (John

8:12; 9:5). God's kingdom is an indisputable reality; it is a city on the mountain top and a light upon the lampstand (cf. Matt. 5:14 ff.). In His high priestly prayer, Our Lord implored His heavenly Father to keep His disciples from the danger of corruption: "Holy Father, keep in Your name those whom You have given Me, that they may be one as We are one . . . I do not pray that You take them out of the world, but that You may keep them from evil" (John 17:11-15).

Though Christ pronounced a serious condemnation on the proud and self-sufficient world, He nevertheless came from heaven to save all mankind. He does not want us to relinquish the earthly domains to the perverse and wicked. His mission is to bring salvation to all the world created by His heavenly Father (cf. John 3:15). His disciples are to work for the expansion of His dominion: "You are the salt of the earth . . . You are the light of the world" (Matt. 5:13 ff.). "The kingdom of heaven is like leaven, which a woman took and buried in three measures of flour, until all of it was leavened" (Matt. 13:33). Our Lord rejoiced over the election of all the redeemed: "You have made them a royal house to serve our God as priests; and they shall reign upon the earth" (Apoc. 5:10). This jubilation over the triumph of the elect also applies to the pilgrim Church striving for perfect holiness of response. In this transition period, the royal priesthood and chosen race of God will unite with all created things to proclaim God's magnificent works of mercy (cf. I Pet. 2:90). The entire creation, yearning after participation in the freedom of the children of God, will experience the liberating power of God's redeeming influence (cf. Rom. 8:19 ff.). The whole universe will profit from man's utilization of his new freedom.

Both our acceptance of God's dominion and our return to God through conversion imply a loving surrender to His redemptive plans in all aspects of life. Although conversion is essentially the heart's response to God's invitation of grace, nevertheless, its effects manifest themselves also in relation to all earthly realms since salvation is meant for the entire creation. *The sincere petition: "Thy kingdom come," requires a keen interest and solicitude for the world around us. Religion is not merely a private affair, although conversion is essentially a change of heart and "a life hidden in Christ"* (Col. 3:3; cf. I Pet. 3:4). The heart's transformation shall manifest itself in an unselfish concern for the eternal salvation of others. Conversion is not confined to the self-centered aim: "How shall I find a merciful judge for myself?" *Conversion is not an isolated incident; it rather is a complete acceptance of God's all-embracing dominion.*

Just as the advent of God's kingdom affects the entire world, so does the conversion of an individual or a community of people effect *a genuine transformation in their environment.* Such a renovation is inherent in the very nature of conversion, since it is a summons to God's kingdom and liberating dominion. The same holds true of the influence exerted by an individual. Man's existence is intimately interlinked with his environment. God's invitation for membership in His kingdom is a uniquely personal one, addressed to a person in a specific family situation, vocation, and neighborhood; to a soul whom He has endowed with singular gifts of nature and grace. Consequently, man's transition from "the world of sin" into "the world of God's beloved Son," although accomplished in his inmost heart, cannot fail to make its redeeming influence felt on his immediate surrounding. The desire for a wholehearted conversion, therefore, implies the firm determination to imprint the mark of God's loving dominion on the world. The full acceptance of God's spiritual dominion demands a basic re-orientation of our hearts and an *unquestioning readiness to advance God's interests in our daily lives.*

Since Christ is the universal Redeemer, my personal salvation, namely, the sincerity and stability of my own conversion, greatly depends on the fulfillment of my apostolic mission in my particular sphere of action.

The same solidarity of salvation applies to charity, the foundation law of God's kingdom. An irresponsible abandonment of the earthly domains to the prince of evil would not only involve a serious injustice to God's legitimate sovereignty and the honor and glory of our Redeemer, but would furthermore endanger the eternal salvation of innumerable souls through a corrupt and perverse atmosphere. Sincere brotherly love should urge each Christian to influence his immediate environment for good because it is the scene of action where both he and his neighbor are to work out their salvation. The full realization of the powerful influences of the milieu should strengthen our spirit of collaboration and mutual support.

5. *Progress in God's Kingdom and Conversion*

"The kingdom of God is like a grain of mustard seed, which a man took and cast into his own garden; and it grew and became a large tree, and the birds of the air dwelt in its branches" (Luke 13:19). Contrary to the teaching of some Protestant theologians, God's kingdom is not a phenomenon of the future but a present reality which impels towards its final consummation in the second coming of Christ. In His first coming, Our Lord not only announced God's kingship but established it with His own precious blood and guaranteed its future victory by His glorious resurrection. In the meantime, the principles of growth and development apply to both God's gracious sovereignty on earth and man's conversion of heart. The law of gradual unfolding holds true of the individual's spiritual re-orientation to God as well as to the conversion of the whole world.

The resolute transition from the spiritual death of sin to a life in Christ is God's powerful work of re-creation accomplished by the efficacious word of God. On man's part, renewal in grace requires a revolutionary change of heart and a decisive openness to God's beneficent action and holy will. Spiritual restoration in the adult is usually preceded by a long chain of actual graces and an ever increasing receptiveness to God's saving influence. Man's spiritual development is a gradual growth process. Its final consummation will be achieved either in a loving submission and conformity to God's holy will at the hour of death, or in the purifying flames of purgatory.

Personal progress in the life of grace cannot be isolated from the promotion of God's kingdom because conversion is essentially oriented to the kingdom of God. There is an intimate relationship between personal sanctification and the salvation of the world. The lives of the saints and their far reaching spiritual influence on others in the extension of God's kingdom are evident proof of the unfathomable mystery of the solidarity of salvation in the Mystical Body of Christ. A grateful appreciation of this union of interests is the sound foundation for the spiritual-moral development of the Christian. *Progress in the life of grace is based on our cooperative efforts for God's kingdom through work and prayer.*

It is evident that the relationship between the promotion of God's kingdom and personal conversion is based on the principle of mutual solidarity. The invitation to the active apostolate and, in particular, the pastoral care of the environment is not a work of supererogation at the end of conversion. Since conversion is man's response to the approaching sovereignty of God, his active interest in the "messianic kingdom" is of prime importance. At every level of conversion and advance in virtue, the Christian should gratefully recall the essential unity of interests in the promotion of God's glory and the salvation of men. His interior renewal and liberation from selfishness will prove itself in the fulness of divine charity. Just as the sacrament of baptism which makes us members of the Mystical Body of Christ finds its consummation in confirmation, which is the sacrament of the apostolate, so does the interior maturity of the Christian tend towards its expression in an ever increasing zeal for God's glory and the salvation of souls.

Since God's kingdom within us and around us is constantly threatened by the still unconquered powers of evil, there can be no real progress in conversion and the extension of God's reign without a continuous re-orientation to God (second conversion).

Section III. The Eschatological Separation and Decision

The eucharistic celebration announces the death and resurrection of Our Lord "until He comes" (I Cor. 11:26). Both the sacraments, which express the foundation laws of the Christian life, and conversion are marked by a definite eschatological significance. *Conversion is the beginning of the process of separation at the end of which Christ, the triumphant Victor over sin, death, and Satan, will cast those at His left into the unquenchable fire of hell while those at His right He will lead into His everlasting kingdom. Conversion receives its truly joyous character and, at the same time, its radical determination, from the escha-*

tological fulness of salvation. Scripture gives us the bold outlines of the coming judgment day and final victory of God's love. At that time God's boundless charity and almighty power will have attained their full redemptive realization in Christ, while Satan will continue to fight with the utmost desperation for man's eternal ruin. Who, under such circumstances, could live leisurely and irresolutely between the two opposing powers? Who could dare to gamble over life and death by sinning after Christ has gained the victory of life for us in a new world which guarantees our victorious resurrection?

The biblical message of conversion points to *two opposing forces*, the one representing the saving sovereignty of God and the other, the destructive influences of Satan. Similarly, there is a combat between two conflicting powers in each soul; namely, the struggle between a *perverse and arrogant self* (which Holy Scripture calls "the carnal self"), and *the man redeemed and renewed by Jesus Christ*. The outcome of this struggle greatly depends on the reciprocal relationship of these two camps during this last interval.

"The last hour" (I John 2:18) still belongs to the interval during which the kingdom of God—an already living reality—remains partially veiled from our eyes. The death and resurrection of Our Lord are definite indications of the final outcome of the obstinate struggle between good and evil. The powers of the end-time are truly present and efficacious in the sacraments, which bring us into personal communion with the crucified and risen Lord, the final Judge of the world. Yet only through faith can the believer perceive Christ's unceasing presence. To the unbeliever He remains completely hidden and disguised under the scandal of the cross. The separation of men into two opposing camps is an ever continuous process which ends for the individual by death and irrevocably terminates for all mankind at Christ's second coming. In the meantime, God permits the wheat and the cockle to grow together (cf. Matt. 13:36-43). Similarly, the Church continues to gather in her "fish-net" both the good and the bad fish (cf. Matt. 13:47-50).

The world is still in nostalgic pain and ardent expectation of Our Lord's second coming in order to behold the revelation of the glory of the children of God. This present life does not reveal a clear-cut separation between the "world" and "the kingdom of God" neither in man's hearts nor in the various earthly realms and domains.* *The interval between the first Pentecost and Christ's second coming is marked by conversion, or evolution and separation. The light and power of love which has appeared in Christ will separate genuine love from its counterfeits.*

The complex problem, how to reconcile the radical finality of the last judgment with the apparent embryonic stage of the intervening time, has resulted in several serious misinterpretations, as for example the so-called "mystique of sin" and the Protestant expression: "sinner and at the same time just."

According to Luther man remains essentially a sinner in his inmost being even after justification through faith. As "sinful and justified at the same time," he belongs both to the world of iniquity as well as to the kingdom of heaven. Consequently, Luther believed that faith justifies and touches man's heart and mind in a very personal, interior experience. Yet this justification, as the exclusive work of God's benevolent judgment with its results reserved for the life to come, does not intrinsically belong to man but is to be sought entirely outside of his own powers. The famous Protestant theologian, Helmut Thielicke, in keeping with

* Cfr. B. Häring, *Macht und Ohnmacht der Religion,* pp. 51-86.

Luther's idea still emphatically proposes that in the life of man justified by faith the old tree of sin continues to bear its bitter fruits with a certain "automatism" which, however, will not be imputed to the one justified remaining firm in faith.

Even in Catholic circles there has appeared in recent years a certain tendency towards a so-called "mystique of sin." While in past centuries the biographies of the saints presented their heroes in a halo of unquestioned holiness which completely overshadowed their real struggle, the new trend seems to obscure the triumphant character of God's all-sufficing grace. It should be understood that any clear-cut delineation between man's sinfulness and heroic virtue will prove both unrealistic and unacceptable. The keynote of the apostles' sermons, which emphasized the victorious transition from the darkness of sin to the radiant light of God's glory (I Pet. 2:9), is replaced today by a resigned type of pessimism which nurtures the complacent attitude that a losing fight in the moral struggle is the expected and natural thing for the majority of men.

On the other hand, we are far from subscribing to the "mystique of sin" if we squarely face the facts of a moral decline in certain eras and places. The Apocalypse gives testimony to the fact that in some early Christian communities both light and darkness appeared side by side (Apoc. 2-3). But the Seer of the Apocalypse is evidently alarmed and shocked at the incongruity inherent in the Christians' manner of life and their relapse into sin and vice as if they had never been redeemed.

Neither does Graham Greene endorse this so-called "mystique of sin." For example, in his novel, *The Power and the Glory,* he portrays his "whiskey priest" as a person who is handicapped by unfortunate, inherited tendencies which, aggravated by a fugitive life, led him into the habit of drinking despite his genuinely charitable attitude towards his neighbor. The author depicts him as a weak but kindhearted hero who trembles at the mere thought of suffering and martyrdom. However, it would be quite a different story to represent the above character as an ideal modern saint. Such an attempt would certainly distort all psychological and sociological truths inherent in the novel.

Recent biographies of saints, far from portraying an "inborn saintliness," show their heroes with all their natural faults and foibles as conditioned by heredity and environment. The utmost sincerity of these writers, bordering occasionally on severity, forms the dark background which by contrast tends to emphasize the victorious character of God's grace. Such descriptions should, however, stop short of exaggerations wherein the unfortunate, warped tendencies obscure both the moral greatness of the saint and the power of God's grace.

Although the Pharisaical pride of believing ourselves to be better than the rest of men is to be condemned, our gratitude and appreciation for God's gift should engender a joyful optimism so that liberated from the kingdom of darkness we shall become "the light of the world" while walking as children of "God's light." *In baptism we declared our decisive opposition to sin.* Therefore, the Apostle's words apply: "How shall we who are dead to sin still live in it?" (Rom. 6:2). "Consider yourselves also as dead to sin, but alive to God in Christ Jesus" (Rom. 6:11).

In view of Christ's death and resurrection, both the individual soul and the *Church, the community of all the baptized,* are embraced in God's loving dominion. Despite Satan's attempts to rule the world, the Church, as the saving sign of God's sovereignty, has been firmly established in this world. In the Church, the salvific deeds of Christ become truly re-presented and efficacious for salvation.

Therefore, the Church is "the judgment over this world," and, at the same time, our rock of security: "Now will the prince of the world be cast out" (John 12:31). The Church is the dispenser of grace and the loving Mother of her militant children to whom Scripture alludes in the song of heavenly triumph: "The kingdom of this world has become the kingdom of Our Lord and of His Christ and He shall reign forever and ever" (Apoc. 11:15). God's saving grace and dominion would be far more effective if it were not for the obstacles which men place in its way through their sinful neglect and laxity. It is partially the fault of those baptized and justified by God's grace that the powers of the New World do not achieve their full efficacy in their own hearts and consequently do not permeate man's environment.

The end of time, which in reality is the interval between the first and the second coming of Jesus Christ, is both a time of salvation and an era characterized by tension. This tension is generated by Christianity's present polarity between fulfillment and unfulfillment. Although this demonstrates that our present state is essentially one of imperfection and unfulfilled expectation, it nevertheless demands our sincere acceptance of the glad tidings of God's kingdom and an unceasing struggle for the all-embracing dominion of God in order to hasten man's final salvation.

Catholic teaching shows God's works of conversion and sanctification diffused by the radiant optimism of the Easter Message and the second coming of Christ "in power and glory." *Accordingly, the Christian is summoned to a radical determination and an inexorable struggle against the iniquity of the world and the evil in his own heart.* All the signs of the approaching consummation of the world including the sacraments, the Church itself, the whole course of salvation, the predictions of Holy Scripture, and the holiness of the saints achieved in struggle and persecution, are truly joyful tokens of hope for those redeemed while for the proud and the "unprofitable servant" they represent bad omens of judgment.* Those failing to do penance and change their heart in view of the marvelous graces of God's kingdom, which is nearing its triumphant vindication, will indeed be judged with greater severity than the sinful cities of Sodom and Gomorrah (cf. Luke 10:11 ff.).

The entire interval between the first and second coming of Christ is "the last hour" (I John 2:18), or the hour of the great separation and momentous decision. If Christ's second coming is delayed, it is due in some measure to *God's forbearance* which provides time for mankind to seek reconciliation. The judgment for those who fail to utilize this last hour of God's overflowing grace and patience will be rendered with utmost severity (cf. Rom. 2:4 ff.; II Pet. 3:9). "How shall we escape if we neglect so great a salvation?" (Heb. 2:3).

PART TWO

The Road to Conversion

The Christian moral code is more than a mere enumeration of rigid principles and more than a summation of basic rules. Since conversion is a *growth process* and the Christian law is essentially a *Law of Life*, the decisive measures and degrees leading to conversion and its perfection deserve a detailed discussion. The term "road" is not meant to imply a sequence of acts or steps on the way to the summit of virtue. Despite a certain precedence and succession of events in the process of conversion, the various phases are greatly interdependent and complementary.

* The Book of the Apocalypse speaks of these mysteries in symbolic language, as for example, "the Woman clothed with the sun."

Conversion signifies a liberation from sin and a turning to Christ and His kingdom. A brief description of both the kingdom of darkness and of light is rather inadequate. Guided by the testimonies of Holy Scripture, we shall try to depict how the gradual liberation from the powers of sin will lead us to a life in Christ and a more active and intimate relationship to God's kingdom. In this connection, it should be noted, however, that the conversion of the individual is related to the fulness of salvation of the whole Mystical Body of Christ. A thorough understanding of the Christian's solidarity of salvation should aid man in his striving for liberation from the solidarity of evil.

SYNOPSIS OF PART TWO

(1) While sin is wickedness and personal entanglement in the solidarity of guilt, sorrow for sin is a reconciliation to God and His kingdom of love. (2) While sin is the embodiment of darkness and falsity, the contrite acknowledgment of wrongdoing is the road to God's kingdom of light and truth. (3) While sin is synonymous with guilt and injustice, its atonement and satisfaction are the bridge to a new justice in God. (4) While sin is the essence of lawlessness, conversion points the way to the New Law in the spirit of life.

Section I. Contrition

1. The Pernicious Power of Sin

Contrition is the most essential act of conversion. A clear perception of its true nature and purpose will aid us to fathom the full malice of sin as the most dreadful outrage against the supreme majesty of God.

Sins of commission are actions committed through thought, word, or deed in the full awareness that they are opposed to God's will and commandment. Sins are grievous or mortal if man, in the full realization that the particular desire, word, or deed unfailingly disrupts his friendship with God (seriously offends God), nevertheless persists in his perverted desire or action.

Viewed from this particular aspect of the inherent nature of sin, it would seem that relatively few people are guilty of mortal sin. Evidently, there are many who, in their perverted actions, are unaware that they grievously offend God. Much wrongdoing occurs without full knowledge of its inherent injustice.

What are the logical conclusions which we ought to draw from such facts? Should we rejoice that so many men are ignorant of the evident contradiction between their actions and God's revealed will, because this reduces the number of subjective sins? Would it be better to be unenlightened regarding God's law and thereby avoid its transgression? Such an opinion would be far from the actual truth! Even if law is the occasion of sin because of man's perversion and estrangement from God (cf. Rom. 5:20), the clear perception of God's will still remains an undeserved grace which enables man to recognize his deplorable and sinful existence.

Law, as such, cannot liberate the soul enslaved in sin. Yet the demands of the Law are part of God's plan of salvation. In view of the Law, the recognition of our insufficiency and weakness should draw us closer to Christ and His salvific deeds. Men are saved not so much by the awareness of their sinfulness in the violation of God's commandments, but rather by their sincere sorrow for sin in view of God's saving love and mercy. The sinful deed in itself gives evidence of the depravity of the human heart. This unfortunate condition is further aggravated if the soul, empty of

God's grace and salutary contrition, remains unmindful
of its sad state of iniquity.

"Sin" in biblical language does not refer to any particular
transgression of God's law, but rather to man's deplorable
servitude under the power of sin and to the world's enslavement by the vicious snares of evil. The essence of sin
and its deleterious consequences consist in the soul's estrangement and total separation from God. Each sin must
be seen as a dreadful link in the long chain of wrongdoing,
beginning with the first sin in paradise and continuing
through the ages down to our own contemporaries. The
sinner who fails to exercise his God-given freedom in a
firm opposition to evil, both in his own heart and in the
world around him, will eventually be overcome by the
powers of sin. "Everyone who commits sin is a slave of sin"
(John 8:34; cf. Rom. 6:16).

St. Paul, in his letter to the Romans, paints the dismal
picture of the pagan world, which despite a certain knowledge of God, refused to honor Him. In consequence of
sin, man's heart and mind became darkened and perverted
(cf. Rom. 21:32). Sin, in its essence, is a voluntary rejection
of God and, consequently, a radical separation from the
very fountain of all goodness and all freedom of choice.
The inevitable outcome of repeated transgressions of God's
law is the final tragedy of a complete estrangement from
God. As soon as sin has gained indisputable possession over
man's heart, the pernicious influences from a wicked world
with its evil spirit ("Weltgeist"), and Satan's cunning, will
tend to destroy the soul.

The sin, which has not been resolutely banished from
the heart by sincere contrition, will prove itself as a leaden
weight tending towards degradation and as a fatal link in
the uninterrupted succession of wrongdoings which will

eventually chain the sinner to the corruption of the world
and the malice of the devil.

Sin is gross self-seeking and a despicable attempt at self-deification (cf. Gen. 3:15). After its commission, sin un-masks itself as a monstrous *enmity against self* and a fatal
violation of God's saving and protecting order in the world
(cf. Gen. 3:16 ff.). The sinner, in his attempt to become in-dependent of God, turns away from his Father's house (Is.
1:2-4; Jer. 2:13; Luke 15:11 ff.—The Prodigal Son). Yet his
alienation from the bosom of God delivers him to the tyran-nical dominion of Satan.

Venial sin, although not radically opposed to the soul's
basic orientation to God, is a dangerous delay in finding
and possessing Him. It lacks the malice of full reflection
and consent in the disobedience to God's will. Its basic
feature is an imperfect attitude towards God and His ex-press will. It does not surrender the soul to the slavery of
Satan. Yet repeated and unrepented venial sin is the prel-ude to the soul's complete estrangement from God, because
it tends towards a gradual decline and eventual extinction
of divine love.

Sin not only jeopardizes personal salvation but, in vary-ing degrees, it also endangers the spiritual welfare of other
members of the Mystical Body of Christ. *Every sin inten-sifies the solidarity of evil in the world.* The evil effects of
sin must be rectified by genuine sorrow.

2. The Object of Contrition

Authentic sorrow for sin should not become contaminated
with morbid feelings of guilt which not only deprive the
soul of the keen joy of reunion in the Father's house but also
tend to block the heart's contrition at the sight of personal

sin and the injustice in the world. Strictly speaking, sorrow for sin applies only to personal failings. Furthermore, there is no sin unless the wrongdoing is the result of a conscious and culpable lack of responsibility.

Genuine sorrow for sin demands an explicit detestation of all conscious offenses against God, both individually and collectively. The more contrition illumines the soul's hidden and perverted motives, the more it will act as a purifying and vitalizing force by opposing the baneful consequences of those sins which, instead of having been repented, were repressed into the subconscious mind.

A heartfelt contrition for sin is not only grief at the sight of particular, deliberate, sinful actions and their evil motives, but also sorrow for every hidden and involuntary wrongdoing because it recognizes such sins as the evident proofs of the accumulated malice in the heart and the evil consequences of unrepented sins. A contrition of the heart voices itself through the sorrow-stricken conscience, not so much by saying: "I have committed such and such a sin," but rather in the humble acknowledgment: "I am such a sinner." Past sins, which have not been eradicated by sincere contrition and atonement, will prove their sinister influence in repeated sinful acts unless conscience is on the alert. In sincere contrition we admit that timely sorrow for our failings and a greater fervor in the atonement of our sins would have prevented the renewal of "unfruitful works."

In case of serious doubt as to whether adequate reflection and full consent of the will were present in particular transgressions of God's law, it may be assumed that the strict obligation for confession is not binding and that Holy Communion may be received without previous reception of the sacrament of penance. Although the person may be excused from confessing the sin, he ought to make a serious effort towards a change of heart through the spirit of compunction and the humble admission of his guilt before God. He should realize that his sins are associated with his lack of sincere contrition. He ought to meditate on the serious consequences of his lack of charity and scandalous behavior.

Although it is true that many partially voluntary and previously repented faults and sinful habits are not to be imputed as mortal sins, their renewed appearance in the rebellion of the lower passions and in semi-voluntary acts should sound a serious warning of the need for salutary sorrow and humble compunction of the heart.

Occasionally, personal guilt may be minimal or absent, even in serious transgressions of God's law, if the latter are the inevitable consequences of original sin, heredity, and environment. In such unusual circumstances, contrition takes on a different aspect because there is no accountability for such actions. We should beware, however, of blaming our sins and shortcomings on heredity or environmental factors.

In every situation we should examine our own conscience as to possible sinful omissions. We should recall our serious responsibility for the extension of God's kingdom and the improvement of the milieu so that those of good will may be aided to fulfill God's will. Very often, hereditary influences persist because of man's resistance to grace and his vacillating opposition to evil.

True sorrow and regret at the sight of men's offenses against God should not only restrain us from passing rash judgment on others, but should fill our hearts with the realization of our own misery which, under similar circumstances, might provoke our downfall. Our solidarity with all the members of the Mystical Body of Christ, and particularly those in our immediate surrounding, should call for the serious self-examination: "How many offenses against God would have been prevented if I had done my share in promoting God's reign in the world?" Such serious reflections, far from leading us into fruitless dejections, should open new dimensions of personal freedom in God's service.

3. Sorrow for Sin as Event of Salvation

To achieve man's salvation, Christ paid the ransom of untold agony, suffering, and dereliction. "Behold, the Lamb of God, who takes away the sin of the world!" (John 1:29). "For our sakes He made Him (Christ) to be sin who knew nothing of sin so that in Him we might become the justice of God" (II Cor. 5:21).

Sin manifested its pernicious power in its sinister victory over life because sin introduced death into this world (cf. Rom. 5:12; 5:21). Death's greatest triumph seemed to be assured in Christ's own dying. Mankind could perceive some realization of its own God-forsaken state in Our Lord's utter dereliction on the cross. Although Christ permitted His soul to be inundated by all the misery and torture of a sinful world, His death spelled utter defeat for sin. His dying proved to be the greatest victory over the powers of sin, over a thoughtless estrangement from God, and over a powerless acceptance of a hopeless death. Although Christ's death in propitiation for the sins of the whole world was filled with untold bitterness and ignominy, it was the most sublime and heroic act of all history, a supreme manifestation of an obedient love to the Father, a sacrifice of charity, and a road to His glorious resurrection (cf. I Cor. 15:55 ff.).

In every salutary repentance, Christ's death and resurrection become present again as efficacious events of salvation in order to unmask the powers of sin. Christ's death is the greatest salvific deed of all times and all people (cf. Rom. 6:10). Conversion makes it actually present and effective here and now in our behalf. "Thus do you consider yourselves also as dead to sin, but alive to God in Christ Jesus" (Rom. 6:11).

Contrition is an ever-present, salvific happening through its relationship with the sacraments of conversion, baptism, and penance. The sacraments are Christ's saving actions which are ever-continuing and effective realities for us in the eschatological struggle against the evil powers of sin. Through the efficacy of Christ's sufferings in the sacraments, contrition gives us an interior participation in the death and resurrection of Christ. Contrition is a fruit of the virtue of faith because it appraises sin and its dreadful consequences by God's just condemnation of its malice in the bitter Passion and death of the Redeemer. Contrition also contains the element of Christian hope since it discloses to the sorrowing heart that Christ's death and resurrection have saved it from the righteous anger of God's judgment. Salutary sorrow for sin assumes a "sacramental form" in so far as the contrite soul, in view of the sacraments, trustfully turns to Christ's efficacious charity. The repentant Christian knows that faith, hope, and God's gratuitous gifts bring him within the radius of God's saving presence of which he has been assured in the sacraments of conversion (baptism and penance), and in the sacraments of the living (Holy Eucharist, confirmation, anointing of the sick, matrimony, and holy orders).

Contrition brings the Christian to a keen realization of the injustice and malice of sin. It makes him share in the bitter grief of soul which Christ had experienced in the Garden of Olives and on the cross. Just as Christ's Passion and death has transformed our dying into a fountain of life, so does salutary sorrow for sin transfigure the barren remorse of conscience. *Contrition makes the old self die in order that our new self re-created in Christ may live and reign.* Sorrow for sin becomes a true participation in the death and resurrection of Christ in its relationship to the sacrament of baptism in which we die to sin in order to live with Christ (cf. Rom. 6:11). Without supernatural sorrow for sin, the salvific act of dying with Christ in baptism does not achieve its full efficacy. Without heartfelt contrition for past sins, the reception of baptism in adults is fruitless (though not invalid since it bestows the baptismal character). Even if the contrition which precedes baptism is merely attrition (contrition of fear), the sacrament of baptism develops the seed of charity which is contained in such imperfect contrition. This means that baptism confers the inner ability or characteristic power of the children of God to grieve over sin for love of God. The same relationship exists between contrition and the sacrament of penance.

The true nature of contrition as well as its intrinsic relationship to the sacraments reveals that contrition is not only a basic prerequisite for the fruitful reception of the sacraments of conversion, but that the sacraments themselves are outward signs of grace and consequently imply a commission to an ever-increasing sorrow for sin. This truth is important for a better understanding of the Church's practice to baptize infants. The child before the age of reason has not committed sin and, consequently, has no personal share in mankind's solidarity of guilt. Yet, the intrinsic character of the sacrament as an ever-continuing event of salvation unites the baptized with the death and resurrection of Christ, and therefore produces in him an ever-increasing conformity with Christ's sorrow for the guilt and the unrighteousness of the world and thus consummates the victory over sin. For the baptized, heartfelt contrition for sin is both an undeserved grace and a solemn commitment inherent in the sacrament of baptism.

The sincere detestation of personal sin and grief over the sinfulness of the world are based on the salutary action of baptism, which St. Paul describes as a dying with Christ and an intimate participation in Christ's resurrection (cf. Rom. 6). The soul's purification is greatly dependent on contrition or salutary grief for sin. In addition, the patient endurance of all sufferings and trials will eventually effect our spiritual dying with Christ as forecast in baptism.

"Blessed are they who mourn, for they shall be comforted" (Matt. 5:5). "For the sorrow that is according to God produces repentance that surely tends to salvation, whereas the sorrow that is according to the world produces death" (II Cor. 7:10). The terrible nature of sin unveils itself in Our Lord's agony in the Garden of Gethsemane and in His utter dereliction on the cross, epitomized in His soul-stricken plea to His heavenly Father. All the world's miseries, including our bodily death, are nothing in comparison with the horrors of spiritual death in sin. Sincere contrition for sin contains the seed which is meant to blossom into a new life of holiness under the efficacious influence of Christ's resurrection. In return for such compunction, God has promised us heaven's consolations of which the reawakened love, purified in the crucible of sorrow, is a foretaste even in this present life.

"Blessed are the poor in spirit," blessed are those, who humbled by God's grace, realize their utter poverty of heart and fully rely on God's mercy "for theirs is the kingdom of heaven" (Matt. 5:3). The humble recognition of our estrangement from God through sin guarantees our participation in Christ's own life because it disposes the soul to die to all self-sufficiency and to surrender to God's all-sufficing grace.

Our explanation shows that the sinner's contrition and his salutary grief at the sight of the sinfulness of the world are distinct from a mere "moral contrition" which disposes man to condemn a particular misdeed because it violated a specific, personal value in his new orientation to values. This confirms rather than denies the fact that true sorrow for sin embraces a new relationship to moral values.

4. Contrition as a Road to Freedom

Since man's moral accountability only embraces the evil actions accomplished with sufficient reflection of the mind and consent of the will, there arises the question: What is the moral responsibility of those souls who because of their entanglement in vice are no longer aware of the sinfulness of their life or who lack the will power to change their evil ways? To some extent this important question has been answered in our discussion on the salutary effects of contrition. Grief of conscience is the road to spiritual freedom. For the sake of deepening our understanding of the relationship between contrition and freedom, we shall briefly summarize the concepts on freedom outlined in Chapter II.

If man surrenders himself to evil, namely, to a perverted aim, he does thereby not relinquish his will power. In fact, the very decisiveness of the wicked man's evil designs puts to shame the half-hearted efforts of the virtuous in the pursuance of the good. This determination of will in the sinner should not overshadow the fact that he is void of "the blessed freedom of the children of God" and that in addition he seriously jeopardizes his moral freedom which permits him to love and embrace the good.

Every mortal sin implies a loss of the blessed freedom of the children of God because the latter is the expression of

man's filial love of God and of a loving submission to the
Holy Spirit who inspires us to cry out: "Abba! Father!"
(Rom. 8:15). Mortal sin is the complete rejection of God
the Father.

*On the other hand, the loss of moral freedom is a grad-
ual one.* Since man is an imperfect being whose intellect
is incapable of an immediate and full grasp of truth, and
whose will is too inadequate to express itself fully in a
single act of choice, he cannot forfeit his freedom in one
decision towards good or evil. In contradistinction to man's
limitations, the purely spiritual nature of the angels implies
not only a penetrating intellect which permits an instan-
taneous perception of the truth, but also a will which is able
to express itself fully and irrevocably in one single act.
Yet since mortal sin is a "fully human act" in the voluntary
choice of evil, it possesses an inflexible and decisive power.
Through mortal sin man relinquishes his supernatural po-
tentiality towards good. By the law of progressive moral
decadence he delivers himself into the "slavery of sin." His
repeated chances for a new beginning in virtue are the
gratuitous gifts of his Creator who, so to speak, subsidizes
every step in the direction of the good. In constraining the
sinner from utter destruction, God, after each relapse into
sin, tries to establish a new relationship by appealing to
those aspects of man's personality which, untouched by
vice, are still receptive to the good. Yet in full accord with
both the nature of man and the essence of sin, the intrinsic
consequence of vice is complete moral degradation and
ruin. The pernicious power of sin reveals itself in a gradual
destruction of moral freedom. Nevertheless it should be
remembered that this holds true only in regard to partially
or totally unrepented sins. Such sins progressively obscure
the recognition of moral values and harden the will in evil.

Each new beginning after a defeat in sin becomes more difficult the more the soul delays to atone for it by repentance.

Each faithful cooperation with grace increases the habitual virtuous state of the heart and the will, which in turn enhances the ease and joy in the performance of the good because of an inner relatedness to virtue. Virtue is synonymous with growth in moral freedom. On the contrary, repeated sins or evil actions, which have not been atoned for by sincere contrition, will eventually breed evil habits which insidiously tend to destroy man's moral freedom. Nevertheless, God is able to touch even the faintest degree of the soul's freedom and to reawaken the stifled possibilities for the good through miracles of His grace. The most decisive and most indispensable step in the process of spiritual "rehabilitation" is contrition for sin. It alone makes possible the transition from the slavery of sin to authentic freedom. *Salutary sorrow for sin breaks the bondage of man's sinful existence.*

The restoration of moral freedom through sincere repentance is a gradual process unless hastened by a special miracle of grace. Contrition should gradually deepen and thus break the fetters of a blind self-infatuation. Thereby, the soul's powers become liberated for a well-ordered self-love and a harmonious striving for perfection. The fear of the Lord and a sincere concern for personal salvation will open the road to a purified love of God which engenders true "love of self in God." Supernatural love of God and self can gain access to the soul of the sinner only after the pernicious power of sin has been recognized and personal guilt has been acknowledged in the presence of God.

Salutary grief and a return to true value assures the victory of true compunction in the soul. The initial assent to the good, although not fully victorious over the powers of the soul, is the first step towards a restoration of freedom. The sinner's humble acknowledgment of his own insufficiency to liberate himself from the snares of sin and to regain his lost inheritance is one of the most decisive factors in repentance. "The spirit of grace and petition" (cf. Zach. 12:10-14) is the beginning of conversion. It is this gift of petition, which in the certain hope of release from sin and its bondage, enables the soul to pray: "Blessed be God who has not refused my petition nor turned His mercy away from me" (Ps. 65:20). A contrite prayer and humble supplication for an increase in compunction of heart will insure a new influx of freedom from the mighty hand of God.

Now we are ready to answer the question posed at the beginning of this section: the sin which is the expression of that lack of moral liberty, which has been incurred through unrepented sins, is sinful to the extent that the first sinful act was freely willed. In this connection we are to take into account both the deliberate and voluntary sins of commission, as well as those of omission through a postponement of conversion and failure to respond to God's invitation of grace. *To prevent sin from clouding our conscience and from gaining an enslaving control over our heart and will, we should evoke immediate and sincere contrition after each relapse into sin. The grace of repentance is a precious gift for which we should constantly implore God's mercy.*

5. Contrition and the Examination of Conscience

A crime inventory of a confirmed convict, who summarizes his "successes" and "failures" on the road of vice, is certainly far from an examination of conscience. This analogy points up the fact that a catalogue-like completeness of all evil thoughts, desires, and actions, is not the distinguishing mark of a sincere examination of conscience. Its most fundamental feature is the penetrating gaze into the very depth of conscience which aims to unmask the real nature of sin in the presence of God and His Church. Consequently, contrition is a basic prerequisite for a salutary examination of conscience. Without an all-pervading sorrow for sin, the examination of conscience will fail to penetrate into the innermost recesses of the heart and might even provoke perverse desires in the recollection of the evil committed. The examination of conscience must be the fruit of sincere contrition. Thereby it will deepen both humility and the sorrow for sin while it unfolds the heart's perversity in its numerous offenses.

The above assertion, that the decisive feature in the examination of conscience does not consist in the complete enumeration of past sins, is not meant to minimize the need and the value of a thorough investigation of the heart's inmost desires. Those sins, which have been repressed into the subconscious mind, must be placed in the penetrating light of a conscience, illumined by contrition in order to resist their further obscuring and enslaving influence. The same obligation is contained in the command to confess as far as possible all mortal sins which were committed with full freedom and deliberation.

In this connection it might be well to remember that contrition, the examination of conscience, the good resolution, the confession of sins, and the satisfaction for sins, are more than parts of the outward sacramental sign. We have seen the deep religious meaning of contrition (and, consequently, all other related steps in the process of conversion) in their relation to the sacrament of penance. They derive their redemptive power from the salvific deeds of

Christ made actual in the efficacious, sacramental signs. However, grace continues to operate beyond the moment of the reception of a sacrament.

6. *Contrition and the Resolution of Amendment*

A fitting resolution can produce its effectiveness only to the extent that contrition undoes the malice of sin and restores the lost moral freedom. The Council of Trent emphatically teaches that contrition does not consist only in the mere "relinquishing of all sinfulness with the resolution of beginning a new life, but also in the sincere detestation of the old manner of life." "Contrition is a grief of soul and an abhorrence of past sins coupled with the firm resolution to sin no more in the future" (Denzinger, No. 897). This clearly states that the power of the good resolution and its religious value are based on sorrow for sin. If so many resolutions are ineffective the reason for this misfortune lies chiefly in the fact that such resolutions were not the outcome of the salutary sorrow of contrition.

Contrition is more than a mere factor in formulating an effective resolution. Its deepest essence and urgency consists in the return and conversion of the heart and in the humble prayer before the offended majesty of God. In view of what has been said, contrition is an event of salvation which is intimately united with the death and resurrection of Christ and the sacraments which efficaciously re-present (make present again) these mysteries. As the sacrament of home-coming assures the sinner of reconciliation and re-adoption, contrition represents the most decisive step in this return to the Father's house.

Psychology corroborates the truths about contrition in the light of faith: there can be no direct transition from

the disorder of sin to a new beginning unless the burden
of the sinful past has been consumed in the fire of sincere
repentance.

Mortal sin begets personal guilt and enmity with God.
Therefore, the fundamental resolution towards a change
of life and a return to God's friendship and sonship presupposes the humble acknowledgment of the prodigal son: "I
am no longer worthy to be called your son" (Luke 15:19).
Without this sincere prayer of contrition and a definite detestation of the sinful past, all our assurances for the future to abide by God's law are no more than self-delusions
and a disrespectful familiarity with God.

Even after the misfortune of venial sin, sincere contrition
should precede the soul's humble supplication for pardon. This alone is conducive to overcoming the evil effects
of sin in man's heart and to strengthening the bond of
friendship with God through the good resolution. In the
sacred Liturgy and in the "Our Father," we are instructed
to implore forgiveness of our sins even though we may not
be aware of an actual transgression.

There exists a reciprocal relationship between the effectiveness of a resolution to amendment and the sincerity
and depth of the grief of conscience. "No contrition can
be truly genuine unless, from its very inception, it embodies the designs for a renewal of heart. Contrition only
destroys for the purpose of rebuilding. In fact, it starts re-
constructing where it merely seems to annihilate." *

Our sorrow for sin must deepen and be sublimated if it is
to bear the fruit of a good resolution and a new life in
Christ. In like manner, the good resolution and its implementation must not be delayed, otherwise contrition
may weaken or degenerate into a barren pain or the despair
of a tortured conscience. Since Christian hope in God's

* Max Scheler, *Vom Ewigen in Menschen*, Leipzig, pp. 398 ff.

goodness and mercy embraces the confident trust in the supernatural power needed for a new life and since this hope is the herald of love, sorrow for sin cannot develop into perfect contrition (love-motive) nor even imperfect contrition (fear-motive) without the element of the good resolution (cf. pp. 425 ff.).

Both contrition and the good resolution are perfected simultaneously, although the real vivifying factor is the grief of conscience. In cases where the good resolution fails to arise or to crystallize fully, the best remedy is humble supplication to obtain God's grace, the source of true repentance. Similarly, if our contrition is deficient we ought to question whether we paid adequate attention to the resolution and its implementation.

Contrition and resolution not only mature together but also fuse into each other. Under ordinary circumstances following a life of sin, even the most sincere contrition is unable to restore instantaneously the full value-appreciation and man's moral freedom which were lost through sin and vice. For this reason, the penitent's resolution to amend is often imperfect and incomplete. The sinner's partial, moral blindness, which keeps him from the realization that a particular action or disposition of the soul ought to be repudiated, can only be overcome gradually in our progress of conversion. The so-called "blindness to applicability" will not admit that a particular acknowledged commandment is to be obeyed by us here and now. This can only be overcome by a sincere sorrow for sin and a relentless struggle against pride, sloth, and the powerful fascinations of the lower passions.

An understanding of the principles of growth and development in the moral-religious life demands both a persistent endeavor for a deepening of contrition and a strengthening and broadening of our resolutions. The acknowledgment of a gradual unfolding in the spiritual life should prevent us from an over-exacting attitude towards those of our fellowmen who at times may fall short in their serious efforts towards conversion. In case of a newly converted sinner, especially if he has grown up in an un-Christian surrounding, it would be unwise to confront him from the start with particular decisions and resolutions which might even surpass the ability of those advanced in virtue. Prudence should guide us in our good resolutions. It is true that conversion by its very nature implies, from its inception, a wholehearted response to God's marvelous deeds of salvation. Every prescriptive or prohibitive law requires unconditional fulfillment. However, the laws directing us towards a goal or an ideal (the love of God and fellowman from one's "whole heart" and the admonitions in the Sermon on the Mount) can be recognized and complied with only by degrees (cf. p. 214 ff.). These basic commandments of the New Law require a ready compliance according to the directives of the virtue of prudence. If in exceptional circumstances the invitation of grace should call for an extraordinary deed, the Christian virtue of prudence would demand an unprecedented response in both resolution and action.

The resolution which is born of sincere contrition is a *humble* resolve which implores God's gracious assistance. The humble penitent is cognizant of the fact that even his best resolutions are imperfect. Therefore, he constantly prays that he may advance in the recognition of the good, the detestation of evil, and the determination to amend his life. Sincere contrition and humility are the indispensable prerequisites for the decisive resolve to avoid sin and its proximate occasions.

7. Contrition as a Road to Charity

Salutary sorrow for sin is God's gratuitous gift. It marks the inception of the heart's transformation in grace. It is therefore fitting that contrition is born on the wings of an unlimited confidence in God's goodness (which is synonymous with the virtue of hope) and, by reason of its nature, aims towards love of God.

Since sin is a serious offense against the holiness of God and a gross ingratitude towards His love, contrition demands a humble acknowledgment of the injustice of sin and of personal guilt. The baptized who reverts to his old life of sin, thereby spurns the love of God for the sake of the pleasures of this world from which he had been redeemed (cf. II Pet. 2:20) whereas the contrite heart gradually returns to God's love.

In keeping with psychological developments and through God's merciful providence, there are, at times, natural and very imperfect motives which may give rise to salutary contrition as, for example, a disappointment in a love affair, temporal reverses and failures, embarrassment, or a keen conception of the ugliness of sin. In themselves, these motives for remorse are without salutary value. Yet through the guidance of divine providence such incentives may lead the sinner to true compunction of heart. The same applies to the servile, imperfect contrition which still lacks the "chaste pain" which only the awareness of the loss of God's friendship can evoke. Such a contrition based on fear rather than love does not detest sin as such but rather fears the temporal or eternal punishment for sin. The imperfect motive or the contrition actuated by fear, though without salutary value in itself apart from the sacrament of penance, is nevertheless a valuable milestone on the way to perfect contrition especially if it originates in a still hidden supernatural charity.

The eventual awakening of divine love in the sinner is a work of God's mercy and the victory of His superabundant charity. This becomes apparent in the fact that the confirmation of this triumph according to God's salvific plan reveals itself in a sacramental encounter with Christ or the sacramental word of Christ. Even if divine love together with the life of grace had been restored prior to the reception of a sacrament, the saving action nevertheless occurred in reference to the sacrament.

Contrition is the gift of God's merciful goodness which flows from the love of our Redeemer. It enters into the salvific events of Good Friday and Easter Sunday. This relationship appears strikingly in the sacrament of reconciliation. Since contrition is the gift of the communion of charity, it tends to lead the soul back into the fellowship of love. Consequently, an express or implicit element in contrition is the grief over the infringement of the solidarity of salvation and, therefore, also a renewed orientation to the communion of all the redeemed.

Despite all theological disputes, the truth remains unquestionable that imperfect contrition, although chiefly motivated by fear, plays an important role in the process of conversion despite the fact that it falls short of the goal of perfect love of God (cf. Council of Trent, Denzinger, No. 898). Furthermore, there is no doubt that the road of salutary contrition achieves its final goal only in perfect contrition. Nevertheless, a contrition, arising from the holy fear inherent in the divine nature of hope, like the virtue of hope itself signifies an awakening of charity although far from the perfect love of the children of God.

The Christian lost in sin, but in the full awareness of God's promises and threats of punishments, will aim towards a contrition based on love because all of God's pledges climax in the assurance that He Himself shall be our abundant reward (cf. Gen. 15:1) and that His reward shall be with Him (cf. Apoc. 22:12). Heaven is the kingdom of love. Consequently, the fear of missing it implies a real although imperfect love of God. The dreadful nature of hell does not consist in physical torments but rather in the irremediable estrangement from God. Therefore, the fear of hell implies a certain desire for God's love.

Since the sacrament of conversion marks the eventful return of the "prodigal son," this occasion deserves to be celebrated not only by all the inhabitants of heaven but also by the repentant sinner himself. Charity alone enables the soul to render fitting expression of joy and gratitude. In view of the essence of conversion and the nature of the sacrament of penance, the penitent sinner ought to evoke a grief of conscience motivated by the love of God. Furthermore, the recipient of the sacrament of penance is aided in the evolution of perfect contrition by the grace of the sacrament through which God deigns to restore the divine virtue of charity unless His efficacious action is frustrated by man's culpable attachments to sin. Only perfect contrition is in keeping with the gracious renewal of God's friendship.

The soul who has returned to God is one who has received pardon and the pledge of a singular love either through or in virtue of the sacrament. On the part of the repentant sinner, this calls for an unceasing response of gratitude arising from a humble and contrite heart. This disposition of humility has nothing in common with a scrupulous retrospect into the past, it rather effects a complete liberation from sin and an uninterrupted song of praise in view of God's merciful love.

Section II. The Confession of Sins

Contrition not only possesses the vital power to unmask the pernicious force of sin, but irresistibly urges the penitent to consummate the work of laying bare the full malice of sin. Confession serves this purpose in a very special way. Man's liberation from *"falsehood,"* from the perplexing *"deception"* of sin, and from a *"darkness and obscurity"* which shuns the light, is a gradual process going hand in hand with conversion. We shall focus our attention on the act of disclosing our sins in the sacrament of penance since it is the most obvious phase in the process of conversion. We should strive to see wrongdoing in its dark and sinister way in order to appreciate more fully the liberating work of grace in confession and to recognize it as a means of rendering praise to God's mercy and of reducing the power of sin in the world.

1. The Darkness of Sin

Sin is basically falsehood and servitude to untruth.

St. John the Evangelist presented Christ as the personification of truth (cf. John 14:6), and the Herald of Truth (cf. John 1:14; 8:40 ff.). He referred to the Holy Spirit sent by Our Lord as the "Spirit of Truth" (John 14:17; 15:26). At the same time, he characterizes the opponent of Christ as the "father of lies" (John 8:44). The devil has fallen away from the truth and maintains an attitude of utter hostility towards it, wherefore he "is no longer able to act according to truth." He is "a murderer" from the beginning (John 8:44). Since there is no truth in him, he seeks to ensnare men in the maze of his lies. He has wielded his power of deception and cunning in his dealing with Eve in the Garden of Eden (cf. Gen. 3:1 ff.; Wis.

2:23-24). The same "spirit of untruth" who continues to delude men into sinning is the instigator of all sinful thoughts, words, and actions of men. In imitation of Satan, the sinner likewise becomes a liar. Just as the disciple of Christ "walks in truth" (II John 4:3; 3 ff.) and "does the truth" (John 3:21; I John 1:6; Eph. 4:15), so also does the sinner in his own way become conformed to the "father of lies" and proves himself a "liar." Such an existence can best be described as "love for deceit and falsehood in action," wherefore "their portion shall be in the pool that burns with fire and brimstone" together with Satan himself (Apoc. 21:8; 22:15).

In view of our human frailty and sinfulness, Holy Scripture calls every man a "liar" (Rom. 3:4) because sin connotes a defection from the truth and a simultaneous inclination towards "the father of lies." Sin gradually ensnares man into ever tighter meshes of heresy and apostasy (cf. Rom. 1:25 ff.). As a life of truth and holiness makes us ever more comfortable to Christ Himself, so does a life of iniquity signify an enslavement to the deceptive spirit of a wicked world (cf. Rom. 12:2). Whosoever fully acknowledges the principles of truth in his thoughts and actions shall achieve a deep understanding of the truth and walk in the light of truth (cf. John 3:21). On the other hand, those who refuse to submit to the mild yoke of a "sincere charity" as witnesses of truth and love will be abandoned by God to the guileful deceptions and "lying wonders" of Satan (II Thes. 2:9-11).

Sin is utter darkness in the most pernicious solidarity with Satan's kingdom.

Holy Scripture employs the contrast of light and darkness in order to illustrate the extreme antithesis of truthfulness and deception. St. John poignantly states: "God is light, and in Him there is no darkness" (I John 1:5). Christ came into this world as "the true light" to dispel the darkness of sin. The fact that this world did not receive Him, reveals its deplorable abyss of darkness (cf. John 1:4 ff.). The identification of sin with darkness pertains not only to particular sins but also to the deplorable, sinful state of this world which is at enmity with God. Darkness is a sinister power which will embrace all those who fail to adhere to Christ and His law because without Him men "walk in the darkness" of sin (John 12:35). Christ is the true light separating the good from the wicked. Since the true light has appeared in this world (cf. I John 2:8), we have escaped the inevitable fate of utter darkness. The fact that despite Christ's coming men still prefer to live in darkness rather than in God's radiant light, by refusing to accept His truths, pronounces judgment on the wicked world (cf. John 3:18 ff.). The verdict of guilt which the malefactors already carry in their hearts will eventually be openly confirmed through the judgment of God who will inevitably cast them "into the dark, the place of wailing and gnashing of teeth" (Matt. 8:12; 22:13; 25:13; II Pet. 2:17). The fallen angels are the "principalities and the powers of darkness" (Eph. 6:12). Whosoever through sin separates himself from Jesus Christ, the true light of the world, delivers himself to the evil spirits. Even in this present life, the enemies of Christ carry hell and its darkness in their very hearts.

Evil is a deceptive power in this wicked world where the wiles of the devil corrupt the very air so that the individual, failing to resist them, will be entangled in their web. Darkness is able to envelop those who surrender themselves to its sinister powers to such a great extent that even the light in their own intellect, their very conscience, turns into utter darkness (cf. Matt. 6:23). Un-Christian surroundings and repeated and unrepented sins effect a dulling and eventual darkening of the powers of conscience.

Sin from its very inception is a process of self-deception and a gradual but total dimming of the light of God's truth. The sinner turns his gaze away from the true good because he is fascinated by false values, inciting his pride and his passions. Unless prompt and sincere contrition heals such vile beguilement, the soul is in great danger of becoming completely enshrouded in its pernicious darkness.

Sin shuns from the light. "Everyone who does evil hates the light, and does not come to the light, that his deeds may not be exposed" (John 3:20). This statement of Our Lord applies not only to secret sins but, likewise, in a frightening degree, to those sins committed in public. The sinner who attempts to hide his sin because he fears discovery, thereby indirectly acknowledges the discerning, judging, and eventually revealing gaze of Christ. On the other hand, far worse is the evildoer who openly and boldly perpetrates his wicked deeds as a proof of being "well-informed, enlightened, and up-to-date," or even dares to "parade" his vices as manifestations of his sense of "responsibility."

Tyranny prefers to masquerade under the guise of freedom. Both the mighty and the lowly try to veil their egotism with the cloak of justice and zeal for the good. The contentious person hesitates to admit his base motives. The seducer of an innocent girl, far from disclosing his gross self-seeking, will try to ensnare his victim with feigned protestations of love and affection. The self-centered spouse masks his aversion for sacrifice and his unwillingness to accept the burden of parenthood with pretenses savoring of a keen sense of responsibility.

The more man attempts to justify to himself his sinful actions with sleazy excuses and the more he parades his public sins and vices as virtues, the more will his heart become overshadowed by darkness. This is the case with some unfortunate divorcees who after their legal "dissolution" of marriage and after entering a new alliance try to get the support of public opinion for their scandalous actions. Similarly, those opposing the existence of denominational schools force their Godless issue with a Pharisaical air of righteousness and solicitude for religious freedom. Others advocate unethical methods of birth control under the false pretense of prudence and of social welfare and scientific progress. All this proves that the darkness of individual consciences connive together with the wickedness of an evil world. Even "Satan disguises himself as an angel of light. It is no great thing, then, if his ministers disguise themselves as ministers of justice" (II Cor. 11:14-15). The most abysmal darkness of sin manifests itself in the wicked scheming of the devil and his associates when they slander the Church of Christ, "the very foundation of Truth," by representing her as the incarnation of darkness (cf. Mark 3:22).*

2. The Admission of Guilt Dispels the Darkness of Sin

The victory of truth becomes assured whenever the sinner acknowledges his evildoing before God and his conscience. Such a triumph over sin reveals itself in the humble confession of sins before the Church and one's fellowmen. A sincere acknowledgment of wrongdoing unmasks the deceit and darkness of evil and gives testimony to the light. Although contrition implies the initial recognition of the unfailing justice of God's commandments and the perdition of sin, man's nature demands that the admission of guilt, which is implicitly contained in contrition, find both its perfection and outward expression in the humble avowal of sin before God and His Church.

Man combines within his nature both matter and spirit

* The very word "devil" or diabolus signifies "entangler."

—body and soul. Since man's transgressions of God's laws have affected all earthly domains, it is but fitting that his humble avowal of guilt likewise assume corporeal expression. Furthermore, based on the substantial union between soul and body, man's efforts towards a suitable external expression of culpability are conducive to a more penetrating self-knowledge. Contrition appears in its most tangible form in the verbal expression and admission of our sins. The disclosure of our sins intensifies the humility and sincerity of our contrition. The acknowledgment of our trespasses releases the sinner from his solitude and enfolds him in the solidarity of the truth.

The humble confession of sin is a powerful barrier against hypocrisy and self-deception. Important circumstances may at times oblige us to conceal our failings for the sake of our good reputation and social prestige in order to fulfill our social service. Despite legitimate reasons for shielding our good name, we should be aware of the danger of camouflaging our weakness under the cloak of righteousness. The practice of frequent confessions forestalls such a risk of hypocrisy.

Every contrite confession of guilt possesses a liberating and enlightening influence on the soul. Therefore Holy Scripture admonishes us: "Confess, therefore, your sins to one another!" (James 5:16). Even outside the sacrament of penance, a revelation of wrongdoing possesses deep religious value and significance. In case of an injustice or a serious scandal to others, a humble acknowledgment of our guilt before others may even be a matter of serious obligation. This amendment for our sins may be expressed in words or in actions. History proves that deeply religious people of all ages have felt the need to reveal their guilt not only before God, but to make timely confessions of their wrongdoing before men. Contemporary psychological research is verifying the therapeutic value of open admission of guilt to others. The self-accusation in the sacrament of penance provides an excellent opportunity to attain the personal, social, and religious values inherent in a humble avowal of guilt.

Sacramental confession is an excellent means of bringing the sinner within the radius of God's light because his self-accusation is made in the presence of the Church, "the pillar and mainstay of the truth" (I Tim. 3:15), and the bulwark of protection against the powers of darkness. In the sacrament of penance the Christian acknowledges the Church's teaching and governing authority. He realizes that the Church accepts his humble admission of guilt in virtue of her God-given power and thereby confronts his life with the truths of the all-just and merciful God. In the sacrament of reconciliation, the Church implants a true spirit of sincerity in order that the penitent may resist all temptations to falsehood and deceit arising from a wicked world. The full realization of such an exalted aim depends on the sinner's sincere self-accusation in the sacrament of penance wherein he uncovers the adverse and deceptive influences from a sinful environment and his failure in his personal responsibility. Therefore, the important questions in the examination of conscience are: What influences did my words and deeds create in my environment? Did I endeavor to represent the Church and her testimony for the truth? Or, did I, on the contrary, accommodate myself to the atheistic principles of my milieu and join in irreligous talk? The humble penitent is aware of his obligation in the solidarity of the Church to carry the light of truth into every domain of life. Consequently, he admits his guilt and promises his readiness to fulfill his noble mission of giving testimony to the truth before the world.

3. Sacramental Confession and the Profession of Faith

In baptism we not only received the infused virtue of faith and membership in the Church, but we also accepted the honorable obligation to be witnesses to the truth. At baptism our first grateful response to the inquiry regarding faith was the solemn recitation of the Apostles' Creed. The baptismal profession of faith is to be confirmed and sealed with our confession of the truth in the sacred Liturgy and in our daily life.

In baptism God delivered us from the power and darkness of sin (cf. Col. 1:13). Thus, in full accord with our noble vocation we have become "light in the Lord" (Eph. 5:8). Consequently, St. Paul admonishes us to walk "as children of light! The fruit of the light is in all goodness and justice and truth" (Eph. 5:9). St. Peter, in view of the momentous baptismal transformation, addresses the faithful as "a chosen race, a royal priesthood, a holy nation, a purchased people," with the exalted mission "to proclaim the perfections of Him who has called you out of darkness into His marvelous light" (I Pet. 2:9).

If a baptized, far from becoming a witness to the light, turns back "to the unfruitful works of darkness" (Eph. 5:11), his profession of faith in the Liturgy is no longer sincere. In order to make himself worthy to participate anew in God's praise, the Christian is obliged to expose all darkness within himself through a humble self-accusation: "For all the things that are exposed are made manifest by the light . . . Thus he says, 'Awake, sleeper, and arise from among the dead, and Christ will enlighten you'" (Eph. 5:14). Similarly, the glad tidings: "You are not in darkness . . . You are all children of the light and children of the day. We are not of night, nor of darkness" (I Thes. 5:4-5), is more than a mere admonition for the Christian: "Not to sleep like the rest, but to keep awake and sober" (I Thes. 5:6). In the event that sin has been committed, it urges the sinner to uncover the unfruitful works of darkness in the humble confession of his sins and to open his soul anew to the light of God's grace.

Our baptismal vows embrace the humble admission of our sinfulness and our complete dependence on the grace and mercy of our Redeemer who has rescued us from the darkness of sin. After having been purified from sin and admitted into the marvelous light of Christ's grace, we are called to walk in the light. "If we say that we have fellowship with Him, and walk in darkness, we lie, and are not practicing the truth" (I John 1:6). For the Christian, sin is an irreconcilable contradiction. "He who says that he knows Him and does not keep His commandments, is a liar and the truth is not in him" (I John 2:4). The full measure of iniquity consists in the sinner's refusal to acknowledge his guilt. This disposes his soul to further enslavement by the powers of darkness after he had been confirmed in Christ's marvelous grace. "If we say that we have no sin, we deceive ourselves, and the truth is not in us. If we acknowledge our sins, He is faithful and just to forgive us our sins and to cleanse us from all iniquity. If we say that we have not sinned, we make Him a liar, and His word is not in us" (I John 1:8-10).

The humble confession of our transgressions becomes an absolute necessity because sin tends to obscure the illuminating power of faith. Only thus shall we be able to give testimony of that faith which we have promised at our baptism. In return for our contrite self-accusation in the sacrament of penance, Christ restores our confidence that in Him and through Him we may again become a shining light for the world in order to bring all men to the full and undisputed acknowledgment of God's sovereignty (cf. Matt. 5:16). The sacramental absolution which follows the confession of sins renews the authenticity of the penitent's testimony for Christ. The newly converted Christian is reinstated as a trustworthy witness for the gospel. Just as the baptismal pledge of faith is made in view of our acknowledgment of truth before men for their edification, so also the humble confession of our sins is directed towards an open profession of faith in the power of the absolving word of Christ and the Church. Christ's merciful forgiveness in response to our humble self-accusation imposes a renewed obligation on the penitent to confess his faith before men.

However, our sacramental confession implies not only a renewal of our pledge of fidelity to Christ and His law, but also signifies a promise to renounce our sinful doing before those whom we have scandalized or encouraged in evil. Only thus will our apostolate of witnessing Christ become again authentic and fruitful.

For example, the young man who seduced his fiancée with false assurances of love ought to confess his guilt not only before the priest but likewise to the one seduced. He should admit to her that his action was base selfishness and utter lack of reverence and charity towards her. Similarly, those who have advocated or justified divorce, abortions, and birth control in opposition to the natural law, should in reparation for their sins defend the real meaning of God's commandments so that others may realize their true conversion and become edified by their sincere profession of faith. Such restitution and dedication to the good will also confirm the converted in his virtuous resolutions and make him ever more receptive for the light.

Our continuous struggle against all work of darkness in our own hearts must go hand in hand with the sincere efforts towards the Christianization of our environment.

This interdependence of interests is based on both the essence of an all-embracing profession of faith and the nature of man, who can achieve his life's purpose only in a close solidarity with, in, and through his environment.[*]

Our self-accusation behind the soundproof walls of the confessional runs the risk of insincerity and duplicity if we do not profess our change of heart before those whom we have openly scandalized by our wrongdoing. The sacramental confession is not only an excellent expiatory renewal of our baptismal vows and pledge of faith, but also implies a renewed commitment to transform our life into a continuous echo of the solemn promises made at our baptism. While sin has jeopardized our confession of faith before men and dimmed the resplendent light of Christ in this world, our witness for the truth ought to strengthen and clarify these anew. St. Augustine made the significant observation that the pagans, though unaware of the sacraments of baptism and the Eucharist, ought to recognize the fruits of these sacraments in the good works of the baptized. Thus, the entire life of the Christian will prove itself as a continuous reflection and diffusion of the light of the sacraments.

4. Sacramental Confession as an Act of Divine Worship

Every sin is an outrage against God's majesty and glory. The sinner prefers his own self-will and self-gratification to the express will of God. His sin is an open or implied rebellion against God's loving designs.

Our solemn pledge and profession of faith at baptism,

---

[*] In this connection we wish to point out the excellent book by Rev. P. Viktor Shurr, *Seelsorge in einer neuen Welt* (Salzburg, Otto Muller Verlag). This book, as the title suggests, completes and supplements my own book on pastoral theology.

which we renew daily at Christ's sacrificial banquet, is an official commitment to a life dedicated to the praise of His goodness and love. If we faithfully respond to God's grace and charity, our life will become an authentic testimony of faith and gratitude to God who, in His condescending love, graciously manifests His holy will to us. It is Christ who brings the sinner back to the communion of the faithful.

Through the contrite confession of our sins in the sacrament of penance, we join the hymn of praise offered by our crucified Lord to the justice and mercy of His heavenly Father. In union with Christ we acknowledge in the words of the Apostle: "The law indeed is holy and the commandment holy and just and good" (Rom. 7:12). At the same time, our self-accusation implies a confident hope in God's goodness and mercy: "Give thanks to the Lord for He is good, for His mercy endures forever" (Ps. 135:1).

If the penitent's humble self-accusation becomes a sincere expression of his firm resolution to bear witness to Christ in his daily life, his testimony of faith will be united with Christ's solemn confession rendered under Pontius Pilate and sealed by His own precious blood (cf. I Tim. 6:13). The sinner's confession of guilt and the priest's words of absolution form a hymn of praise to God's justice and mercy revealed in the sacrament of reconciliation.

Man's evident self-seeking and self-glory are defeated by the humiliating and painful acknowledgment of his sinfulness. The dying of the old self, closely associated with the mystical death in the sacrament of baptism (cf. Rom. 6), is the gate to a fuller participation in the glory of the risen Lord. The life of the repentant sinner, who after his humble confession of wrongdoing receives the comforting words of absolution, is again transformed by the splendor of God's love. The sinner becomes reinstated as a worthy

440

participant in the eucharistic celebration and as a trustworthy witness for the faith.

Very often the full realization of the undeserved grace
of conversion is dawning upon the penitent when, in union
with all the faithful, he joins anew in the eucharistic banquet. This explains the keen joy of the newly converted
and his humble gratitude for the grace of conversion
which he desires to make known to all the world.

The keynote of the deep gratitude which pervades the
sacramental confession and absolution is the newly awak-
ened love of God. This charity will prove itself in truly
apostolic zeal (cf. p. 233 ff.). "Again, a new commandment I
am writing to you, and this is true both in him and in you.
Because the darkness has passed away and the true light is
now shining. He who says that he is in the light, and hates
his brother, is in the darkness still. He who loves his brother
abides in the light, and for him there is no stumbling"
(I John 2:8-10). If, in imitation of St. Peter, the admission
of guilt is joined to a sincere avowal of charity (cf. John
21:15-17), such love will inevitably prove itself in a truly
apostolic zeal for the world. The apostle's interest for God's
glory and the salvation of souls is the most efficacious
means of remaining in the light of God's grace.

Through the humble confession of sins, the penitent is
reinstated as an active participant in the liturgical worship
rendered by the Christian community for the greater
honor and glory of God, our common Father. "If you
walk in the light as He also is in the light, we have fellowship with one another" (I John 1:7).

5. The Strict Obligation of Sacramental Confession

Man's readiness to expose his sins in sacramental confession implies genuine contrition and a thorough change of

heart. The acknowledgment of our guilt is a basic prerequisite to our victory over the darkness of sin within and around us. *The confession of our wrongdoing restores the solidarity of salvation in the Church just as the sins of each member represent a serious insult and loss to the Mystical Body of Christ.* Consequently, it is the right and sacred duty of the Church to encourage the confession of sins.

It should be remembered that a clear understanding of the deep significance of the demand for material integrity in confession is more important than a hair-splitting analysis of the requirements of this law. Despite this fact, an understanding of the minimum requirements of God's law will not only minimize the danger of scrupulosity but promote the spirit of Christian freedom which, in due regard for prudence, aims to exceed minimal requirements.

(a) The Minimum Requirement of the Universal Law

The positive divine law obliges every Christian to confess all mortal sins according to their species and number as far as he is aware of these after a thorough examination of conscience.

The positive precept of the Church interprets God's law in regard to the frequency of confession. It warns the sinner from delaying the confession of his mortal sins beyond the span of a year (yearly Paschal time), unless weighty reasons demand an exception. Strictly speaking, the commandment of the Easter duty applies only to those who have committed a mortal sin since their last sacramental confession.

All grievous sins must be confessed according to their *species:* this means that the self-accusation must include all circumstances which change the nature or the species of the sin, or which change a sin which is objectively venial into a subjectively mortal sin. Naturally, this duty is incumbent only to the extent of the penitent's intellectual ability and perception of the true state of his conscience.

It is obvious that the self-accusation: "I have sinned against chastity," is inadequate in the case of adultery because the latter includes the added malice of injustice against conjugal faith and fidelity and is therefore a serious violation of the marriage bond. Similarly, it would be wrong to confess a grievous theft in words which could be construed to imply a minor offense against justice. Likewise, false swearing must be confessed as perjury rather than as a "lie in serious matters." In like manner, it would be insufficient to confess slander as a mere lie when, in reality, it is a malicious injury against the good name of another. Like other mortal sins, those against the virtue of chastity, including all interior, deliberate, sinful thoughts, desires, and intentions, must be confessed according to their species and number.

On the other hand, the strict obligation of the law does not demand the inclusion of all particular circumstances of a transgression, even if these should add to the ugliness of sin, as long as they do not change its nature. Nevertheless, the penitent should answer the confessor's questions with unaffected sincerity if the latter deems it necessary to ask for further information (such as the proximate occasions for sin, the penitent's need for advice, or, perhaps, indications for ecclesiastical censures and penances). A deliberate lie in response to such justified questions would make the sacramental confession invalid. The situation is different, however, if the penitent answered untruthfully to such questions because of the perplexity of the situation. Such a thoughtless and unintentional untruth does not render the reception of the sacrament unworthy or invalid.

Despite the basic requirement for material integrity in

the self-accusation, the penitent should refrain from all unnecessary elaborations in confessing sins of impurity. However, his discretion should not prevent him from seeking advice from his confessor in those situations which imply a proximate danger of sin. If a sinner has made himself guilty of numerous offenses against chastity since his last sacramental confession, it might be inadvisable, and at times even forbidden, to give a detailed account of all individual transgressions according to their species and number, if such an accusation would expose him to repeated and unnecessary temptations. Under these circumstances, the humble acknowledgment that the particular sins have been committed so frequently that they could not be confessed individually without provoking new temptations is, in essence, akin to an enumeration of sins. Following such a generic self-accusation, the confessor may ask questions relative to the avoidance of sin in the future.

All mortal sins must be confessed according to their *number,* because the guilt incurred and the duty of restitution greatly depend on the frequency of the offenses. If the penitent is unable to render an exact account of his mortal sins due to a faulty memory or for fear of arousing new temptations, it will be sufficient for sacramental integrity to state the approximate number of transgressions per week or month. Following such a sincere estimate, all further brooding should be avoided.

The law does not demand the confession of a doubtful sinful act (a doubtful mortal sin). Both the Council of Trent and Canon Law explain the divine commandment regarding confession to this effect, that the obligation to confess all mortal sins expressly exists in regard to those sins of which we know ourselves to be guilty after a serious examination of conscience. Yet we cannot say "that our conscience accuses us of mortal sin" if, after serious humble reflection, we are still in doubt as to the commission of a certain sin or its grievous nature.

The zealous Christian may dispel any prudent doubt in this regard in favor of himself, while a lukewarm Christian, in the habit of committing mortal sin, should prudently decide in his own disfavor because of his lax conscience. In every doubtful case, the scrupulous person should consider himself dispensed from the sacramental self-accusation in the particular area of his scrupulosity.

If legitimate reasons should prevent a penitent from confessing all his mortal sins, it is sufficient for the validity of the sacrament that he prove his good will by putting forth his best effort. Factors which might dispense from an integral confession are the declining physical strength of a dying person, lack of privacy in a hospital ward, language difficulty, or impairment of mental faculties.

In extreme situations, any sign indicating contrition or implying a desire for self-accusation will suffice for confession. If in time of war or threatening disaster there are not enough priests to hear the confessions of those endangered, the priest may extend a general absolution in agreement with the stipulations of the Church. Such an absolution is valid for all those who in sincere contrition resolve to confess all their sins according to their species and number at the next sacramental confession.

Any penitent of good will receives the sacrament of penance both validly and worthily in spite of all personal awkwardness. A penitent's sincere desire for conversion insures the validity of his confession despite the fact that he should forget a mortal sin or fail to realize his true state of conscience. He may at a later date come to the recognition that his past sacramental confessions had lacked material integrity because of a laxity in scrutinizing his conscience.

If in consequence of such knowledge the penitent begins to doubt the worthy reception of the sacraments and the material integrity of his sacramental confessions, he has no obligation to repeat his self-accusation. This is in agreement with the rule of prudence: "If an act has been performed it is prudently presumed that it was correctly and validly performed, unless proven otherwise." Consequently, the obligation for confession extends only to those mortal sins which in all moral certainty have never been confessed in a valid sacramental confession.

The above principle is applicable to all Christians. In addition, the scrupulous person is bound by the virtue of prudence to refrain from all unnecessary retelling of sins in his self-accusation. In the case of doubt, he should remember that the general maxims of prudence apply to him without any exception.

On the other hand, the Christian, who consciously and deliberately has omitted a mortal sin in his sacramental confession because of a false sense of shame or for the sake of shielding his accomplices in sin, has received the sacrament of penance unworthily and sacrilegiously. In a certain sense, his insincerity proclaims in the presence of Christ that he desires to submit his sins to the strict judgment of God's justice at the end of time rather than to the tribunal of His mercy here below. In order to rectify a sacrilegious sacramental confession, all mortal sins since the last worthy reception of the sacrament of penance must be confessed anew.

(b) Certainty of Obligation in Uncertainty of Mortal Sin

In agreement with the universal teaching of the Church and for the sake of forestalling undue scrupulosity, we

446

have emphasized the universal law of God and the Church which, strictly speaking, does not demand the confession of sins whenever there is reasonable doubt regarding their gravity. However, we may not forget the equally important truth that *every Christian has at all times, but particularly in danger of death, the inevitable moral obligation to choose the safe road of salvation. Therefore, in case of doubt, it would be wise to seek the certain road to God's grace.*

Consequently there is the strict and immediate obligation to follow the impulse of divine grace and evoke a perfect act of contrition after each sin, even if in doubt as to its seriousness, and thereby free the soul from the attachment to sin. Whoever has reason to doubt his ability to make a perfect act of contrition is bound to pray earnestly for such a grace if there is no opportunity to receive the sacrament of penance. If at all possible it is well to receive the sacrament of reconciliation and thereby sanctify and consummate the salutary effects of perfect contrition. Yet, the soul after sincere efforts to make a perfect act of contrition would be permitted to receive a sacrament of the living (for example, Holy Communion) which guarantees the state of grace even if the contrition was imperfect or mere attrition.

It should be noted that those prevented from the reception of the sacrament of penance, yet doubtful in regard to the seriousness of a particular sin as well as their ability to make a perfect act of contrition, would do better to receive Holy Communion than to refrain from its reception on the basis of an unreasonable fear. Suppose their sin was grievous and their contrition imperfect—a fact known only to God—they would remain in the state of sin without a sacrament of the living, while its reception would assure

them of the state of grace unless they have reason to doubt
their own good will.

(c) The Integrity of Sacramental Confession

Although the Christian may be cognizant of both the minimum requirements of the universal law and the reasons
for prudent exceptions, he still remains confronted with
the question: "What and how to confess?" Doubtlessly, the
universal law is applicable to all penitents. It meets the
needs of the weak as well as the virtuous. Over and above
the bare minimum of the law, the soul is aware of God's
personal and loving invitation. It knows itself to be called
by name. The "fulness of the law" consists in the heart's
ready assent to each grace which is granted towards its
ascent on the road of purification to the very summit of
consummate love.

As previously indicated, it may at times be advisable or
even necessary to refrain from a detailed self-accusation in
order to devote one's wholehearted energies to a new beginning in the spiritual life. Those tending to scrupulosity
should limit their accusation to the bare minimum according to the advice of a prudent confessor. Regarding offenses
against the sixth commandment, the penitent should abstain from all detailed explanations without shirking the
humiliating experience implied in the confession of sins or
hesitating to ask for advice in future situations.

With increasing progress in the spiritual life, the Christian will tend to examine his conscience not merely in the
light of the strictly prohibitive and prescriptive laws of
God. His examination of conscience, contrition, resolution,
and, if possible, his self-accusation shall more and more be
governed by the sublime goals of charity to God and neighbor. The Christian is not chiefly confronted with restric-

tions and limitations of the law, but lives in God's presence as His well-beloved child; he is guided by the urge of grace in response to the love of Christ. Consequently, he willingly confesses in the sacrament of penance even the venial sins and the sinful motives.

Although venial sins may be remitted outside the sacrament of penance, the Church nevertheless encourages the so-called "confessions of devotion," namely, the freely chosen frequent reception of the sacrament of penance by those who have not committed any mortal sin. Through the graces of the sacrament, Christ sanctifies and consummates our personal endeavor for compunction of heart and liberation from sinful attachments. However, the practice of frequent confession should not become a matter of mere routine. In keeping with the sacred nature of this sacrament, we ought to strive for a continuous increase in the spirit of genuine compunction. This will foster a firm resolution for a change of life.

We might suggest the monthly confession as ideal in frequency for the average Christian. The minimum for any practicing Catholic is the yearly confession within the Paschal time although, strictly speaking, this Paschal confession is demanded only of those in the state of mortal sin as a necessary preparation for their Easter Communion.

In addition to the obligatory, general confession which is mandatory in case of unworthy and invalid confessions, there is also the freely chosen *general confession* in which the penitent includes some or all of his past sins, previously confessed worthily. Such a general confession is advisable at special times of grace or at the beginning of a new state of life, such as during spiritual retreats and missions, before marriage, and on embracing the religious life. Scrupulous persons should be discouraged from any type of general confession even if they should doubt the validity of their previous confessions. Furthermore, in these freely chosen, general confessions, there is no strict obligation to include all mortal sins. In addition, it would be inadvisable to review minute details regarding sins against the sixth commandment, particularly if there is danger of renewed temptation. St. Alphonsus wisely admonishes: "It would be far better to utilize one's time in pious meditation" than in scrupulous self-examinations.

Our recommendation regarding the "confessions of devotion" should not cloud the sublime truth that the Eucharist rather than the sacrament of penance is the true center of the Christian life. Frequent confessions should encourage rather than prevent us from the frequent and devout reception of Holy Communion.

Section III. Restitution and Atonement

1. A Transition from Injustice to the New Justice

Sin is more than a violation of human rights. It is a hideous insult against God's divine majesty and authority. It is an outrage against His absolute dominion and singular jurisdiction over the love and obedience of all mankind created and redeemed by Him. "All lawlessness is sin" (I John 5:17) and, consequently, every sin is an injustice.

In view of the numerous manifestations of God's love and in consequence of the heart's illumination through faith and the precious gift of the Holy Eucharist, mortal sin in the soul of the baptized is a most grievous offense. It is an incomprehensible perversion in which man prefers "the world" and its malice to God's intimate friendship (cf. II Pet. 2:20). The detestable malice of sin appears in its most rebellious form in the apostasy from faith.

The creature's rejection of God, the very essence and

source of truth, is indeed a serious iniquity because the apostate loves the darkness more than God's illuminating light of truth to which he has been called (cf. I Pet. 2:9). The injustice of sin "holds back the truth of God" (Rom. 1:18). The final judgment of Christ will manifest the full malice of all sinners who in the eschatological struggle have turned to "the deceptive powers of injustice" and have "agreed to all injustice" instead "of confiding in the truth" (II Thes. 2:10-12). Moral corruption and apostasy are deeply rooted in man's malice of refusing to give glory to God despite their awareness of His supremacy as their Creator.

Mortal sin is not only an act of injustice but also a state of iniquity and guilt. The sinner is ensnared and enslaved by "the bonds of iniquity" (Acts 8:23). "The man who sins is a child of the devil," he is in conspiracy with God's enemies because Satan is the instigator of all evil (cf. I John 3:7 ff.). Sin and vice must be seen against the dreadful background of its pernicious solidarity with Satan and his kingdom.

Through His bitter Passion and death, Christ merited for us the grace of conversion. He saved us from the enslaving snares of guilt and made us participants in His own justice. Consequently, it calls for man's grateful acceptance of the law of expiation and satisfaction since there is no salvation and participation in God's justice without the atonement which Christ has offered to His heavenly Father.

Through our solidarity with Christ, God grants us a purely gratuitous justice provided that we confess our guilt with a contrite heart. The salutary acknowledgment of our guilt implies not only a grateful trust in the satisfaction of Christ, but also a willingness to share in His propitiation for sins as far as God may demand our cooperation. Conversion is synonymous with an adoption of the sublime intentions of Jesus Christ (cf. Phil. 2:5), it means that in all our thoughts and actions we "put on the Lord Jesus Christ" (Rom. 13:14). Consequently, the baptized, who in view of Christ's expiatory suffering and death has been granted participation in the life of Christ, ought to take upon himself his share of redemptive suffering (cf. Rom. 8:16-17).

Baptism removes all guilt and punishment for sin. Therefore, strict justice does not demand personal atonement for the sins which he has committed prior to baptism. However, his interior conformity with Christ demands a willing acceptance of all God-sent sufferings and a grateful pursuit of voluntary works of expiation and penances in behalf of the world's salvation. With Christ and in virtue of His merits we are enabled to atone for the sins of the world by offering appropriate satisfaction to our heavenly Father and thus participate in the work of redemption.

The sacrament of penance frees us from the entanglement of sin and guilt provided we are willing to make amends for our transgressions which had been remitted in its salvific action. If despite our spiritual rebirth in baptism we have relapsed into sin, conversion demands an authentic desire to make reparation for our wrongdoing. However, as stressed by the Council of Trent, the value of our atonement depends on our conformity with Christ. Albert the Great succinctly states: "Penance receives its power from Christ and at the same time conforms us to Him." The patient endurance of expiatory sufferings is a difficult obligation. On the other hand, the sacrifice of an acceptable reparation offered to God is an undeserved grace merited by Christ's suffering and death. The fact that the baptized, after falling into mortal sin becomes fully reinstated through the sacrament of penance not only as a recipient but as an active participant in Christ's redemptive work, is an unmistakable proof of God's saving grace. In conformity with

Christ's intentions, the penitent responds to God's summons for atonement if, in addition to the willing expiation
for personal sins, he also renders pleasing reparation for all
the sins of the world, fully cognizant of his solidarity with
the entire Mystical Body of Christ. Thus, atonement and
satisfaction for sins must be recognized as an essential aspect of a life based on the new justice bestowed by God.

2. The Salutary Effects of Penance

The Council of Trent explicitly stated that in the wise plan
of "divine clemency" the sacramental "forgiveness of sins is
not granted without man's cooperation through salutary
works of satisfaction because the remission of guilt (in the
absence of atonement) might induce the soul to underes-
timate the malice of sin. Such an attitude would inevitably
lead the sinner into ever greater depths of iniquity and moral degradation in direct opposition to the guidance of the
Holy Spirit. This would accentuate God's wrath on the day
of final retribution (cf. Rom. 2:5). There is no doubt that expiatory works of penance restrain us from further transgression of God's law. They tend to make us more vigilant and
discreet. They heal the wounds inflicted by sin and aid in
the eradication of vicious habits acquired by a life of sin"
(Denzinger, No. 904). This truth expressed by the Council of Trent is evidence of the Church's maternal solicitude for man's salvation in her very insistence on restitution and satisfaction for sins. Our acts of reparation will
achieve their truly salutary effects if done in conformity
with the precepts of the Church and the justice and holiness of God. *Contrition for sins runs the risk of insincerity
unless man humbly admits his duty of reparation through
a contrite acknowledgment of God's supreme justice and
thereby unites himself with Christ's superabundant satis-*

faction for the sins of all mankind. In order to effect its full liberating power, sorrow for sin must transform our life by counteracting our innate selfishness and by rectifying our wrongdoing through a willing acceptance of reparation. God will liberate us for a new beginning if in the true spirit of penance we sincerely atone for our past sins.

In the course of time Christ has opened for us a new period of salvation by taking upon Himself the full burden of sin and iniquity. Far from removing suffering and death from our life by His voluntary sacrifice of atonement, He imparted a new and sublime meaning to all propitiation by His willing and loving acceptance of untold pain and agony in order to make atonement to the justice and holiness of His heavenly Father. Similarly, the faithful imitation of Christ calls for a wholehearted acceptance of all sufferings and trials in order to offer adequate reparation for the sins committed after baptism. Each soul has to bear the consequences of personal guilt. Our readiness to atone for sin, in union with Christ's Passion and death and in loving submission to the divine justice, not only removes the bitterness and hopelessness of the inexorable obligation towards reparation but transforms suffering into a welcome opportunity for expiation and worthy adoration of God.

Seen in the light of strict justice, the sacramental penance ought to be in proportion to the number and gravity of the offenses. However, Holy Mother Church prudently refrains from any severity in due consideration of the individual's state of soul. Ordinarily, both the heart's compunction and readiness for adequate satisfaction progress at a slow and gradual pace. Hence the relatively mild penances imposed by the confessor do not dispense the penitent from freely chosen acts of amendment. The willing acceptance of all God-sent sufferings in the true spirit of reparation is a worthwhile goal on the road of atonement.

In conformity with the spirit of justice and the objectives of true satisfaction for sins, the Church imposes salutary acts of penance in order to counteract man's evil inclinations and predominant passions. "The will becomes liberated through the choice of the things which are opposed to the fascinations of sin because it was attracted towards evil through the inordinate desires for pleasure. The liberation from such attachment can only be accomplished through some punitive and painful measures" (Thomas Aquinas, *Summa Contra Gentes* 3, 158). Thus it is appropriate that the penitent manifests his willingness to perform certain penances in conformity with his particular spiritual needs.

In addition to the penance imposed by the confessor, which in our day is minimal when compared with the penitential practices of the early Christian times, the penitent ought to prove his readiness for atonement by voluntary acts of propitiation. These acts of reparation shall prove their salutary effects if they correspond to the special needs of the penitent. Thus, an appropriate satisfaction for previous negligence in prayer consists in reciting the daily prayers (morning and evening prayers, grace before and after meals) in a kneeling posture. The person who had failed against charity should repair the harm through specific works of charity. The sordid habit of masturbation should be overcome by a sincere endeavor to bring joy and delight to others. The Christian who has scandalized his neighbor by his obvious neglectful or irreverent attitude toward the sacrament of penance should encourage those hesitant to approach the sacrament of reconciliation through his evident reverence and joy in appreciation for its marvelous blessings.

A readiness for penance will manifest itself in adequate restitution for all forms of injustice and scandal. It should find appropriate expression in a grateful attitude of willing forgiveness towards others.

3. The Fruits of Conversion

The essence of conversion does not consist in acts of atonement but rather in a grateful return to God's mercy and a sincere change of heart. The soul's readiness to make amends is both a necessary fruit and basic constituent of an authentic conversion. At the same time, penance is an absolute prerequisite for a continuous increase in the intensity and stability of conversion. The acts of reparation in themselves do not constitute the eminent fruits of conversion. The choicest blessings of conversion consist in the new life based on the law of the imitation of Christ which demands a consuming zeal for the glory of God and the salvation of souls. Since such a life is totally dependent on a sincere readiness to atone for sins through the humble acceptance of the daily tribulations, the penitent should willingly bear the trials of life in the true spirit of penance.

The Christian ought to prove his readiness to penance not only by a total acceptance of the suffering sent by God, but also by freely chosen acts of atonement. The Council of Trent suggests "fasting, almsgiving, prayer, and other works of piety." *Fasting* implies voluntary renunciation and self-imposed penance for the sake of overcoming our inborn sloth and inordinate desire for pleasure. In addition to voluntary abstinence in eating and drinking, prudence requires a discriminate restraint in all types of recreational and leisure activities, such as the reading of newspapers and periodicals; the frequenting of movies; the use of the radio and television; and the habit of smoking. A conscientious adherence to traffic laws might prove both practical and salutary. *Almsgiving* is opposed to man's innate selfishness in the inordinate quest for earthly riches and an unreasonably high standard of living. Almsgiving, as an act of charity, points to the truth that love is to motivate and animate every work of penance. *Prayer*, in its deepest essence, is not meant to be a penance but a loving dialogue with God; an undeserved dignity; and an outward expression of faith, hope and charity. Prayer is essentially an act of divine worship. However, prayer may take on the nature of penance insofar as we are unable to pray worthily and persistently without a genuine spirit of self-abnegation.

The penance imposed by the confessor should be directed towards a specific resolution for the amendment of life. The following are examples of efficacious penances: the prompt reception of the sacrament of penance after committing a particular offense; a charitable donation in the amount spent for intoxicating drinks in reparation for each relapse into the old drinking habit; a special act of fraternal charity and intercessory prayer for every sinful gossip; a hymn of praise in atonement for every blasphemy uttered against God's holy name; and an apology for each outburst of anger or impatience.

Section IV. Conversion to the New Law

1. Sin as a Contradiction Against the Law

St. Augustine defines sin as: *"Any thought, word, or deed in contradiction to the Eternal Law."* Man's culpability is in direct proportion to his awareness of the contradiction existing between the Eternal Law of divine wisdom and the act which he freely chooses. Therefore, man's free and conscious opposition to the clear manifestation of God's

wisdom and love determines the sinfulness of such a violation against His Law.

Even the pagans, though deprived of God's pristine revelations, are still in possession of some basic law. Even if
their knowledge of law is far inferior to the revelations
granted to the chosen people, they still "do by nature what
the Law prescribes, these having no law are a law unto
themselves. They show the work of the law written in their
hearts. Their conscience bears witness to them" (Rom.
2:14-15). Consequently, their sin implies not only a contradiction to the light of their intellect and a violation of
the general order in the world, but at the same time signifies an opposition to the will of God, their Creator who
deigned to reveal Himself through the marvelous order in
creation. Behind their lawlessness and estrangement from
the created order lies their apostasy from the Creator (cf.
Rom. 1:20 ff.).

God has not only given us a magnificent self-revelation
in creation, but has clearly announced His loving will
through His message on Mount Sinai and the teaching of
His prophets. God made the observance of the Law the
fundamental requirement for His Covenant of love. Consequently, all transgressions of the Law are evident contradictions to God's holy will. "Sin becomes more sinful
than ever" (Rom. 7:13). Estrangement from the Law
is synonymous with apostasy from the Covenant of love
and, at the same time, a grievous injustice against God's
unfathomable predilection. "Hear, O heavens, and listen,
O earth, for the Lord speaks: sons have I raised and reared,
but they have disowned Me" (Is. 1:2). Jeremiah compares
the denial of God's Covenant to an adultery: "Like a woman
faithless to her lover, even so have you been faithless to
Me, O house of Israel, says the Lord" (Jer. 3:20).

Sin reveals its greatest resistance to God's loving will in the very fact that it is committed despite the express revelation of the Law through Christ. Since the New Law has been fully revealed to us through Christ's self-sacrificing love and since it offers the life-giving grace of the children of God, lawlessness takes on the nature of a conscious opposition to God. It is the expression of Antichrist himself. Therefore, the Apostle refers to Antichrist as "The son of perdition (II Thes. 2:3), and "The lawless" (2:8). "For already the secret power of wickedness is at work" (2:7). Sin opposes the full revelation of the kingdom of God and the New Law of love. In reference to the eschatological struggle of God's elect with the spirit of lawlessness, Our Lord announced: "And because iniquity will abound, the charity of the many will grow cold" (Matt. 24:12). Passages from Holy Scripture, referring to man's "darkness," the "perdition of sin," the entanglement in guilt, and the state of "lawlessness," chiefly allude to the pernicious power of sin in the individual and in the world at large rather than to a particular transgression. Despite this fact, the power of sin is neither an impersonal force nor a blind destiny since it is the expression of man's free and conscious decisions when confronted with God's clearly revealed, beneficent will. Satan himself is the chief instigator of all sin and vice because he sows the seeds of revolt against the law of love.

"Lawlessness" in the biblical sense means more than the mere external transgression of God's law. This truth reveals itself in the unceasing struggle which Christ had to wage against the "law-consciousness" of the Pharisees who prided themselves in their fulfillment of the law. He rightly accused them: "You appear outwardly just to men; but within you are full of hypocrisy and iniquity" (Matt.

23:28). The Pharisees attempted to make law subservient to their pride and self-interest instead of purifying their hearts for a worthy submission to God's loving will as revealed to them in the Law of the Covenant and in the person of Jesus Christ. The tax collectors and prostitutes, who in the painful awareness of their contradiction with law feel embarrassed in God's presence, are closer to His kingdom and the New Law of love than those who in their utter self-righteousness entrench themselves behind the dead letter of the law in direct opposition to the clearly revealed, beneficent will of God. St. Paul expressly stated that the New Law was challenged not only by the open transgressor, but also by those who treated it as a written precept demanding mere external conformity.

Conversion is effected in man's total renunciation of all resistance to the New Law which he begins to recognize as the Law of Christ's abounding charity.

2. Progress in Accepting the Law of Charity

Conversion is more than a transition from the works of iniquity and lawlessness to an exterior conformity with the law. Conversion is not rooted in the works of the law but is founded on the firm faith in Jesus Christ who is our salvation (cf. Gal. 3:21 ff.). Through faith, hope, charity, and the graces of the sacraments, we not only gain participation in Christ's divine life but achieve a right attitude towards the Law which is Christ's own Law, in fact His personal love, His own person revealing to us the love of His heavenly Father. He who surrenders to Christ ceases to be "lawless"; he is no longer subservient to the external restrictive and accusing law; but possesses the core and center of the law in the charity of Christ who desires all hearts to reciprocate His boundless love. Clearly, God demands much more than the outward observance of a written law.

Our divine Master ardently desires that all men should imitate His sublime virtues and thus enter into the kingdom of His everlasting love. In the words of St. Paul, we are to lead "a life in Christ," a life according to the "law of faith" illumined by the light of grace and directed by the Spirit of Christ. St. John envisions the entire Christian life as a loving response to God who "has first loved us" (I John 4:10). The sacraments of conversion express the same urgent appeal for a total self-surrender to the God of love. They lead us to the summit of Christian fulfillment, to the most personal and intimate encounter with our eucharistic Lord through His redeeming acts commemorated in union with all the redeemed. Continuous conversion which aims towards the perfect consummation of Christian living will manifest itself not only in a more perfect observance of God's external laws, but in a greater docility to God's grace which elevates our whole life with all its moral and religious strivings into the realm of an undivided love of God and neighbor.

Although the borderline positive laws which are expressed in clear-cut prohibitive and prescriptive terms clearly demand a faithful and ready obedience, they nevertheless receive their incentive and consummation only in a perfect love of God and fellowman. Perfect charity is such a sublime goal that it can be attained only in heaven. Yet its growth is man's most urgent and, at the same time, most ennobling and beatifying obligation. Charity is the fulfillment of the whole law which can "be summed up in one single commandment: 'Love your neighbor as yourself'" (Gal. 5:14).

It is only through an undivided love of God and neighbor that the New Law truly becomes "the perfect law of liberty" (James 1:25). Charity purifies the heart and leads it imperceptibly to the heart of God and to that love of neighbor which is the principle of unity, the distinguishing feature of the *New World*.

I. Analytical Index

ing, 33; positive laws of the Church, 35; property laws, 344-345, 355; Sunday Mass obligation, 44-47; supernatural (see supernatural laws); unity of, in Christian life, 43-49; written in minds and hearts, 19-27

Lay Apostolate, 240-257; in care of environment, 252-254; in shaping public opinion, 240; in worldly activity, 248-252

Legal protection in last will and testament (also see justice and injustice), 338

Leitmotif (also see ideal of life, good intention); conscious and hidden, 170; keyed to individual needs, 171; leading idea, 169

Letter of the law, 25

Liberalism; capitalistic, 342-343; fallacies, 343; neo-liberalism, 343

Licentiousness, 375-376; St. Paul's admonitions, 387-388; St. Peter's castigation of, 386-387

Lies; calumny, 318; children's "lies," 318-319; deliberate, 317; detrimental to our neighbor, 317; jocose lies, 318; "little lies," 317-318; sins against charity, 317; slander, 318; symptomatic of personality disorders and pathological states, 319

Lockout, 354

Love of enemies in an unjust world, 340-342

Love of God (see charity)

Luther and justification, 401

Manslaughter (also see accidental homicide), 364

Martyrdom (manifestation of fortitude), 377

Marx, Karl—theory and Christian hope, 66, 196-201

Mary the Mother of Mercy, 203, 205-206

Mass (see sacrifice of Christ)

Masochism, 371

Masturbation, 370-371

Material goods (see earthly goods)

Materialism (dialectic), (also see Marx, Karl), 251

Materialistic pseudo-religion, 68

Matrimony (see sacraments)

Meekness; and compassion towards others, 8; Church history, 70; example of Christ, 70; in Scripture language, 69-71

Mental health and holiness, 79-81

Mental reservation (broad), 321-323

Milieu (see environment)

Morality; aberrations of, 17; code of, 3; man's moral strivings, 16

Motives; attitude of Christian ethics to natural motives, 166-167; compared to humanistic efforts of self-perfection, 214; divine charity, 161-164; dominant motives for moral action, 161-168; interior dispositions and motives, 141-173; related to reward and punishment, 164-167; roots of (see dispositions), 152; social considerations, 167-168

Murder; infanticide, 360; judicial, 360; premeditated, 360

Mystique of sin, 402-403

Name of God and its revelation, 266-267

Natural laws; and new order of grace, 29-30; and pagans and

II. Name Index

III. Biblical Index

480